Exploring Islam in a New Light
A View from the Quranic Perspective

Second Revised Edition

A Guide to What Makes a True Monotheist

Foreword by Professor Riffat Hassan, Ph.D.

ABDUR RAB

brainbowpress

Exploring Islam in a New Light
A View from the Quranic Perspective

Copyright © 2008, 2010 by Abdur Rab

ISBN: 978-0-9825867-1-6

$19.95

ISBN 978-0-9825867-1-6

51995>

9 780982 586716

Cover Design: Uğur Şahin

Printed in the United States of America by LightningSource

10 9 8 7 6 5 4 3

A bold, modern, and in-depth description of the message of Islam, and an impassioned call for reform of the practiced faith in light of the Quran.

"This is a surprising, inspiring, and ultimately, refreshing book. It is simultaneously a solid introduction to Islam, an ecstatic spiritual journey, and an analytical call for reform. Abdur Rab is not only a reliable and authoritative voice on modern Islam but he is an original and thrilling thinker. This is one book that is definitely well-worth the time investment and indeed it should be read widely by Muslims and non-Muslims alike."

–Dr. Khaled Abou El Fadl, Chair of Islamic Studies, Alfi Distinguished Professor of Islamic Law, UCLA School of Law.

"At a time when misconceptions about Islam are on the rise, even among Muslims, Abdur Rab has provided a compelling argument for returning to the Qur'an for a deeper, more complete, more original understanding of the meaning and message of Islam. The result is a book that posits not a NEW interpretation of Islam, but a more authentic one."

–Reza Aslan, Professor of Creative Writing, University of California, Riverside; author of *No god but God: The Origins, Evolution, and Future of Islam.*

"Abdur Rab offers a comprehensive vision of Islam using the Quran as his sole religious textual source. He intentionally avoids the *hadith* literature, which he believes, and argues, has done much damage to the message of the Quran. His work provides many very thought-provoking insights and should be a significant contribution to the 'Quran only' movement in modern Islam."

–Jeffrey Lang, Ph.D., Professor of Mathematics, University of Kansas; author of *Losing My Religion: A Call for Help.*

"Another valuable addition to a list of books that question the sectarian teachings […] A scholarly contribution to the message of Quran alone or rational monotheism movement." [Part of his review of the book]

–Edip Yuksel, Author; Professor of Philosophy, Pima Community College; founder of Islamic Reform; co-founder of Muslims for Peace, Justice and Progress (MPJP).

"Dr. Rab has […] produced a thoughtful, wonderful book that is constructively revolutionary." [Part of his review of the book]

–Khaleel Mohammed, Ph.D. (McGill), Professor/Undergraduate Advisor, Department of Religious Studies, San Diego State University.

"[This] book brings Islam nearer to modernity, more particularly challenging […] aspects of practiced Islam so far thought unchallengeable. In that respect [the author's] contribution can be called revolutionary."

–Dr. Rezaul Haq Khandker (late), a former official of UNDP, New York, USA

[…] [T]he book is original in many respects. The author deserves high compliments [...] The author's skill in explaining concepts in a simple way is commendable."

–Dr. M. Shahjahan, Professor of Economics, the University of Arkansas

4

ABOUT THE AUTHOR

Abdur Rab, Ph.D., graduated with Honors and received a Master's degree from Dhaka University and a Ph.D. from Harvard. He spent decades in economic research and consulting, analyzing various public policy issues, while serving the Pakistan Institute of Development Economics, the Industrial Development Bank of Pakistan, and the Bangladesh and former undvided Pakistan governments, and various international organizations. He served the Pakistan Tariff Commission as a Member, and the Bangladesh Planning Commission as a Section Chief and a Senior Consultant. He worked as an Industrial Development Officer with the United Nations Industrial Development Organization (UNIDO), Vienna. He served as Financial and Monetary Adviser for the government of Uganda under a World Bank assignment, and as Senior Industrial Economist for the Qatar government under a UNIDO assignment. Under a UNDP assignment, he contributed to part of a business plan for a trade and development bank of the Economic Co-operation Organization (whose founding members are Iran, Turkey and Pakistan). He also offterred his consulting services to various development projects in Bangladesh supported by donor agencies such as the World Bank, USAID, and the Asian Development Bank. He also did consulting as an agricultural trade specialist for the US-based International Fertilizer Development Center (IFDC). Abdur Rab grew up in a traditional Bengali Muslim family. Deeply religious since childhood, he experienced a paradigm change in his religious approach after he came in contact with a virtually unknown but versatile Bengali spiritual guide Shah Aksaruddin Ahmad, whose Quranic teachings were resisted by influential Islamic leaders of the traditional, Hadith-following sects. Under his guidance, Abdur received some preliminary lessons in spiritual exercises. Inspired by him, Abdur closely studied the Quran, the Hadith, and other relevant Islamic literature of modern scholars. He presently lives with his family in the United States. His website is: http://www.exploreQuran.org.

FOREWORD

In the aftermath of September 11, 2001, more attention has been focused on Islam and Muslims than perhaps at any other point in modern history. Much of this attention – particularly in the case of mainstream U.S. television channels – has been negative, associating both Islam and Muslims with violence. The negative stereotyping and imaging of Islam and Muslims is not a new phenomenon. It is as old as the first chapter of Islamic history, when the new religion began to move into territories largely occupied by Christians, and Muslims were seen not only as "the Other" but as "the Adversary". However, the worldview which became dominant – particularly in the West – since the onset of the "war on terror", polarizing the world into two absolutely opposing camps, has generated a discourse which constitutes a new challenge both for Muslims and non-Muslims. Dualistic thinking which permeates this discourse seems, at times, to be cosmic in magnitude, and makes it seem as if the so called "clash of civilizations" between the "West" and "the world of Islam" posited by Samuel Huntington, has indeed come to pass.

While popular Western media continues, in general, to portray Islam as a religion spread by the sword and characterized by "Holy War," and Muslims as barbarous, backward, frenzied, fanatic, volatile, and violent, important initiatives have been taken by a number of scholars of Islam to present a knowledge-based account of various aspects of the Islamic tradition. Of significance amongst scholarly works written by Muslim scholars against the backdrop of the contemporary situation, is Dr. Abdur Rab's *Exploring Islam in a New Light : An Understanding from the Qur'anic Perspective,* a wide-ranging book in which the author shares his own understanding of Islam as he has studied and lived it.

The Qur'an is regarded as the highest source of authority by the majority of Muslims. However, most Muslims also consider the Sunnah (practical traditions) and the Hadith (oral traditions) of the Prophet Muhammad to be sources of normative Islam. Dr. Rab belongs to a school of thought which holds the view that the Qur'an embodies the core message of Islam which is best understood if one focuses solely on the Qur'an. He argues against the use of Hadith for a number of reasons and points out that his book "is a renewed systematic attempt to show that there are serious problems with the so-called Prophetic traditions. It looks at the accumulated evidence against the reliability and authenticity of the

Hadith in terms of theological (Qur'anic) sanction or authority, historical basis, and objective criteria such as consistency with the Qur'an, reason and scientific truths. The ideas that seriously distort religious conceptions and practices, demonize and weaken women's position in society, encourage fanaticism and fatalism, block progress and modernization, encourage intolerance, violence and terror and extol the virtues of aggressive *jihad* ("holy war") against other communities – all come from the Hadith.."

It may be stated here that the modernist reformist thinkers of the nineteenth and twentieth century, especially in the Indian sub-continent, also put great emphasis on the Qur'an, and that their rallying cry was "Back to the Qur'an, forward with *Ijtihad.*" However, most of them accepted the Sunnah as an integral part of Islam and did not reject Hadith as a source of Islam though they advocated the use of only authentic "*hadith.*" In more recent times, there have been scholars, such as Kassim Ahmad of Malaysia, and Ghulam Ahmad Parwez of Pakistan, who have taken a position similar to that of Dr. Rab on the Qur'an vis-à-vis the Hadith.

Dr. Rab states why he considers the Qur'an to be divinely inspired. In his view, "The book suggests that the religion professed by the Qur'an is essentially humane and scientific in nature. Some of the awe-inspiring features of this Qur'anic message are its eloquence, profundity, comprehensiveness, logical coherence and rational orientation, immutability and dynamic flexibility in the face of changing contexts."

Dr. Rab believes that "The Qur'an inspires us to envision and build a human society where peace, security, justice and compassion and an environment conducive to the uplifting of all humankind prevail." In the light of its teachings, Dr. Rab explores various subjects such as the relation of religion to science, how human beings can achieve spiritual progress, what constitutes righteousness, and the significance and purpose of religious practices such as prayer ("*salat*"), spending in God's way ("*zakat*"), fasting ("*siyam*"), and pilgrimage ("*hajj*"). Dr. Rab's concept of the above-mentioned four "pillars" of Islam is much broader than the conventional one, being grounded in the ethical and mystical core of Qur'anic teaching.

Dr. Rab regards Ego, love, will and knowledge as "the fundamental building blocks of the way forward to spiritual progress or evolution,"

7

and believes that these four factors combined with planning and execution lead to creative action. In his view, Heaven and Hell are not created by God but by our own deeds, and the purpose of religion is to "transform this earth into a Heaven and create a still better afterlife" through our deeds.

Dr. Rab states that "the true image of Islam countenances neither intolerance nor violence nor harsh punishments," and that the Qur'an does not warrant a rigid application of the "Shari'ah" (traditional Islamic law). He looks at issues of marriage, divorce, the status of women, and the treatment of slaves, pointing out what he considers to be permissible or impermissible in Islam.

In his book, Dr. Rab, a distinguished internationally-recognized economist, explores the implications of Islam for the economic system which he summarizes as follows: "The Qur'an calls for a free and exploitation-free egalitarian economic system…While there should be recognition of private initiative and enterprise, and hence of private property and ownership, this should be subject to an understanding that all things ultimately belong to God. One important implication of the Qur'anic directions is that there should be an equitable distribution of economic resources, especially land, if these are found to be starkly unequal in a society. An important message of Islam is that none should fully enjoy his own fruits of labor but should share them with his fellow beings through an appropriate distribution system. … Contrary to what is generally believed among Muslims, the Qur'an does not really condemn interest *per se* that is being universally used for lending and borrowing purposes and also as a monetary policy instrument and an essential device for efficient allocation of productive resources. What it condemns is interest that is charged to people who deserve humanitarian treatment."

In the final chapter of his book, Dr. Rab reflects "on the rise of religious fanaticism among 'Muslims'" which he largely attributes to the Wahhabi ideology patronized by the Saudi Arabian government. He advocates that traditional "*madrasahs*" should be "thoroughly remodeled on the pattern of modern schools." Dr. Rab believes that the "true revival of Islam" can only take place "when Muslims understand and return to their only Holy Book, the Qur'an."

In the Preface to *Exploring Islam in a New Light: An Understanding from the Qur'anic Perspective* (First Edition), Dr. Rab has correctly stated that "This book is a marked departure" from a conventional interpretation of Islam. In his words, "It is an attempt to look afresh at the meaning and role of religion per se in general and provide a primer on the message of Islam in particular solely on the basis of the Qur'an." Whether or not one agrees with all of Dr. Rab's views, his book is a serious modern attempt at understanding Islam profoundly from within. Dr. Rab's deep and dedicated study of the Qur'an makes his book – first and foremost – a labor of love. It is also a book that offers valuable insights on a number of issues of interest and concern to contemporary Muslims. Though Dr. Rab has written his book as a committed Muslim, his book has much to offer to all readers who are keen to see and understand Islam as it is embodied in the Qur'an which has been the major source of inspiration to the most outstanding modernist reformist Muslim thinkers such as Sayyid Ahmad Khan and Muhammad Iqbal.

Riffat Hassan

(Dr. Riffat Hassan, Professor of Humanities at the University of Louisville, Louisville, Kentucky, U.S.A. and President of *The Iqbal International Leadership Institute* in Lahore, Pakistan)

ACKNOWLEDGMENTS

All praise be to God, the Sustaining Lord of the Universe, without Whose grace and help, nothing worthwhile is possible!

I owe this work, in large part, to the labor of love of many minds. My greatest inspiration and guiding light has been my spiritual teacher Shah Aksaruddin Ahmad whose life-long dream had been to portray Islam exclusively in the Quranic light, but whose efforts to publish some works along this line were nipped in the bud due to opposition from the Bangladesh *ulama*. At his direction, his student Panaullah Ahmad beautifully articulates similar ideas in his book *Creator and Creation*. These ideas are the basic ingredients of my book. I have profited substantially also from selected works of many modern Islamic scholars.

I am very grateful to Professor Riffat Hassan of the University of Louisville, Kentucky for kindly writing a foreword for the book. I am also very thankful to Brother Edip Yuksel for kindly offering to publish this second edition through his press as well as for his insightful and appreciative comments on the revised manuscript. I gratefully recall the special debt I owe to my former boss at the Bangladesh Planning Commission and a former senior official of UNDP, late Dr. Rezaul Haq Khandker, for his guidance on my work right from the beginning with critical, insightful, and encouraging comments. In addition, I wish to acknowledge with my gratitude the following scholars for comments, endorsements, or reviews of my book:

1. Dr. Khaled Abou El Fadl, Chair of Islamic Studies, Alfi Distinguished Professor of Islamic Law, UCLA School of Law;
2. Reza Aslan, Author, Professor of Creative Writing, University of California, Riverside;
3. Jeffrey Lang, Author, Professor of Mathematics, the University of Kansas;
4. Edip Yuksel, Author; Professor of Philosophy, Pima Community College; founder of Islamic Reform; co-founder of Muslims for Peace, Justice and Progress (MPJP);
5. Khaleel Mohammed, Author, Professor of Religious Studies, San Diego State University;
6. Aisha Y. Musa, author, Professor of Religious Studies, Florida International University;

7. Layth Saleh Al-Shaiban, Author, and Manager of the website: www.free-minds.org;
8. Arnold Yasin Mol, Author, CEO of Deen Research Center, the Netherlands;
9. M. Shahjahan, Professor of Economics, University of Arkansas;
10. Haroon A. Khan, Professor of Political Science, Henderson State University;
11. Mominul Hoque, former Professor of Sedimentology and Petroleum Geophysics, the University of Nigeria;
12. A.M. Muazzam Husain, former Professor of Agricultural Economics, Agricultural University of Mymensingh, Bangladesh; and
13. A.H.M. Nuruddin Chowdhury, retired Senior Economist, the Asian Development Bank, Manila.

I also wish to thank British Muslim convert Sam Gerrans who wonderfully came in my way, and volunteered editing (the first edition) of this book along with some substantive trimmings. Last, but not least, I acknowledge the support and encouragement in various ways that I received from my family – my wife, children and their spouses.

PREFACE TO THE SECOND EDITION

This second revised edition has been prompted, sooner than it would otherwise have been the case, by a kind offer extended by Brother Edip Yuksel to have my book published by his Brainbow Press. Its subtitle has changed from "An Understanding from the Quranic Perspective" to "A View from the Quranic Perspective", and so has its logo. While the substantive themes of the book remain basically the same as before, it incorporates some revision of texts here and there. A new chapter has been added with the title "The Significance and Scope of Spending in God's Way (*Zakat* or *Sadaqa*)", which is practically a revised consolidation of material that was spread in a few earlier chapters of the book. Other improvements incorporated in this edition are reformatting of the Quranic verses and quotes of other scholars cited; rephrasing of a selection of cited verses keeping in view the Quran translation done by Edip Yuksel and his colleagues, and that done by Muhammad Asad. This edition also omits the index and the section on the glossary of terms (the latter is omitted considering the fact that such terms are explained in the body of the text). Editorial improvements along with the correction of a few errors noticed on verse number citations along with their simplification are other features of this edition. For a summary of major observations about the book, the reader is referred to the Preface to the First Edition. Two other summaries about the book are available – one on the author's website www.exploreQuran.org and another on the following web links:

> http://www.deenresearchcenter.com/Blogs/tabid/73/EntryId/78/My-Book-A-Snapshot.aspx;

> http://www.scribd.com/doc/23084237/Exploring-Islam-in-a-New-Light-A-Snapshot-An-Understanding-from-the-Quranic-Perspective-by-Abdur-Rab.

A full and updated reproduction of endorsements and reviews of the book received from a number of eminent scholars is available on the author's website. An earlier consolidated version of the reviews and endorsements can be seen on the following web link:

> http://www.islamicreform.org/index.php?option=com_content&view=article&id=75&Itemid=82.

PREFACE TO THE FIRST EDITION

Perhaps at no other time in history has the question "What Islam?" or "Whose Islam?" been so important. And perhaps never before has attention been so much focused on a particular religion. In the wake of the events of September 11, 2001, Muslims are undergoing an identity crisis and passing through a critical juncture. There has been a frantic effort on their part to find the heart and soul of Islam. Suddenly, bookstore shelves are stuffed with books on Islam, written by both Muslims and non-Muslims. Some books have appeared with even misperceived contents or inappropriate titles; notable examples: Islam Unveiled, The Trouble with Islam, The Two Faces of Islam, and Islam: Opposing Viewpoints, as if, Islam has a wrong, dark side. Whatever the interpretation of a religion, it cannot and should not be faulted for any wrongs done by its followers. No religion in the proper sense of the term teaches immoral values, violence or crimes. The question is: Have Muslims and non-Muslims been able to find what Islam truly represents? Or, does the plethora of books simply confound them?

Undeniably, religion is a subject that is often least understood or most misunderstood. Its understanding grows with the level of knowledge and wisdom one acquires from spiritual endeavor. Unfortunately, Islam, as it is often understood, is a religion that is currently dreaded. Terrorists are most often associated in the public's mind with people who boastfully declare themselves as Muslims. Arguably Islam can be, and is indeed, generally interpreted and understood in diverse ways, though not nearly in as many ways as Christianity. But its conventional interpretation dominates and guides most Muslims, and is, unfortunately, to put it quite appropriately in the words of a contemporary writer, "not far different from that of the terrorists but without the justification of violence," an interpretation that "serves to suppress individual creativity and innovation" and risks Muslims becoming "a permanent global underclass."[1]

This book is a marked departure from this conventional interpretation. It is an attempt to look afresh at the meaning and role of religion per se in general and provide a primer on the message of Islam in particular solely on the basis of the Quran. This message is essentially spiritual, humane, and scientific in nature. Much of the book focuses on this message, embracing an interpretation that responds to the social and economic

13

challenges of modern time. A second related major topic covered is the authenticity and reliability of the Hadith and its consequent harm done to Islam.

The Quran is a unique and wonderful book, unaltered and unadulterated since its compilation (by the Prophet Muhammad's trustworthy companions). Its message exhibits certain characteristic features that make it a compelling reading for both Muslims and non-Muslims, especially in the backdrop of recent terrorist attacks linked to some extremist Muslims. Some of the awe-inspiring features of this message are its eloquence, profundity, comprehensiveness, logical coherence and rational orientation, and immutability and dynamic flexibility in the face of changing contexts. The basic purpose of the Quran is to civilize and purify humankind and make it wise (62:2; 36:2). Man needs to develop and purify his soul and conscience (91:8–10) and attain higher levels of understanding, enlightenment, and power. The role of this religion is to help man evolve so as to live a flawless, enriched, progressive, and blissful life. The Quran inspires us to envision and build a human society where justice, peace, security, friendship, and an environment conducive to the spiritual uplifting of all humankind prevail.

Understanding a Divine Book is always an intractable job, perhaps more so when it is in Arabic, a language whose words often give diverse meanings. That is precisely the reason why translations of the Quran in other languages do not all give the same meaning, but the differences in them are neither numerous nor so acute in most cases. Most translations have been affected by available traditional interpretations, which are not always fully representative of the original meaning. The Quran needs a re-interpretation, free from any undue influence from any quarters. Certainly it needs a re-interpretation to rid Islam of the influence that has come from the Hadith, which unfortunately has not always been in tune with the Quranic spirit. At the same time, it is not necessary to insist that one needs to know the Arabic language in order to understand the Quran, though learning the language of the Quran is an advantage. This author thinks, however, that a reader, who does not know Arabic, should consult several translations, and in case of differences found, should reflect on such differences and make his own judgment about the appropriate meaning. If one sincerely tries to understand the Quran, the Quran reveals itself to the reader.

14

Contrary to the views held in some circles, especially among those embracing modern life styles and by atheists, agnostics and skeptics, religion is the most living, civilizing and nourishing force for humankind. The basic role of religion is to guide man on a journey of spiritual evolution, as distinguished from material wellbeing. Religion is for real human progress; not an object of scorn and ridicule. Meaningful progress among humankind and its true happiness can come only through a true religious sense, which is not just observance of some tailor-made rituals, but which embraces genuine submission and devotion to God and godly values, and the doing of righteous deeds.

Perhaps the most intricate part of religion is to understand why we need God. According to science, God means external intervention, which is incompatible with observed scientific relationships. Here lies the crux of the issue, which has deluded not only scientists but also religious zealots who care nothing for reason. Religion is not devoid of reason. The religion professed by the Quran is essentially scientific in nature. It inspires us to reflect on and take lessons from the creative process and changes taking place throughout the universe. God is One Who does not do anything of His own accord to interfere in our affairs, a conception that is in accord with the idea that He is impartial and neutral, and importantly, also consistent with the scientific idea that everything has its cause. We ourselves change our affairs. If we do good work we get a reward in some form, which is rather reflection or perfection of the good work in a changed form. If we do bad work we suffer a punishment, which is in a way correction of the bad work. Consciously or unconsciously, deliberately or involuntarily—in some way or other, we are all engaging and changing ourselves in an unrelenting process of evolution, which is scientific (84:19). What scientists have ignored is that prayer works. Prayer is essentially desire, mental power that also has an effect. God is ever present in all of our work. God helps those who help themselves. We accelerate our progress by seeking God's help. This is the real meaning of *salat* or prayer.

Religion cannot be defined rigidly in ritualistic terms. The outward appearance of what one does with religious practices can be utterly deceptive. Being religious is much more than just practicing of some rituals. It involves bringing about a revolutionary change in one's mindset, attitudes, and behavior pattern. It is a complete surrender to God and godly values. To follow the path of religion is essentially a spiritual quest to understand God and His attributes, and understand how He creates or acts. It is a spiritual quest to understand one's own self, one's own purpose in life, and the latent potential self-development. God is the supreme ideal for us. Serving Him really amounts to emulating Him in all of our thoughts and deeds. Religiosity is really one's sincere endeavor to attain self-purification and acquire spiritual wisdom to lead one's life flawlessly. Heaven is nothing but a state where we have nothing to fear and grieve (43:68; 46:13) —a very lofty stage indeed for an individual to attain. But for that, one needs to turn to God with one's whole heart and soul.

"Turning to God alone" means that we do nothing but what is right, good, just and kind, and all that God stands for. The book discusses the meaning and significance of religious practices such as prayer (*salat*), fasting (*siam*), and pilgrimage (*hajj*) and that of spending in God's way (*zakat* or *sadaqa*). It provides a broader conception of zakat or sadaqa than is conventionally being understood. This conception needs a major reformulation in light of the Quran and the functions of a modern state, and should embrace in a significant way the government taxation and expenditure system. The purpose of such a system should be to alleviate poverty, help people stand on their own feet, and bring about other human and social developments. The over-arching objective of all the religious practices and spending in God's way is to bring the worshiper closer to God through good work, devotion and self-purification.

The book presents a formalized way of looking at some fundamental building blocks of the way forward to spiritual progress or evolution: Ego, love, will and knowledge. These factors or faculties underlie all creative action or evolution, including spiritual evolution. Love is a major propelling factor. The more intensely one can develop one's devotion and love, the nearer one can approach God. Love needs to be freed of lust. Any indecent or lewd thought or action on the part of a person robs him of the golden opportunity to go forward spiritually. Likewise, one also needs to develop one's will and increase one's knowledge to go forward spiritually. The book also calls for understanding Heaven and Hell in a new light. In a vital sense God does not really create any Heaven or Hell for us; it is we who create them by our own deeds. It is through our deeds that we can transform this troubled, dull and dreary earth into a Heaven and create a still better afterlife (16:30, 97). This is essentially the purpose of religion.

The book calls for understanding the meaning and significance of salat solely in light of the Quran. *Salat* is really one's overall effort for purification and spiritual development, and preparation to become a God's true servant or an ideal successor species (khalifa) on earth, worthy of respect by all others. It is remembrance and glorification of God with sincere devotion and a platform for seeking His help to spiritually evolve, and acquire inspiration and knowledge to walk aright and get success in real life. Real prayer must always go hand in hand with consistent work in day-to-day life. However, *salat* as generally practiced by Muslims has been largely reduced to a mere ritual devoid of real prayer, prayer that is an exercise for self-purification on the part of the worshiper, and prayer that God answers.

The most recurrent theme of the Quran is that righteousness is the key to success. True righteousness or religion consists in emulating the virtues and qualities that define God. To be righteous, just observing some liturgies is not enough; one needs also to be morally and ethically fully upright. One needs to have a right *iman* or mindset, which involves much more than a mere belief in One God and His Messenger Muhammad. The process involves embracing various elements of beliefs and thoughts and nurturing the right attitudes of modesty and tolerance, as well as getting rid of wrong attitudes such as fatalism, intolerance, greed, fear, etc. Then come in other actions we do. We need to be careful about all of our actions of the mind and the body. Islam demands that we do nothing but what is right, good, just, kind, appropriate, or productive, and that we contribute to, and proceed toward God who epitomizes all that is true, good, just, kind, noble, perfect, and beautiful. The Quran wants us to be right, just, and kind to all. The true image of Islam countenances neither intolerance nor violence nor harsh punishments. The Quran condemns violence and terrorist acts in the strongest possible terms. The rigid application of the so-called *shariah* (traditional Islamic) law is also not justified in the light of the Quran.

The issues of marriage, divorce, and the status of women and the treatment of slaves also need to be properly understood in light of the Quran. The institution of marriage is a sacred bilateral contract between a man and a woman, where there should be mutual love, respect and understanding and sexual restraint between spouses. There is no room for free-style living or for same-sex marriage in Islam. Polygamy is allowed only with restrictions and could be seen as a safety device in exceptional circumstances. The book calls attention to the lousy way divorce often

17

takes place in Muslim societies, whereas the Quran calls for going in a very gradual way. It calls attention to the infamous *hilla* system that requires a divorced wife to marry another person in order to remarry her former husband after taking divorce from the second husband. The Quran does not really sanction such an abhorrent practice. God is gender-neutral. So the status of women in Islam is not subordinate to that of men. Islam condemns slavery in unequivocal terms. A good Muslim will never enslave a person, but will rather free him or her, or keep him or her as an equal member of his family. Social egalitarianism is a major hallmark of Islam. This is the only way we evolve and elevate all men and help develop their latent talents and bring about all round progress in society, which is precisely the way we can manifest the creative splendors and glories of God.

The Quran also calls for a free and exploitation-free egalitarian economic system. Strict observance of justice and fairness necessarily implies ensuring a system that has the least distortions in economic activities (production, trade, etc.) and prices (prices of goods and services, of capital, etc.) that come from controls, restrictions and monopolistic practices, etc. While there should be recognition of private initiative and enterprise, and hence of private property and ownership, this should be subject to an understanding that all things ultimately belong to God. One important implication of the Quranic directions is that there should be an equitable distribution of economic resources, especially land, if these are found to be starkly unequal in a society. An important message of Islam is that none should fully enjoy his own fruits of labor but should share them with his fellow beings through an appropriate distribution system. Such a system must necessarily encompass public welfare and development expenditures. Contrary to what is generally believed among Muslims, the Quran does not really condemn interest per se that is being universally used for lending and borrowing purposes and also as a monetary policy instrument and an essential device for efficient allocation of productive resources. What it condemns is interest that is charged to people who deserve humanitarian treatment. So-called Islamic interest-free banking is a misnomer, an unsound institution and a drag on the development of Muslim countries.

This Quranic conception of religion or Islam has unfortunately been seriously misrepresented and undermined by later religious literature, most notably the Hadith that surfaced long after the death of the Prophet Muhammad (peace be upon him). Regrettably thus, Islam perceived in

18

terms of both the Quran and the Hadith generates a mixed message. Due to the widely pervading influence that has come from the Hadith, the civilizing and progressive message of the Quran has been largely lost. This book tries to rid Islam of some of the misconceptions that have bedeviled it. It is time we looked afresh at the question of reliability of the Hadith literature as religious guidance, and as part of our religious tradition. Because of the reliance on the Hadith, Islam continues to be widely misperceived in many respects. Generally, those who portray Islam in a good light do so by tapping its "best traditions."[2] The issue, however, is not really about choosing between good and bad traditions; the issue is really about whether we can still afford to continue with traditions that often misguide us. A religious book needs to be completely holy to command compliance. It is time that all Muslims took a dispassionate look at the reliability of the Hadith. This book makes a renewed systematic attempt to show that there are serious problems with the so-called prophetic traditions. It looks at the accumulated evidence against the authenticity and reliability of the Hadith in terms of theological (Quranic) sanction or authority, historical basis, and objective criteria such as consistency with the Quran, reason, and scientific truths. The ideas that seriously distort religious conceptions and practices, insult and at the same time idolize the Prophet of Islam, demonize and weaken women's position in society, encourage fanaticism and fatalism, block progress and modernization, encourage intolerance, violence and terror and extol the virtues of aggressive *jihad* against other communities—all come from the Hadith. Not surprisingly, it is from some Hadith texts that the extremist groups among Muslims get their inspiration for committing intolerant, violent, and terrorist acts against other communities, and for committing most heinous crimes against humanity in the name of religion in various parts of the world.

Finally, the book touches on the rise of religious fanaticism among "Muslims" and the directions for true Islamic revival. As pointed out by some modern writers, a disconcerting development has been the rise of a special ideology known as Wahhabism, promoted by an eighteenth century cleric Abd al-Wahhab and vigorously patronized by the Saudi Arabian government. The Wahhabis have been responsible for the perpetration of numerous barbarous crimes against humanity over the last three centuries. The appearance of much of the terrorism today can be traced to this special ideology, which is being taught in typically traditional madrasahs (Muslim religious schools), where no modern education is imparted. The true revival of Islam can come when these madrasahs are thoroughly remodeled on the pattern of modern schools, keeping religious education as an additional subject. The true revival of Islam can come only when Muslims understand, and return to, their only Holy Book, the Quran.

These are some of the things this book is about. I am sure the book will sound ultra-modernist to many of our Muslim brethren. However, let us not give the final verdict now. Let us reflect. Let us ponder the Quran, and try sincerely to understand its message. That is really the message of the Quran:

38:29   (This is) a Book We have revealed unto thee, blessed, that they may ponder its verses, and that those with understanding may take heed.

CONTENTS

Foreword .	6
Acknowledgments	10
Preface to the second edition	12
Preface to the first edition	13
Chapters	
1. Introducing the Quran: why it is important to read and understand the Quran	23
2. The meaning and *raison d'etre* of religion and its relation to science	53
3. Understanding religion in light of the Quran: the road to spiritual progress	67
a. Annex to chapter 3: a partial list of God's names and attributes	93
4. Formalizing understanding on religion and conceptions of heaven and hell	99
5. The essence of *salat* in light of the Quran	116
6. The significance and scope of spending in God's way *(zakat* or *sadaqa)*	157
7. Righteousness in light of the Quran: getting our *iman* right	170
8. Righteousness in light of the Quran: getting our actions right	205
9. Marriage, divorce, the status of women and the treatment of slaves in light of the Quran	232
10. Some implications of the Quranic message for the economic system	266'
11. Reevaluating the hadith: survey of earlier hadith criticism, and theological and historical tests of hadith authenticity	288
a. Annex to chapter 11: criteria used for hadith evaluation	329
12. Reevaluating the hadith: the objective test of hadith authenticity	332
13. Epilogue: the rise of religious fanaticism and the direction for true islamic revival	386
Appendix: select themes with Quranic references	398
Works cited	428
Endnotes	

I. Introducing The Quran: Why It Is Important To Read And Understand The Quran

… Now hath come unto you from God Light and a profound Book whereby God guideth whosoever seeketh His good pleasure unto paths of peace, and bringeth them out of darkness into light by His leave, and guideth them onto a straight path. – *Quran*, 5: 15-16

Do they not then ponder the Quran? Or are there locks upon their hearts? – 47: 24

INTRODUCTION

Man is yet to unravel the mystery of why comprehensive divine guidance comes through a particular man at a particular time in a particular region. Islam, the newest of major world religions, was born through the Prophet Muhammad (pbuh[3]) in the seventh century on the Arabian Peninsula, which was a most corrupt spot of the time. Orphaned at a young age[4], Muhammad grew up to enjoy great respect from his community for his excellent judgment, trustworthiness and character – qualities that earned him the nickname of *al-ameen* (the trustworthy). The divine guidance needed to come through a person like him, in the words of one commentator, "to repel the maximum of evil with what was the best."[5] Another noted contemporary Muslim scholar states: "Muhammad had to be humanity's greatest genius, for history has known many unusually gifted minds but none that transcended their time and place as he must have."[6]

In times of recess from work,[7] Muhammad used to go for long periods of retreat to a cave of Mt. Hira on the outskirts of Mecca and engage in contemplative meditation. One glorious night, he heard the divine call – the first of many revelations brought by the angel Gabriel. The experience was a nerve-racking one. This led him to meet with one Christian cousin of his wife Khadijah, Waraka ibn Qusayy, who, after hearing his experience, had both reassuring as well as disquieting words for him:

Surely, by Him in whose hand is Waraqa's soul, thou art the prophet of this people. There hath come unto thee the greatest Namus (angel or Gabriel) who came unto Moses. Like the Hebrew prophets, thou wilt be called a liar, and they will use thee spitefully and cast thee out and fight against thee.[8]

Waraka ibn Qusayy's prophecy, save that regarding his prophethood, proved true for the intermediate period of Muhammad's mission. Later, Muhammad would win over his people. Though his message in Arabic was initially meant for the Arabic speaking people of the mother-city of Mecca and the surrounding region (42:7), it ended up being a universal message for all mankind (3:138; 38:87; 81:27; 68:52; 14:1; 34:28). The Quran, which contains this message, was revealed piecemeal over around 23 years of his life (610-632 C.E.).

As God's trustworthy emissary for delivering His message to mankind, Muhammad took adequate measures for its preservation, preaching, and dissemination. During his lifetime, as the Quran itself mentions, he had the revelations written by scribes (25:5) on parchments and other writing materials. They were also preserved orally, as some of his devoted followers memorized them. After his death, his trustworthy companions had them compiled in book form. Thus the Quran is the only Divine Book that enjoys the advantage of remaining unaltered and unadulterated in its original text. As Kassim Ahmad notes:

> [...] history has fully shown that at the time of the Prophet's death, only the completed written Quran, duly arranged into chapters by the Prophet, existed as his only legacy. It was not yet compiled into book form, but complete writings of it on parchments and other writing materials were kept in the Prophet's house and other houses of the Prophet's scribes. The Prophet also taught many Companions to memorize the Quran following the chapter arrangements he himself had made. During the second caliph Abu Bakr's administration, Abu Bakr himself ordered the Prophet's secretary, Zaid ibn Thabit, to compile the Quran into book form, taking care that all its contents were corroborated by two or more witnesses. When the third caliph, Uthman, prepared his official version of the Quran for dissemination throughout the length and breadth of Islam, he based it on this version.

Thus, the Quran fully satisfies the requirements of a well-corroborated text.[9]

In the beginning of his preaching, Muhammad's own tribe, the influential Quraish, treated him with a kindly indifference. But as his following began to grow, and as it became clear to the Meccans that the new message was revolutionary not only in its conception of God, but also in its ideas of moral principles and social egalitarianism – directly attacking not only their gods but also their wealth – they began to oppose him. At first, they imposed an economic and social boycott on Muhammad and the entire Banu Hashim clan to which he belonged.[10] Though the boycott was lifted after some months, with the death of Muhammad's uncle Abu Talib, Muhammad lost the personal protection Abu Talib had afforded him during his lifetime from the wrath of the Quraish. Muhammad was openly abused on the streets of Mecca and harassed in other ways. His followers were increasingly harassed and persecuted. In the fifth year of the Prophet's mission, he advised his poorer converts, who were subjected to ruthless oppression and unable to defend themselves – those that could afford to – to migrate to Abyssinia, the country of the Christians, where the One God was worshipped. Some years later, Muhammad was impelled to find a safe haven for himself. In the meantime, a delegation of people, who came from Yathrib (present-day Medina) met with Muhammad and embraced Islam. On invitation from the Medinan people,[11] Muhammad then advised his followers to migrate to Medina.

When the Quraish plotted to kill the Prophet, he and his close companion Abu Bakr also left Mecca and fled to Medina, which became the center of the new faith. Muhammad and his converts later were led to fight a number of battles against the invading forces of Mecca. The Meccans finally surrendered to the Prophet and his forces, most of them becoming converts to the new religion. Gradually over time, the message of Islam spread far and wide. Currently about one and a quarter billion people of the world are Muslims, being the second largest religious group globally after the Christians. They comprise the second largest community in Europe, and the third largest in the USA.[12]

After the September 11, 2001 terrorist attack – one of history's deadliest and most savage – it is no wonder that, to put it in the words of a noted expert of comparative religion, "most Americans and Europeans think of Muslims as strange, foreign, and frightening, inevitably linked to

24

headline terrorist events" despite the fact that "Islam is similar in many ways to Judaism and Christianity. [...] This state of affairs needs to change – and can change with better information and deeper understanding. We must put an end to the spiral of fear, hatred, and violence, spawned by ignorance that no longer only afflicts other countries but has come home to America."[13]

It is time that both Muslims and non-Muslims read the Holy Book of Islam to understand its message. After September 11 there has been some interest in Islam among the American Christians. Muslims also need to rediscover afresh what they acknowledge to be the central book of their religion. They need to do so, because sadly, most of them do not care to read it; some read it only in part; and only a distinct few care to make any real effort to understand it. Muslims who do not know the Arabic language are typically taught by their religious teachers to recite the Arabic text of the Quran without understanding its meaning. They are led by their religious leaders to believe that whether or not they understand the text of the Quran, the recitation *per se* is a virtue (*thawab*). People are taught to memorize some short *surahs* (chapters) from the Quran to recite in their prayers. But, with few exceptions, they do not understand what they recite. As a consequence, most Muslims are not only ignorant of the basic teachings of the Quran and of the guidance it provides, but they are also deprived of the vast treasure of wisdom that this Holy Book has to offer to those who make some sincere effort to understand it. Through ignorance, non-Muslims and, worse still, Muslims harbor misconceptions about Islam. This book attempts to highlight the central tenets of the Quran, and point out some of the misconceptions that the majority of the Muslim community has about Islam.

WHY IT IS SO IMPORTANT TO READ AND UNDERSTAND THE QURAN

The Quran is divinely inspired

The historian von Grunebaum states that Muhammad had "a system of ideas which drew its strength from an experience of God. This was clear even to his opponents, although they might not accept it."[14] The Quran clarifies the ways God communicates to man:

> **42:51** It is not fitting for a human being that God should speak to him unless through revelation (*wahy*), or

from behind a veil, or unless He sendeth a messenger to reveal His message by His leave.

The Quran is divinely inspired, and Muhammad was God's Messenger, and a trustworthy deliverer of His message (5:99). This point is reiterated in glowing expressions in various other places of the Quran:

42:52-3 ... And thus *have We[15], by Our command, sent inspiration unto thee* (Muhammad). ... We have made it a Light, wherewith We guide such of Our servants as We will; and verily thou guidest unto the Straight Path – the Path of God. ...

53:1-18 By the star when it setteth, your comrade (Muhammad) erreth not, nor is he misled. Nor doth he speak of his own desire. *It (the Quran) is naught else than divine revelation revealed to him.* One Mighty in Power taught him. Endowed with Wisdom, He appeared (in stately form), while He[16] was in the highest part of the horizon. Then He drew nearer and approached, and was at a distance of two bows or even closer. And He revealed unto His servant (Muhammad) what He revealed. His heart lied not what he saw. ... *His eyes turned not aside, nor did it wander; for he saw the greatest of the signs of the Lord.*

36:5-6 This (the Quran) is a revelation from the Almighty and the Most Merciful, *in order that thou mayst warn a people whose forefathers were not warned, and who (therefore) are unaware.*

69:38-48 But nay! By all that ye see, and all that ye see not. *This is indeed the utterance of an honored Messenger.* It is not the utterance of a poet; little it is that ye believe. Nor the utterance of a soothsayer; little it is that ye heed. It is a revelation from the Lord of the universe. ...Verily it is a Reminder for the righteous.

Considerations that support the revealed status of the Quran include the following:

- The then socio-cultural development of the Arabian Peninsula, and Muhammad's own lack of any literary background;
- The personal conviction of knowledgeable people;
- The accuracy of scientific observations in the Quran;
- The phenomenon of "religious experience" as a credible basis of revelation; and
- The veracity and coherence of the Quran.

About the first of these considerations, Jeffrey Lang remarks: "if Muhammad were the Scripture's [the Quran's] author, then he is undoubtedly the supreme human anomaly, and if he is not, then the true author somehow entirely escaped the view of history."[17] He continues: "The whole style of the Quran, its stress on reason, its logical coherence, its ingenious employment of ambiguity and symbolism, its beauty and conciseness, suggests an author whose insight and wisdom come from far beyond the primitive confines of the then backward and isolated Arabian Peninsula."[18]

Those who think that the Quran is not from God, but written by Muhammad, are directed to what the Quran itself says on this point:

29:48   And *thou (Muhammad) wast not a reader of any Book before it, nor didst thou write it with thy right hand*; for in that case the followers of falsehood might have doubted (it).

Lang goes on: "The conjecture that the Quran is the creation of someone possessed, or out of his mind (7:184, 68:5-6, 81:22) or is a forgery (10:37, 11:13) is refuted by pointing to its unparalleled profundity, coherence and eloquence."[19] Further verses emphasize these points:

16:103   We know indeed that they say: "It is a man who teacheth him." (What?) The language of him whom they falsely point to is outlandish, and this is clear Arabic speech!

17:88   Say: If the whole of humankind and Jinn banded together to produce the like of this Quran, they could not produce the like thereof, even if they were helpers one of another.

In several of its verses the Quran also reminds us that knowledgeable people feel a deep conviction, sometimes with tears in their eyes, that the Quran is indeed divinely inspired (29:49; 34:6; 32:15; 13:36; 5:83; 17:107-108). Look at two of them:

29:49 Nay, *these are clear revelations in the hearts of those who have been endowed with knowledge.* None but the wrongdoers reject our revelations.

5:83 And *when they listen to what hath been revealed to the Messenger, thou seest their eyes overflow with tears in recognition of the truth therein.* They say, "Our Lord, we believe; write us among the witnesses."

Some commentators marvel at the accuracy of scientific observations held in a Book that came in the seventh century covering such topics as water being the source of every living thing, the movement of heavenly bodies, the vastness of space, the expansion of the universe, human reproduction, and other matters. Interestingly, a number of the observations mentioned in the Quran have only recently been found to be accurate.[20]

However, these arguments do not suffice to convince the skeptics. A more basic question lying at the heart of religion is whether there is any real basis in divine revelation as a source of religious guidance or, – which boils down to the same thing – whether a God exists. This question has occupied great minds. But neither philosophy nor science (which includes modern psychology) has yet helped solve the mystery. This should not be taken to mean that the whole truth has been vindicated, but rather that science and philosophy remains inadequate. The condition known as "religious experience"[21] – which is indeed a high stage of spiritual attainment – can enable one to receive divine revelation. Such experience *ifso facto* also proves God's existence. This is a special kind of human experience that comes only to a few, who have earned some special or extra-ordinary human abilities. The Quran illustrates this point as follows:

74:52-3 Nay, but each one of them desireth that he should be given scrolls (of revelation) spread out. By no means! Verily they fear not the Hereafter.

6:124 And when a sign cometh unto them, they say, 'We will not believe until we are given that which God's messengers are given.' *God knoweth best with whom to place His message.* ...

68:4-6 And *thou (Muhammad) indeed possessest a great moral character.* And thou wilt see and they will see which of you are really afflicted with madness.

Religious experience, which is the basis of divine revelation, has been brushed aside by scientists "as psychic, mystical, or supernatural", but as Muhammad Iqbal has aptly observed, this description "does not detract from its value as experience; [...] religious experience has been too enduring and dominant in the history of mankind to be rejected as mere illusion."[22]

The Quran proclaims itself to be a book of true guidance and states that believers recognize the truth of its message (5:83). To be divine revelation, the Quran has to be fully reliable, without doubt, and with no scope for falsehood to touch it.

2: 2 This is the Book, *wherein there is no doubt, guidance unto those who guard against evil.*

16:102 Say: *the Holy Spirit hath revealed it from thy Lord with truth,* ...

41:42 *No falsehood could enter it before or afterwards,* a revelation from the Wise, the Praiseworthy.

Another point that supports the truth of the divine message received by a prophet is that it is cleared of any illusion.

22:52 We have not sent any messenger or a prophet before thee (Muhammad), among whose desires Satan injected not some wrong desires, but *God bringeth to naught that which Satan suggests. Thus God affirms (establishes) His revelations,* for God is Knower, Wise.

This verse points out that prophets are also not immune from receiving false messages, but such messages get erased with divine help. Some vested-interest groups have misused this verse to suggest that the Prophet Muhammad received verses which were initially included in the Quran to satisfy the Arab pagans who worshipped the deities Lat, Uzza and Manat as God's daughters, and that later on these verses were withdrawn.[23] The Quran specifically mentions these gods, however, strongly dismissing them as false:

> **53:19-23** Have ye considered the Lat and the Uzza, and another the third (goddess), Manat? What! For you the males, and for Him the females? That would indeed be an unfair division! *These are nothing but names, which ye have named– ye and your forefathers, for which God hath revealed no warrant.* They follow naught but conjecture and what they desire. ...

The Quran also confirms that devils did not reveal it; it is not in their power to do so (26:210-211). The integrity of the Quranic message is confirmed by another of its important characteristics, i.e., its internal consistency or coherence.

> **4:82** Will they not then ponder the Quran? *Had it been from other than God, they would have found therein much inconsistency.*

Indeed, if the Quran is the revealed Word of God, it is inconceivable that there should be any incoherence in it. God never acts or creates incoherently; there is no flaw in His system of creation (67:3-4). Flaws could, of course, enter a Divine Book through human errors or lapses, but in the case of the Quran there appears to be no evidence of that sort. Historical information of that period to justify this could be considered tenuous or biased. There are, however, certain internal structural features of the Quran that suggest its amazing factual accuracy and internal logic. For example, the Quran mentions 12 months in one verse (9:36), and the word "ShaHR" (month) in singular form appears exactly 12 times in it. The frequency of word "YWM" (day) in singular form is found to be exactly 365 in the Quran, which is consistent with the total approximate number of days in a solar year. These and other instances of numerical harmony with Nature or other kinds of symmetry found in the Quran are a testament to the special and inimitable character of its text and to its coherence.[24]

Criticisms of the claim that the Quran is internally consistent are found to be either superficial or malicious based on an inadequate comprehension or appreciation of its message, or such inconsistency arises because of flawed translation of its message. Critics suggest, for example, that some verses in the Quran that speak of God preordaining things or speak about His Will or Knowledge (which point to predestination), are inconsistent with other verses that speak of free choice available to man. We will address such claims as we proceed.

Though this could be viewed as circular reasoning, the assurance the Quran itself gives us about its protection from any possible corruption and change deserves mention as part of the Quran:

15:9   Surely We reveal the Reminder (the Quran), and *We will assuredly guard it* (from corruption).

18:27   And read that which hath been revealed unto thee of the Book of thy Lord. *None can change His Words.*

The assertion that the Quran is perfectly preserved in its original text is confirmed by Western researchers. The French physician Maurice Buccaille, while comparing the Quran with the Old and New Testaments, states:

> Thanks to its undisputed authenticity, the text of the Quran holds a unique place among the books of Revelation, shared neither by the Old nor the New Testament. [There were] alterations undergone by [both] the Old Testament and the Gospels before they were handed down to us in the form we know today. The same is not true for the Quran for the simple reason that it was written down at the time of the Prophet.[25]

To recapitulate, factors such as unparalleled profundity and literary brilliance of its text, unimaginable in a backward socio-cultural backdrop of the then Arabian Peninsula and Muhammad's known lack of literary background, its coherence, and immaculate accuracy of its scientific observations, together with its unalteration since its compilation, and the conviction of knowledgeable people about its veracity adequately assure

31

the Quran's divine status. I do not think that we need a mathematical wonder as a further proof to establish this status. It is worth mentioning, however, that recent discovery by noted Egyptian-American scholar Rashad Khalifa, further explored by his close associate Turkish-American scholar Edip Yuksel, both great champions of the Quran-only movement in modern Islam, suggests some interesting mathematical features of the structure of the Quran using the number "Nineteen" mentioned in verse 74:30. According to them, there is something unique and extra-ordinary about the literary construction of the Quran. While I find some of their findings quite valid, I have difficulty accepting their full thesis, since a major part of their otherwise fascinating discovery is predicated on the premise that the last two verses of *Surah* 9 (9:128, 129) do not belong to the Quran, but are man-made insertions.[26] While I greatly respect and admire Edip Yuksel for his bold, imaginative leadership in the current Quran-only movement, in my personal correspondence with him, I have expressed my reservation about this finding saying that the omission of two verses of the Quran would remain an issue[27], and that the number "Nineteen" might be better interpreted to denote the degrees or stages of progress in knowledge and power one needs to acquire to decisively conquer Hell fire mentioned in adjoining verses.[28]

Not all divine revelation has reached humankind through compiled books. Earlier revealed books mentioned in the Quran are the Psalms, the Torah, and the Gospels. Other known divine oriental books, all of which proclaim the message of One God, include the Vedas (the Rig, the Atharva, the Sama and the Yajur), the Bhaghavad Gita, and the Zend Avesta. The Tripitaka, the book of Buddhism, emphasizes the need for and importance of striving for truth and enlightenment on the part of every human being who is a true seeker of truth.

Another point we need to note in this context is that since God is the Maker of everything and since everything in the heavens and the earth is interconnected, the Words of God are present everywhere and revolve round a common message, which is the Mother of the Book (*ummil kitab*). The Quran refers to such a message as high in dignity and full of wisdom (43:4), and in a "well-guarded tablet" (*lah-i-mahfuz*) (85:21-22). All divine scriptures, therefore, essentially belong to this Mother Book, which is an inexhaustible fountain of God's Words:

18:109 Say: Though the ocean were ink (to write) the Words of my Lord, verily *the ocean would be used up before the words of my Lord were exhausted*, even though We brought the like thereof to help. (Also see 31:27)

The Quran is a book of wisdom and comprehensive guidance, but it introduces no new religion

The Quran has been revealed with the avowed objective of purifying humankind – to make us realize our flawed ways and help us mend our ways – and remove our ignorance and make us wise (62:2). It is a book of wisdom (10:1; 31:2; 36:2; 43:4). It provides humankind adequate guidance and knowledge to walk aright (12:111; 16:89), and to evolve spiritually. At the same time it provides valuable information about the universe, living beings, and things, about the messages brought by earlier prophets, and about the fate of nations that did not heed their advice. It is indeed a wonderful book. The more one reads, and reflects on, its verses, the deeper is the meaning one can extract from it. Unlike science, which has made tremendous progress in enhancing human knowledge and enriching human life, the religion professed by the Quran provides extensive moral and ethical guidelines to bring about overall moral and spiritual uplifting of humankind at large. Such a remit goes far beyond the role that modern science has been able to play, or even to recognize as essential for humankind.[29]

The Quranic guidance is comprehensive in its scope. It covers every aspect of individual and social life that is of any religious or spiritual significance. Being the last of all revealed books, the Quran takes account of all human errors in the past, and recounts the salient histories of God's prophets providing invaluable lessons for humankind. An excerpt from John L. Esposito aptly describes the scope of the Quranic concerns:

> The Quran envisions a society based on the unity and equality of believers, a society in which moral and social justice will counterbalance oppression of the weak and economic exploitation. [...] The scope of Quranic concerns reflects the comprehensiveness of Islam. It includes rules concerning modesty, marriage, divorce, inheritance, feuding, intoxicants, gambling, diet, theft, murder, fornication and adultery. The socio-economic reforms of the Quran are among its most striking

33

features. Exploitation of the poor, weak, widows, women, orphans (4:2; 4:12), and slaves is vividly condemned. [...] False contracts, bribery, abuse of women, hoarding of wealth to the exclusion of its subordination to higher ends, and usury are denounced. The Quran demands that Muslims pursue a path of social justice, rooted in the recognition that the earth belongs ultimately to God and that human beings are its caretakers. While wealth is seen as good, a sign of hard work and God's pleasure, its pursuit and accumulation are limited by God's law. Its rewards are subject to social responsibility toward other members of the community, in particular to the poor and needy."[30]

The Quran also emphasizes the point that it does not introduce any new religion to humankind but, rather, re-introduces the same religion which had been revealed from time to time to different communities.

16:36   And *verily We have raised up in every nation a messenger.* ... (See also 35:24).

41:43   *Naught is said unto thee (Muhammad) except what was said unto the messengers before thee.*

5:48   And unto thee have We revealed the Book with truth, *confirming whatever Book was before it.* ...

The earlier revelations have been either lost or tainted by vested interest groups. The Quran was revealed to the Prophet Muhammad to correct the human errors that have crept into the scriptures of Judaism and Christianity (See 5:15 below). The Quran recognizes the earlier prophets and upholds the religions that were brought by the Prophets Abraham, Moses and Jesus. Since the source of all divine knowledge or revelation is the same God, true religion (*deen*) with God, i.e., Islam, has always remained the same (3:19). "Islam" means "peace" as well as "submission to God." Correspondingly, a Muslim is one who is for peace, and who surrenders to God, and follows His guidance. All earlier prophets and their followers were Muslims just like Abraham, who, the Quran states, was neither a Jew nor a Christian, but one who submitted to God (i.e., was a Muslim) (3:67). Thus, Islam, the religion of the Quran, represents the oldest as well as the newest, the original as well as the final of all major religions.

42:13   *He (God) established for you the same religion as that which He established for Noah, that which We have sent as inspiration through Abraham, Moses, and Jesus,* namely that you should remain steadfast in religion and make no divisions within it. ...

22:78   *... It is the religion of your father Abraham. It is He (God) Who hath named you Muslims (Submitters) both before and in this (revelation)*; that the Messenger may be a witness before you and ye may be witnesses before humankind. ...

To the People of the Book in particular, i.e., to Jews and Christians, to whom the Torah and the Gospels were sent, the Quran specifically proclaims:

5:15   O People of the Book: *Now hath Our Messenger come unto you revealing unto you much of what ye have concealed of the Book, and passing over much. Now hath come unto you from God Light and a Profound Book.*

27:76   Verily this Quran explaineth to the Children of Israel most of that in which they differ.

The Quran also mentions that it was prophesied in earlier scriptures, and that this is acknowledged by knowledgeable people among the Children of Israel (26:196-197). It further states that the followers of the Torah and the Gospel find the Messenger, *Nabiul Ummi* (the gentile Prophet[31]), mentioned in their books, a prophet who forbids them what is wrong, makes lawful to them what is good and prohibits them what is bad, and relieves them of their burdens and the shackles they used to wear (7:156-157).

The latest revelation, while confirming the earlier ones, points out at the same time the corruptions made in the word of God at various points in history. Particularly worth noting are the human distortions seen in the presentation of Elijah and Jesus as the Son of God in Judaism and Christianity respectively, and the introduction of the idea of a trinity in Christianity. The Quran strongly denounces the ideas of sonship (2:116; 19:35; 6:100-101) and the trinity (5:73, 116). Its most important message is that there is no god but One God who neither begets, nor is begotten

(112:1-3); who has no daughters or consorts (6:100-101; 72:3), nor any partners (6:22-24). Worshiping any living being other than God limits the vision of God Who is All-Transcendent, Mighty, and Wise, and Most Worthy of Praise.

> **3:79-80** *It is not for any human being unto whom God hath given the Book, wisdom and the Prophethood that he should afterwards say unto mankind: Be ye worshipers of me instead of God.* But rather (he would say): Be ye worshipers of the Lord, by virtue of your teaching of the Book and your study thereof. And *nor would he enjoin that ye take the angels and the Prophets for Lords.* What! Would he enjoin disbelief after ye have surrendered (unto God or become Muslims)?

Polytheism, idolatry, and association of anyone or anything with God (*shirk*) are the worst forms of unbelief in Islam (31:13; 4:48), a great deviation from the strict monotheism that Islam has restored one final time.

The Quranic message is immutable whilst flexible

The consideration that the Prophet Muhammad did not bring anything new to mankind as emphasized at (41:43) points to another related characteristic that the religious principles or values that he brought could not also be transient in character, for in that case religion would have little significance for humankind. These are values that are of enduring or eternal benefit to mankind. God's words are essentially Principles or Laws, which can be equated with the Laws of Nature in the physical realm, and are inexorable:

> **10:64** *... No change there is in the Words of God;* that is indeed the supreme triumph.

> **35:43** ... Thus *no change wilt thou ever find in God's ways of treatment* (*sunnah*); yea, no deviation wilt thou ever find in God's *sunnah.*

God's Laws emanate from Him, i.e., are subject to Him; and He is also subject to His own Laws. This implies that God binds Himself to His own Laws. God compensates us for our deeds in ways that always remain the same, and He never does the least injustice to anyone (46:19). Divine revelation thus transcends time and space. Von Grunebaum has aptly expressed the unchanging character of divine revelation:

> Originality is not a religious value. Religious truth is experienced, and is 'rediscovered' because of its content; it has 'existed' unchanged since time began. The Prophet, in his own view and in the view of the Community, is not an originator of teachings but an awakener and a warner, and where necessary a creator of a form of life and community fitted to his newly acquired understanding of God, since this understanding can only be made concrete in the execution of commands and prohibitions. Understood thus, Muhammad was a creative religious spirit and an emissary of God.[32]

Some consider this unchanging character of the divine message static and an obstacle for progress. However, this is a superficial view. The divine message is both unchanging and flexible. The immutability of God's Law cannot preclude it from being flexible or elastic at the same time since it needs to allow for all possibilities and complications which may arise. Indeed the principles that the Quran lays down are immutable, but they accommodate flexibility to deal with varying contexts and circumstances. The Quran asks us to judge between people with justice (4:58 and other verses). This is a general principle we all need to follow. But its practical application to particular cases may vary with the specific contexts and other specifics of such cases for which the Quran does not give any specific guidelines. At the same time where it provides specific guidelines, as in the case of the law of requital, the Quran enunciates a fundamental principle, for example in avenging – without committing excesses ourselves – wrongs done to us by others (2:178, 194) and at the same time urges us to forgive others' faults (5:45), wherever appropriate. The Quranic prescriptions for dispensing criminal justice are flexible between two extremes: the highest possible exemplary punishments and straightaway forgiveness depending on circumstances. The Quran forbids some foods, but allows them in moderate amounts in unavoidable circumstances (2:172-173; 6:145). The principles enunciated in the Quran are compatible with changing contexts and circumstances. But such principles need to be applied judiciously in particular circumstances. That is also the reason why God sometimes introduces better advice replacing an earlier message in order to better suit changing circumstances, but the amendments do not affect the central themes or principles, however:

> **2:106**   Whatever Sign (*ayat*) We abrogate or cause to be forgotten, We bring in (in its place) a better one or the like of it. Knowest thou not that God hath power over all things?

Unfortunately, this verse has caused confusion and a wrong impression among Muslims who toe the traditionalists' line that some verses were abrogated or replaced by later ones.[33] This is a serious misconception:

> **2:85**   *Believe ye then in part of the Book and disbelieve ye in part thereof?* What then is the reward of such among you who do this except disgrace in the life of this world, and on the Day of Resurrection they would experience the most grievous punishment. And God is not heedless of what ye do.

It is also worth noting that while divine revelation or God's Word has remained unchanged, its interpretation has changed from person to person and over time, due to the essentially dynamic nature of the Quranic text as well as the human element involved in interpretation. As pointed out by modern reformist thinkers like Muhammad Iqbal, individual interpretations of the Quranic message by early scholars, which gave four [or five] different schools of law, cannot claim any finality.[34] He notes that the principles that are immutable should be distinguished from those regulations that are the product of human interpretations and are thus subject to change.[35] There has been a surge in new thinking in recent years about how to interpret the Quran or Islam, which emphasizes the value of *ijtihad* (new interpretation and thinking) in understanding Islam in order to effectively come to grips with the challenges and realities of modern time. As a contemporary Egyptian writer Nasr Abu Zayd appropriately comments, the Quranic revelation is "a cultural and social phenomenon [...] [T]o faithfully and completely comprehend Islam's universal message, one must understand the seventh-century cultural and linguistic environment of Prophet Muhammad, the Arab-speaking human being to whom God revealed the Quran. [...] *The Quran is divine as revelation and human as interpretation.*"[36] The orthodox Islamic view, Abu Zayd claims, is "stultifying; it reduces a divine, eternal, and dynamic text [of the Quran] to a fixed human interpretation with no more life and meaning than a trinket, a talisman, or an ornament."[37] This modern view of the nature of the revealed text is related to the long-running theological debate about whether the Quran is the eternal, uncreated, and exact word of God (the position of the traditionalists), or is a created, or humanly understood version of divine revelation or inspiration (the rationalists' and modern dominant position).[38] The Quran itself bears witness to the fact that many of its verses are allegorical in nature (3:7), and amenable to multiple interpretations, and thus they should not be always understood in a strictly literal sense.

The Quranic message is universal, and an inimitable miracle in itself

The Quran was revealed in Arabic primarily to warn and guide the Arabic-speaking people of Mecca and adjoining regions (42:7). A messenger came from among them to read to them the divine revelations, to purify them, and make them wise – people who were unlettered, and in clear error (62:2). But at the same time the Quran is also a book of guidance and wisdom for all humankind relevant to all times:

> **14:1** *A Book (the Quran) We have revealed unto thee (Muhammad), in order that thou mayst lead humankind out of Darkness into Light* – by the will of their Lord – to the path of the Mighty, the Praiseworthy. (Also see 34:28)

> 38:87 *It (the Quran) is naught else than a Reminder for the whole universe.* (Repeated in 68:52 and 81:27)

The great miracle of the Quran, as the nineteenth-century Muslim thinker-reformer of India Sir Sayyid Ahmad Khan aptly observes, is its universality. "Each generation continues to find the Quran relevant despite the constant increase in human knowledge. Too heavy a reliance on hadith for the interpretation of the Quran puts at risk this eternal and universal quality. Hadith-based *tafsir* [commentary] tends to limit the meaning of the Quran to a particular historical situation, thus obscuring its universality."[39]

This characteristic of universality highlights the point that the Quran is amenable to reaching non-Arabic speaking people through appropriate translations into different languages, and that there is a need for such efforts to be pursued in competent quarters. The Quran categorically states that it was revealed in Arabic for a reason:

42:7   And thus *We have inspired unto the thee the Quran in Arabic, in order that you mayst warn the mother-city (Mecca) and those around it*, and warn of a Day of Assembling whereof there is no doubt; (when) a host will be in the Garden and a host in the Fire.

14:4   And *never have We sent a messenger except in the language of his people* in order that he might make (the message) clear to them. ...

41:44   Had We revealed this Quran in a foreign tongue, they would certainly have said: Why are not its verses made clear? What? A foreign (tongue) and an Arab (Messenger)? ...

Ironically, while the Jewish and Christian scriptures were translated into Greek and Latin at an early date and disseminated in vernacular languages, the Arabic Quran was not translated into other languages in Muslim countries until modern times.[40] After the Bible, the Quran is probably the most translated book of religion in the world. It should be noted, however, that for readers who do not know Arabic, it will be advisable for them to consult several of the available translations, as translations are found to differ in regard to various verses of the Quran. In cases where such differences are found – such differences are found only in sporadic cases of verses and are not too substantive in most cases – the reader should reflect on the meaning of the verse(s) concerned and make his own judgment about its (their) proper meaning. "The Quran stands on its own, requiring the application of a dedicated and enlightened mind for its understanding."[41] God Himself has made the Quran so clear, easy and self-explanatory that the reader should be able to get its full message himself without the help of any commentaries.

Indeed the Quran is an inimitable miracle the like of which could not be produced even with the combined efforts of all humankind and Jinns (17:88).

29:51   *And is it not enough (of a miracle) for them that We have revealed unto them the Book,* which is read to them? Surely it is a Mercy and a Reminder to those who believe. (Also see 74:35-37)

Jeffrey Lang, a Mathematics professor and a contemporary Muslim convert and noted Islamic scholar had these glowing words to describe the profound nature of the Quran, even when he was an atheist and not yet a convert:

> I did not recognize any specific wonders of a mathematical nature in my first reading [of the Quran]. However, I will say I was in awe of the genius that produced it. Its marvelous precision and economy of expression suggested an amazing logic. Its superb wisdom, cloaked in the most exquisite phraseology, pointed to knowledge that is beyond any one man's life experience. Its ability to reach with the same words and to make surrender to its calling both the learned and the illiterate could only come from a profound understanding of human psychology. While reading the Quran, I felt I was being continuously educated –that it was taking me to higher and higher vistas of thinking – about life, about humanity, about reasoning and spirituality – even though [at that time] I did not accept its central premise of the existence of God.[42]

The Quranic religion is a science

Admittedly, "the essence of religion is faith", as Iqbal puts it.[43] But faith, as he notes, goes with ideas which should have a rational foundation.

> Now, since the transformation and guidance of man's inner and outer life is the essential aim of religion, it is obvious that the general truths which it embodies must not remain unsettled. No one would hazard action on the basis of a doubtful principle of conduct. Indeed, in view of its function, religion stands in greater need of a rational foundation of its ultimate principles than even the dogmas of science. Science may ignore a rational metaphysics; indeed it has ignored it so far. Religion can hardly afford to ignore the search for a reconciliation of the opposition of experience and a justification of the environment in which humanity finds itself.[44]

While religion is firmly rooted in divine revelation, its principles must have a rational foundation, since what comes through divine revelation – what God prescribes for humanity for its transformation or evolution – has to be based on the soundest of logic. Especially significant is the Quranic appeal to humankind to reflect on the creation of the universe, and on their surrounding environment, and on the alteration of the day and night:

44:38-9 And *We created not the heavens and the earth, and whatever is between them, in sport*. We created them not but for a serious end; but most of them know not.

3:190-1 *Verily in the creation of the heavens and the earth, and in the succession of the night and the day, are signs for men of understanding,* who, standing, sitting, and reclining, remember God, and reflect on the creation of the heavens and the earth, and say: O our Lord! Thou hast not created this in vain.

29:20 Say (O Muhammad): *Travel through the earth, and see how God hath brought forth all creation; hereafter He wilt give it another birth.* Lo! God hath power over all things.

God's signs or messages are evident throughout creation, history, and nature. The Quran urges man to take lessons from the universe, and its creation and change. "The Quran opens our eyes to the great fact of change, through the appreciation and control of which alone it is possible to build a durable civilization."[45] Change points to causal relation. The Quran thus presents a religion, the principles of which constitute a science. It is a religion that makes man conscious of how he can change both his lot and the lot of his society, and how he can make all round progress: temporal and non-temporal, worldly and spiritual. "And in this process of progressive change", as Iqbal puts it, "God becomes a co-worker with him, provided man takes the initiative."[46] The Quran states:

13:11 Verily God changeth not the condition of men until they change their own selves (*nafs*).

8:53 God never changeth the blessings (*niamat*) with which He hath graced a people until they change their own selves.

42

The Quran itself, Jeffrey Lang rightly observes, encourages a rational approach to faith, as evidenced by the tenor of arguments offered in many of its verses, e.g., in the many verses that say that people should apply their *aql* or reason and where Abraham had arguments with disbelievers, which cornered the disbelievers.[47] Indeed, if one reads the Quran carefully and ponders its verses, one can find in it a science or philosophy. It describes how man can evolve spiritually to achieve real progress and success, or how he can falter in his way, how he can be distressed and hurt, or even become impoverished materially. The following verses are especially worth pondering:

53:39   *Man hath only that for which he maketh effort.* (See also 20:15)

2:286   God tasketh not a soul beyond its capacity. *For it (is only) that which it hath earned, and against it (only) that which it hath deserved.*

42:30   And *any misfortune that befalleth you is because of your own deeds.*

3:117   *It is not God Who doeth them any wrong, but it is they who are wronging themselves.*

25:70   *Excepted (from grievous retribution) are those who believe, repent, and do righteous deeds*; for such God would change their bad deeds into good ones.

28:84   *Whoever cometh with any good work will gain further reward from it*; but as for one who cometh with any evil deed (should know that) the doers of evil deeds will be requited to the extent of what they did.

19:76   *God increaseth the guidance of those who go aright.*

2:26   *God leadeth astray only the evildoers.*

6:132   *For all there are ranks according to their deeds.* Thy Lord is not oblivious of what they do.

2:148   *Strive together toward all that is good.*

The Quran points out that it is only one's work that determines one's fate, and that it is only with sincere effort that man can achieve progress and success. God does not do anything on His own to reward or punish man or any creature. As Ahmad aptly remarks, God never really rewards or punishes anybody. It is actually the creature who does this work to fulfill or correct its own deed or misdeed.[48]

Is it then an echo of what scientists say: God does not intervene? In a way, yes, and it is at this juncture that science and religion meet. But while science sees no divine presence in human affairs, religion shows how the All-Pervading and Responsive God acts even though we may interpret this divine action in different ways.[49] "Response, no doubt, is the test of the presence of a conscious self", says Iqbal.[50] Religion shows how man can receive God's mercy and help in his work and life. Believers experience such divine mercy and help in their multifarious situations and activities. Those who pray to God with heart-felt sincerity and devotion can receive His kind response (2:186; 40:60; 27:62).

A question may arise: if it is work alone that determines one's fate, then what meaning is there to the Quranic message that God is Forgiving and Most Merciful? The way God forgives is worth pondering:

> **16:119** Then, verily thy Lord – to *those who do evil in ignorance, repent afterward and do right (mend their conduct)* – to *them thy Lord is Forgiving, Most Merciful*. (See also 6:54)

> **3:135** And Who forgiveth save God only those who, when they commit sins or wrong themselves, remember God and implore forgiveness for their sins, and *who do not knowingly repeat their sins?*

> **11:3** And *seek ye forgiveness of your Lord, and turn to Him repentant; He will* provide you goodly provision until an appointed time, and *bestow His abounding grace upon those who deserve it. ...*

It is evident from these verses that God does not forgive in the way most think. God does not forgive one without one's adequate repentance, which is also a punishment. Thus, none escapes the punishment of evil deeds. Three preconditions that make a man or a woman eligible for getting God's forgiveness are: first, that he/she does not commit the wrongdoing knowingly; second, that he/she mends his/her ways; and third, that he/she does not repeat the wrongdoing. God does not favor anybody, or bestow any mercy on any unless he deserves it.

If work determines one's fate, it then also follows that there should be no such thing as predestination by God or fatalism, i.e., the belief that all events are preordained by God. There has been a lot of confusion and misunderstanding among both Muslims and non-Muslims about the question of predestination by God, surrounding the Quranic word *taqdir*, which literally means "measure" or "proportion" or "destiny". The following Quranic verse, among some, may be quoted, which has been misunderstood by many:

25:2   He (God) hath created everything in due measure (proportion or destiny).

This verse is related to other verses that describe God's will and knowledge, which have also given rise to confusion that is of the same nature as that with predestination. The idea that has often been mistakenly advanced is essentially that God knows in advance all events, He predetermines all events, and He wills all events and, therefore, all events take place in accordance with what God knew, planned and willed. But if this idea is true, the Quranic verse that "Man hath only that for which he maketh effort" (53:39; 20:15) cannot have any meaning. For, if God decides beforehand what man will do, He cannot legitimately make him responsible for anything he does and the whole system of rewarding for good work and punishing for bad work completely breaks down, there remaining no role for religion to play for man. God has endowed man with free will and freedom of action; He has given him freedom to choose between good and evil (18:29; 76:3). The only sensible meaning that can be attached to the verse 25:2 concerning God's assignment of measure to everything and other related verses relating to His knowledge and will is that man has to work with his own given situation and his given possessions including his own qualities, which may have been influenced by his own previous actions or by actions of others, including his predecessors, and in a situation which is external to him. Thus man works with certain favorable or unfavorable conditions or constraints, which so to say, are given for him or, if you will, which are already willed or predetermined by God. Also, there are certain conditions or factors given for a man that may be beyond his knowledge and control, which are given by God. Man needs to accept such factors as given and work within that context. He cannot be held accountable for such givens. However, with sincere determined efforts, man can often succeed in turning the surrounding adverse conditions into favorable ones for him.

Note also that God's foreknowledge of events does not necessarily imply that He predetermines them. For example, a man planning to kill another person, or to steal something, at a particular time is known to God, but it cannot be said that this planning and the actual events of killing or stealing when they take place are predetermined by God. He certainly has not preordained someone to be a killer or a thief. Simply put, divine knowledge is irrelevant to the claim that God predestines our choices and state in the afterlife.[51] Also, as Iqbal forcefully and beautifully points out, God's fore-knowledge is that of open possibilities of future events, not of events as such as a fixed order of things – a notion that admits of freely exercised creativity on the part of humankind as participants in the divine course of events. "The future certainly pre-exists in the organic whole of God's creative life, but it pre-exists as an open possibility, not as a fixed order of events with definite outlines," he notes.[52]

However, even as things happen according to the natural laws of causation, which are after all God's laws, when such things were determined beforehand and are given for the present, we may term such events as God-willed or God-given. So it is also true to assert that our fate is predetermined in part, and that our free choice or room for action is not fully free after all. We often bind ourselves by our own actions or actions of others. So this is a fully logical thing.[53]

Thus, what the Quran professes for man is based on a rational foundation.[54] What ostensibly appear to be miraculous activities of prophets and saints, or God-sent boons or scourges that are described in the Quran cannot be explained in the generally understood or applied sciences, but they are explicable in the science that God has expounded in the Quran, which can be perceived only by men of insight and transcendental knowledge. The Quran itself suggests that, as Jeffrey Lang aptly puts it, faith is undermined when reason is ignored or poorly applied.[55] The Quran thus characterizes people who reject faith as those who are devoid of *aql* or reason (2:171; 5:58, etc.), and encourages men to apply their reason to see the truth of the revealed word (2:44, 76, etc.). Citing Quranic verses, Lang further remarks: Those who benefit the most from the Quran are 'persons of insight,' 'firmly rooted in knowledge,'

46

'use their reason,' and 'stand on clear evidence and proof'. While those who oppose revelation are 'deluded,' 'in manifest error,' 'ignorant,' 'foolish,' 'have no understanding,' 'only follow surmise and conjecture,' and blindly adhere to tradition.[56] The Quran also repeatedly asks us to think and ponder. Thus as Lang further notes: The message is plain enough: to gain truer faith, we need to free ourselves from inherited notions and examine our beliefs rationally.[57]

In a vital sense then, religion is a science that can be considered superior to conventional science, just as prophets can be held to be superior to scientists.[58] It should naturally be the case, since prophets are the best servants and emulators of God, Who is Most Wise and the Greatest of all scientists.

The Quran is easy to understand, detailed and self-explained, and complete

In many places, the Quran states that its message is clear and easy, straightforward with no ambiguity, detailed, and self-explanatory. Many of its messages are repeated, yet each time conveying the meaning to the reader in a newer light, or giving a deeper understanding and insight:

44:58 Verily We have made this (Quran) *easy in thy tongue* that they may take heed. (See also 54:17, 22, 32, and 40.)

39:27-8 And verily We have set forth for mankind in this Quran *every kind of similitude*, in order that they may reflect. A Quran in Arabic *without any crookedness* (or ambiguity), in order that they may become upright.

12:111 It is no invented story (*hadith*); this (the Quran') is a confirmation of previous revelations, *a detailed exposition of everything,* and a guidance and a mercy for people who believe. (See also 6:114 and 16:89.)

6:115 *Perfected (or complete) is the Word of thy Lord. ...*

The Quran explains everything of religious importance to us. One can gauge how detailed its messages are by simply looking at some of the minutest details of its admonitions relating to such matters as how we should conduct ourselves in what many might think to be even ordinary or petty matters of etiquette or behavior. For example, the Quran teaches us to be duly polite to others in conversation and arguments; to salute or to return salutation; to be polite to superiors, and to speak to them in a voice not higher than their voice, and not walk ahead of them; to enter a house not without the due permission of its occupants; to seek permission to enter rooms of couples at specified private times; not to ridicule, or make faces at others; not to back-bite; to record loan or other transactions in order to avoid possible future misunderstandings; and similar things we should or should not do, which benefit us enormously in our day-to-day affairs, and add to our overall spiritual development. Such ordinary matters are detailed in the Quran, in addition to the bigger issues. What else one needs for guidance in life? It is hard to imagine why one should not regard the Quran as a complete guidance for mankind.

The Quran is self-explanatory. No human explanation is necessary to understand it, not even from the Prophet Muhammad:

> **75:16-9** Move not thy tongue herewith (the Quran) to make haste with it. Lo! It is for Us to put it together and read it. And when We have read it, just follow thou the reading. Then lo! It is upon Us to explain it.

Muslims in general mistakenly consider that the Hadith literature complements and explains the Quran, and is an essential aid to understanding it. We will, however, argue later that the Hadith, instead of clarifying things, rather confuses them.[59]

It should also be noted that while none should find it difficult to understand most of what the Quran contains, there are also verses in it that are allegorical, which are not easily understood by all. Only knowledgeable, i.e., spiritually advanced, people understand them. Those who do not understand such verses do not have to be too concerned about their meanings. The Quran mentions about these verses and states that some people who do not understand such verses create confusion among people with them:

> **3:7** He (God) it is Who hath revealed unto thee (Muhammad) the Book wherein are clear revelations – they are the fundamental part of the Book – and

others (that are) allegorical. But those in whose hearts is doubt pursue that which is allegorical, seeking dissension and seeking to interpret it. None knoweth its true interpretation except God and those who are of sound knowledge (who) say: We believe in it; the whole is from our Lord; but only men of understanding really heed.

As many Quran scholars point out, the Quranic verses convey two types of meaning: one *zahir* or apparent (or literal) and another *batin* or hidden (or deep or esoteric). The Quran thus becomes an inexhaustible source of knowledge to those who truly seek knowledge.

The Quran is to be understood, and pondered, not blindly recited

The Quran was revealed in Arabic precisely and specifically to enable the Arabic-speaking people to understand its message:

43:3 *Verily We have revealed the Quran in Arabic, that ye may learn (or understand).*

38:29 (This is) a Book that We have revealed unto thee, full of blessing, *that they may ponder its revelations, and that men of understanding may reflect.* (Also see 10:24.)

It is really unfortunate that many of those who do not understand the Arabic Quran, recite it in Arabic without trying to understand its meaning. And there are even *hafizes* (memorizers) in some non-Arab countries who have memorized the whole Arabic Quran without understanding its meaning. And a lot of emphasis has been placed by religious teachers on the pronunciation of the Arabic text of the Quran. All this they do by wrongly thinking that the recitation of the Holy Quran *per se* is a virtue (*thawab*), an idea that is borrowed from the Hadith. It is ironic that, in Bangladesh for example, the Quran is recited in Muslim families by hired *qaries* (Quran reciters) over the bodies of their dear and near ones who have just died. This is a practice which is hard to comprehend. The dead cannot hear it, nor do those who are around the dead body. Neither the *qaries* nor those who hear them understand anything of the Quranic message in the foreign language. Such a practice is against the very message and spirit of the Quran, which specifically urges us to listen to its message (i.e., with understanding) when it is recited so that we may receive God's mercy (7:204). It is unthinkable that reading a religious book without understanding should make any sense. The Divine Book has been sent precisely for humankind's guidance, to purify people, and to make them wise. How can they get guidance, purification and wisdom without understanding its message? Such people as recite the Quran without trying to understand the message serve no good cause; they serve God on the verge and incur a manifest loss (22:11). The Quran clearly points to the need for understanding its verses, and repeatedly urges the readers to reflect on them (see: 38:29 and 10:24 cited above). As it is sufficient, self-contained, and amenable to understanding according to its internal logic, none should excuse himself on the grounds that the Quran is so difficult that it is not worth trying to understand it.

A final note on the healing power of the Quranic verses

The Quran is, in a special sense, a healing for the believers. By inspiring them to shun all misdeeds, including wrong attitudes and feelings, and to do good deeds, and purify their body and mind, it does exercise an influence as a healing or preventive antidote for them from their diseases, physical or mental.

> **10:57** O humankind! There hath indeed come unto you an admonition from your Lord, a *Healing for (what is in) your hearts*, and a Guidance and a Mercy for those who believe. (Also see 17:82.)

This does not mean that every Tom, Dick, and Harry can cure diseases by uttering some Quranic verses like a mantra. If this were true, all and sundry would be able to cure diseases, or, say, remove snake poison by simply uttering some Quranic verses. Since all cannot perform this feat, it means that the power of healing is not in the verses themselves but in the persons themselves. Only certain people, who can acquire some extra-ordinary power through meditation, *dhikr* (remembrance) of God, or *jappa* (repeated chanting of some name), or because of endowment with special inborn gift, can display such healing power by uttering Quranic verses, or through other means.

CONCLUSION

The Quran is indeed a wonderful book, unrivalled by any in the world. Confirming and upholding earlier divine messages, and excelling in eloquence, profundity, coherence, and scientific orientation of its message, it embodies the latest genuine, comprehensive guidance to humankind in Arabic. Its main purpose, to quote Iqbal again, is to awaken in man the higher consciousness of his manifold relations with God and the universe.[60]

Religion as practiced today by most Muslims has little of what the Quran has to offer. It is time we all rediscover the Quran anew.

II. THE MEANING AND *RAISON D'ETRE* OF RELIGION
AND ITS RELATION TO SCIENCE

Let there arise from amongst you a community who invite to all
that is good, enjoin what is right, and forbid what is wrong. It
is they who are successful. – 3:104

And We created not the heavens and the earth and whatever is
between them for just play. *We created them not but for a*
serious end; but most of them know not. – 44:38-39

The meaning and *raison d'etre* of religion

Religion is of the highest importance to humankind. It is the most living,
civilizing, and nourishing force for it. It is primarily concerned with the
development of man's psyche and personality. It provides him the
necessary knowledge to distinguish between right and wrong in all of his
actions. It shows how he can purify and develop his soul and conscience,
and attain higher levels of understanding, enlightenment, and power.
Success comes to one who purifies his soul:

> **91:8-10** And (God) inspired it (*nafs* or soul to know) what is
> wrong for it and (what is) right for it. *He indeed*
> *succeedeth who purifieth it; and he indeed faileth*
> *who corrupteth it.*

The basic role of religion is to guide man on a journey of spiritual
evolution. Man cannot live a life worth living by bread alone. He cannot
be content with material progress alone. Neither wealth nor men are of
any real help to man (26:88-89; 34:37). On the other hand, spiritual
progress can help one make material progress as well. The Quran
describes this in the parable of two persons, one of them materially rich,
but without faith and the other poorer but with faith. The rich person had
two gardens, interspersed with croplands, which gave good harvests. One
day the rich person boasted of his wealth to the other, saying that his
wealth would never run out, and expressing disbelief in God and
afterlife. The pious man admonished him that he should not deny God
and His powers, saying that God might give him (the pious man) better
than what the other person had, and that God could bring his harvests to
naught. And when the boastful man visited his gardens and croplands, he
found all the crops destroyed by a storm (18:32-42).

Though his species marks a distinct improvement over all others, man is prone to making mistakes, and by thus doing can become worse than even animals. God has breathed of His own Spirit (*ruh*) into man (15:29; 32:9; 38:72); He made him worthy of reverence by Jinns and angels (2:30-34; 7:11). His distinct superiority over all other living beings is due to his faculties of understanding, thinking, and judgment. He has been endowed with a heart (the central organ) or a mind (and also a brain, which is closely interlinked with the heart) in order to feel, think, and exercise intelligence; and he has eyes to see and ears to hear (16:78; 32:9; 46:26; 90:8; 22:46; 69:12). But if a man does not exercise his faculties and act accordingly, the consequences are not good for him:

25:44   Or *thinkest thou (O Muhammad) that most of them listen or understand?* They are like the cattle; nay, but they are further astray from the path!

7:179   Already We[61] (God) have cast into hell many of the Jinns and humankind, *those who have hearts with which they comprehend not, eyes with which they see not, and ears with which they hear not.* They are like the cattle; nay, they are worse! These are they who are neglectful.

Just as wealth does not count as a criterion in judging how good or religious a person is, his bodily and intellectual developments are also no good indicator of how religious or pious he is. Our schools and universities may produce scholars and technocrats, but they do not necessarily turn out good and wise men and women.

Religion proclaims a message of peace, tolerance, justice, mercy and compassion. It teaches us to live in peace and harmony with others in society. Even scientists who do not believe in God recognize the great importance of the moral and ethical lessons that religion teaches. Indeed the very foundation for maintaining harmony and beauty in human relationships would have been severely shaken if moral values were not honored by humankind, and nurtured in society in some way. Albert Einstein was struck by the wondrous structure of the universe, and its underlying laws, and "admitted that our actual knowledge of these laws is only imperfect and fragmentary, so that actually, the belief in the existence of basic all-embracing laws of Nature also rests on a sort of faith." He was "convinced that a spirit is manifest in the laws of the Universe – a spirit vastly superior to that of man, and one in the face of which we with our modest powers must feel humble".[62] He further observes:

> The most important human endeavor is the striving for morality in our actions. Our inner balance and our very existence depend on it. Only morality in our actions can give beauty and dignity to life. To bring this [as] a living force and bring it to clear consciousness is perhaps the foremost task of education.[63]

> Our time is distinguished by wonderful achievements in the field of scientific understanding and the technical applications of those insights. Who would not be cheered by this? But let us not forget that knowledge and skills alone cannot lead humanity to a happy and dignified life. Humanity has every reason to place the proclaimers of high moral standards and values above the discoverers of objective truth. What humanity owes to personalities like Buddha, Moses, and Jesus ranks far higher than all the achievements of the inquiring and constructive mind. What these blessed men have given us we must guard and try to keep alive with all our strength if humanity is not to lose the dignity, the security of its existence and its joy in living.[64]

It is the violation of the pristine values and lessons of religion that causes human corruption, strife, and misery in the world. The twentieth century has witnessed the occurrence of two great world wars, and human strife and conflicts have been recurrent and frequent in various regions of the world with incidences of genocide, human torture and persecution, and other forms of gross human brutalities and injustice. And while the world has seen unprecedented economic prosperity and material progress of human beings, there still remain many disadvantaged and impoverished groups in society, for whom a moral duty devolves on the more affluent. Moreover, the need for strict observance of morality on the part of man, or for its effective enforcement by society has not diminished at all in modern time with educational, scientific, technological, and industrial progress, but seems rather to have increased.

It is from religion that we get guidance and inspiration for doing right and noble things. Our deeds consist of two kinds: (1) what we do inwardly through our beliefs, feelings and thoughts; and (2) what we do outwardly through our outward behavior and actions. We are accountable to God for both:

2:284   … And *whether ye make known what is in your minds or conceal it, God will bring you to account for it. …*

Beliefs matter, since our beliefs determine our personality and behavior patterns. An example is trust between people, which is based on the belief that neither would deceive the other. Religion as proclaimed by the Quran requires belief in one All-Transcending God, the Day of Resurrection (or Afterlife), and His creations of angels and Jinns, His revelations, and the prophets who have received such revelations (2:177; 6:100).[65] Likewise we need to be careful about the feelings that we harbor. Feelings such as ingratitude, pride, imprudence, complacency, lust, apathy, hatred, hostility, cowardice, jealousy, greed, and generally fear, anger, bitterness, and suspicion are of the wrong kind, which retard one's spiritual development, and hence are condemned by religion. Feelings such as contentment, gratitude, love, appreciation, and empathy are of the right or appropriate kind, elevate human personality and help one spiritually. Feelings of complacency or the arrogant feelings of self-achievement and smug self-satisfaction, imprudence and pride are at the root of self-destruction. Citing some Quranic verses, Ahmad describes this last point beautifully:

[N]one should ever think that he or she reserves all the intelligence and others are but fools. Smug self-satisfaction pulled down Iblis (a Jinn) from his leadership of the angels and the feeling of insignificance by giving rise to a growing thirst for knowledge lifted earthly man and woman far above the angels.[66]

Feelings of pleasure, displeasure, happiness, sadness, and grief may be good or bad depending on the circumstances, which give rise to such feelings. For example, displeasure at one's own work or achievement may inspire one to do further work, while pleasure or happiness at the plight of others is the wrong attitude. Frustration reflects an extreme form of dissatisfaction with one's own situation, performance, achievement, or progress, but is the wrong way of looking at the result of one's own effort, and should be avoided. Frustration is degrading to one's soul, as it implies the complete lack of confidence in one's own self, i.e., in one's own capacity and potential, which in effect reflects a lack of faith in God Himself.

It should also be noted that since religion is a serious matter, man is more accountable for those actions that are made seriously, i.e., with a deliberate intention, than for those actions that are made unintentionally or accidentally (2:225; 4:92-93). However, showing off, hiding, or meaning something else in one's mind, amounts to hypocrisy. Hypocritical behavior is a greater wrong, and is more damaging to one's soul than an open rejection or opposition of faith. As Ahmad points out in light of the Quran, a hypocrite expends more energy or effort, or suffers more pain to mend his misdeeds.[67] The Quran states:

> **4:145-6** Surely, the hypocrites are at the bottom of the fire, and thou wilt find no helper for them, except for those who repent, mend (their action), and hold fast to God, and make their religion sincere to God. ...

The kind of *iman* or mindset one has is an important determinant in how far and how fast one can proceed on the path of progress, material or spiritual.[68] The collective mindset of a nation determines how fast it can develop. The relative underdevelopment of the Muslim community in general in various regions of the world today is, in some significant measure, to do with the kind of mindset they generally have, which can be traced largely to the influence that has come from the Hadith literature.[69]

On a mental plane, man at times may find himself totally lost, not knowing where to find answers to how he can live a life worth living and get some solace or relief to his distress. Man needs to seriously consider where he gets answers to these questions and situations. It is religion – and right religion, of course, which provides answers to these questions. Religion teaches man to never lose hope (39:53). Religion provides hope to the frustrated, and light to those groping in darkness (28:57).

Note also that every man or woman has a purpose to fulfill in life. Scientists, if not all of them, seem to suggest that man, or for that matter, any living creature or any inanimate thing in the universe does not have any end or purpose. The Quran, however, asserts the opposite (See 44:38-39 cited at the top of this chapter, also 23:115). Man thus needs to seriously wonder why after all he exists in this world. Man's first appearance in the universe heralded a new golden era in the history of creation and creativity. He has been made in the best of forms (95:5), fit as a successor on earth, and superior to all other species:

> **2:30-34** Behold, thy Lord said to the angels: I am about to place a successor (*khalifa*) on earth. They said: Wilt thou place there one who will do mischief and shed blood, while we hymn Thy praise and glorify Thee? He (God) said: Surely I know what ye know not. And He taught Adam the names of all things; then He showed them to the angels, and said: Inform Me of the names of these if ye are right. They said: Be thou glorified! We have no knowledge save what Thou hast taught us. Lo! Thou, only Thou art the Knower, the Most Wise. He said: O Adam! Inform them of their names. (When he informed them of their names), He (God) said: Did I not tell you that I know the secrets of the heavens and the earth, and I know what ye bring to light and what ye hide? And behold! We said to the angels: Prostrate yourselves before Adam. They fell prostrate, all except Iblis. He refused, and was too proud, and so was of those who disbelieved.

Evidently man, as the most competent successor species on earth, has a most responsible, dignified role to play. He can best perform this role by serving God and emulating Him – by creating or acting in the way God Himself does, i.e., by learning the secrets of divine creation or action or the divine laws, which are at work. Note, however, that God does not need anything from us, including our praise and adoration of Him:

> **35:15** O ye men! *It is ye that have need of God, but God is one Who is self-sufficient*, Most Worthy of Praise.

> **3:97** ... And as for those who deny the truth, (know that) verily, *God standeth in no need of anything in all the worlds.* (See also 47:38 and 55:29)

> **51:56-8** I have not created the Jinn and humankind except to serve Me. *Neither livelihood do I need from them nor*

do I require that they should feed Me. Verily God is the provider of livelihood, Lord of Power, the Strong.

Religion is guidance for real human progress – not only to elevate man morally and spiritually, but also to emancipate him from the shackles of slavery, serfdom, and indignity, to liberate him from any want or poverty, and to lift him from ignorance, and make him intelligent and wise. Religion is for creation of a just, secure, and peaceful society, for creation of equal opportunities for all, for abolition of all forms of unfair discrimination in society, and for creation of an enabling and conducive environment for all men and women to pursue their endeavor for spiritual advancement, and thus for overall uplifting of humanity at large. There is no end to human evolution and progress. Hence, one cannot remain complacent with any given state of progress. For that would be the recipe for either his or her stagnation or downfall. This is precisely the reason why man needs to serve God, follow Him as his only most reliable Guide, or as his ultimate goal. Only by submitting to and following God, as the Supreme Being, man evolves himself properly. This is at the heart of the theory of religion. Religion is thus a progressive concept, and men of religion are progressive people. Those who think that religion is "an opiate", or that religion is 'a reactionary concept", miss its real meaning and purpose.

What religion can do for an individual man is best exemplified by the life of the Prophet Muhammad himself. Being an orphan, he rose from a humble beginning in life. By nature he was honest and trustworthy, which earned him the nick-name *"al-ameen"* (the trustworthy) quite early in life. He was a man of excellent character. (68:4-6). By dint of his tireless efforts for knowing the truth through meditation and prayer, he received divine revelation. He brought light to himself as well as to the world at large. The Prophet Muhammad thus received abundance of good in his life, and became the ideal to follow for all human beings. The story of the Prophet's rise to spiritual eminence or abundance from a humble beginning is reflected in the following Quranic verses:

108:1-2 Surely *We have given thee (Muhammad) abundance*. So, pray to thy Lord, and sacrifice.

93:3-8 The Lord hath not forsaken thee (O Muhammad), nor is He displeased (with thee). And verily the future will be better for thee than the present. And soon thy

Lord will give thee that with which thou will be well pleased. *Did He not find thee an orphan, and give thee shelter? And He found thee diverted, and He gave thee guidance. And He found thee needy, and He gave thee independence from want.* (See also 94:1-8)

33:21 *Indeed in the Messenger of God ye have an excellent example* for him who looketh unto God and the Final Day, and remembereth God much.

What religion does for a society is also best illustrated by the example of change that was brought about in the Arabian Peninsula and its adjoining areas immediately after the Prophet's mission had been accomplished. The revelation of Islam came at a time and at a place when and where anarchy, violence, vices and corruption were rampant. People could not trust one another let alone love one another. Peace and security was starkly lacking. Society had little concern for the poor and the deprived. Women were being treated little better than property. But the change Islam brought about was nothing short of revolutionary. Muslims became as brothers one to another, with amity, friendship and love among them, and a state of peace, security and justice was established.

5:15-6 There hath come unto you Light from God and a profound book, wherewith God guideth all who seek His good pleasure unto ways of *peace and security.*

8:26 And remember when ye were few, deemed weak in the land, and fearful that people might snatch you; but He gave you a *secure refuge* and strengthened you with His aid, and gave you of His good things that ye may be grateful.

28:57 Have We not established for them (the followers of the guidance) a *secure sanctuary, to which fruits of all kinds are brought* — a provision from Us? But most of them know not.

3:103 And recall with gratitude (O Believers) God's favors unto you: for ye were *enemies, and God created love in your hearts, and ye became as brothers by His grace*; and ye were at the brink of a pit of fire, and He saved you from it. ...

59

6:45   *So of the people who were unjust, the last remnants were cut off.* Praise be to God, the Lord of the Universe.

However, the initial shine of those who embraced Islam gradually faded, Muslims later became divided into many sects despite God's clear directive in the Quran to remain united and steadfast on the path of God (3:103, 105). They started fighting among themselves. A long period of decline and degeneration set in for them, which, as many Muslim scholars have pointed out, was due to their closing of the door of *ijtihad* (independent thinking and interpretation) and blind following of the past traditions (*taqlid*).[70]

The relation of religion to science

Considering the enormous influence that science wields on mankind as a way of searching for truth, its relation to religion should be understood in the proper perspective, since religion also seeks to lead mankind to the path of truth.

According to the Nobel Laureate physicist Richard Feynman, there are three aspects of religion: metaphysical, ethical and inspirational. "The first is that it tells what things are and where they came from and what man is and what God is and what properties God has and so on".[71] The ethical aspect of religion is concerned with how man should behave in a moral way. "And one of the powerful aspects of religion is its inspirational aspect. Religion gives inspiration to act well."[72] It is in the areas of metaphysical and ethical aspects that conflicts of religion could be seen to arise with science.

In regard to metaphysical aspects, religion could be seen to conflict with science, depending on how one interprets the views that religion was said to have propounded. Those who claimed to be the leaders of religion at the time came out with ideas attributed to religion such as that the earth was at the center of the universe, that it was stationary and not round came into direct conflict with later scientific discoveries. Also the idea that man was created and was not a descendant of animals and a late-coming outcome in a long and vast, evolving drama is inconsistent with the theory of evolution. However, the Quran nowhere mentions that the earth is at the center of the universe, though it says that God has made

60

the earth habitable for mankind and that He has made everything in the universe subject to the service of man. Nor does it say that the earth is stationary, and not round. It says that God has spread the earth for mankind, but that could not be taken to mean that it was flat. The Quran urges mankind to reflect on the creation of the universe and of everything in it, and on the alternation of the day and night (10:6). It speaks of creation, of course, but it mentions that creation of everything was or is done in periods (*ayums*) or stages. Such a conception is perfectly in accord with evolution. Specifically relating to man, it explicitly states that man has been created in stages:

> **71:13-4** What is the matter with you that ye revere not the greatness of God, when *it is He Who created you in (diverse) stages?*

And the Quran also speaks of human evolution or spiritual development, and there is hint of evolution of all creatures. With respect to man, the Quran states:

> **84:19** *Ye shall certainly march from state to state.*

It is generally thought that religion is largely a matter of faith, while science deals with pure reason and the two do not meet. However, this viewpoint must be a gross simplification. Religion, as we have argued before, cannot be devoid of reason, though it demands unqualified faith in, and devotion to, God without seeing Him. One might say, there is a conflict here. As Feynman points out, science encourages doubt before one can accept anything as true after sufficient evidence to that effect has been gathered.[73] On the other hand, one can know God not by doubting Him, but by putting full faith in, and accepting Him as reality, and by fully submitting to Him. Many scientists, probably a majority of them, do not believe in a God who interferes with our affairs, as science does not prove His existence. But science does not, and cannot, disprove His existence either. Many other scientists do in fact believe in God, and they find their belief in God consistent with scientific approach. Their conception of God may, however, be different from that of a conventional or ordinary believer of God. It should be noted, however, that though religion requires faith in God without seeing Him, it encourages man to strive for knowing Him through prayer and meditation, through observing divine signs in Nature (3:190), and through his personal experience of the objective world (41:53), and to try to receive His response or impulse (5:35; 17:19). Those who have been able to receive the Divine impulse, or undergo a deeper religious experience, for them God is a known Entity. They do not grope in the dark. There cannot, however, be any question that most men do in fact grope in the dark, and for them religion is largely a matter of faith.

Many scientists do not want to recognize the reason for believing in God, simply because they see that everything in this universe – all natural phenomena and movements as well as the relative position and structure of all celestial bodies in the universe – is all explicable, interconnected, or governed by a logical system of causes or laws. They hardly see any scope for a divine presence here, as Einstein said, "[...] profound interrelationships in the objective world can be comprehended through simple logical concepts"[74]. He did not see any connection of religion to his theory of relativity.[75] He did not believe in "a personal God who would directly influence the actions of individuals, or directly sit in judgment on creatures of his own creation [...] in spite of the fact that mechanistic causality has, to a certain extent, been placed in doubt by modern science".[76] This was a reference to the quantum theory. Einstein appeared to have been dissatisfied with the quantum theory, with its denial of determinism and its limitations to probabilistic, statistical predictions, though he was himself a pioneer in the development of this theory. He was convinced that there was need for a different understanding.[77]

On close reflection, it can be said that religion does not really call for a belief in a personal God who interferes with human actions of His own volition. God is neither personal nor does He interfere with our actions. As argued before, God does not act for any person unless that person himself acts, or unless that person has been acted upon by hereditary or other (societal or environmental) factors. One might wonder why then we need God? The answer lies in the fact that, contrary to what many scientists say, prayer to God is not meaningless. God responds when we sincerely ask for such a response, and that one can find Him to be the best source of real enlightenment, guidance, power, and all kinds of benefits one can cherish. Even some stalwarts among scientists have missed this conception of God. Prayer is also a kind of action, which must have a reaction. Scientists should strive to comprehend the power of prayer, the power that can be developed of the human mind, and the mysteries of what the prophets and saints of religion have done by way of what appeared to be miracles to others. The power of prayer is also quite in the logical scheme of things, and belongs to God's own immutable Laws, to which God Himself is subject. God's immutable Laws or, if you will, the Laws of Nature, are really the systematic relationships that scientists themselves have discovered or are in the process of discovering. As mentioned in the previous chapter, God has given man free will and choice between good and evil (18:29; 76:3). He does not do anything of His own accord to interfere in our affairs, a conception that is in accord with the idea that He is impartial and neutral, and importantly, also consistent with the scientific idea that everything has its cause. We ourselves change our affairs. If we do good work we get a reward in some form, which is rather reflection or perfection of the good work in a changed form. If we do bad work we suffer a punishment, which is in a way correction of the bad work. Consciously or unconsciously, deliberately or involuntarily – in some way or other, we are all engaging and changing ourselves in an unrelenting process of evolution, which is scientific. God is ever present in all of our work. He helps those who help themselves. We accelerate our progress by seeking God's help. This is the real meaning of *salat* or prayer. So in a vital sense, religion is perfectly in accord with science, and according to religion also, there is determinism surrounding all events.

Recent developments in psychology and parapsychology provide some valuable insights on psychic, mystical or religious experiences. Philosopher, mathematician, scientist and psychologist Michael Scriven calls to task those who maintain that all psychic claims (about, say, extra-sensory perception or ESP, telepathy, clairvoyance, precognition, etc.,) must be either fraud or error, since such an attitude implies that current scientific models will never be superseded.[78] Stanislav Grof, an innovative psychotherapist who has attempted to integrate divergent schools of Freud, Jung and Reich with insights from the leading edge of contemporary physics and biology, contends that in extraordinary circumstances the human mind is capable of accessing information from anywhere in time and space.[79] According to him,

> The traditional point of view of Western materialistic science is that we are Newtonian objects, made up of atoms, molecules, cells, tissues and organs, that we are highly developed animals and biological thinking machines. If we seriously consider all the data amassed in the last few decades by modern consciousness research, we discover that this point of view is incorrect, or at least incomplete. It is just one partial aspect of a

much more complex picture. It can be maintained only when we suppress all the evidence from parapsychology and the study of non-ordinary states of consciousness, such as mystical, psychedelic, and near-death experiences, or trance phenomena and meditation. In all these situations, we can also function as fields of consciousness which can transcend space, time, and linear causality.[80]

Other modern writers such as William James and Ralph Metzner have acknowledged paranormal experiences. Helen Palmer contends that certain paranoid and neurotic states can open the mind to a range of intuitive and psychic experiences.[81] Note, however, that paranormal claims made by people can often be false as well, and gullible people can be victimized by fake *faqirs* (people who can show exceptional psychic powers) or *peers* (spiritual teachers). Hence one should always guard against possible false paranormal claims made by other people. In fact, those who possess such exceptional powers generally do not publicize their powers.

It thus appears that the day may not be very far off, when science, psychology and religion will have a common meeting ground, and the veracity of claims about God and the value of prayer will be confirmed beyond any shadow of doubt.

The fundamental difference between science and religion is in the sphere of ethical or moral values. It is not in the realm of science to tell what is good or what is bad. "The sciences do not directly teach good and bad [...] moral values lie outside the scientific realm."[82] Science cannot pass a judgment on the questions of "What should I do?" and "Should I do this?" Science can only confine itself to saying what will happen if I do this? Science cannot make us really know if killing of man is bad. "[...] only knowing that it is a depression doesn't tell you that you do not want it [...] it is impossible to decide moral questions by the scientific technique; and [...] the two things are independent"[83]. The questions of what is good and what is bad, what is right and what is wrong, have thus to be settled outside the purview of the current state of science, since, we can say, science to date has not progressed far enough to judge logically whether the outcome of a certain action can be termed good or bad. It is religion that remains the source of such knowledge. As Ahmad puts it:

Real knowledge can never come to the human mind unless man is reconciled to God. Science has to be wedded to religion and then religion will wed science. One at the cost of another becomes a mirage which keeps man always disillusioned.[84]

The contribution that the prophets of religion have made to human progress and civilization is far superior to that of the scientists. Even aside from the moral teachings they handed down to us, some of the miraculous feats that the prophets and saints performed foreshadowed the progress that was humanly possible and that science later transformed into reality. The healing power of the Prophet Jesus who could heal the blind and the leprous and even revive the dead (5:110) blazed the trail of the wonderful progress that medical science could achieve later. Also, as Ahmad notes, the Prophet Solomon's ability to control the wind and fly (21:81) pointed to the future possibility of air travel. The experience of the Prophet Jonah in the water and the fish (37:139-145) was a forewarning of the possibility of the future submarine. The Prophet Abraham's exhibited power of controlling the fire, into which the idolaters threw him (21:68-71), presaged the future firefighting devices.[85] Ahmad again notes:

Prophets therefore have been the fore-runners of all progress and culture, and religion in reality is not and should not be the object of scorn and ridicule.[86]

It may be noted, however, that scientists who do not believe in the divinity of ethical values nevertheless generally do not find any difficulty in accepting moral and ethical values. It is only a matter of time when scientists will gladly embrace the logic of religion, and science and religion will have a happy marriage.

III. UNDERSTANDING RELIGION IN LIGHT OF THE QURAN: THE ROAD TO SPIRITUAL PROGRESS

The command belongeth to God alone; *He hath commanded that ye serve none but Him*. That is the right religion, but most men know not. – *Quran*, 12:40

Muslims appear [...] to have almost killed the spiritual message of Islam and the powerful spiritual potential of Islam's rituals by putting so much stress on rules, regulations, punishments, formalities, and politics to the near exclusion of the spiritual and ethical dimension, which is the predominant message of the Qur'an. – Jeffrey Lang, *op. cit.*, 2004, p. 470

The basic role of religion is to guide man on a journey for his spiritual evolution. The effort for such progress critically hinges on, and consists in, one's turning to God and devoting wholeheartedly to His service.

The meaning of "turning to God" and the conception of God

We are in need of God for our own sake – for our own spiritual progress. Our religious or spiritual endeavor involves turning to God and serving Him alone. It means forsaking the path of evil and going along the straight and righteous path (*sirat al-mustaqim*), which is the path of God (11:56). It also means that we need to surrender to Him, i.e., become Muslims or Submitters. If we further analyze this concept of "turning to God alone", it should be evident that it means that we do nothing but what is right, good, just and kind, appropriate and productive, and all that God stands for. It means that we should strive to move closer to God who alone epitomizes and represents all that is true, good, just, kind, noble, perfect, and beautiful. Numerous verses of the Quran point to such attributes or qualities of God. God is True (4:87, 122) and He represents Truth (18:44; 24:25). God is Just (39:75; 40:20), and also Beneficent, Merciful or Kind (1:1, 3; 2:163 and numerous other verses). His are the most beautiful names (*asma-ul-husna*) or attributes (59:24). God represents the Highest Ideal. He is unique, unrivalled and unsurpassable.

> **2:163**   And *your God is one God; there is no god save Him,*
>   the Beneficent, the Merciful.

112:1-4   Say, He is God, the One. God, the Absolute. He begetteth not nor is he begotten. And, *there is none like unto Him.* (Also see 42:11)

This oneness or uniqueness (*tawhid*) of God symbolizes the perfection of virtues, and signifies that He is our ultimate goal – our first priority, and the only one to be most revered and served, and that all other things must be subordinate to Him, or to His cause. It also means that we should endeavor to acquire such virtues. As we grow in various virtues of God such as mercy, compassion, forgiveness, "love, truth, justice, kindness, and so on, [...] the greater our ability becomes to receive and experience God's attributes of perfection."[87]

We benefit by following God's path because His is the highest and unsurpassable ideal, and because His path is flawless, most bountiful, and blissful. He is the source of all life and livelihood, and the sustainer of all things, and the source of all creation, and creative power. He hears everything, sees everything, and knows, and has record of all events. Nothing can be hidden from Him. He is Most Wise, and the source of all knowledge. He has power over all things, and is the source of all power. He is the source of all good to us. We can gain in sight, hearing, knowledge and power if we seek His help. The final judgment belongs to Him alone. "He encompasses everything, enters everything, and as He is bigger than, or transcends, everything, He is not visible anywhere although He pervades everywhere."[88] No human vision comprehends Him, but He comprehends all vision.

58:7   Seest thou not that *God knoweth all that is in the heavens and the earth*? There is not a secret consultation between three, but He is the fourth of them, nor between five, but He is the sixth, nor between fewer or more, but He is with them wherever they may be. And afterward on the Day of Resurrection, He will inform them of what they did. *Verily God is Knower of all things.*

42:10-2   *Whatever it is wherein ye differ, the verdict thereabout belongeth to God.* Such is my Lord, in Whom do I (Muhammad) put my trust, and unto Whom I turn – *the Creator of the heavens and the earth.* He hath made for you pairs of yourselves, and pairs among the cattle, whereby He multiplieth you. Naught is as the likeness of Him, and *He is the Hearer, the Seer. His are the keys of the heavens and the earth. He enlargeth and restricteth livelihood for whomsoever He willeth. He is indeed the Knower of all things.*

6:103   *No vision comprehendeth Him, but He comprehendeth (all) vision. He is the All-Subtle, the All-Aware!*

3:26-7   Say: O our God, Master of Sovereignty (or Kingdom)! Thou givest sovereignty to whomsoever Thou pleasest; and Thou withdrawest sovereignty from whomsoever Thou pleasest. Thou honorest whomsoever Thou pleasest, and Thou humiliatest whomsoever Thou pleasest. *All good is in Thy hand. Thou indeed hast power over all things.* Thou makest the night to pass into the day, and Thou makest the day to pass into the night. And *thou bringest forth the living from the dead, and Thou bringest forth the dead from the living. And Thou givest sustenance whomsoever Thou pleasest without any limit.*

Whether we believe or not, He is the Ultimate Reality. He responds to our prayers. This divine response, sometimes manifested in religious experience leading one to receive divine revelation, is ample proof that God exists. Being the Highest Ideal in all qualities, He is Most Deserving of all praise. That makes Him most worthy of our service and emulation.

1:2-4   *All praise belongeth to God, the Lord of the universe,* Gracious, Merciful, and Master of the Day of Judgment.

2:255   *God! There is no god but He, the Living, the Self-sustaining.* No slumber can seize Him, nor sleep. His are all things in the heavens and in the earth. Who is there who can intercede with Him except with His permission? He knoweth what is in front of them, and what is behind them. They can comprehend naught of His knowledge except what He pleaseth. His throne extends over the heavens and the earth, and he is never tired of preserving them. He is the Most High, the Supreme.

59:23-4 *He is God; besides Him there is no god, the Knower of the Invisible and the Visible.* He is the most Gracious, the Most Merciful. He is God; besides Him there is no god, the Sovereign Lord, the Holy One, the Peace, the Most Faithful, the Guardian, the Most Powerful, the Compelling, and the Superb. Glorified be God from all that they ascribe as partners (unto Him)! He is God, the Creator, the Originator, and the Fashioner. His are the most beautiful names. All that is in the heavens and the earth glorifieth Him. He is Mighty, Wise.

57:1-4 *Whatever is in the heavens and on earth glorifieth God*, for He is Mighty, Wise. To Him belongeth the sovereignty of the heavens and the earth; it is He Who giveth life and death; and He hath power over all things. He is the First and the Last, the Manifest and the Invisible; and He hath full knowledge of all things. He it is Who created the heavens and the earth in six stages, and then he established Himself on the Throne. He knoweth what entereth within the earth and what cometh forth out of it, what cometh down from heaven and what mounteth up to it. And *He is with you wherever ye may be. And God seeth all that ye do.*

The Quranic idea that God is present everywhere is not pantheism. His presence with every being or everything does not mean that every being or every thing is God. A confusing belief is held among certain religious groups that everything is God, or that the universe and Nature are themselves divine. But this conception of God is in direct conflict with the Quranic conception, which at no time confuses God with His creation.

24:35 *God is the Light of the heavens and of the earth.* His Light is a like a Niche, wherein is a Lamp. The Lamp is in a Glass, the Glass as it were a brightly shining Star, lit from a blessed Tree, an Olive, neither of the East nor of the West, whose oil almost gloweth, though fire touched it not: Light upon Light. God guideth unto His Light whom He pleaseth. God setteth forth parables for men, and God is Knower of all things.

Many misjudge God about His will from such verses in the Quran that say that He gives sustenance to whomsoever He pleases (2:212; 3:27); that He guides whomsoever He wills (2:213, 217, and more verses); that He purifies whomsoever He pleases (4:49; 24:21); and honors whomsoever He pleases and humiliates whomsoever He pleases (3:26). From such verses and others, a reader may infer that nothing is really possible without God's will, help or grace. In a vital sense this conclusion is quite correct, but only if we have a proper perception of the conception of God. The truth is that God does not will or predestine in the generally understood sense, which negates human free will, and the relevance of his effort. God says that He will test who is best in conduct (11:7; 67:2). He cannot have a legitimate basis for testing us, if He wills or predestines our fate.

> **36:47** When it is said unto them: Spend of that with which God hath provided you, those who disbelieve say to those who believe: *Shall we feed those whom God, if He willed, could have fed? Ye are naught else than in clear error.*

In this verse God rebukes those who skirt their duty to help the poor, and the helpless on the plea that if God willed He could have fed them (See also related verses 107:1-7; 90:12-16). This clearly suggests that God does not make one rich or poor of his own volition, and that it is the duty of the rich to feed the poor. He never does any wrong or injustice to men; it is men who do it to themselves (3:117). Additional statements in the Quran reinforce the point that God does not will or act in the popular sense. God says that if He willed He could have guided all of us (see: 6:149), that if He willed He could have made mankind one nation (see: 5:48), and that if He willed all would have believed (see: 10:99). The import of these verses is that God does not directly determine our affairs. He has given us free will (18:29; 76:3). It is up to us alone to shape our destiny by deciding where to go and what to do. God turns us whichever way we choose to turn (4:115). He does not help anyone unless he or she deserves it by his or her own individual effort, or by a sustained combined effort of heredity and/or environment. A good example of the fruit of a sustained combined effort of heredity is the Prophet Jesus who was a prophet from the day he was born (19:29-34), while the Prophet Muhammad was predominantly the result of his individual effort.

It should also be noted that though it is our own initiative that matters most in changing our lot, it is the power of everything, whether good or evil, which derives from God.

> **4:78-9** If a happy thing befalleth them they say: This is from God; and if an evil thing befalleth them they say: This is of thy doing (O Muhammad). Say (unto them): *All is from God*. What is the matter with these people that they fail to understand a happening. *Whatever of good befalleth thee (O man) is from God; and whatever of evil befalleth thee is from thyself.*

It is thus not good for us to take any credit for any good that comes to us. All credit for good things belongs to God, i.e., to the forces that lead to the good, which are essentially the forces of God.

The Quran is clear that God has no family to favor:

> **19:35** *It befitteth not God that he should take unto Himself a son.* Glory be to Him! When He decreeth a thing, He sayeth unto it only: 'Be', and it is. (See also 112:3)

> **6:100-1** And they make the jinn associates with God, while He it is Who created them, and *they falsely attribute to Him sons and daughters without knowledge*; glory be to Him; exalted He is above what they attribute! Wonderful Originator of the heavens and the earth! *How could He have a son when he hath no consort?* He hath created everything and He is Knower of all things. (Also see 72:3)

The Quran makes it clear that it is work, and work alone that determines one's fate; it is replete with verses that emphasize righteousness as the sole determinant of who will be rewarded (20:15; 53:39; 2:148, 286; 42:30; 28:84; 6:132; 46:19; 17:19; 5:35).

46:19   And *for all there will be ranks according to what they do*, that He may compensate them for their deeds; and no injustice will be done to them.

17:19   And whoever desireth the Hereafter (the future) and striveth for it with the due effort, being a believer, for such *their efforts will surely be appreciated (rewarded)*.

5:35   O ye who believe! Be mindful of your duty to God, and seek the way of approach unto Him, and *strive in His way in order that ye may succeed*. (Also see 2:148)

The Quran points out that God helps only those who help themselves. At the same time God is also Ever Forgiving and Most Merciful. His Mercy lies in the fact that man can recover from any sliding back through wrongdoing if he is truly repentant about his wrongdoing, and in the fact that with good work he can erase the effect of bad work, and make onward march toward spiritual evolution. "Man is prone to [making] mistakes but the real man is he, whose failures turn into pillars of success."[89] God forgives the sins of those who turn to Him truly repentant, and who do not persist in their sins (3:135. Last-minute repentances are not acceptable, however, from one who continues doing evil until death and says:

4:17-8   I surely repent now. Nor (is it acceptable) from those who die as nonbelievers. It is they for whom We have a terrible punishment in store.

Addressing the Prophet Muhammad, the Quran further states:

9:80   Ask forgiveness for them (O Muhammad), or ask not forgiveness for them – *even though thou ask forgiveness for them seventy times, God will not forgive them. That is because they disbelieve in God and His Messenger, and God guideth not wrongdoing people.*

Jeffrey Lang notes that it is the doer himself "who benefits or loses the most from a good or evil act. [...] The harm that evildoers experience as a result of persistent wrongdoing is intrinsic. Evil deeds hamper growth in virtue and erode spirituality, so that those who stubbornly reject righteousness do violence to their [own] being and experience spiritual decay. [...] One of the great risks taken by the unrepentant sinner is bringing damage to his moral and spiritual center, or what the Qur'an refers to as the 'heart'. [...] The Qur'an asserts that the hearts of these persons become dark, veiled, rusted, and hence impenetrable to guidance, while the hearts of the virtuous become soft, sensitive, and receptive to God's guiding light. The more we persist in wrongdoing, the more desensitized we become to the evil of it. [...] It is the evil that human beings acquire that cover their hearts like rust (83:14). It is because the deniers follow their own low desires or lusts that their hearts are sealed (47:14-16). God does not make people deny [H]is signs; rather their hearts grow hard by their own wickedness (2:74)."[90]

Ahmad adds: "Only a prayer or wish not to commit a wrong again is not sufficient amends. One must efface past mistakes by encountering bitter facts of life in course of living. [...] Repentance therefore is no effortless task or is not merely an expression of remorse said in a closet or before the Confessional or upon the hands of one's Peer, Guru or religious teacher. The possible hypocrisy in it is to be annihilated."[91] Indeed, penance or suffering on one's part is a necessary corrective process to remove one's dross and move toward purification.

When one deserves to be helped, God helps. There is no basis in the belief that all happens according to a predestined plan, which implies that man is preordained to act in certain ways, and is powerless to do anything about the course of events. God does not act irrationally. "He has not certainly predestined a man to be a thief or a good man. [...] man only comes to naught by worshiping predestination in the act of foolish acceptance of the so-called inevitable."[92] At the same time events can, of course, be predetermined based on underlying predetermining factors – a matter of causation. There are references in the Quran to certain past events, e.g., calamities that struck wrongdoing people during the times of certain prophets which were willed and pre-announced by God. But it would be wrong to think that God predestined these events without any reason. These events were instances of a natural reaction to certain immoral behavior patterns of people, and thus logically predetermined. Where things are predetermined, God knows them in advance, and so God willed them in a way. It is on the basis of such predetermining factors that those who walk in the way of God can also correctly predict future events. Scientists who discover natural laws behind events can also foretell many things (e.g., the movements and relative location of planetary bodies on a future date).

God is subject to His own immutable laws – the Laws of Nature. There is full logic in His system of creation. The Quran states:

> **67:3-4** Thou (Muhammad) canst see no flaw in the creation of the Most Gracious. So turn thy vision again; seest thou any flaw? Then turn thy vision again and yet again; thy vision will return unto thee dazzled and fatigued.

Whatever God does is a creation. So if there is no flaw in His creation, that *ifso facto* implies that He does not, and cannot engage in any irrational or whimsical action. So He cannot predestine or seal the fate of any man or woman. However, part of the fate or destiny of a man may be already predetermined because of the work that has already gone forth – that has been done by the person(s) concerned, or by his/her/their parents and ancestors (hereditary factors) and/or due to what society has already done. Such predetermined aspects of destiny of a man due to hereditary or other factors may act adversely as a constraint on one's own development, but one can often overcome such adverse factors with sufficient determined endeavor. With things that are given and unalterable, human beings have to work with certain limitations. But this is not to suggest that God predestines everything. The doctrine of predestination is inconsistent with the rationality that the Quran so powerfully espouses, and also "with assertions in the Qu'ran concerning God's justice, mercy, compassion and transcendence."[93] Though with God-given factors, so to say, man is not as free as he might think, and though there is some element of destiny that influences his fate, this should not obscure or belittle the importance or value that attaches to human endeavor.

Man is largely the architect of his own destiny. The history of human endeavor so far amply proves the point that virtually nothing is beyond man's reach and control. Man can now predict, and in some cases even control natural events. Indeed the Quran affirms that God has subjected the universe to the service of humankind:

31:20   See ye not that *God hath subjected unto you whatever is in the heavens and the earth,* and hath made His bounties available unto you in abundance, seen and unseen? Yet there are among those who dispute about God, without knowledge and without guidance, nor without a Book to enlighten them. (See also 45:13)

16:12-4   He hath subjected unto you the night and the day, the sun and the moon, and the stars are subjected by His command. Verily in this are signs for men who apply sense. And whatever He hath created in the earth of diverse colors. Verily in this are signs for men who take heed. And He it is Who hath made the sea subject, in order that ye may eat thereof meat that is fresh and tender, and that ye may extract ornaments to wear, and thou seest the ships that plough it, that ye may seek of His bounty, and that ye may be grateful.

God has endowed man with faculties and qualities, which if developed properly, can work really wonders. Should man ever succeed in reviving or resurrecting a dead man, it should not bring religion into disrepute, since the true vision of religion does not mean that man should not acquire God's creative powers. Indeed if Jesus could make a bird of clay into a real bird, and revive a dead man (apart from healing the blind and the leprous) (5:110), if Moses could turn a stick into a real moving serpent, which devoured the false serpents of the Pharaoh's sorcerers (7:106-107), if Abraham could restore life to birds cut into pieces, and thrown over the hills (2:260), then why man should not succeed in restoring the dead to life? At the present time scientists have already succeeded in cloning animals, and in cloning a human embryo for therapeutic purposes, and it is believed that cloning a human baby is within reach in the near future. However, scientists should wonder whether cloning a human baby is worth the effort morally and ethically, and whether it will serve any noble human purpose. Why do scientists not concentrate on producing children in the way Mary, the mother of Jesus (3:43-47), and the barren and old wives of Abraham (11:69-73) and Zachariah (3:40) conceived?

It is also worth noting that God acts through His agents, His own creation – Nature and human beings, angels and Jinns. He intends when some of

His agents – I, you or some of they – intend to do something. By becoming God's servants, we act as His agents – we act in conformity to His nature or way of creation, i.e., His law, method or ideal. This is real service to God. This way alone we live in God's way, and this way we evolve spiritually. This is true religion:

> **30:30** *So set thy purpose truly for religion as a man by nature upright, the nature (made) of God, in which He hath created man.* There is no change in the way God createth. That is the right religion, but most men know not.

If the Way God creates or acts is true religion, and if there is no change in this way, then true religion must be one that comes from the divine source, and must reflect the Way God acts, which is immutable and valid for all time and space. God wants us to act in His Way. Thus prophets have brought to mankind essentially the same religion from the same divine source, and they could not introduce anything of their own that could be labeled as their way or *sunnah*, as they were obligated to follow and profess only God's Way or *Sunnah*.[94]

Knowing God by His attributes

To know God, We may conceive Him by His various attributes. He has manifold attributes, and has many corresponding beautiful names.

> **7:180** And *God's are the most beautiful names; so call upon Him by them.* And leave the company of those who distort His names. They will be requited for what they do.

We need to reflect on the various names or attributes of God since these names provide the clues to the great variety of ways in which we can develop our own personality, and march ahead spiritually. For example, God is Loving, Beneficent, Kind, and Forgiving. Thus we need to develop our character in such a way that we become loving, beneficent, kind, and forgiving in our conduct. He is Truthful and Just. He is not unjust to anybody, and does not deceive anyone. He is appreciative of whatever good one does, and rewards one accordingly. We also need to be truthful and just in our conduct. We cannot deceive anybody; we cannot cause the slightest injury to anybody without legitimate cause.

We also need to appreciate others' work in the same manner as God does. God is All-Seer, All-Hearer, and Most Wise. We also need to develop our seeing or perceiving and hearing capabilities, and we need to enhance our knowledge and wisdom. Striving to reflect God's attributes or qualities in one's life is the greatest *salat* or prayer one can perform. Elevating us in such qualities will be our true spiritual development.

Another good example of God's attributes is that He is independent and free of want. We also need to try to be independent as far as possible. This means that we should not be parasites or beggars. A begging action or mentality degrades one's soul. We can attain nearness to God when we shun such mentality, try to become self-reliant, and are independent of others' help. We will then be free of want or become rich, and enjoy a life of abundance. True Muslims cannot remain poor if they really follow God's way. At the same time, this does not mean that we do not come to others' help when others really need our help. God is most kind, and helpful to those who need and seek such help. So we need to do the same to others who are in need of help. Serving God really means serving His creation in the same way and spirit as God serves it. God is helper to those who need and seek help. He is Reliever of our misery, and Protector from all kinds of danger. However, while trying to help the helpless in God's way, we should be conscious of the need for helping others in a way that we would like for ourselves should we need help. Since we would like to be self-reliant, our help that reaches others should also be aimed at making them self-reliant. That should be the hallmark or whole purpose of help or assistance. Help or assistance should be for a temporary or transitional phase. Otherwise, help or assistance will make one a permanent beggar, which is like making one a slave to others. That would be against the spirit of religion.

Some of the other attributes of God are as follows. He is the source of our true guidance and enlightenment. All are directly or indirectly subservient to Him, dependent on Him, and subject to His inexorable laws. Directly or indirectly every being and every thing glorifies God, or to say the same thing in other words, every particle of the universe manifests or demonstrates the glories of God. So the Quran says:

17:44   *The seven heavens and the earth, and all that is therein glorify God*, and there is not a thing that doth not celebrate His praise. And yet ye understand not how they celebrate His glory! ...

God is Most Responsive, Acceptor of Repentance, and Oft-Forgiving. There are many other attributes of God. The Quran mentions numerous attributes of God.[95] One needs to reflect on these names to try to understand God in His true *jat* and *sefat* (personality and qualities), and to mold one's character accordingly. It helps one to envision God in very many ways, and be conscious of such attributes or qualities. When we emulate all such qualities of God, we become His real worshipers. He and His angels bestow their blessings and mercy on His faithful and devoted servants who glorify Him, which essentially means coveting and emulating His qualities (33:41-43).

Knowing God's Way basically means knowing His Laws. One essentially knows God and achieves nearness to Him through knowing His Laws, which are the Universal Laws. By knowing such Laws, one gains the knowledge of the secrets of all creation, events or action which are logical chains of causation. Indeed, it is this knowledge that is most valuable to mankind to enrich their life.

No room for polytheism or idolatry

In the conception of God as outlined above there is no room for either polytheism or idolatry. It is one God Who is the source of all knowledge, guidance, power, and all good, and the perfection of all qualities. It is all good that we need to strive for. Thus the central message of religion is *la ilaha illallah – There is no god but God* (2:163). To be truly religious, we need to tenaciously reflect this fundamental faith in all of our behavior and actions. The most significant implication of this belief is that we accept all that God represents or stands for – truth, reason, justice, knowledge, guidance, power, and all that is good, beneficial, noble, and beautiful. We thus need to serve only Him.

This is not to say that we should not respect, and follow our fellow men who are more respectable and knowledgeable than us. In fact, following those who walk in the way of God implies the same thing as following God Himself. And not respecting those who are more respectable and knowledgeable than us really amounts to disrespecting God Himself. That is precisely the reason why God has urged us to follow the prophets, and those who have authority or justification to be followed, and to show due respect to the Prophet:

4:59	O ye who believe! Obey God and obey the Messenger, and those who have authority from among you; and if ye have any dispute concerning any matter, refer it to God and the Messenger if ye are believers in God and the Last Day. That is better and more seemly in the end.
33:56-7	Verily God and His angels encourage and support the Prophet. O ye who believe! Ye also encourage and support him, and greet him with due respect. Verily (as for) those who malign (or harm) God and His Messenger, God hath cursed them in this world and in the Hereafter, and hath prepared for them a disgraceful retribution.
49:1-5	O ye who believe! Put not yourselves forward before God and His Messenger, and be careful of (your duty to) God. Verily God is Hearer, Knower. O ye believe! Raise not your voices above the voice of the Prophet, nor speak aloud when ye speak to him as ye speak aloud one to another, lest your works be rendered null and void while ye perceive not. Verily those who lower their voices in the presence of the Messenger of God, those are they whose hearts God hath tested for righteousness. Theirs will be forgiveness and immense reward. Verily those who call thee (Muhammad) from behind the private chambers, most of them lack sense. And if they had patience till thee couldst come forth unto them, it would be better for them. And God is Forgiving, Most Merciful.

How detailed these admonitions are to us! The Quran does not leave untouched even minute details of etiquette we should exhibit in our behavior to more knowledgeable and respectable people. We need to appreciate the qualities of, show due respect to, and bless and support, superior persons. Such appreciation, blessing or support has a special spiritual significance. By extending such appreciation and support, we in the process enlist their blessing or support in return. Our remembering the Prophet, and expressing our appreciation and reverence to him by salutation has significance only if we become in the process conscious of his great qualities, and if we develop our love toward him in order to enlist his love and blessings for us. Muslims generally use the *milad* institution to verbally shower praise and blessings on the Prophet. However, such an institution has been reduced to a largely barren one, as it has failed to contribute to any spiritual uplifting of the participants. There is little discussion of the qualities and teachings of the Prophet, and of the guidance he has brought us through the Quran.

God and His angels also support believers who remember Him much:

> **33:41-3** O ye who believe! Remember God with much remembrance. And glorify Him in the morning and the evening. He it is Who blesseth you, and so do His angels, that He may bring you from darkness into light. And He is full of mercy to the believers.

Note also that respect for a person should not degenerate into worshiping him. No one deserves God's status, as all are God's servants, and prophets are also His worshipers. Worshiping prophets is like worshiping idols, and such worship idolizes them. Worshiping any living being other than God limits the vision of God Who is Infinite. So the Quran emphatically reminds us:

> **3:79-80** *It is not for any human being unto whom God hath given the Book, wisdom and the Prophethood that he should afterwards say unto mankind: Be ye worshipers of me instead of God.* But rather (he would say): Be ye worshipers of the Lord, by virtue of your teaching of the Book and your study thereof. And nor would he enjoin that ye take the angels and the Prophets for Lords. What! Would he enjoin disbelief after ye have surrendered (unto God or become Muslims)?

At the same time, the Quran makes it also amply clear that we can respect and follow others only when, and to the extent, they follow God. We have been urged to follow the Prophet precisely because he followed only God. Thus the Quran affirms:

> **6:50** Say (O Muhammad, to the disbelievers): I tell you not that I possess the treasures of God, nor do I have

knowledge of the unseen. Nor do I tell you that I am an angel. *I follow only that which is revealed to me*

46:9 Say (O Muhammad, to the disbelievers): I am not new among messengers. Nor do I know what will happen to me or to you. *I only follow what is revealed to me*; and I am no more than a plain warner.

It is clear from these Quranic verses that the Prophet Muhammad followed only what was revealed to him; and what was revealed to him is in the Quran. It follows that if we follow the Quran, which incorporates all divine revelations to the Prophet, we follow his *sunnah* (way) as well.[96]

True religion, the basic postulate of which is that God must be Supreme and All-Transcending, thus necessarily rules out multiple gods. The Quran gives the reason why we should eschew the idea of multiple gods:

21:22 If there were therein (in the heavens and the earth) other gods beside God, verily there would have been chaos in both. Glorified be God, the Lord of the Throne, from all that they ascribe (unto Him)! (See also 17:42-43)

No human being, or for that matter, no prophet, no angel, no other creature[97], or no piece of God's creation such as the sun, the moon, any star, fire, or any other thing can be a god, as all living beings and things are subservient to God, and directly or indirectly yield to, or recognize, God's sovereignty (2:107; 64:1).

For the same and even more compelling reasons, there is also no place for idolatry in Islam. Idolatry represents in essence the act of being bogged down with something powerless to do anything or effect any change.

17:56 Say (O Muhammad): Cry unto those whom ye assume (to be gods) beside Him, yet they have no power to rid you of misfortune, or to change. (See also 46:5)

While certain diversity in religious practices can be compatible with the true spirit of religion, differences in faiths underscore the need for distinguishing between what is the intent of true religion, and what is apocryphal, peripheral, artificial, or wrong. Clearly, idolatry and polytheism are aberrations from the true religion based on monotheism.

Religion is much more than just beliefs and rituals. It is also a code of moral and ethical conduct. All religions preach moral and ethical standards, or norms of human conduct. It is striking that greater similarities can be observed among all religions in respect of moral and ethical precepts than in beliefs and rituals. For example, all religions teach fundamental codes of behavior such as truthfulness, honesty, humility, acts of kindness and charity, and forsaking of such behavior as indecency, insincerity, deceit, greed, vanity, persecution, and murder. It is a great pity that many followers of different religions often neglect the moral and ethical side of religion, which is a great sin in the eye of God. The avowed objective of true religion is to rid mankind of all impurities in them and purify and prepare them for self-evolution. It will be a great folly to think that one can be truly religious by following only the rituals, and neglecting the moral and ethical side of religion.[98]

The way forward to spiritual enlightenment

The attributes of goodness are godly qualities. Unless man strives to attain such qualities in his life, his life becomes devoid of meaning, and he becomes a candidate for moral and spiritual degradation. For, man who wishes to become truly religious needs to strive for real progress, and should never be satisfied with his current state of progress, for progress is infinite.

The essential message of religion is spiritual. As Ahmad puts it, man needs to develop in such a way that he is able to receive and grasp the divine message or revelation, "either from the Divine Book [...] or from the universe or Nature, which is the other form of the very same Book"[99]. Ahmad further notes:

> [T]he word (of God) reigns everywhere. But blessed is he who chooses to catch it. Want of effort or half-hearted effort can never reach it. The mind of one who makes little or no effort gropes in the dark, as the word does not reach him.[100]

One needs to have transcendental knowledge to avoid pitfalls and shocks of life, and evolve progressively. In his quest for spiritual development, man needs to take his cue from his own change as well as from the change that is constantly taking place around him. Man needs to take lessons from the change of day and night, and all the creation that is in the universe.

> **10:6**   Verily in the variation of the night and the day, and all that God hath created in the heavens and the earth, there are signs for those who are righteous.

It is not for just a joke that God has urged us to reflect on the creation and structure of the universe. One can wonder how vast the universe is! Scientists reckon that the universe has a mind-boggling number of galaxies, and stars – our "sun being among a hundred thousand million suns in our galaxy, itself among a billion galaxies"[101]. Nothing in the universe is stationary. All heavenly bodies, including this earth, are floating and moving on their orbits in a vast space! Do we ever wonder that we are also floating, and moving in space together with the earth and the sun and our galaxy, the Milky Way? There is perfect order in the universe. These must be signs for those who want to understand the creation, and understand its mystery. Ahmad observes:

> The infinite lengths of slow motion and quick motion pictures presented every day by the celestial cinema, the motley different growths in the animal and vegetable kingdoms opened their kindergarten schools long, long ago to impart the idea of acceleration, that is progress. [...] So it is clear that on every pin-point of this vastly vast universe, progress has been writ large to unmistakably inspire the mind of the universe, that is man in a nutshell, with the sign, idea, urge, word, formula or principle of action of ever-expanding greatness. Men who have been able to read the sign, catch the idea, feel the urge or hear the word to get nearer and nearer the principle or code of action till it has been discovered have kept the torch of progress burning.[102]

Alongside the changes in the outer world, changes are constantly taking place also in the inner self of human beings. When I carefully look at my own inner self, I find myself changing ceaselessly. The philosopher Bergson describes this change in the following words:

I pass from state to state. I am warm or cold. I am merry or sad, I work or I do nothing, I look at what is around me or I think of something else. Sensations, feelings, volitions, ideas – such are the changes into which my existence is divided and which colour it in turns. I change then, without ceasing.[103]

"Thus, there is nothing static in my inner life; all is a constant mobility, an unceasing flux of states, a perpetual flow in which there is no halt or resting place."[104] As Ahmad puts it, "Nothing does exist as it is or in tact. You cannot show a thing that has not undergone any change."[105] The Quran affirms the fact that man is changing:

84:19   Ye shall certainly march from state to state.

What religion does is to teach man to reflect on this change, and to consciously direct his own change into a progressive one to evolve spiritually. He needs to be conscious of whether he is changing in the right or wrong direction, and whether he is changing with the desired speed. The process of evolution, which man undergoes deliberately or unconsciously, is expressed in the following verse:

84:6   O humankind! Verily thou art ever toiling on toward thy Lord, a hard striving until thou meetest with Him.

Man needs to make conscious efforts to make a change in the right direction, and with desired intensity of effort. He needs to work hard to achieve desired progress. The kind of hard work that man needs to do to achieve desired spiritual evolution is illustrated well by what the Prophet Muhammad himself was urged by God to do, and what he actually did.

94:5-8   Verily with hardship goeth ease; with hardship surely goeth ease. So *whenever thou (O Muhammad) art relieved, strive hard*, turning exclusively to thy Lord.

73:1-8   O thou (Muhammad) wrapped up in garments! *Rise (and strive with meditation and prayer) during the night, save a little. A half thereof or a little less. Or a little more*, and read the Quran in measure. Surely We will send thee a weighty message. Surely the rising by night is at a time when the impression is keener, and the speech is more certain. Indeed thou art preoccupied with other matters during daytime. So remember thy Lord, and devote thyself to Him with a complete devotion.

73:20 Surely thy Lord knoweth that thou standest (for prayer and meditation) nearly two-thirds of the night, or half of it, or one-third of it, and so do a party of those with thee. God measureth the night and day, and He knoweth that ye are unable to count it, and turneth unto you (in mercy). Read thee of the Quran as much as is easy for thee. He knoweth that there are (some) sick among you, while others travel in the land in search of God's bounty, and others are fighting in the cause of God. So *study the Quran as much as is easy (for thee), and establish prayer, and purify*, and lend unto God a goodly loan.

These messages confirm that even the Prophet Muhammad, who received Divine revelations of the Quran after a lot of hard work and meditation, was urged by God to continue striving hard to stay in the path of, and attain further, spiritual progress. It was by dint of his hard work that he could attain ascension (*miraj*) and receive divine revelation, and even approach God face-to-face.

17:1 *Glorified be He (God) Who made his servant go on a journey by night from the Inviolable Mosque to the Farthest Mosque*, the precincts of which We did bless, in order that We might show him some of Our Signs. Surely it is He Who is the Seer, and the Hearer. (See also 53:1-8 cited in Chapter 1)

The Prophet Muhammad is an excellent example for us to follow:

33:21 *Verily in the Messenger of God ye have an excellent example* for him who hopeth for God and the Final Day, and who remembereth God much.

Those who can make sufficient progress on the spiritual path can develop a sixth sense whereby they can hear things that are not audible by the ordinary ear, and see things that are not visible by the ordinary eye. They can see with eyes that lie within their hearts:

> **22:46**   Have they not traveled in the land, and *have they hearts wherewith to understand and ears wherewith to hear?* For *indeed it is not the eyes that are blind, but it is the hearts, which are within the bosoms, that are blind.*

At another place, the Quran mentions that historical events carry a good reminder or message for him who has a heart, and who lends ear, and is a witness (50:36-37). Ahmad describes such people who are able to apply their sixth sense as:

> [...] the keepers of the conscience of the whole universe. They bring themselves as also others out of darkness into the light. Such persons are clairvoyant. They are the protectors of the standard or are landmarks of progress upon progress. [...] [E]xcept very few clairvoyant persons, none else numbering millions who are the rest of the inhabitants of the earth see or hear the happenings behind the Screen of Death. They form the Highest Civil List of the Walis or the Keepers of God's secrets [2:257; 7:196; 10:62; 58:22]. They are the successful persons from whom sprang the Prophets.[106]

Every creature has the potential to reach the stage where he can receive divine impulses and transcendental message or knowledge. The Quran refers to bees receiving divine inspiration (*wahy*) about the places where to build their hives (16:68). Man should be able to do better in this regard. Indeed reaching the stage where one can receive divine inspiration or revelation is a coveted spiritual goal for all of us. One can also reach the stage where he or she can act or create in the manner of God, and he or she can realize whatever he or she wishes to do. One has the potential to reach the stage where he or she achieves what is called "Bak-Siddhi" in Bengali, or the power of the word to translate into whatever is intended by the word. Realizing that potential should be everyone's goal. That way man gets real knowledge and some real power to lead his life in a decent, productive, flawless, and progressive manner. And that way he acquires some of the godly qualities, and becomes a God's ideal servant and a source of real happiness and abundance not only for himself but also for others. That God's righteous servants (should be righteous enough) receive divine communication is affirmed in the Quran in the following reassuring words:

41:30-2 The angels descend on those who confirm "Our Lord is God", and lead a righteous life (saying): *Fear not nor grieve, but receive the good news of the Heaven that ye are promised.* We are your protecting friends in the life of this world and in the Hereafter. There ye will have all that your souls desire, and there ye will have all that ye ask for – a welcome gift from the Forgiving, the Merciful.

One needs to make sincere efforts to make real spiritual progress. But at the same time it should be noted that for making such efforts, one does not need to forsake the world, forsake one's family, and go to a jungle. However, one needs to earmark some time at day and/or at night to contemplate, pray and meditate in seclusion, keeping away from the normal disturbances and interruptions of daily life.

Prayer (*salat*), meditation or remembrance of God (*dhikr*) that is basically prayer – the best according to the Quran (29:45), fasting (*siam*), charity (*zakat*), and pilgrimage (*hajj*) are some religious rituals or institutions, which are prescribed for us in the Quran, along with essential, consistent, and complementary righteous deeds, to make progress on the spiritual front. The topics of *salat* (including *dhikr*) and *zakat* are discussed respectively in Chapters 5 and 6.

In a wider sense, the other two institutions, fasting and pilgrimage to the Holy Kabah in Mecca, are essentially parts of the prayer of the believing Muslims. During the fasting and the pilgrimage, Muslims have been urged by God to be especially devoted to God so that they get further golden chances to receive spiritual enlightenment. Here we make some brief references to these religious institutions.

Fasting has been prescribed to help believers guard against evil and become upright:

2:183 O ye who believe! Fasting is prescribed for you as it was prescribed for those before you, *that ye may become upright.*

The basic purpose of fasting is thus to help man attain piety. It provides one a golden opportunity to devote himself fully to prayer and meditation, as he or she has to not only refrain from eating and drinking, but also to abstain from any sexual activity during the day-long fasting, and the latter activity also during the period of one's retreat for worship in the mosque (See 2:187). Fasting should help one learn sexual restraint, which is an essential ingredient for spiritual progress. Fasting has been prescribed for a full month during the Ramadan. However, if one is unable to fast because of sickness, or if one is on a journey, he or she can fast the equal number of days later, or if this still is not possible he or she needs to feed one poor person. If one does good deeds of his own accord, it is better for him; and it is still better if one fasts (2:185).

We have been urged also to perform pilgrimage in the well-known sacred lunar months, which are known to be *Zil Hijja, Muharram, Safar,* and *Rabi al-Awwal,* or failing that to send an offering that is easy to obtain (2:196-200). Here also the emphasis for the pilgrims is for attaining righteousness and piety, as the Quran has urged complete abstinence, no misconduct, and no angry conversation during the period of the pilgrimage, and complete devotion to God:

> **2:196-7** Perform the Pilgrimage and the visit (to Mecca) for God. And if ye are prevented, (send) gifts that are easy to obtain. And shave not your heads until the gifts have reached their destination. And whoever among you is sick or has an ailment of the head, (for him) a ransom of fasting, or almsgiving, or sacrificing of an offering. And if ye are safe, whoever wisheth to continue with the visit and the Pilgrimage (should provide) such offerings as are easy to obtain. And who cannot find (such offerings), then a fast of three days while on the pilgrimage, and of seven days when ye have returned; that is ten in all. That is for him whose folk are not present in the Sacred Mosque. Be careful (of your duty) to God, and know that God is stern in punishing. The pilgrimage is (in) the well-known months, and (for) whoever wisheth to perform the Pilgrimage therein, there (should be) *no lewdness, no misconduct nor quarrelling during the Pilgrimage.* And whatever good ye do God knoweth it. So make provisions for yourselves, but *the best*

provision is to attain righteousness. Therefore, be careful (of your duty) unto Me, O human beings of understanding.

Fasting and pilgrimage are additional religious rites for the worshipers to perform so that they can purify themselves, and make spiritual progress. If, however, these institutions do not help them make some headway in fulfilling these objectives, such institutions degenerate into mere rituals devoid of any real meaning. Among Muslims, there are many who perform fasting and pilgrimage, but at heart they have not become Muslims in the proper sense of the term, because they have not refrained from doing the heinous things they did previously.

Muslims regard the *kalima* (belief in one God), prayer, fasting during the month of Ramadan, and the pilgrimage as four of five obligatory duties. The fifth obligatory duty is considered to be *zakat*[107] or charity to the poor and deserving. However, it should be emphasized that whatever is mentioned in the Quran as worth doing or following by us should be regarded as *fard* (or obligatory). Indeed the whole Quran has been made *fard* for us. Whatever God exhorts us to do, whatever He forbids us to do, and whatever He designates as acts of righteousness for us, are all binding on us:

> **28:85** Verily He (God) Who *hath made the Quran binding (fard) on thee* (O Muhammad) will bring thee back to the destination. Say: My Lord knoweth best who it is who bringeth true guidance and who is in manifest error.

It is misleading to limit the main obligatory religious duties only to five things, and omit altogether so many other things of right conduct or righteousness, which have been mentioned, and emphasized in the Quran. One cannot be a good Muslim without strictly observing such prescriptions of righteousness.[108]

Also it is important to note that the prayer and other rituals, as described above, should be considered as means to an end, not ends in themselves. They are important aids for a believer to attain piety, self-purification, and spiritual development. However, the performance of rituals can be deceptive as an indicator of real religiosity if they are not observed with the right earnestness and devotion and if they are not accompanied by good deeds at the same time. It is ironic that the *ulama* (traditional learned men in Muslim religion) lay a lot of emphasis on the nominal performance of the rituals rather than on their observance in spirit; and they make these rituals difficult for the believers by introducing unnecessary rules, regulations, punishments, and complications in terms of attaching levels of compulsiveness to various rituals such as *fard* (obligatory), *wajib* (semi-obligatory), *sunnah* (in line with what the Prophet is alleged to have done), *nafl* (optional), etc. They present the rituals in such a way as if these are the things God wants from us as a matter of duty to Him, and as the principal means of attaining God's pleasure and mercy to go to Heaven. Failure to perform such rituals is depicted as something that earns wrath and punishment from God. But this conception is at odds with the statement of God that He does not need anything from us (35:15; 51:56-58; 47:38). What we need to realize is that we should not observe the rituals as a matter of obligation to God, but should do them for our own sake – for our own benefit. Being led by a feeling of obligation to God does not lead the worshiper very far in his spiritual pursuit. Thus spontaneity on one's part in observing the rituals is of the essence of the real worship of God. "True submission [to God] is predicated upon the principle of personal freedom. [...] Is there any merit in imposed religion or forced prayers?"[109] Indeed, it does not help the worshiper much if he feels compelled to observe the rituals under some duress, explicit or implicit community pressure, or just because the *ulama* so insist.

A misperception entertained among Muslims is that performing *hajj* is so important – if one can financially afford it in one's lifetime – that one must travel to Mecca from far-flung corners of the globe to perform it at any cost, even though there may be more pressing demands to be met at home for such causes as caring for the family and parents, poor relatives, and other poor and needy people. A careful study of the Quran does suggest that we should prioritize what we should do keeping in view our limited time and resources. God rebukes the worshipers who neglect the necessary caring of orphans, and poor and needy people (107:1-6). Also, the *ulama*, influenced by the Hadith, assign so much virtue to the performance of *hajj* that many old, sick people undertake arduous travel and ritual requirements to perform *hajj* thinking that it will wash away their life's sins, while the spirit or lesson to be taken from *hajj* is meant for younger people so as to lead a better, righteous life. And the *hajj* institution has been corrupted by certain things such as the kissing of a black stone in the Kabah – an idolatrous practice counter to the spirit of the Quran, and the throwing of pebbles at a pillar at another place, symbolizing an imaginary Satan, while the real Satan is with us, when we entertain evil thoughts from ourselves, or wrong whispering suggestions from others (112:4-6). Some Muslim scholars also point out, the *hajj* institution, where millions of Muslims merge together from all over the world, provides a good forum where Muslims' problems and Islamic ideas could and should be discussed for promoting world peace, justice, and progress in general, and amity, solidarity, peace, justice, and progress for the Muslim *ummah* in particular. However, this potentially beneficial feature of the *hajj* institution is currently conspicuous by its absence.

ANNEX TO CHAPTER III

A PARTIAL LIST OF GOD'S NAMES AND ATTRIBUTES

abqa	Most Abiding, Lasting (20:73)
adil	Just (3:108, 117, 182; 4;40; 8:51; 39:75; 40:20; 46:19; etc.)
afu	Pardoner (4: 43,99,149; 22:60; 58:2)
ahad, wahid	One (2:133, 163; 4:171; 5:73; etc.)
ahkam al hakimin	The Wisest of Judges (11: 45; 95: 8)
ahya	Giver of life, Quickener, Reviver (41:39)
ajaab	One Who answers, responds (2:186; 40:60)
akhir	Last (57:3)
akram	Glorious, Most Bountiful (96:3)
allah, ilah	God, (only) Who is worthy of worshiping (12:40)
ala, ali, ald, mutaali	High, Exalted (2:255; 4:34; 13:9; 22:62; 31:30 etc.)
alim	Knower (2:32,77,224,227,256; 3:34, etc.)
alim al ghaib	
wa al shahadah	Knower of the hidden and the open (2:33; 59:22, etc.)
amana	Faithful
aqata	Overseer
arham al rahimin	Most Merciful of the Merciful (7:151; 12:64,92, etc.)
awwal	First, Foremost (57:3)
azim	Great, Supreme (2:255; 42:4; 56:74; etc.)
aziz	Mighty, Powerful (2:129,209,220; 58;21, etc.)
badii	Incomparable, Unique (42:11; 112:4)
bari	Originator, Evolver (2:117; 6:101; 59:24)
bais	Resurrector (7:57; 22:5-6; 30:19,50; 35:9; 41:39; 43:11; etc.)
baqi	Eternal, Everlasting
barr	Benign, Beneficent, Source of goodness (52: 28)
basir	Seer (2:96,110; 4:58,134; 8:72; 17:1,18, etc.)
basit	Expander
batana, batin	Inward, Hidden (57:3)
dhahara, dhahir	Manifest (57:3)
dhaifu	He Who gives manifold increase (2:261)

92

dhu al fadl	Bountiful (2:105,243; 3:74; 8:29, etc.)
dhu al fadl wa al azim	Lord of Abounding Grace (2:105; 3:174, etc.)
dhu al ikram	Full of Honor (55:27, 78)
dhu al jalal *wa al ikram*	Full of Majesty, Bounty and Honor (55:27, 78)
dhu al maarij	Lord of the Ways of Ascent (70:3)
dhu al quwah	Lord of Power (51:58)
dhu al rahmah	Full of Mercy (6:133,147; 18:58)
dhu intiqam	Lord of Retribution (3:4, 14:47, 39:37)
fadl	Graceful, Bountiful (2:105,243)
fadl al azim	Lord of bounties unbounded (3:74, 174)
fasil	Decider, Judge (6:57)
fattah	The One to decide, Judge, Opener (34:26)
fatara, fatir	Originator, Maker (6:14; 12: 101, etc.)
ghaffar	Oft-Forgiving (20:82; 38:66; 39:5, etc.)
ghafur	Forgiving (2:173,182,192,218,225,226,235; 3:31, etc.)
ghani	Free of wants (263,267; 4:131; 6:133; 10:68, etc.)
hada, hadi	Guide (2:26; 6:71,88; 25:31;27:63; 87:3; etc.)
hafiz	Presever
hai	Living (2:255; 3:2; 20:111, etc.)
haimana	Preserver
hakama	Most Just Judge
hakim	Wise, Knowledgeable (2:32,129,209,220,228,240; etc.)
halim	Forbearing (225, 235, 263; 3:155, etc.)
hamid	Praiseworthy (2:267; 4:131, 11:73; 14:1,8, etc.)
haqq	Truth (18:44; 20:114; 22:6.62; 23:116; 24:25; 31:30; etc.)
hash	Blameless
hasib	One Who calls to account, Reckoner (2:284; 4:6, 86; 6:62; 13:40-41; 15:92; etc.)
jabbar	Compeller, Irresistible (59:23)
jalal	Majestic (55:27,78)
jalil	Sublime
jamaa	Gatherer (3:9; 45:26}
kabir	Great (4:34; 13:9; 17:43, etc.)
karim	Honorable, (23:116; 27:40,44,49; 82:6)
khabir	Aware (2:234, 271; 3:153,180; 6:103; etc.)
kafi, hasbi	Sufficient (2;137; 3:173; 4:6,45,70,79,81, etc)

khair	Best (20:73)
khair al fasilin	Best of Deciders or Judges (6: 57)
khair al ghafirin	Best of Forgivers (7:155)
khair al hakimin	Best of Judges (7: 87; 10:109, etc.)
khair al rahimin	Best of the Compassionate (23:109, 118)
khaliq, khallaq	Creator (2:21,29,117; 6:73,102; 130:16; etc.)
latif	Subtle (6:103; 22:63; 31:16)
muhsi	Reckoner
majed	Noble
majid	Full of glory (11:73; 85:15)
malaka, malik	Master, Lord (1:4; 3:26; 20:114, etc.)
malik al mulk	Master of the Kingdom, Owner of Sovereignty (3:26)
malik yawm al din	Master of the Day of Judgment
matin	Firm, Steadfast (51:58)
mawla, wali	Protector (2:107,120,257,286; 3:50,51,68, etc.)
mubdi	Originator
mugni	Enricher
muhaimin	Preserver of Security, Protector (59:23)
muhi	Giver of life (2:258; 3:156; 7:158; 45:26; etc.)
muhith	One who encompasses (4:126; 17;60; 40;7; etc.)
muid	Restorer
muiz	Honoror
mujib	Responsive, Answerer of prayer (11:61; 37:75)
mumin	Faithful (59:23)
mumith	Giver of death (45:26)
muntaqim	Avenger
muqit	Maintainer, Sustainer
muqsit	Equitable
muqtadir	All-Prevalent, Most Powerful (18:45; 43:42; 54:42)
musaddeq	Confirmer (2:41)
musawwir	Fashioner, Bestower of forms and colors (59:24)
mutaqabbir	Majestic, Supreme (59:23)
mawla	Protector (8:40)
nafi	Propitious
nima al mawla	Best of Protectors (8:40)
nima al nasir	Best of Helpers (8:40)
nima al wakil	Best Guardian (3:173)
nasir	Helper (2:120; 3:150; 4:45; 8:40; etc.)
nur	Light (24:35)

qabid	Constrictor
qadir, qadira	Capable, Powerful (2:20; 3:189; 4:149)
qahhar, qahir	Subduer, Overpowering (6:18,61; 12:39; 38;65; etc)
qarib	Near (2:186; 11:61; 34:50)
qawi	Strong (8:52; 11:66; 22:40,74; 33:25; etc.)
qayyum	Self-Subsisting, Eternal (2:225; 3:2; 20:111)
quddus	Holy One (59:23; 62:1)
rab	Lord, Sustainer, Cherisher (1:2; 6:45,164)
rabb al alamin	Lord of the Worlds (1:2; 2:131; etc.)
rabb al arsh	Lord of the Glorious Throne (9:129; 17:42, etc.)
rabb al izzah	Lord of Honor (37:180)
rabb al ma'arij	Lord of the ways of ascent (70:3)
rafee	Exalter
rahim	Compassionate, Merciful (1:1,3; 2:160,163, etc.)
rahman	Beneficent, Gracious (1:1, 3; 2:163; 13:30, etc.)
rashid	Guide to the right path
razzaq, raziq	Provider of sustenance (5:22,58,114; 23:72; 34:39, etc.)
raqib	Watcher (5:117)
rauf	Compassionate (2:143,207; 3:30; 9:117; etc.)
sabur	Patient
salam	Peace, Peaceful, Source of Peace (59:23)
samad	Absolute, Independent of others (112:2)
sami	Hearer (2:137,224,256; 3:34; 4:58, etc.)
sar al hisab, hasibin	Swift in Reckoning (2:202; 3:19,199; 5:4; 6:62; etc.)
sar al iqab	Quick in punishment (6:165; 7:167)
sawwara	Shaper, Fashioner
shadid al ikab	Enforcer of punishment (2:165,196,211; 3:11; etc.)
shahid	Witness (4:33,79,166; 5:117; 6:19;10:46, etc.)
shakara, shakur	Appreciator, Thankful (2:158; 4:147; 35:30,34, etc.)
ta'ala	Exalted, Bountiful (40:3)
takabbara	Majestic, Superb
tawwab	Oft-returning (2:37,54,160; 4:16,64; 9:104,118; etc.)
uluwwa	Exalted (17:43)
wahhab	Bestower (3:8)
wahid	One (38:65; 40:16)

wajed	Finder
wakil	Disposer of things, Trustee, Guardian (3:173, etc.)
wala, wali	Patron, Protecting Friend (2:107,120,257; 3:150; 22:78)
warith	Inheritor (15:23)
wasih	Embracing, Caring (2:115,247,261, 268; etc.)
wadud	Loving (11:90; 85:14)
zu inteqam	Lord of retribution (3:5)

Additional description of God's qualities

Acceptor of repentance and Forgiver of sins (40:3; 42:25)

Bestower of love on the righteous (19:36)

Bringer of the hidden to surface (2: 29, 72; 27:25; 31:16)

Curser of the unfaithful (2:88-89)

Decider and giver of judgment with truth (39:75; 40:20)

Deliverer from misery, Savior (2:49-50)

Determiner of measurement and proportion, Ordainer of laws and results (87:3)

Feeder of creatures (29:60)

Feeder, but not fed (6:14; 51:57-58)

Giver of bounties to the righteous (42:26)

Giver of free choice to man between good and evil (2:286; 18:29)

Giver of respite to the wrongdoers to help them grow in wrongdoing (3:178)

Giver of shelter to orphans (93:6)

Giver of what one earns or deserves (2:286)

Guide through darkness (27:63)

Helper of the rejecters of faith to go astray (2:8-10, 26)

Increaser of faith, guidance of the righteous (2:58; 19:76)

Listener to the righteous (27:62; 42:26)

Maker of the laws of nature (25:61-62)

Mindful, not unmindful, of what we do (2:74, 85, 140, 144, 149; 3:99; etc.)

Non-breaker of promise (3:9; 30:6)

Non-harmer; Who does not wrong us, or cause any misfortune (2:57; 3:117; 42:30)

One Who neither begets nor is begotten (112:3)

One Who leads astray only the wrongdoers (2:26)

One Who does not change people's condition until they change themselves (8:53; 13:11)

One Who will test who among us are best in conduct (11:7; 67:2)

One Who does not task a soul beyond its capacity (2:286)

Refuge from all ills and mischief (113:1-5; 114:1-6)

Reliever of suffering (27:62)

Revealer of divine message (2:4, 23; etc.)

Reviver of the dead (2:28, 73, 243, 259-260; 3:27; etc.)

Sender of rain and reviver of the earth (29:63)

Sender of recorders over men (6:61)

Setter of order and proportion (87:2)

Settler of our affairs (55:31)

Showerer of signs for understanding people (2:73)

Source of all good (4:79; 16:30, 53)

Source of all grace and bounties (3:73)

Source of all honor (4:139; 10:65; 63:8)

Turner of one to whatever direction one turns to (4:115)

IV. FORMALIZING UNDERSTANDING ON RELIGION AND CONCEPTIONS OF HEAVEN AND HELL

And *vie (ye) one with another for forgiveness from your Lord, and for a Paradise* as wide as the heavens and the earth, prepared for the righteous. – 3:133

Basic propellers forward – the general theory of evolution

How one can move forward on the religious or spiritual path is a question that warrants some more scrutiny. The essence of religion can be described in terms of just a few building blocks, or propelling factors, the development of which helps man become truly religious, or attain spiritual development or evolution. To systematize our thinking, and understanding about this question, we take recourse to a theory, which we might label as the General Theory of Evolution. This is essentially a Quranic idea, borrowed from my religious teacher Shah Aksaruddin Ahmad.[110] Any action is like a creation. An advance that we make on the spiritual front, or any knowledge that we acquire is the result of our having developed four primary and fundamental factors, faculties, or qualities:

EGO (personality, living entity, or self-consciousness)
LOVE (feeling of need or likeness)
WILL (desire or prayer)
KNOWLEDGE

It can be said that ego, or living entity, or self-consciousness, when developed to express itself in some way, translates into feeling a need, or likeness, or love (for something or somebody). With likeness, or love, a will to do something is developed. Will needs to be combined with knowledge to do something, as the knowledge of what to do and how to do is essential to proceed. "Then when EGO, LOVE, WILL, and KNOWLEDGE are of equal dimensions, concentration or potency, they conjointly lead to action or creation."[111] It may be noticed that the process of accomplishment into creation, or action also involves the employment of two additional factors, which are:

Planning and
Command or Execution

These six factors or, as one might also label them as stages, can be conceived as the basic factors that underlie all creative process. The Quran states:

> **32:4** God it is Who created the heavens and the earth and all that is between them in six "*ayums*" (days or stages); then He established Himself on the Throne.

The significance of this theory of evolution (action or creation) should be evident in the context of spiritual development. Let us pause and reflect a bit on the factors. We will concentrate our discussion on the four basic factors or faculties. A harmonious development of these basic faculties is of the essence of the process of progressive religious or spiritual development. A lack of balance and a deficiency in the development in these faculties will result in stalling, hampering, or even reversing of the process of spiritual development. One example of an unbalanced development is excessive development of the love faculty without sufficient concomitant development of, say, knowledge might risk one becoming insane. On the other hand, insufficient development of the love faculty often lies at the root of insufficient spiritual development. Sufficient development of the will enables one to realize what one wants to do or get done. Differences in the behavior patterns of different people should be largely explicable in terms of the differences in the combination and development of these four basic faculties.

Another point to note about these four factors is that none of them can exist or manifest itself without the other three being embodied in each of them in some way. In other words, these faculties cannot exist separately and independently of each other, although each one of them can be felt separately when it is expressed in a pronounced manner. Each of the four faculties affects the other three. Hence lack of development of any of these faculties is bound to hold back one's spiritual development.

Ego must of necessity be a building block of any action or creation, since action or creation cannot be conceived to originate without an originator, i.e. without the power of one who can exert that power. No work of art is imaginable without an artist's personality, or mind, or creative power behind it. Ego embodies in itself the actor's living entity, self-consciousness, ability, power and self-confidence to act. Iqbal defines "ego" as "directive energy" that manifests "itself in the act of perceiving, judging, and willing" and "is formed and disciplined by its own experience." He refers to it as an independent human soul (*ruh*) that flows from the command (*amr*) of the Ultimate Ego, i.e., God (17:85).[112] Each man or woman has a distinct individuality. That is why each man is accountable for his own actions, not for another's actions:

29:6   And *whoever striveth, he striveth only for his own soul* (*nafs*); for God is independent of anything in the worlds.

17:15   *Whoever goeth aright goeth aright for his own self; and whoever goeth astray goeth astray only to his own harm.* No bearer of a burden beareth the burden of another. (Also see 6:164)

Ego here is not meant to imply egotism, which is an exaggerated view of one's own self, or of one's own importance. Such an attitude is unacceptable, and deplored in religion, as it retards one's spiritual development. In fact one needs to feel very humble before those who have a greater level of spiritual attainment and wisdom, and much more so before his or her All–Transcending and Supreme Lord. The aim of one should then be to proceed toward a stage where he can merge his own Ego with the Ultimate Ego, which is God's Ego. Whatever he does then is perfectly in tune with the Divine Ego or Will (see: 53:3; 18:79-82).

Now to act, one must feel the need for action. Thus the second essential ingredient is need, or likeness, or love. The more intensely one feels the need, or loves a thing, to do, the more effort one would employ to achieve his or her goal. Love or devotion is a key component of one's spiritual advancement. It was through love, a creative impulse, that God felt the need to express Himself. He felt the need for creation, and when He exercised His further will to create the universe, and all living creatures, the universe came into existence, along with all living beings. It is love that permeates all creative activity. God is full of love. He loves those who are righteous (2:195; 3:76, 134, 148; 5:13, 93; 9:4, 7), who purify themselves (2:222; 9:108), who are just (5:42; 49:9; 60:8), and those who fight in His cause (61:4), and who are patient and perseverant (3:146). He loves those who sincerely turn to Him for guidance:

11:90   Ask forgiveness of your Lord, and turn unto Him in repentance. Verily, *my Lord is Merciful, Loving.*

Those who have firm faith in God are staunch in their love of God. Those who wish to earn the pleasure of the Prophet and hence of God, need to love the Prophet and God as they love their near and dear ones. We need to wholeheartedly love God to earn God's love. It is love that begets love:

2:165   *...Those who believe (firmly in God) are staunch in their love for God...*

42:23   This is of the good news God giveth unto his servants who believe and do good deeds. Say (O Muhammad): *I ask of you no reward for it but the love (like that) of near kinsfolk.* And whoever earns any good, We add further good for him. Verily God is Forgiving, Grateful.

3:31   Say (O Muhammad): *If ye love God, then follow me; God will love you and forgive you your sins,* for God is Ever-Forgiving, Merciful.

Indeed noble actions are inspired by love rather than by any selfish motive. With such actions we can do the maximum good for all. Love reigns everywhere, and prevails eventually. The path of human progress is toward love, and those who love God will ultimately prevail over those who reject Him, i.e., over those who abandon the path of progress toward good, or godliness:

5:54   O ye who believe! If any from among you turneth back from his religion (should know that in his place), *will God raise a people whom God Loveth as they Love Him,* (who are) humble toward believers, and stern toward rejecters, striving in the way of God, and never afraid of the blame of such as blame. That is the Grace of God, which He bestoweth on whom He pleaseth. And God is All-Embracing, and All-Knowing.

Noble or righteous deeds on one's part in turn enhance one's feeling of love:

19:96   Verily the Beneficent (God) *endoweth with love* those who believe and do righteous deeds.

To do righteous deeds, what we need to do is try to emulate God and acquire His qualities, which also implies that in the process of such endeavor we also develop our love. The flipside of this is that the more sinful we are and the more we persist in sinfulness, the more hardened and rusty our hearts become. Those who are endowed with love, which is an embodiment of divine love, are very blessed indeed, for such persons are not very many on earth. They are forerunners of spiritual progress for themselves as well as for others in society. God loves them (3:31), and God and angels support them (33:41-43).

One who is on a spiritual training knows how difficult it is to develop the faculty of love. A true aspirant should endeavor to increase his love for God by good thoughts and deeds. He needs to live strictly in conformity with moral principles, which is conducive and critical to spiritual development. Thoughts and acts of indecency give rise to a feeling of rancor or enmity, and blunt the nobler human qualities. Those who become dwellers of Heaven get rid of their feeling of rancor or jealousy in their hearts among themselves (15:47). Love has to be freed from any touch of lewdness, if it is to be instrumental for one's spiritual development. Feelings or acts of base desires or lusts on one's part rob him or her of the golden opportunity to go forward spiritually. Such passions need to be controlled with determination. Development of true love on one's part in turn helps one effectively control such passions.

4:27   And God wisheth to turn to you in mercy, but those who follow their low desires (or lusts) wish you to deviate a great deal. (See also 79:40-41)

7:28   And when they commit some indecency, they say: We have found our fathers doing so, and God hath enjoined it on us. Say (O Muhammad): Verily God never enjoineth what is indecent. Say ye concerning God which ye know not? (See also 25:43-44)

5:5   … And so (lawful unto you) are the chaste from among believing women and chaste from among those who have been given the Book before you, when you have given them their marriage dowries; and *seek chastity, not lewdness, nor taking them as paramours. ...*

Adam and Eve found themselves ousted from their heavenly state of love and happiness, and there arose enmity between them, when they transgressed their limits and became conscious of their nudity (7:19-24; 20:117-124). The Quran exhorted the Prophet Muhammad not to pay attention to that with which human beings enjoy worldly life:

20:131 And strain not thy eyes toward that with which We cause parties of them to enjoy the splendor of this worldly life, that We may test them thereby. The provision of thy Lord is better and more enduring.

Thus those who sincerely desire to go forward in the way of God, i.e. the spiritual path, need to keep their desire for carnal pleasure in check. As Ahmad puts it, they need to "cure" their sex, which means that they need to attain the state when their sexual urge is fully contained:

The Prophet [...] had also to cure the sex in him as also his wives for God is neither male nor female and Muhammad is nothing but His last Prophet to illustrate this view of life in the most beautiful way.[113]

Hunger and thirst under check lead to moral living; when let they end in carnal lust, and sensuousness turns into sensuality which is nothing but conscious nudity.[114]

Thus failure on one's part to keep carnal lust in check is a major stumbling block to developing one's pure love, which in turn is a major driving force for spiritual progress. To strive on one's part to restrain any evil propensity is an integral part of one's striving or struggle (*jihad*) for attaining righteousness or piety.

The Prophet Muhammad was exceedingly kind and loving to the believers, as the Quran confirms:

9:128 There hath come unto you a Messenger from among yourselves, grievous unto whom is any misery that befalleth you, full of concern for you, to the believers compassionate and merciful.

In view of the beneficial divine message he has brought us, he has indeed been a mercy to the whole universe:

21:107   And *We (God) have sent thee (Muhammad) not but as a mercy for the whole universe.*

Love for anything symbolizes appreciation for that thing, or attraction to that thing, and concentration of one's attention upon that thing. That evokes a natural reaction from that thing, which translates itself in the form of a desire on the part of that thing to reveal itself to the person who appreciates it. Observing Nature and appreciating its splendor and beauty has thus a good meaning to the Nature observer. Such observation is a source of insight and power to the observer. Abraham reached his goal of reaching God through observing Nature (6:75-79). And thus it is not for nothing that God has urged man to observe Nature in the Quran (3:190-191; 2:164; 31:29).

We may be relatively brief on the two remaining faculties: Will and Knowledge. If one likes to have something, his likeness or love for that thing needs necessarily to be accompanied by his will to have that thing. The degree of love dictates, or translates into, the degree of will one needs to employ. Will translates into effort, mental or physical. One cannot make progress simply by a pious wish. One needs to strive hard in the way of God to achieve success. It is lack of effort or half-hearted effort that holds us back in the path of progress. The Quran urges us to strive in the way of God. The importance of will is evident from the adage "Where there's a will, there's a way." The will leads to the way. The way signifies the knowledge of how to proceed. Will or determination to improve one's condition, to march forward on the path of progress, has indeed been a linchpin in the progress of human civilization. Will or desire is really prayer. We pray to seek something. Whether we formally pray or not, we may mentally keenly desire something, and try to get that thing by practical means. That is also prayer. However, the will should not degenerate into greed – hankering after others' property, or exploitation of others' sweat, or desire for any kind of transgression of limits. That kind of will or desire is degrading to human soul, and impedes spiritual progress. The Quran has condemned and forbidden such behavior (2:188; 17:34; 2:190, 5:87).

104

Knowledge represents both an input and an output. For seeking knowledge we need knowledge as one of the basic inputs. When one exerts one's ego, employs one's love and exercises one's will, one can do all this only when one has knowledge of how to proceed. So knowledge enters the equation simultaneously with the other three faculties. Differences in the level of knowledge among people are an important distinguishing characteristic between people. It is knowledge, with which man has been endowed, that characterizes mankind's superiority over all other living beings. Knowledge of how to proceed in spiritual pursuit is without doubt the key to progress (58:11). God exhorts mankind to travel through the earth to gain knowledge about how creation is originated (29:20). And those who have been able to acquire knowledge or wisdom have indeed received a great good:

29:20   Say (O Muhammad): *Travel through the land, and see how He originated creation; then God bringeth forth the late growth.* Verily God hath power over all things.

2:267   *He (God) giveth wisdom unto whom He pleaseth, and he unto whom wisdom hath been given hath indeed received a great good.* But none take admonition except men of understanding (or intelligence).

The Prophet Muhammad was urged by God to pray for an increase of his knowledge (20:114). Also, God lifts to higher ranks those who have knowledge:

58:11   God will exalt those to high ranks who believe among you, and those who have gained knowledge.

Indeed God requires us to acquire knowledge to pursue our goals, and not rush into things whereof we have no knowledge or verification:

17:36   And, (O Man), *pursue not that of which thou hast no knowledge*, for surely the hearing, the sight and the heart, each of these shall be questioned about that.

It is lack of knowledge, imperfect knowledge, or guesswork on one's part that leads one to confuse things, and err. Knowledge is thus a *sine qua non* of proceeding properly with any action. Man needs to have clear, and flawless knowledge to live in a flawless way. That is why it is so important for man to strive to attain divine knowledge, which is flawless and inexhaustible.

Note also that knowledge comes only to those who earnestly seek it. It does not come to those who think that they already know enough. As Ahmad puts it:

> [The] portals of the gate of knowledge open only to the hard knocks of those whose quest after knowledge does never quench.[115]

Ego, love, will, and knowledge together create the driving force or energy or power which underlies all creative activity. All of these faculties or factors are invisible elements which can turn into invisible or visible end products. Modern science partially recognizes this. Einstein's celebrated equation $E = mc^2$ does demonstrate that matter can turn into energy. The reverse process should also be possible!

The relevance of matter (or body) and mind – or of space and time – to the arena of the creative process needs to be pointed out at this point. Our action is an interaction of body and mind. For spiritual progress, one needs to work with one's whole body and mind. The four basic creative faculties or qualities of ego, love, will, and knowledge as described above must be embedded in body and mind. We need to work with body (space), and mind (soul, perseverance, or time), which are reflected in ego, love, will, and knowledge, to result in real fruitful action, or creation.

Those who sincerely seek God, i.e., seek His nearness, need to strive hard with prayer and meditation – which are reflections of will – along with all righteous deeds. They need to make their four driving forces – ego, love, will, and knowledge – work to their maximum possible advantage. Should one find any of these driving forces lacking, one should ponder how he could grow in that force. For example, lack of love must be due to some wrong deeds, or due to the lack of sufficient good deeds, or due to the lack of will, or sincerity of devotion, and concentration in prayer and meditation. One needs to submit or surrender whole-heartedly to God – the Source of all goodness, knowledge and power, and guidance and mercy.

106

It is a great pity that a religion, which has proclaimed such messages of love, will, knowledge, etc., has reached so poorly its self-proclaimed followers. It is Muslims today who appear to lack such qualities the most. Rather most of them are steeped in moral, cultural, and spiritual degradation, ignorance, poverty, inter-communal intolerance and violence, and sectarian strife and killing. Muslims pay little attention to the valuable lessons of their Book of Wisdom, the Quran.

The conceptions of Heaven and Hell

Those who walk in the way of God – do right deeds and attain spiritual enlightenment – attain great or real success. They become dwellers of Heaven, or the heavenly state. On the other hand, those who reject faith – do misdeeds – live in Hell, or the hellish state. We need to have some idea about Heaven and Hell. But at the outset it is important to underscore the point that it is neither the fear of Hell nor the lure of Heaven that should really drive one to do good deeds, and strive for spiritual uplift. One should be temperamentally inclined to do good deeds regardless of the fruits of such actions. Prophets did not work expecting any rewards (6:90). Work in expectation of rewards for good work, and in fear of punishment for misdeeds befits only those who are not mature, or intelligent enough. Those who are inherently good and intelligent do not need to be lured by Heaven, nor do they need to be intimidated by the fear of Hell. God does, of course, point out the consequences of good or bad work, but that for our own enlightenment, not to lure, or scare us. Selfish work, or work in expectation of some return does not always promise to be ideal work, as it does not guarantee the best result. As Ahmad puts it:

> The ideal worker or creator is he or she who bestows his or her whole attention or being in the work undertaken to deny selfishness or participation in the result thereof. By so doing a creature emulates God the Creator.[116]

This is not to say that one should be oblivious of the consequences of one's work. Indeed, those who are inherently good are conscious of the fact that their ultimate fate will be good. They are conscious that what they do is good and is bound to have a good end result. Wise men know whereto they are destined. They harbor sure conviction, and they see signs in the earth as well as within their own selves (51:20-21). It needs

107

also to be noted that those who are striving in the way of God should not be too much concerned about the immediate effects of their efforts. If their persistent efforts do not show any signs of progress, they should rethink their efforts, as there may be something wrong with, or something lacking in, their efforts, and they should accordingly try to make renewed efforts. Nobody should be obsessed with the absence or presence of any signs of progress that one experiences in his spiritual endeavor. Continuation of a meaningful effort is more important than the immediate result one succeeds or fails in perceiving. And in the process, when one succeeds in getting some real spiritual fruits, he should steadfastly stick to such achievements to make sure that there is no retreating.

In a vital sense God does not really create any Heaven or Hell for us; it is we who create them by our own deeds. And as the Quran assures us, as noted above, no one should despair of God's Mercy and Forgiveness, and hence of moving out of a hellish state to a heavenly one. There should be no such thing as condemnation of anyone to a permanent hell. No sin is so great that it should condemn one to Hell forever. Many have translated some Quranic verses to suggest that the wrongdoers will live in Hell forever. It must be a mistake to translate, and understand the relevant Quranic verses in such a way. Living in Hell for good does not advance the cause of evolution. It is by virtue of our corrective deeds, which is our own evolution, that we can transform Hell into Heaven. It is through our deeds that we can transform this troubled, dull and dreary earth into a Heaven, and create a still better afterlife (see: 16:30, 97). This is essentially the purpose of religion.

The conceptions of Heaven and Hell, as described in the Quran, are most often taken literally in physical terms, and are thus misconstrued. But their subtle or allegorical meaning is more significant. What is Heaven or, more appropriately, the heavenly state? Using the Quranic ideas, we can say that one characteristic of this state is that it is a state where man does not have to fear, regret or grieve anything, and where there will be no remorse or sorrow for him:

> **46:13**   Verily *those who say: Our Lord is God, and remain steadfast (on the path of God), there shall be no fear for them, nor shall they grieve.* (See also 43:68)

35:34   And they (the dwellers of the Garden) will say: *Praise be to God Who hath removed from us (all) sorrow!* Our Lord is indeed Ever Forgiving, Grateful.

If we reflect on these verses, we should not fail to perceive the deep implications of qualifying for a no-fear, no-grief, or no-sorrow state. This we can realize in our day-to-day activities. If we plan and decide some action properly, and execute that action properly – indeed it needs to be a good action – we find ourselves not regretting our action. This is how we create our own Heaven. But if we do plan an evil deed, and execute it, and even if we plan a good deed, but execute it half-heartedly, or improperly, we find ourselves regretting that action of ours. That is the Hell we create for ourselves, and we suffer accordingly. We start enjoying the bliss of Heaven, or suffering the sting of Hell from the very time of our action, i.e., from this world, while we are still living. The after-effects, or long-run, and afterlife effects are of still greater importance.

16:97   Whoever doeth right, male or female, and (who) is a believer, verily We will grant him (or her) a life (in this world) that is good, and verily We will bestow on them a reward in keeping with the best of what they did.

16:30   And it is said unto those who are upright: What is it that your Lord hath revealed? They say: All that is good. *There is good in this world for those who do good deeds; and the home of the Hereafter is even better.* Excellent indeed will be the abode of those who are upright.

The *ulama* generally convey the impression that we should not be interested in this world, but only in the Hereafter. But such an assertion belies what the Quran states. The Quran clearly states that those who are righteous receive good results in both worlds. Another verse of the Quran confirms that the dwellers of Heaven enjoy the likes of fruits they enjoyed before (i.e., on earth) (2:25). Muslims should wonder why they should live a pitiable life in this world, when God promises that His righteous servants are made inheritors, and rulers of the earth (21:105; 24:55; 7:128-129; 10:14). Of course, if we seek this world alone, we lose the good of the Hereafter; but those who sincerely seek the good of both worlds do get both (2:200-202).

Another important characteristic of the Heavenly State is that it is a state where the dweller gets whatever he wants, as the Quran states:

> **25:16**   Therein (in Heaven) abiding, *they (those who are righteous) will have all that they desire.* It is a promise (which is) binding upon thy Lord. (Also see 42:22)

No fear or regret, and getting whatever one wants are probably the most important godly qualities or gifts that man can ever covet. For, man can find himself not fearing or regretting anything, only when there is no fault or flaw in the feelings, thoughts, and actions that he does. And he can get anything he wants only when he attains a very high level of creative power, or talent and perfection. These characteristics of the heavenly dwellers clearly point to the necessity for man to attain real spiritual progress to be able to display such heavenly qualities.

The Quran provides other descriptions of Heaven. It is a state where man does not have to taste death again after his first death (37:58-60; 44:56), but lives forever in a perpetual state of bliss. It is a place or state where there is no boredom or weariness (35:35), where there is peace and security (6:127; 15:46), where there is abundance of fruits (food and drink) (56:32), where there is no futile conversation and no lying 78:35), where there is purity and no foul play (56:25), where there is peace and salutations of peace (19:62; 56:26), where there is no feeling of rancor, but only brotherhood (7:43; 15:47), where there is grace and beauty (55:70), and pure companionship and love (56:36-37), where it is neither too cold nor too hot for the dweller (76:13), and where there is the light of those who are admitted there, and where they pray for perfection of the light, which is nothing but striving for perpetual progress (66:8).

These and more characteristics of Heaven described in the Quran speak of things, which a human being always cherishes. These are the things which we need to have in this very world so that the world can be transformed into a heaven. Heaven is a state from which no one wants to go backward (18:108). That implies that the heavenly state represents a maximum vantage point for human evolution, which is implied also by the verse where the dwellers of Heaven pray to God to perfect their light (66:8).

If we have an idea of Heaven, it is not difficult to know what Hell is. It must be the place or state where all the good things that the dwellers of Heaven have, or enjoy are conspicuous by their absence. The other name of Hell is Fire (2:24; 3:131; 4:56; 6:27; 25:11). The following verses are especially worth noting:

40:71-2   While the fetters and the chains (shall be) on their necks, they shall be dragged through the boiling water; then *they will be thrown into the Fire.*

10:54   And *if each soul that doth wrong had all that is in the earth, it would seek to offer it for ransom*; and they will feel remorse within them, when they see the punishment. And it would be judged between them fairly and they would not be wronged.

These verses reflect the suffering that one needs to undergo to atone for one's misdeeds. The sinner would be prepared to part with everything of his possession – even if he possessed all that is in the earth – to atone for his misdeeds. The greater the degree of misdeeds, the greater is the scale of suffering. This is the necessary evolutionary or corrective process of purification for one who makes mistakes, or commits misdeeds.

Evidently, Hell is a state that is most resented by all, and all really wants to escape such a fate. If a man is wise, he will not knowingly jump into such a frying pan. It is so important for all to know how to evolve spiritually to avoid pitfalls in order for him no to regret his actions later. Indeed, we should think in terms of turning this dull and dreary earth into a garden of bliss. The Quran hints at a Heaven as a changed earth, and says that this Garden is as wide as the heavens and the earth:

14:48   One day *the Earth will be changed into a new Earth, and so will be the Heavens*; and they shall come unto God, the One, the Supreme. (See also 3:133)

Indeed this earth is changed into a safe and good place to live when, and as long as, good and pious people inhabit it. This becomes evident by what God Himself says in the Quran:

111

29:31-2 And when Our messengers (angels) came to Abraham with the good news (of a son to him), they said: 'We are indeed going to destroy the people of that township, for its people are wrongdoers.' He said: 'But Lut is there.' They said: 'We know well who is there; *we will certainly save him and his family except his wife*; she is of those who lag behind.'

The angels then advised Lut and members of his family to leave the township before it was destroyed. God does not send a punishment to a habitation as long as there are good people there. This is more evident from the following verse addressed to the Prophet Muhammad himself:

8:32-3 And when they said: 'O God! If this (the Quran) is indeed the Truth from Thee, then rain down on us a shower of stones or inflict on us some grievous punishment'. But *God would not send down a punishment on them while thou wast among them, nor will He punish them while yet they seek forgiveness.*

Indeed, it is God's immutable decree that the good people – the believers – are saved from God's wrath or destruction:

10:103 Then shall We save Our Messengers and believers, in like manner (as of old). It is incumbent upon Us that We save believers.

This earth or its designated regions are continually purified and changed into a New Earth by replacement of bad people with good people:

10:13-4 And We did destroy generations before you when they did wrong. Their Messengers came to them with clear signs, but they would not believe (and rectify themselves). Thus We requite the guilty folk. Then we made you successors in the earth after them, that We might see how ye behave.

21:105 And verily We have written in the Book that after the Reminder My righteous slaves will inherit the earth.

47:38 And if ye turn away (from the right path), He will replace you by some other folk who would not be the likes of you.

It is precisely because of the presence of the virtuous people among us that this earth is being saved from utter ruin and destruction, and it is being turned into an increasingly safer and better place to live. Their tireless well-meaning work and prayers are saving mankind from decay and destruction, and are turning the earth into a Heaven for them. Because of the good work being done by good people and because of their good wishes or prayers, as time rolls on, we should be moving forward to seeing better and better days ahead, though this progress may be punctuated by periodic lapses. Ultimately over the long run, the good and the true prevail over the bad and the false, and the earth gets rid of the bad and false or meaner elements (see: 5:56; 8:7-8; 9:48; 20:68-70; 26:45-48; 21:18; 58:19-22).

8:7-8 And God willed that He should cause the Truth to triumph by His words, and cut the root of the disbelievers; that he might cause the Truth to triumph and bring vanity to naught, however much the guilty might oppose it.

21:18 Nay, We hurl the Truth against falsehood, and it doth break its head, and behold, it (falsehood) vanisheth!

5:56 And whoever taketh God and His Messenger and the believers for friend – the party of God, they certainly are the victorious.

Civilization marches forward, not backward over the long run. One need not predict doom, destruction, or dire consequences for the fate of this world. Such predictions ignore the clear indications God has given us in the Quran. *Qiyamat* (resurrection) should not be interpreted as destruction of the earth. It must be understood in a different light. The time of *qiyamat* is one when the dead will rise from their death or slumber (36:51-52), when to every soul will become clear what it earned in the past (81:14), when the curtain will be lifted from them, and they will be able to see clearly (50:22), and when the guilty people will fully

113

realize and accept their guilt (6:130). This should augur well for the time that follows.

Man has evolved as the best species among God's creation, and deserves to be His best servant, and to live in the Eternal Garden of knowledge and bliss. Adam and Eve received the knowledge of how to live there forever. However, when they let themselves to be misguided by the devil, and erred, they fell from God's grace to the earthly life. They were not condemned to be completely lost. When they realized their fault, and repented, they received guidance from God. God told them that if they followed that guidance, they would have nothing to grieve or fear and that they would regain the heavenly state (2:36-38). God, the Most Merciful, thus has prescribed guidance or religion for human beings to lift them from their earthly state to the heavenly state, and to create conditions in society that facilitate the process of such human evolution.

V. THE ESSENCE OF *SALAT* IN LIGHT OF THE QURAN

O ye who believe! Remain conscious of God, *seek a way unto Him, and strive in His way that ye may succeed.* – 5:35

When my servants ask thee concerning Me, then *surely I am nigh (unto them); I answer the prayer (dua) of every suppliant when he crieth unto Me.* ... – 2:186

INTRODUCTION

Belief in God and His worship, which includes *salat* or prayer seeking His help, are the most important metaphysical aspects of religion. These are also aspects that most distinguish religion from conventional science.

Most of the building blocks of the existing *salat* system have been taken from the Quran and the Hadith. But the full form in which it is practiced appears to have been developed over time by the *ulama* long after the death of the Prophet Muhammad. The existing practice of *salat* has certain inherent shortcomings that could be largely attributed to the influence that came from the Hadith (see below). To rid *salat* of its current deficiencies, we need to understand and formulate it exclusively on the basis of the Quran alone.

Salat is a principal medium of worshiping, and remembering God, and seeking His nearness:

20:12-4 Verily I am God, there is no god but I. Therefore serve Me, and *establish prayer for My remembrance.* (See also 96:19)

96:19 Nay! Obey not thou (O Muhammad) him (who is misled, and who misleadeth), but *prostrate thyself, and draw near (unto God).*

In practice for most Muslims, however, *salat* has become more or less a routine ritual mainly because of the way it has been defined to be performed. The main elements of this definition are five-time prayer everyday, a *rakah* (prayer cycle) system with certain physical postures and movements such as *qiyam* (standing), *ruku* (bowing), *sajdah*

115

(prostration), and sitting with a particular sequencing of such postures and movements, and recitation of the *surah fatiha* (first chapter of the Quran) in the standing position along with recitation of an additional *surah* or some verses thereof, and recitations of certain words of glorification of God in physical postures and movements of bowing, prostration, standing and sitting, and recitation of a *tashahud* in the sitting position, which is a text with words of praise for God and blessings upon the Prophet and righteous believers, and affirmation that God alone is worshipped and that Muhammad is His Messenger[117], and a *taslim* or wishing of peace and God's Grace for all around the worshiper – all of which is done in the language of Arabic.

From the Quran we get the timings of prayer as well as certain features of its physical form. It calls for standing, bowing, and prostrating. However, it does not suggest any combining or sequencing of these postures. It calls for only two or three sessions of prayer in particular verses. It provides timings, which add up to three: (1) morning, (2) afternoon since the decline of the sun until dark of the night, which includes dusk, and (3) some watches of the night. The Quran does not prescribe any *rakah* system. Nor does it specify any particular words of prayer or glorification that one has to utter in *salat*. A Divine Book need not specify every detail. But this should not be taken to mean that the Quran does not provide sufficient guidance on *salat*. Thinking or believing so will amount to contradicting the Quran itself (12:111; 16:89). The Quran has given us detailed guidance about how to do the ablution (*wudu*: washing face and hands up to elbows, and wiping head, and feet up to ankles) which we should do before performing *salat*, about when we should take a bath, or do the *tayammum* (wiping face and hands with earth) (5:6; 4:43) instead of the ablution, about the decent dress we should wear for the *salat* (7:31), and about the *qiblah* (the direction of the Kabah at Mecca) we should face for the *salat* (2:144). In addition, the Quran describes the inherent purpose and spirit of prayer. It illustrates the nature or content of prayer that we can use for different reasons. It also provides many examples of prayers of past prophets and believers. Whatever guidance is provided in the Quran on *salat* must, therefore, be regarded as sufficient for us, even though the Quranic conception of *salat* is generally perceived to be sketchy, and different from its prevailing conception, and practice.

Evidently some form of *salat* has been in vogue since the time of the Prophet Abraham (21:73), who is the father of the religion of Islam

(22:78). God has asked specifically the Prophet Muhammad, and indirectly us, to follow Abraham (3:95; 2:135; 4:125; 16:123). Hence, as many scholars think, the *salat* practices that were observed by the Prophet Abraham (21:73) could be presumed to have been known, and followed by our Prophet and his followers as well. However, the exact form of *salat*, including its timings, they followed do not appear to have been documented anywhere.

It is apparent that the prevailing conception of *salat* was drawn largely from the Hadith, where the clues of many of the elements of the prevailing practice can be found, though the description of the various elements there is neither all consistent, nor does it appear fully complete on all the elements. The five-time *salat* idea is directly traceable to a Hadith, though that Hadith is not credible (see below for elaboration). There are many Hadith texts suggesting the concept of *rakah*, and their numbers in various *salat*, the prescriptions for recitations from the Quran, those for several physical postures and movements, and some suggestion on what to say with physical postures and movements, along with the *tashahud* that is to be recited in the sitting position of the *salat*. What is remarkable is that the Hadith readings concerning *salat* are mostly ritualistic in nature, which give a lot of prominence to details of physical postures and recitations, but which give virtually no guidance on the spirit and substance of *salat*.

THE QURANIC CONCEPTION OF *SALAT*

Every creature has an instinctive yearning for upgrading itself, which is its prayer for evolution. In a broad sense, *salat* or prayer is nothing but desire, most often reflected in, or accompanied by, actions. Sincere prayer is strong determination backed up by necessary action. We often experience receiving external help in the process of our work. Some of this help may indeed strike us as surprising, and we may characterize such help as divine help. But all help that we get is divine help. Only those who recognize help as such are grateful to God (14:7; 27:19, 40). But human beings are seldom grateful (2:243; 7:10 and numerous other verses).

Prayer needs to be addressed only to God (72:18), and prayer to false gods is of no avail to the worshiper:

117

13:14   Real prayer (*dua*)[118] is unto (true) God. *Those to whom they pray beside God never respond to them,* except as one who stretcheth forth his hands toward water (wishing) that it may reach its mouth, but it never reacheth it. The prayer of those without faith (in God) is in vain.

We may also note that all creatures perform *salat* or glorify God in some way or other:

24:41   Hast thou (O Muhammad) not seen that God, He it is Whom all beings in the heavens and the earth glorify, and the birds in their flight? *Each one verily knoweth its salat (prayer) and the glorification,* and God is aware of what they do.

Also one needs to note that prayer can be for good or evil:

17:11   Man prayeth for evil as he prayeth for good, for man is ever in haste.

This verse suggests that one's prayer may not always be for one's own good, and for the good of others. God also says in the Quran that one can pray for, or desire, only this world, or he can pray for both the worlds. Those who pray for, i.e., desire, this world alone will not be eligible for any reward in the Hereafter (2:200-202). All this suggests that we need to be careful about the content of our prayer, which should be directed to enhancing our individual and collective good, and good that takes into account the present as well as the future rather than just concentrating on the present. None should wish or pray ill for others. Such wishing does not serve any good purpose, but spiritually hurts the person who makes such wishes. However, in special circumstances, wishing or praying for delivery and protection from the persecution, or bad influence, of wrongdoing people may result in the ruin or harm of such people, which is part of the grand design of God to establish greater good on earth by replacing bad people with good people, or by punishing the former, and rewarding the latter (54:89; 26:169; 7:89; 10:88; 10:13-14; 21:105; 47:38).[119]

The devil also prays. Iblis brought his own downfall by becoming proud – by refusing to recognize that some other being could be superior to him (2:34). He vowed to misguide mankind, and sought from God respite till the Day of Resurrection, which God granted him (7:14).[120] But the devil rejected God, and he hardly needs to care for a god. So it is just that his desire translated into a prayer to God.

Salat is prayer of a personal, devotional, and spontaneous type, not bound by any rituals or formulas. For this reason, the believer should be allowed to fashion his own way to relate to his Creator, taking the cue from the guidelines that can be found in the Quran, however sketchy they might appear to be.[121]

According to the Quranic conception, the essence of *salat* lies in one's full surrender and devotion to God, his or her seeking of His countenance and help, and one's sincere endeavor for purification and spiritual development. This approach can be viewed, and analyzed under the following heads:

- The vision or purpose of *salat*;
- The content of *salat*;
- The form of *salat*;
- The language of *salat*;
- The timings and times of *salat*; and
- God's response to *salat*.

The vision or purpose of *salat* in turn can be seen to encompass the following elements:

- It is remembrance and glorification of God (His worship).
- It is devotional in kind, and has to flow from one's own heart.
- It is for seeking divine help.
- *Salat* is not just prayer; it is prayer coupled with consistent work.
- *Salat* is to be established or kept up.
- We need to pray for our own sake, not because God needs or wants it.
- It is essentially one's overall effort for purification and spiritual development.
- It is preparation for one to become a God's true servant and emulator to go nearer to Him.

119

All these points are elaborated below.

The vision or purpose of *salat*

Salat is (1) remembrance and glorification of God (His worship), (2) essentially devotional in kind, and (3) a conduit to seek divine help. It is to be envisioned as something that leads the worshiper to lead a more purified and evolved life that enables him to walk aright, avoiding mistakes and misdeeds. It has to be (4) backed up by consistent and complementary actions in real life. Also there needs to be (5) spontaneity on our part to pray for our own spiritual development. These points are worth some elaboration.

Salat is remembrance and glorification of God (His worship)

The Quranic conception of *salat* is implicit in the very first *surah, the fatiha,* of which the first four verses, including the first verse containing *basmalah* (In the name of God, the Most Gracious, the Most Merciful), are words of remembrance and glorification of God (worship), and the remaining three verses constitute general prayer of the believer to God to lead him to the righteous path. Remembrance and glorification of God is in itself part-and-parcel of prayer, which helps us keep away from evil (29:45). God revealed to the Prophet Moses when he heard the voice of God at the valley of Tuwa of Mount Sinai that he should pray to remember God:

> **20:11-4** So when he came to it (a fire), he was called: O Moses! Verily I am thy Lord, take off thy shoes; verily thou art in the sacred valley Tuwa. And I have chosen thee. So listen to what is revealed. Verily I am God; there is no god but I. Therefore serve Me and *establish prayer for My remembrance.*

God has specifically urged the Prophet Muhammad and also us to remember Him much and glorify Him often; and His remembrance is characterized as the best act of prayer (29:45). God has advised the Prophet Muhammad and us to remember Him to find refuge from devilish thoughts and actions (7:200; 41:36; 23:97-98; 114:1-6). God and His angels bless those who remember and glorify Him much. And our hearts do find rest and satisfaction in God's remembrance (13:28).

7:205 And do thou (O Muhammad) *remember thy Lord within thyself humbly and with awe and in a voice not loud* in the morning and the evening, and be not thou of the neglectful. (See also 20:12-14 cited at the beginning of this chapter.)

73:7-8 Indeed thou (O Muhammad) art preoccupied with other matters during daytime. *So (during night) remember thy Lord, and devote thyself to Him with a complete devotion.*

33:41-3 O ye who believe! *Remember God with much remembrance, and glorify Him early and late (or day and night).* And He it is Who blesseth you, as do His angels, that He may bring you forth from darkness into light; and He is Full of Mercy to the Believers. (See also 3:191 and 76:25-26)

29:45 *And surely remembrance of God is the best.*

13:28 Verily *in the remembrance of God hearts do find rest.*

God promises forgiveness and a great reward to good believers who, among other good things they do, engage much in God's remembrance (33:35). God is most Kind and Responsive to His servants who call upon Him sincerely. That is God's promise. And God does not make a vain promise (30:6).

And importantly, we remember and glorify God inherently to admire His qualities, and at heart to seek such qualities. This way we seek our spiritual evolution, and that is precisely the significance of such remembrance and glorification. The whole universe glorifies God in some way or other. The faithful servants of the Beneficent God are those who, among other things, spend the night before their Lord prostrating and standing (25:64).

57:1 *Whatever is in the heavens and on earth glorifieth God;* for He is Mighty, Wise.

17:44 ... And *there is not a thing that doth not celebrate His praise*; but ye understand not their glorification. ...

52:48-9 ... And *celebrate the praises of thy Lord when Thou risest (from bed). And celebrate His praises also for part of the night, and at the setting of the stars.* (See also 15:97-98 and 30:17-18)

Believers need to pray and remember God at all times – even when they are at war. The Quran exhorted the Prophet Muhammad, when at war, to lead the prayer for a party of his soldiers, while others were in arms, and after they had finished prostrating, to lead the prayer for another party who had not prayed (4:102). In the verse that followed next, the Quran further states:

4:103 When ye have performed your prayer, *remember God standing, sitting, and reclining.* ...

We are urged by God to remember and glorify Him by conceiving Him by His numerous attributes or beautiful names. We may choose any of such names to call upon Him:

7:180 And God's are the most beautiful names; *so call upon Him by (any of) them. And leave those who distort His names.* ... (See also 17:110)

We need to strive to develop the various godly qualities and capabilities as best as we can. Since God wants us to call upon Him by any of His beautiful names or attributes (17:110), it will be very good prayer for one if he or she devoutly chants any of such names to remember and glorify Him, at the same time visualizing Him in His various attributes, and seeking His mercy and help to acquire such qualities (For some elaboration, see the box below).

Examples of Some Mental Glorification and Prayer while Chanting God's Name

While chanting His name (e.g., the name "Allah"), one may at the same time be mentally contemplating or visualizing Him in terms of His various qualities such as that He is Rahman (Most Gracious or Kind), Rahim (Most Merciful), Haiyu (Ever Living),

---

Qayyum (Self-Sustaining, Eternal), Basir (All-Seeing), Sami (All-Hearing), Hakim (All-Knowing), and so on, and at the same time he or she may be mentally seeking His mercy and guidance, and His corresponding various qualities. One may mentally pray at the same time "O my Lord, Most Kind and Merciful! Touch me with Thy Mercy and manifest Thyself with all Thy qualities in me, so that I can understand Thee and I can make others understand Thee! O my Lord, Ever Living! Respond to me! Without Thy response I am like a dead man! Make me live a life worth living – give me new life! O my Lord, All-Seeing! I am blind! Give me sight! O my Lord, All-Hearing! Bestow on me real hearing capacity! O my Lord, Most Wise! Increase my wisdom!" So on and so forth. Such remembering and glorifying God along with mental prayer leads one to receive God's mercy, which we may call "the energy of mercy", and through him or her, such energy can reach others as well. This process thus leads one to achieve spiritual progress, and helps others also achieve such progress. Such remembrance and glorification of God has thus a special meaning and significance, and that is the reason why God characterizes remembrance of Him as the best of prayers (29:45), and He exhorts us to remember Him most often, and also after usual or formal prayer (4:103). It will be good for one to allocate some appreciable amount of time in the morning, afternoon, evening, and/or at night (30:17-18; 33:41-43; 52:48-49) to remember and glorify God. One should judge how much time one should devote to such remembrance and prayer by observing what the Prophet Muhammad and his close associates used to do. The Quran mentions that they used to spend about one third to about two thirds of the night for remembrance and glorification of God, and for studying the Quran (73:20). Besides, the Prophet and we have been admonished by God to remember and glorify Him in the morning and evening, and during parts of the day and at night (20:130; 30:17-18; 33:41-42; 52:48-49).

It is through rigorous spiritual exercises with persistent devoted remembrance and glorification of God that one can hope to achieve self-purification, spiritual progress, and knowledge to understand and experience the divine. If one carefully reads the Quran, one will notice that it lays enormous emphasis on the need for spiritual uplifting of humankind. God wants us to grow in purification and piety, and God wants to complete His Grace on us, and manifest and complete His Grace and Splendor throughout His whole creation. To manifest His Mercy (*rahmat*) and Grace (*niamat*) in His creation is what God Himself considers as His duty or rule, and accordingly the rule of His Mercy reigns everywhere:

9:32   Fain would they like to extinguish the Light of God with (the blowing of) their mouth, but *God would not allow that, but will perfect His Light,* however much the disbelievers are averse (See a similar verse also at 61:8).

5:6   God wisheth not to place any burden (or difficulty) on you. But *He wisheth to purify you, and to perfect His niamat (grace) for you, that ye may be grateful.*

6:12   Say: 'Unto whom belongeth all that is in the heavens and the earth?' Say: 'Unto God. *He hath prescribed for Himself (the rule of) Mercy'*

7:156   *My (God's) mercy embraceth all things; so I will ordain it (specially) for those who are righteous, pay the poor-due and those who believe Our revelations.*

God is very close to His devotees. He is closer to them than even their own heart and life vein:

8:24   O ye who believe! ... And *know that God cometh in between a man and his heart.*

50:16   ... And *We are closer to him than his jugular vein.*

We need to remember and glorify God earnestly (33:41-43). God sees everything everywhere, manifest or hidden. We also need to strive to see or perceive as far as possible on our part. Spiritual development helps one become clairvoyant, i.e., to see beyond the way one sees with one's normal eyes (22:46; 51:20-21). God hears everything everywhere. We also should try to develop our hearing capacity beyond the way we can hear with our normal ears. It is thus that prophets hear God's words, and receive His revelations. We need to emulate prophets in like manner. God is most wise. We also need to increase our wisdom. Thus remembering and glorifying God is the best of prayers to receive God's mercy, gain spiritual knowledge and development, and to draw near to Him.

Salat is devotional in kind, and has to flow from one's own heart

Devotion is a crucial element of the vision of *salat*. *Salat* should flow from one's own heart or mind. God knows best what is in our heart or mind:

17:25   *Your Lord knoweth best what is in your minds.* If ye are upright, then verily He is Ever Forgiving unto those who turn (unto Him).

One needs to pray with his whole body and mind. God wants us to call upon Him sincerely at every place of worship (7:29). He urged the Prophet Muhammad to remember Him and devote to Him whole-heartedly (73:8). He exhorts us to remember Him with a love and devotion that is like or more than the love and devotion we show to our parents:

2:200   Remember God *as you remember your fathers or with a more devotional remembrance.*

There are men and women who call upon God sincerely, when they are in some serious trouble, but when God's grace shines on them, and their distress is gone and good times return, they forget their Lord and become ungrateful; but the prayer of such people at bad times illustrates well what genuinely sincere or devotional prayer means (39:8, 41:51). God asks us to call upon Him with awe or reverence and hope:

7:56   *And call upon Him (God) with reverence and hope.* Verily the mercy of God is nigh unto those who do good.

Salat requires expression of a special attitude of mind – a mind not proud, but which is one of devotion and humility. People who are proud and arrogant lack such an attitude:

40:60   And your Lord sayeth: Call upon Me; I will respond to your (prayer); but *verily those who are too proud to serve Me will enter Hell, disgraced.*

7:55   (O humankind!) *Call upon your Lord humbly, and in private.* Verily He loveth not transgressors. (See also 7:205)

Those who think that they know enough learn or gain nothing. Thus God proclaims that one of the preconditions for success is praying to God with a mind that is full of humility, reverence or devotion to God. Indeed, as the Quran confirms, praying meaningfully is not really possible except for people who are sufficiently humble:

> **2:45-6** And *seek (ye God's) help through perseverance and prayer. This is indeed hard except for the humble (or reverent)*, who know that they will have to meet with their Lord, and that unto Him they will return.

Humility grows when one recognizes, and is fully conscious of, one's own deficiencies and past mistakes, and when one truly seeks to improve himself. True believers are humble enough to submit to God's remembrance and to accept the truth (57:16). Knowledgeable persons are humble enough to recognize such truth, with prostration in tears, and this further increases their humility (17:107-108):

One meaning of *salat* is "sacrificing oneself". Sacrificing one's self to God means one's discarding of all mundane distractions, and surrendering or submitting fully to the will and service of God, and devoting fully to His worship. The sincerity of the prayer of the devotees of God needs to be reflected in all of their thoughts and actions. They sacrifice and devote whole-heartedly all their worship, their actions, their life, and their death to only God and His service, just as the Quran wanted the Prophet Muhammad and, indirectly us, to do (6:162).

> **6:71-2** Say (O Muhammad): Verily the Guidance of God is the (true) guidance, and we are *commanded to surrender to the Lord of the universe*, and to *establish prayer* and to be upright, and He it is unto Whom is our destination.
>
> **73:8** And remember (O Muhammad) the name of thy Lord, and *devote thyself to thy Lord whole-heartedly.*
>
> **6:162** Say (O Muhammad): *Truly my prayer and my sacrificing actions, my life and my death – all are for God, the Lord of the Universe.*

Saying something verbally without feeling and meaning it at heart really boils down to saying nothing, and is meaningless. God pays no attention to such uttering (2:225). The Quran refers to men who serve God on the verge, and not whole-heartedly, as those who become content with good when they receive it, but make an about-face in times of trial and tribulation. Such people are losers in this world as well as in the Hereafter (22:11).

Also importantly, one needs to pray in order to increase one's devotion and love for God. Prayer cannot be conditioned by a ritual. Devotion is what really counts, not observing particular norms of a ritual. The real spiritual purpose is served when one inclines to God spontaneously with real devotion, and when one sincerely strives to increase such devotion and love. The worshiper should find his own way of devoting and relating to God with the guidance that he can find in the Quran. Whole-hearted devotion and concentration in prayer also means that the worshipers should get rid of extraneous thoughts and distractions. The worshipers should not be like those who rush to places of business interest, unduly leaving the place of worship (62:9-11). Business or trading does not derail God-loving believers from properly remembering Him, and establishing *salat* (24:37).

Salat is for seeking divine help

Prayer is for seeking divine help. The rationale of such seeking is inherent in the fact that we are needy in some way or other, and directly or indirectly dependant on God Who is free of wants and independent of all His creations (2:263, 267; 4:131; 6:14, 133; 35:15; 47:38). He also admonishes us to seek His help through perseverance and *salat* (2:45, 153). None can really help us if God does not come to our help; and beside God, we have no real refuge.

> **2:153** O ye who believe! *Seek help through perseverance and prayer (salat)*. Verily God is with the perseverant. (See also 2:45-46 and 3:26)

> **2:107** Knowest thou not that God's is the kingdom of the heavens and the earth; and that *ye have not, beside God, any (real) friend or helper*? (See also 3:160)

127

72:22   Say (O Muhammad): None can protect me from God (if I were to disobey Him); *nor can I find refuge except in Him.*

Through the last three verses of *surah fatiha* (1:5-7), which we always use in *salat*, we ask for God's general help for His mercy and guidance to *sirat al mustaqim* (the straight path):

Thee (alone O God) we serve; *Thee (alone) we ask for help!*
Show us the straight path;
The path of those who have received Thy Grace (manifold boons); not the path of those who have earned Thy wrath nor of those who go astray!

We benefit by seeking divine help for anything we need or want, and for facilitating all of our work. We, of course, feel the need for very many things, including help to be able to seek and find employment for livelihood, do our work successfully, or to do it more and more efficiently and perfectly. In short, we need to seek God's help to lead our life flawlessly, and to enrich it by receiving His manifold bounties. Among the things we should seek, increasing love and devotion for God, and spiritual knowledge should count as the most important. Progress in this regard is more effective for one to move along the *sirat al-mustaqim*. We need to seek such a path with diligence and perseverance, along with consistent thoughts and actions, as God exhorted the Prophet Muhammad and us to do (94:1-8; 2:148).

5:48   *So vie (ye) one with another in virtuous deeds.* The goal of you all is unto God.

17:19   *And whoever desireth the Hereafter (the future), and striveth for it with the due effort, being a believer, for such their efforts will surely be appreciated (rewarded).*

Perseverance or patience signifies that help does not always come automatically, instantaneously, or with ease. Help often comes after enormous effort and waiting, and at times with vicissitudes of events in life, which one needs to endure with patience. About such vicissitudes, God says:

128

2:155-7 And *We will certainly try you with something of fear and hunger, and loss of wealth and lives and crops; but give good news to the perseverant*, who say when a misfortune striketh them: Verily we are for God, and verily unto Him we are returning. Such are they, on whom are blessings from their Lord, and mercy. Such are those who are rightly guided.

Perseverance that is required of believers is well exemplified by that which the prophets and believers with them showed, and which is noted in the Quran:

3:146-7 How many of the Prophets fought (in God's way), and with them (fought) large bands of worshipers of the Lord? *But they never lost heart because of what befell them in God's way, nor did they weaken (in spirit), nor were they brought low. God loveth those who are patient.* Their only utterance was: Our Lord! Forgive us our sins, and anything we may have done that transgressed limits. Make our foothold firm, and help us against those who are disbelievers.

The victory of the Muslims over the persecuting and attacking disbelievers during the Prophet's lifetime is a good example to cite. The Prophet and the believers along with him prayed to God for such victory (2:286). The final or ultimate victory, however, did not come instantaneously. They had to undergo trying periods. Believers faced a lot of obstacles, torture, and persecution. Many had to migrate to other countries. At one point, the Prophet and his close associates also had to migrate to another land. There were several battles between the believers and the disbelievers. The great victory then finally came when the disbelievers were decisively overcome, and Islam took root in the land.

Salat is not just prayer; it is prayer coupled with consistent work

Since *Salat* is essentially for seeking *sirat-al-mustaqim* that enables the worshiper to walk aright, avoiding mistakes and misdeeds, it must necessarily be complemented, or backed up, by consistent and complementary actions. In other words, *salat* encompasses both prayer and consistent actions, or overall efforts for the coveted goals. The Quran states:

29:45   And keep up prayer; *verily prayer keepeth (one) away from indecency and evil.*

A good worshiper needs to make earnest efforts to keep away from all kinds of evil thoughts and deeds. He cannot commit any wrongdoing. He needs to engage in only good, appropriate, decent, and noble deeds in feelings, thoughts and other actions. The prayer of a person will be devoid of any meaning if he or she is oblivious or neglectful of the necessity of doing the appropriate things in any occasion. One glaring example of prayer that will go to waste is that of those who neglect their duties to help the indigent and the helpless, and whom God curses:

107:1-7   Hast thou observed him who rejecteth religion? That is the one who mistreateth the orphan; and encourageth not the feeding of the poor. So *woe to the worshipers who are heedless of their prayers, those who act to be seen, but refuse the acts of kindness*!

In our everyday prayer, we seek God's guidance for going along the right path – for doing the right thing. So we worshipers cannot do, or even think of doing anything that is contrary to the spirit of prayer. We cannot lie. We cannot deceive others. We cannot steal or plunder. We cannot commit any act of indecency. We cannot even profess wrong faiths, and nurture wrong feelings. We cannot cause even the slightest injury to others without any legitimate reason. Any such act renders our prayer null and void. Are they real Muslims who pray even five times a day, but who at the same time do not hesitate to engage in deceitful and corrupt practices? One is corrupt, not simply when he or she takes bribes, but also if he or she distorts facts, does not tell or accept the truth, works insincerely, provides wrong information and advice, does not judge properly, conveniently forgets past promises, deliberately avoids repaying debt, and deceives others and institutions in any way.[122]

That verbal praying without meaning it by heart and without reflecting it in all of one's thoughts and actions does not make any sense is captured beautifully in the following words of Shah Aksaruddin Ahmad:

Just saying verbally is not enough; just saying is not enough
That for God is your *salat*,
Your actions,
Your life,
And your death (6:162);
Just saying is not enough.

For God only you shall pray;
For God only you shall live;
Lead your life on earth following the Quran alone;
And you will have nothing to fear, and you will not grieve.[123]

Salat is to be established or kept up

The Quran repeatedly exhorts us to establish or keep up prayer in the verse "*akimus-salat*", which means "establish or keep up prayer", and not "read or recite prayer" (2:3, 43, 177; 4:162; 5: 12, 55; etc.). Establishing or keeping up prayer implies that we should keep praying for the things we want until our prayer has been fulfilled, and that along with the prayer we should also act in accordance with the spirit of that prayer. When we seek God's guidance to walk aright, we need to act also in a just manner, and cannot commit any wrongdoing. It also means that we need to keep praying always to remember and glorify God as well as to seek His mercy, help, and guidance. That means that we must remain in the prayer mood all the time, not simply while in prayer but also in all of our actions. Muslim religious teachers generally interpret establishing prayer as observing the timings of the prayer. However, establishing the real intent of the prayer in all actions of the worshiper is really what matters, and is much more important than just establishing the timings of the prayer.

We need to pray for our own sake, not because God needs or wants it

As noted above, we are needy in some way or other, while God is free of wants and independent of all of His creations (35:15; 3:97; 2:267; 4:131; 6:14, 133. Once we realize this conception of *salat*, we can easily see that God does not need to care about whether we turn or pray to Him or not.

29:6 And whoever striveth, *striveth only for his own soul, for God is fully independent of anything in the universe.* (See also 31:12)

It is quite clear then that whatever we do, we do for our own sake, not for God. The idea prevalent among Muslims that we have to perform prayer because God wants us to do this as an obligatory duty to Him is a misconception that needs to be dispensed with for good.

Salat is one's overall effort for purification and spiritual evolution

The craving and effort of a creature for rising to a higher state is its real prayer. This is prayer for spiritual development, which is the *raison d'etre* or *summum bonum* of prayer. It comes through our striving for self-purification. Purification does not come unless one washes away one's dross by repenting and atoning adequately for one's past mistakes. *Salat* is a place where one can at least partly, if not fully, wash away one's blemishes by expressing deep regret and repentance before God and by imploring His forgiveness. Human beings are prone to making mistakes. They need to regret, repent for such mistakes and mend their ways so that they can lead a flawless and blissful life afterward. No worshiper should be under an illusion that God forgives just on the asking. Getting forgiveness is not a painless process. One needs to sufficiently repent and atone for one's mistakes, and at the same time mend his or her conduct, and not repeat the mistakes. God forgives the sins of only those who turn to Him truly repentant, and who do not persist in their sins (3:135; 16:119; 66:8). One needs to turn to God with sincere repentance:

66:8 O ye who believe! *Turn unto God with sincere repentance.* It may be that your Lord will remove from you your evil deeds and admit you into Gardens underneath which rivers flow.

Every man or woman should engage in a relentless striving or struggle (*jihad*) for good against evil. It is those who earnestly seek good can successfully overcome evil. By overcoming evil only, one can purify himself or herself. True prayer is for one's purification and for bringing one out of darkness into light. Purification is the key to success.

132

87:14-5 *He succeedeth who purifieth himself,* and remembereth the name of his Lord, and prayeth. (See also 91:9-10)

To proceed along the path of purification and spiritual progress, one needs to live a moral life, including freeing one of any indecent or lewd thought or act. The Quran emphasizes the importance of living a moral life. Strict adherence to righteous conduct of oneself – living strictly in conformity with moral principles – is critical to fostering the faculties such as ego, love, will and knowledge, which are conducive to spiritual development.[124]

The most important and meaningful purpose of *salat* is to understand God, and understand how He creates or acts, which is really understanding of His Laws or, if you will, the Laws of Nature. Those who gain such understanding are spiritually enlightened, wise and blessed. To the service of such people, God subjects all that is in the whole universe (31:20; 45:13). Seeking divine help at the most meaningful level can thus be summed up in seeking to increase only one's love and knowledge leading to the approach to God, which is termed as knowledge of *marefat* or spiritual knowledge, also variously known as Yoga, Sufism or Mysticism. Thus *salat*, which is also *dhikr* (or remembrance of God), should, at the most meaningful level, be devoted to seeking enhancement of one's love and learning of *marefat*. Such seeking is a major hallmark of prayer. Other objectives are secondary in nature. Love and knowledge are two most precious gifts with which God's righteous believers are blessed (19:96; 2:269). Those who are so blessed either do not have to worry about other things or they can get access to other things they need much more easily than others.

At the same time, love of God should translate into love of humanity. Serving God means serving humanity in the same way as God serves humanity. So love, and goodwill for others should be a hallmark of a good believer's *iman* (mindset) and prayer. Prayer should be meaningfully directed to developing one's love for God, and love for His service, which is really service for all humankind.

Salat is preparation for one to go nearer to God

God has established man as a *khalifa* (successor species) on earth, worthy of reverence by angels (2:30-34). We need to call upon God for

133

our evolution to a state where we can work as a worthy species on earth. We can achieve such an evolution by seeking, and sincerely striving for, the path of approach to God Who is the perfection in all qualities (See 5:35 cited earlier). In order to seek the path of approach to God, we need to shun all misdeeds, and do good deeds, including performing true prayer. And true prayer works the other way round as well: it helps one keep away from evil deeds (29:45). If prayer does not help one keep himself or herself from evil thoughts and deeds, and does not drive or inspire him or her to do good and noble deeds, and to make progress on the spiritual path, he or she should think that he or she has not performed real prayer, or that his or her prayer remains incomplete.

Striving for our spiritual evolution will help us acquire something of God's qualities. Of course, acquiring His qualities does not make us gods; it only brings us closer to Him to be able to comprehend Him in a better way, and to unearth some of the mysteries of the creative process that is at work and spread throughout the universe, and thus to reap some of His *niamat* or boons for us.

The content of *salat*

The content of *salat* should be shaped by its vision, and is similar to that vision. It should contain all that is consistent with that vision. The content of *salat* consists in what one expresses in it, including the devotional content in such expression. One should fully understand what one says to God. The content should be directly prayer to, or glorification of, God, but no recitation, and the content should be consistent with the spirit of prayer or glorification. Recitations from the Quran, unless these are words of glorification of God or invocations meant at heart by the worshiper, are not consistent with the vision and spirit of *salat*. The content is also expression of our gratitude to Him for all that we get or enjoy. God loves only the grateful (39:7). He gives more to people who are grateful to Him:

> **14:7**　　And (remember) when your Lord hath it proclaimed: 'If ye are grateful, I will certainly give you more; but if ye are ungrateful, My punishment is truly severe!'

Understanding what one prays is a critical requirement of real prayer. One needs to be fully aware of, and understand, what one says or prays. That is why God has forbidden us to go to prayer when we are drunk:

134

4:43   O ye who believe! *Go not near unto prayer when ye are drunk till ye know what ye say.*

Those who pray without earnestness and to be seen by others do not really pray:

4:142   ...When they stand up to pray, *they stand without earnestness, to be seen of men, but little do they hold God in remembrance. ...*

In *salat* we address none other than God. We need to be careful about what we say to Him, for we cannot afford to say things, which sound rather unbecoming of us. The requirement of understanding requires that we say things from our own heart, and not recite things like a parrot. Recitations from the Quran are not consistent with the vision and spirit of *salat*. It makes hardly any sense – it is rather imprudence on our part – that we should recite God's revelations to God! The revelations are for our own guidance. There is virtue in reading and studying the Quran for our guidance. However, this does not warrant us to recite the Quran in *salat* thinking that that would also be a virtue.

While recitations from the Quran *per se* do not make any sense, we can, of course, use certain verses of it, which are in essence words of prayer, or of God's glorification. But when we use them, we need to own them – i.e., to use them as our own words, flowing from our own heart. The last three *surahs* of the Quran – *ikhlas, falaq* and *nas* – begin with the word "*qul*" which means "say". With this word God teaches us some words of prayer or glorification for Him. However, if instead of the texts that God wants us to say, we say the whole *surah* in the *salat*, including the word "*qul*", it will foolishly miss the true intent of God's advice, and look as if we are commanding God to say these things. We should use these *surahs* as our words of prayer without the word "*qul*" or "say". That will be more sensible and dignified. God has urged us to ponder and reflect on His revelations and thus exercise our wits (38:29; 10:24). It does not require much of our intelligence to understand this sensible thing. Likewise, in glorifying God, we cannot say in prayer "Say: O God! Master of the Kingdom! Thou givest kingdom (or power) to whomsoever Thou pleasest and withdrawest kingdom (or power) from whomsoever Thou pleasest..." (3:26). We should omit the word "Say" if we want to

135

use these words of glorification of God. Recitations of many *surahs* or verses thereof in the prayer (e.g., Surah Lahab (111), Surah Nasr (110), Surah Kafirun (109), Surah Kauthar (108), Surah Maun (107), etc.), which are not consistent with the spirit of prayer or glorification, but which are found to be widely used by Muslims in *salat* are thus clearly irrelevant and inappropriate, and hence need to be avoided in *salat*.

The form of *salat*

No particular form or mode of prayer is worth considering as sacrosanct or important by itself. Any of the forms that are mentioned in the Quran such as standing, bowing, prostrating, sitting, reclining, or any combination of them should be all right so long as prayer is done sincerely. Without sincerity or devotion in prayer, the forms are of no religious significance.

Since one should pray with application and devotion of one's whole body and mind, the mode, way or form in which one prays may take on some significance, but only when one prays sincerely. However, this should not be taken to mean that there is something inherently sacrosanct about any particular mode or form. A form or a physical expression should be a spontaneous expression to what one feels at heart. Thus God mentions in the Quran that God-loving people, who are overwhelmed with glorification of God when they hear anything of His revelations, fall down prostrate in tears in recognition and approbation of the truth and grandeur of such revelations (17:109; 32:15; 19:58). Here, prostration is a spontaneous physical expression. Thus in prayer, a spontaneous physical movement with devotion to God in whatever form one wants to make, will be a plus point, and will enable one to pray more effectively, and will increase one's humility (17:107-108).

With an empty heart, no particular form or mode of prayer *per se* is worth considering as sacrosanct and important. God is not interested in the particular outward form in which we pray. God says in the Quran:

2:177   *It is not righteousness that ye turn your faces to the East and the West.*

22:37   *It is not their (the sacrificed animals') flesh nor their blood that reacheth God, but it is your piety that reacheth Him.*

These verses do imply that no particular form is essential or important by itself. "[B]id goodbye to all systems, come out of their rigid shells (Quran V-48 Maida) to remember God [...] for, is not remembrance of God the greatest achievement? (Quran XXIX-45 Ankabut) [...] The right religion is above its form whatever it might be."[125] Indeed, one may stand, bow or prostrate before God numerous times without making any real headway whatsoever in terms of piety or spiritual development. God in fact looks at, and knows best, what is in one's mind, not at the outward form or posture one takes (2:284, 225; 17:25).

Conventionally *salat* is defined and performed in the form of some *rakah*s, each *rakah* constituting a prayer cycle. Undoubtedly, it is a very good and beautiful form, which combines standing, bowing, prostrating and, in the second and last *rakahs*, also sitting in a particular sequencing. One does not need the reference of the Hadith to sanctify its use. It can be logically assumed that this practice has been followed, and came down to us from generation to generation. Yet it would not be an appropriate approach to consider the *rakah* as an indispensable form or part of prayer. The form does not really matter to God; what really matters is the content of what the worshiper prays. Hence attaching importance to the *rakah* is misplaced. The Quran mentions about standing, bowing, prostration, etc., but suggests no particular combination or sequencing (9:112; 22:77; 3:43; 48:29; 3:43; 48:29; 7:206; 9:112; 25:60; 96:19; 53;62; 38:24; 39:9; 41:37; 32:15; 22:18, 77).

A hard and fast rule that one must observe some postures in a definite sequence, and that one must complete at least two *rakahs* for a *salat*, and that such and such number of *rakahs* is required for such and such *salat* does not appear quite relevant in light of the Quran. The *rakahs* do not reach God, just as our turning to any particular direction, or the flesh and blood of sacrificed animals do not reach God (2:177; 22:37).

Also, can we discount the devotional practices or modes of worship or prayer that other communities resort to? God says:

> **22:67** For every community We have established its own devotional rites, which they are to perform. So let them not dispute with thee on the matter, but do thou

137

invite to thy Lord. Most assuredly, thou art on the right path.

The Quran also states that people from other communities, be they Christians, Jews or Sabians, or by implication, be they of whatever communities, those who believe in God and the Last Day and are righteous will have their reward with God (2:62). This verse also implies that we should not think that any particular form is an indispensable part of prayer.

God has characterized remembering Him as the best of all prayers (29:45). This remembering and, along with it, praying can be done either standing, sitting, or even reclining, or lying down on one's sides (3:191; 4:103). Many *dhakeran* (those who remember God) remember and glorify God in a sitting position. Sufis are found to remember and glorify God mainly in a sitting position punctuated by some standing positions. The Turkish *dervishes* do the same by a form of whirling.

The language in which we pray

Praying in a language, which the person who prays does not understand, cannot make any sense. Muslims who do not understand Arabic are also generally taught to pray in Arabic. The Quran has forbidden us to go near prayer when we are intoxicated and we do not know what we pray (4:43). This Quranic verse clearly underscores the importance of one's understanding of what one says in the prayer. Unfortunately, however, it appears that the verse has been misinterpreted in different quarters to mean that the person should only recognize what he recites in the prayer, and whether or not he understands the language in which he recites the prayer does not really matter. However, this sort of reasoning is clearly unacceptable in light of the Quran. God is not kind to those who do not apply their sense. The Quran likens those who are disbelievers to those who do not apply their sense:

> **2:171** The likeness of those who disbelieve is that of those who repeat naught but sounds of what they hear of shouts and cries, without understanding; deaf, dumb, blind, for they use not reason.

138

If we do not understand, and mean what we utter, then we really convey nothing to God. Also, *salat* is also not a place for recitation from the Quran. Recitation *per se* makes no sense, since it raises the question: recitation to or for whom? *Salat* is for speaking our own heart or mind to God. If we use certain verses of the Quran that are in tune with the spirit of prayer and glorification of God, we need to use them as expressions of our own mind. For the same reason, only verses relevant to prayer can be used, not those which have little or no relevance to prayer. God has urged us to exercise our wits. It does not require much of our intelligence to understand this sensible thing. Muslim worshipers use or recite many *surahs* or selected texts of the Quran in the *salat*, which are grossly unrelated to the context of prayer. Such recitations are clearly irrelevant and inappropriate.[126]

The language or utterances should be one's own. The idea that the language of *salat* has to be Arabic for all people is not a tenable proposition. One should pray in any language one fully understands, and is comfortable with. It cannot be right to insist as the *ulama* do that God requires us to pray in only one language, Arabic, and that Arabic is God's or heavenly language. This assertion is clearly contradictory to the spirit of the Quran, which states that God never sent a messenger except with the language of his (own) folk, that he might make (the message) clear for them (14:4).

This verse clearly points to the notion that it should be all right for any person to pray in a language of his or her own. Certainly earlier Prophets and their followers prayed in their own languages. The fact that Islam was revealed in the Arabic world does not mean that all Muslims whether Arabs or non-Arabs must pray in Arabic. How does God know what we are communicating if we ourselves do not know what we are saying? If we do not know what we are communicating, it is then not in our hearts and minds. God really looks at what is in our hearts and minds, i.e., what we really mean (17:25).

Arabic or, for that matter, any human language cannot be conceived as an exclusive or special language of God. He has revealed His message to all the prophets in their own languages. Hence, it is unthinkable that it should not be all right for us if we pray in either our own mother tongue or any other language we are comfortable with. Indeed, we can pray with our heart and soul, and concentrate our full attention to the content of what we say only when we pray in a language that we well understand.

The timings and times of *salat*

According to the prevailing conception, *salat* is to be performed five times or in five sessions everyday at specified timings. However the emphasis should rather be laid on the content and sincerity of prayer and one's compliance in terms of consistent actions in real life than on strict observance of the timings. The Quran advises believers to perform prayer at specified timings:

> **4:103** Prayer hath been enjoined on the believers at specified timings.
>
> **11:114** And *establish salat (prayer) at the two ends of the day (morning and evening), and some part of the night*. Verily good deeds erase (the effects of) bad deeds. This is a reminder to those who take heed.
>
> **17:78** *Establish salat at the declining of the sun until the dark of night*, and (the reading of) the Quran in the morning. Verily (the reading of) the Quran in the morning is witnessed (most effective).

Some translators or interpreters have interpreted "*le-dulukis shamsi*" in the verse above at (17:78) to mean "setting of the sun" rather than "declining of the sun". If we grant that it means "declining of the sun", then the last two verses cited above together specify (1) *morning*, (2) *afternoon* including *evening* (since the declining of the sun until the dark of night also includes *evening or dusk*), and (3) *some part of the night* as the timings of *salat*. Thus according to the Quran, the specified timings really add up to three, rather than five, since the evening mentioned in the Quran can be considered as included in the afternoon extending up to the dark of night, and since *zuhr* (afternoon) and *asr* (late afternoon) are also included in the afternoon mentioned in the Quran. However, it has become customary to count the timing given in the Quran at (2) above (as in verse (17:78) as combining three timings such as *zuhr*, *asr* and *maghrib* (evening) rather than just one. Together with the morning and night, these timings add up to five. Note, however, that the Quranic verse (24:58), which mentions about private times of married couples, mentions about morning and night prayers, and it mentions about the time *zuhr* (noon or afternoon), when the couples take rest but does not mention about any prayer at that time. The verse at (17:78) clearly lays more emphasis on the establishing of *salat* during the afternoon, and on the studying of the Quran in the morning. A question may naturally arise, why *salat* timings are regarded as mandatory while the morning timing for studying the Quran mentioned in this verse is not so regarded. In other words, the timings given in the Quran should be considered as suggestive in nature for our benefit. Just as prayer should be a spontaneous activity on our part for our own sake, not imposed as a matter of obligation to God, observance of such timings should also be taken in that light.

The verse at (2:238) refers to midmost prayer, which is interpreted by many as the late afternoon (*asr*) prayer. However, interpreting this verse in this way will be inappropriate, and will rob the verse of its true message, which is that one should be mindful of the main or central theme of his or her prayer. Even if one interprets this verse as referring to the late afternoon prayer, this timing can be considered as included in the afternoon that is mentioned in the verse at (17:78). It may be noted, however, that the Hadith, from which the contention of the five-time *salat* appears to have been taken, is not credible enough (see below). And importantly, it is also to be noted that, according to historical records, the requirement of five-time daily *salat* was not laid down during the Prophet's lifetime; what was enjoined was three-time *salat*.[127] Shiite Muslims observe the five prayers at three timings rather than five.[128] Admittedly, however, it is not of much significance to squabble over the number of times one should pray. Praying five times with the same amount of devotion is admittedly an act of greater devotion and piety than praying a lesser number of times. What is more important and worth emphasizing, however, is that a worshiper should be more concerned with maintaining the spirit of *salat* than with strictly observing its timings.

Also, the above timings of the Quran should be taken in the same light as the timing of the night, less than half or more than half of the night, which God enjoined on the Prophet for prayer and meditation, and for studying the Quran (73:1-8). God enjoined this timing for the Prophet precisely because he was preoccupied with other things at daytime. Following this, the Prophet and his close associates devoted one third to two thirds of the night to prayer, and remembrance and glorification of God, and studies of the Quran (73:20). Separately, specific timings have

141

been mentioned in the Quran for remembrance and glorification of God, which are the morning, afternoon, evening, and night (20:130; 30:17-18; 33:41-43; 52:48-49).

The Quran does not specifically mention that one has to observe all the timings. In the Quranic light the emphasis should be on the devotional content of prayer, and one's compliance in terms of consistent actions in real life rather than on strict observance of all the timings since we can observe the timings without really establishing the real purpose of *salat*. One can notice in the Quran that there is specific instruction for us to complete the period of *siam* (fasting), provided we are not sick or on a journey, and to fast other days afterward if we miss certain days to fast in the Ramadan for such reasons, or to feed poor people (2:185), while in the case of *salat* there is no such specific instruction to complete all the timings. There is a reason for this. One may devote a lot of time to *salat* in one or two sessions, which may obviate the need for keeping all the timings. Insisting that all the timings must be observed by us as a matter of course enjoined on us by God would serve no real spiritual purpose. The *real* spiritual purpose is served when one observes the timings spontaneously, and inclines to God with real devotion.

God responds to our prayer

The Quranic conception of *salat* also embraces the idea that God responds to one's prayer. The Quran proclaims that God responds to every devoted worshiper when he cries to Him (2:186). This is evident indirectly also from the following verse:

> **13:14**   Unto Him (God) is true prayer. *Those unto whom they pray beside God respond to them not at all.*

God is most Kind and Responsive to those who are believers and upright, and who call upon Him with sincerity and perseverance. As Ahmad puts it, "Increase your belief, work hard with endurance and craving for achievement of whatever is best and know that God guides those who endure even unto death (Baqarah 2:153)".[129] God responds to the devoted call of the worshipers in some way, and increases mercy for them, and the real devotee and worshiper of God is able to feel or perceive such response.

> **40:60**   And your Lord saith: *Call upon Me; I will respond.*

42:26 *He (God) respondeth to the call of those who believe and do deeds of righteousness,* and increaseth for them His Grace (or Bounty).

27:62 *Is it not He (God) Who listeneth to the distressed when he crieth unto Him, and Who relieveth his suffering?*

41:30 (As for those) who say: 'Our Lord is God,' and then remain upright, the angels descend upon them (saying): *'Fear not nor grieve, but hear the good news of the Heaven that ye are promised'.*

We have numerous examples before us from the past prayers of distinguished men and women, and of the corresponding divine responses they received, and benefited from. Indeed every person with a strong faith in God experiences God's response in some way or other. What can one say or make of precognition one may experience, which is a kind of divine response? This is foreknowledge of future events, which one may receive through dreams, or some extra-sensory perception such as visions, revelations, or through some other ways. One is surprised when one has such an experience, and sees things happen exactly the way they could perceive beforehand. Such precognition is a definite response from the divine source, which the devotee may have earnestly sought, or which has been communicated to him because of his piety, even though he may not have thought about it at all in the immediate past. God-loving devotees often receive divine reminders of impending bad news or dangers through dreams or visions or other ways. They receive such extra-ordinary information so that they can take necessary precautionary measures. Or they may be informed in advance of good news, so that they can be reassured, especially if they are worried enough.

The Prophet Zachariah and the Prophet Abraham received good news of a son to them through messengers in response to their prayer. The Prophet Muhammad was reassured by God, and he received revelation from Him of the impending victory over the disbelievers, and he was advised to inform the believers accordingly (3:124-127; 61:13), God was so kind and responsive to him that he was repeatedly consoled by Him through revelations not to grieve over what the disbelievers did to him, and also assured of the more rewarding and blissful future that awaited him (16:127; 18:6; 27:70; 31:23; 35:8; 36:76; 93:3-7).

143

18:6   *Then wouldst thou only, per chance, fret thyself to death, following after them in grief, if they believe not in this Message?* (See also 27:70; 31:23; 36:76 and 93:3-8)

4:113   *But for the Grace of God upon thee (O Muhammad) and His Mercy, a party of them would certainly have resolved to lead thee astray, but they lead only themselves astray,* and *they will not (be able to) harm thee at all. ...* The grace of God upon thee hath been great indeed.

Only persons who have reached a very high point of spiritual pursuit and development can receive such exceedingly kind, loving, reassuring and encouraging divine messages. Such messages were given to the Prophet to boost his self-confidence, and to encourage his spirits to go forward without hesitation or worry. The Quran affirms that other believers can also receive reassuring divine messages: God's angels come to His righteous servants (should be righteous enough) with the message that they need not fear nor grieve, and that Heaven will be their reward; and that the angels are their protecting friends in both this world and the Hereafter – a welcome gift from God for the righteous people (41:30-32).

The way or method through which one receives such messages varies from person to person, and depends on the level of piety, and spiritual knowledge and development one has acquired. Dreams are a crude form in which one may receive God's messages. But it is not always easy to read or interpret dreams, as dreams may be of different kinds, and all of them may not be of equal significance, and also because what the dreamer dreams is in an allegorical language. God speaks in such languages. Many can realize the meaning and significance of their dreams only after the events have taken place. Only knowledgeable people can correctly interpret dreams in advance (12:36-49, 101). Those who are advanced enough spiritually may see God's signs or messages through visions (they are clairvoyant), or they may hear the words of God, or directly receive God's revelations through intuition or urges, or receive such revelations through an angel. We may receive God's word or guidance also through intuition, or flashes of thoughts or feelings in our mind, and we receive such guidance when we remember things, or remember to do certain things, which we need or aught to remember, just as forgetting to do things we aught to have remembered, which is really attributable to our own negligence or lack of earnestness or determination can be recognized or characterized as the Devil's handiwork (18:63).

Salat or prayer needs to be established in a way that is effective to elicit God's response in some way. *Salat* remains either inadequate or incomplete if it does not succeed in receiving some divine response – feel or catch some divine impulse, or receive divine revelation. As Ahmad puts it:

> Prayer or so desire is not therefore ideal until and unless one can decipher the real swing or message either from the Divine Book, i.e., Revelation or from the universe or Nature which is the other form of the very same Book.[130]

As Ahmad further notes, *salat* should also help proper psychological development for practical works of utility.[131] While prayer helps one to be pious and knowledgeable, it is also pious and knowledgeable people who benefit the most from it.

Individual *versus* congregational *salat*

Prayer is largely a matter of individual effort for one's own spiritual evolution. The Quran states that whatever one does is for his own self (29:6; 6:164; 35:18). And it also states that one does not share the burden of others (6:164; 17:15; 35:18; 39:7; 53:38). God also exhorts every human being to be conscious of his or her responsibilities in life as none else is responsible for his or her fate (5:105).

One should therefore primarily focus on his own spiritual development and salvation. However, this does not mean that one does not benefit from the blessings from others, or that one should not bless others. The Prophet was asked by God to pray for the believers (3:159, 47:19). Following the example of the Prophet, we should also pray for other believers. Likewise, the believers have also been asked to encourage and support the Prophet (33:56-57; 48:9-10). God and His angels also encourage and support the believers so that they can be brought from darkness into light (33:41-43). These verses clearly imply that believers should mutually support and help one another, and that we should strive for the good of all of us together with the good that we seek for ourselves at the individual level. Wishing or praying for the common good of a group of people is best done in a congregation of them. Congregational prayer also provides some social or community benefit in terms of fostering communal amity, friendship and solidarity. The congregation of worshipers from all strata of society, high or low, rich or poor, praying shoulder to shoulder before God – a serene, heavenly sight to watch – exhibits a sense of equality and fraternity of humankind.[132] The Quran urges believers to join the prayer of the congregation day and disperse for business after duly completing it:

> **62: 9-10** O ye who believe! *When the call is made for the prayer on the day of congregation, then hasten unto the remembrance of God, and leave your business; that is better for you if ye did but know*! And when the prayer is ended, then disperse in the land, and seek of God's bounty, and remember God much that ye may be successful.

Hence congregational prayer is of considerable significance. In practice, Muslims prefer congregational prayer led by an *imam* (leader) to individual prayer in what they unnecessarily consider as *fard* (obligatory) prayer. Additional significance is derived if such prayer is led or conducted by spiritually capable and advanced people. The Prophet and his close associates used to pray, remember and glorify God together (73:20), and he used to lead the prayer even in the battlefield (4:102). Thus, congregational prayers, or acts of remembering and glorifying God which are led and conducted by capable spiritual teachers are often instrumental in inspiring those who are initiated, and who are beginners or novices in the process of spiritual pursuit and transformation. However, it should always be borne in mind that spiritual guides can only inspire others, and give them some knowledge and guidance; they cannot by themselves raise others in spiritual development unless they themselves put in their own efforts. The effort one individually puts in is always the real determinant of what one achieves.[133]

PROBLEMS WITH THE CURRENTLY PRACTICED *SALAT*

The foregoing analysis of *salat* in light of the Quran should enable one to perceive that *salat* as prescribed by *shariah,* and conventionally conceived and practiced by Muslims suffers from a number of inherent deficiencies, and this mainly due to the influence of the Hadith. Some of the misconceptions or problems with the currently practiced *salat* are:

- Holding the notion that *salat* is a duty imposed on us by God, or something we owe to God, which we need to pay off;

- Laying emphasis on five-time observance of *salat* every day, rather than on maintaining the spirit of the prayer;

- Sanctifying recitation of Quranic verses in *salat*, which is not relevant to the spirit of prayer or glorification of God;

- Attaching undue importance to the *rakah* system, and assigning virtue to the number of *rakahs* one performs;

- Introducing different categorizations of *salat* as *fard* (obligatory), *sunnah* (allegedly in conforming to what the Prophet did), *wajib* (near-obligatory) and *nafl* (optional);

- Conceiving and using only the Arabic language as the only usable medium of communication; and

- Projecting *salat* as a ritual that automatically washes away one's sins.

Most of these points have already been covered. As pointed out above, we need to perform *salat* for our own sake, not because God has told us to do this. To understand this conception in the correct perspective is very important since the difference in conception has made a big difference to the whole approach to religion and prayer. Most Muslims offer *salat* as a matter of course, but they pay little attention to what they pray, and they do not pay enough attention to the requirement that the essence of what they pray must be reflected also in all of their thoughts and actions. God says in the Quran that He responds to the prayer of those who pray sincerely and humbly (2:286; 40:60; 27: 62). However, most Muslims pray as a matter of course, but do not care whether they receive any divine response to their prayer. So if they pray their whole life without getting any response to their prayer, and they have never found whether their prayer was ever effective in some way, they should ponder whether in effect they have really prayed! Poor faith in God does not make one eligible to receive God's mercy and response. Only strong faith in God expressed in sincere prayer with full devotion to Him can elicit such response.

The weakness of the notion that *salat* has to be performed five times every day can be demonstrated by scrutinizing the relevant Hadith texts. The gist of a first Hadith text – a narration from Abu Dhar who reportedly heard from the Prophet – that is widely cited in support of the five-time *salat* contention reads as follows:

> One day the angel Gabriel descended through the roof of the Prophet's house, split open his chest, and washed it with Zam-zam (a spring at the Kabah) water. Then the angel brought a golden tray full of wisdom and faith and having poured its contents into his chest, he closed it. Then he took the Prophet's hand and ascended with him to the heavens, where he met with several Prophets, including the Prophet Moses. Gabriel ascended with him to a place where he heard the creaking of the pens. Ibn Hazm and Anas bin Malik said that the Prophet said that God then enjoined fifty prayers on his followers. While returning with this order of God, he passed by the Prophet Moses (PBUH) who told him that it was too much for his followers and advised him to go back to his Lord and plead for a reduction of the number. When the Prophet returned to God and pleaded for a reduction, God reduced the number to one half, but on his way back when he met again with the Prophet Moses (PBUH), he was advised to go back again to God with a request for a further reduction. God again reduced the number to one half. On his way back, the Prophet was again advised by the Prophet Moses (PBUH) to go back again for a further reduction. God at this time prescribed five *salat*. Even at that time he was advised by Moses (PBUH) that the number of *salat* was still too high, but at that point the Prophet (PBUH) gave up, as he was too ashamed to ask God again. (*Sahih Bukhari*, Vol. 1, Book 8, # 345)

The relevant part of a second Hadith text narrated by Malik bin Sasaa on the reductions of the number of *salat* at each earlier step is as follows:

> Then fifty prayers were enjoined on me. I descended till I met Moses who asked me, 'What have you done?' I said, 'Fifty prayers have been enjoined on me.' He said, 'I know the people better than you, because I had the hardest experience to bring Bani Israel to obedience. Your followers cannot put up with such obligation. So, return to your Lord and request Him (to

reduce the number of prayers.' I returned and requested Allah (for reduction) and He made it forty. I returned and (met Moses) and had a similar discussion, and then returned again to Allah for reduction and He made it thirty, then twenty, then ten, and then I came to Moses who repeated the same advice. Ultimately Allah reduced it to five. When I came to Moses again, he said, 'What have you done?' I said, 'Allah has made it five only.' He repeated the same advice but I said that I surrendered (to Allah's Final Order)' (Narration by Malik bin Sasaa, *Sahih Bukhari*, Vol. 4, Book 54, # 429).

The differences in the two Hadith texts respectively by the two narrators but included in the same compilation by Bukhari are both striking and puzzling. While the first version speaks of reduction by one half from the original fifty *salat* at first step, then by another half at the second step and so on to five *salat* at the last step, the other version speaks of reduction to forty *salat* at the first step, then to thirty, then to twenty, then to ten and at last to five. The inconsistency in the two versions of the Hadith reveals weakness in their reliability in support of the five-*salat* contention.

The Hadith is not credible also for more substantive reasons. It demeans both God and the Prophet, and directly contradicts the Quran in more than one way. First, it misjudges how God acts. Is it conceivable that God should prescribe or reveal something, which He will need to change soon afterwards? The Quran clearly gives the idea that God does everything with firmness, and His ways of treatment or *sunnah* never change (See 35:43 cited earlier); nor do His words.

10:64   *... There is no change in the Words of God. ...* (See also 30:30; 17:77 and 18:27)

Second, can we ever conceive that God can ever impose in the first place any burden on man that is beyond his capacity to bear? The Quran makes it clear that God never tasks any soul beyond its capacity (2:286; 6:152; 7:42; 65:7). Third, what reason is there to think that any Prophet should judge God's certain prescribed direction or advice as beyond man's capacity, when God says He never imposes any such burden on man? The Hadith also indirectly casts aspersion on the wisdom and judgment of the Prophet Muhammad shown considerably poorer to that of the Prophet Moses. Also, the story of the back and forth journey of the

Prophet to and from God, or the divine sphere, appears suspect, not simply because it belies the conception of God as Omnipresent. The question also arises if this number of *salat* times was so important, why has this prescription not been included in the revelations of the Quran, when it states that it does not leave anything of concern to us untouched (12:111; 16:89).

The unnecessary insistence on observance of five-time *salat* as a matter of compulsion has resulted in the notion that if one misses the so-called *fard salat* at a given time, he or she can make it up by so-called *qada* (make-up) prayer. How this missed prayer can be made up by so-called *qada* prayer is beyond one's comprehension. Such a conception sends the wrong message that *salat* of a certain prescribed form at a specified time is something that we owe to God, and it must be paid off some how. This is contrary to the Quranic message that God does not need anything from us. Attaching importance to the times of prayer rather than to the content of prayer, and to its establishment in terms of one's *amal* or work consistent with the spirit of prayer must be considered as misplaced and misleading.

The Hadith has done a great damage to the conception of *salat* by also suggesting that it should be performed using recitations from the Quran. The Quranic verse (73:4) is cited in support of the contention that the Quran also prescribes recitation of Quranic verses in *salat*. However, this verse is wrongly cited as this verse, or the other associated previous and succeeding verses (73:1-8 cited before) do not explicitly mention *salat*. It will be more appropriate to interpret these verses along with the other related ones as emphasizing that we should devote ourselves to worship and prayer, along with reading or study of the Quran.

Another verse that is also sometimes cited to support recitation of the Quranic verses in *salat* is: Recite that which hath been revealed unto thee of the Book, and establish *salat* (29:45). However, this verse could not be interpreted as necessarily meaning that the recitation has to be done in the *salat*. The two are separate activities, and are better done separately. Recitation, reading, or study of the Quran is more appropriately done outside the prayer. Of course, as mentioned above, it is quite reasonable to think that the Prophet used some verses of the Quran in *salat*, which are in the nature of prayer or glorification of God, but when he used them he used as his own words. To assert that the Prophet used to recite any verses of the Quran regardless of their relevance to the spirit of *salat* was a wrong attribution to him. The Quran urges us to reflect on, and understand, His signs or revelations, and apply our sense (10:16, 24; 38:29; 45:13). The Prophet who followed nothing but the Quran (6:50; 46:9) must have applied his good sense while using verses from the Quran in *salat*. Worshipers should be under no illusion that reciting verses from the Quran in *salat* regardless of its relevance to the context of prayer is a virtue.

Another weakness of the prevailing *salat* conception is its emphasis on the *rakah* system with particular physical postures and movements and with their particular sequencing. As discussed earlier, the Quran speaks of standing, bowing, reclining, sitting, and/or prostration that can be used in *salat* or *dhikr*. Any of these forms or any of their combination should be considered as good for purposes of *salat* or *dhikr*, which is also prayer. It should be left to the worshiper whether he should use the *rakah* or any other form of his choosing, but it is certainly not right to assert as the *ulama* do that a *salat* cannot be performed without the *rakahs*. Muslims are also led to believe that the number of *rakahs* of prayer one does counts as a virtue in itself. This is a misconception, because it is the content of prayer or devotion of the worshiper that really reaches God, not the *rakahs* just as the flesh or blood of a sacrificed animal does not reach God (22:37).

Also, the existing conception embodies or introduces unnecessary complication by distinguishing between different kinds of *salat* (*fard*, *sunnah*, *wajib* and *nafl*), and attaching different levels of virtues to certain recitations. Postulating that one has to perform certain *rakahs* at every time as *fard salat* is incomprehensible, as what is not mentioned in the Quran cannot be declared as *fard* or obligatory. *Salat* is *salat*. How one can gain anything by considering some *rakahs* as *fard*, some as *sunnah* (i.e., conforming to the Prophet's practice, or in some cases *wajib* or almost obligatory), and some as *mustahab* (preferred) or *nafl* (optional) is beyond comprehension. *Shariah* has created unnecessary complications for the worshiper also by introducing rules that certain factors cause annulment of ablution (*wudu*) or of prayer, or diminish their virtue (*makruh*). A true worshiper needs no such categorization of prayers, or attention to such minute things to pray effectively. The Quranic concept of prayer is simple and straightforward. One only needs to pray sincerely and devoutly; and God responds to such prayer. Also, as explained above, insisting that we should pray only in Arabic whether

151

we understand or not is clearly misperceived. Ahmad appropriately comments: Muslims "worship in their barren mosques with hearts empty of faith for want of proper understanding."[134]

There are also other ideas borrowed from the Hadith embedded in the existing *salat* conception, which send wrong messages to Muslims. Such messages relate to things such as that such and such *salat*, or such and such recitation, gives such and such virtue to the worshipers, including, in many cases, forgiveness of all past sins, regardless of whatever sins one has incurred. Such messages are clearly at odds with the spirit of the Quran, which emphasizes righteous deeds, effective repentance and atonement for past misdeeds, and no recurrence of misdeeds along with prayer.

In the *tashahud*, which is taken from the Hadith, and recited in the sitting position of the last *rakah* of *salat*, the text includes such wordings as "Peace be on you, O Prophet, and Allah's mercy and blessings be on you." This expression of blessings on the Prophet by directly addressing him is counter to the very idea of prayer that the worshiper should address only God.[135]

CONCLUSION

In sum, there is not much prayer in the current practice of *salat* in accordance with God's advice "Seek help through perseverance and prayer" (2:153). It has been relegated largely to a mere ritual often devoid of any real seeking of help from God. By upholding the imaginary virtues of reciting from the Quran, and by emphasizing physical postures and movements, and insisting on the use of one language by all worshipers, the prevailing conception has robbed *salat* of its true, substantive, and essential intent and traits, as propounded and required by the Quran.

To become a good Muslim, it is both necessary and important for one to understand and perform *salat* in light of the Quran. There can be no question that the *rakah* system, which is being universally practiced by Muslims, is indeed a very beautiful form. Yet what is important to recognize and appreciate is that this system is not of the essence of *salat*; the essence of *salat* lies in keeping to the spirit of *salat* and living up to it. As generally being understood and practiced by Muslims, this system needs to be freed of its inherent deficiencies that it currently suffers from, and appropriately reformed in order to conform to the Quranic guidance. The foregoing analysis suggests just that reform.

Salat is to be considered as purely personal and devotional in kind, and should be performed spontaneously, not as a ritual to be performed as a matter of obligation to God. God does not need our *salat*; we need to do it for our own sake. *Salat* is to be performed for one's spiritual development, to achieve purification of one's soul, and gain wisdom. It has to be coupled with consistent work in life. It should be devoted to understanding God and how He acts, and understanding His Laws. *Salat* needs to be devoted to eliciting divine response in some form or other. The real purpose of prayer is to help one lead a flawless and enriched life.

It needs to be noted that this conception of *salat* in light of the Quran that has been presented in this chapter is drawn from the ideas of Shah Aksaruddin Ahmad. It will be quite fitting, therefore, that we conclude this chapter with some of his words about *salat*, which capture the gist of what *salat* is:

(1)

Know by the Quran
How you should do your *salat.*
God's message in the Quran is:
'Akimus *salat*'.

'Establish *salat*'
Is what God the Pure has said.
What is the use doing it like doing a rite?

Salat is no child's play
Five times night and day.
Seek power and help; seek forgiveness of your sins
Humbly and devoutly.

Seek in *salat what you need,*
But act you must accordingly
Going along the path that helps you get what you seek.

(2)

Salat is to get one's peace

153

Keeping away from indecency and evil.
Nigh is God
Who hears the call of the heart,
If one implores Him humbly and devoutly.

He forgives one's sins,
And removing one's dross
Purifies one's mind.
Sorrow and grief goes away;
No regret remains in one's heart.

Seeking power and help
Do your *salat* without recitation.
God will wash away your mind.
You will get peace and happiness and all that you need
In this world and also in the Hereafter.

Instead of doing the *salat* of the Quran,
Why recite the *Namaz* (Persian equivalent of *salat*) like doing
one's rite?
Make no mistake, even by mistake.

(3)
Through *salat* burn all your sins
And all the dross of your heart.
Present in your front is your Lord,
Salat is the platform for imploring God.

Salat is giving away (one's heart and soul),
Forgetting one's self,
Salat is commitment
To serve God,

To seek the straight path,
The path of those
Who received God's *niamat* (bounties),
To go along that path
To get that *niamat*.

Salat is meeting with the Lord –
Miraj (ascension) in this world.

By remembering the *alhamdu* mantra (the *surah fatiha*)
Dances the heart
Filled with love, and the soul is sacrificed![136]

VI. THE SIGNIFICANCE AND SCOPE OF SPENDING IN GOD'S WAY *(ZAKAT OR SADAQA)*[137]

Ye will not attain piety until ye spend of what ye love. And whatever ye spend, God is well aware of it. – 3:92

That which ye give in usury in order that it may increase people's property hath no increase with God, but that which ye give in charity (zakat), seeking God's pleasure, hath increase manifold. – 30:39

Introduction

One of the central tenets of Islam relates to spending in God's way – *zakat* (or *zakah*)[138] or *sadaqa*. For those who can afford, prayer on their part needs to be coupled with deeds of material sacrifice, or spending on the less fortunate in society, or for other noble purposes, which is spending in God's way – an act that has been much emphasized in the Quran. Such spending is characterized as part and parcel of righteousness, and its virtues are enormously extolled.

Spending in God's way (*zakat* or *sadaqa*) is narrowly defined in traditional Islam. However, properly understood in the Quranic light, it is found to embrace a much broader meaning and scope. Some of the salient features such spending should embrace are as follows:

- The basic purpose of such spending should be to make the poor and disadvantaged people in society stand on their feet – not to perpetuate a beggars' class in society, which is really a social nuisance, degrading to humanity.

- Such spending according to the Quran well exceeds the 2½ percent of assets (excluding one's homestead) generally understood as the *zakat* amount. And it should come out of both earnings (income) and wealth.

- Such spending covers not only welfare payments for the indigent and the needy, and poor relatives but also those for other causes, lumped up as God's cause, which covers a whole host of things such as defense against external aggression; dispensation of criminal justice; maintenance and promotion of law and order and peace in society; economic policymaking; and promotion of social and employment-generating economic development; and similar other purposes, including the development of supportive infrastructure. Developments in many of these areas are vital for effectively dealing with the problem of the poor and unemployed.

- Finally, the state has an important role to play in such programs besides what individuals can do at their own levels on top of taxes they pay to the government to cover welfare needs at the state level.

The Significance of Spending in God's Way

Some of the reasons why those in society who can afford to engage in such spending should do so are as follows:

- Such spending is part and parcel of the very service to God;
- It is through such spending that we bring about greater egalitarianism in society;
- Such spending is self-purifying, and it brings real contentment and happiness for the giver; and
- Such spending also makes economic sense.

The rationale for spending on others is to be found in the consideration that man can hardly live alone in happiness without sharing his earnings and possessions with others, and also in the fact that all that we earn and possess is really the Grace of God, and belongs to God only. Whether one calls it *zakat* or *sadaqa*, spending on the poor and our disadvantaged fellow beings, or for God's cause is part and parcel of the very worship of God – for expressing our gratitude to God for His manifold blessings we enjoy (6:141), and for our livelihood that really originates from Him (2:57, 126, 172, 212; 3:27, 37; 4:130; etc.).

There is also a deep philosophical reason for humanitarian spending on the part of the rich people in society. They are just custodians of their wealth and income[139]; they need to spend that wealth and income for godly purposes – to serve only God (12:40). Such spending amounts to serving humankind, and serving humankind is essentially serving God. There is no merit in the amassing of wealth, as it has no value as a measure of virtuousness of a human being before God (34:37). Those who are stingy in humanitarian spending, and amass or hoard wealth would eventually find that wealth too burdensome for them – such wealth would be tied to their necks like a collar on the Day of Resurrection (3:180). The Quran directs us to be fully alive to the need for ensuring distributive justice in society. It strongly urged the Prophet Muhammad, who was an orphan and a needy person, not to be oblivious of the needs of the orphans and the needy (93:6-10). The Quran envisions for us an egalitarian society. A society is neither egalitarian nor healthy for its all-round development when some people swim in wealth while others are ill-fed, ill-clad and ill-housed, and when they cannot provide for their health and education even at a basic level. Spending on the helpless and disadvantaged groups in society helps overall moral and spiritual uplifting of all humankind, which is the only way we elevate all men and women, and help develop their latent potentials, and bring about all round progress in society.

Zakat means "purification" – through sharing a portion of one's blessings with others for free, i.e., *pro bono* – where the giving is without expectation of any return (See 76:8-9; 92:20-21). Blessings could be in any form such as friendship, professional skill, knowledge, manual work, beautiful voice, and real or monetary resources.[140] *Sadaqa* or *infaq* could be regarded as that kind of *zakat*, which involves material sacrifice on one's part. However, both *zakat* and *sadaqa* could be interpreted to mean the same thing for all practical purposes – sharing of one' resources (or spending) – material or non-material – for God's cause. Spending for a benevolent cause, i.e., in God's way, is a way of purifying oneself (92:17-21), and often a way of atoning for mistakes or misdeeds, or for inability to perform other desirable acts. The Quran emphatically proclaims that we cannot attain piety until we spend of that which we love (3:92). God-loving people spend for the poor, the orphans, and the captives out of love for, and pleasure of, God – which is essentially their own pleasure, and they seek or expect no reward or thanks in return (76:8-9; 92:20-21).

3:92   *Ye will not attain piety until ye spend of what ye love.* And whatever ye spend, God is well aware of it.

92:17-21 *As for the righteous, he will be spared it (the blazing Fire), one who giveth from his riches for self-purification. He seeketh nothing in return, but*

158

seeketh (only) the pleasure of his Lord, the Most High. It is he who verily will find contentment.

9:103   *Take (O Muhammad) contributions (sadaqa) from their riches to purify them, and make them grow (in spirituality), and pray for them.* Verily thy prayer is reassurance for them.

We need to submit ourselves completely, i.e., our body and mind, our thoughts, our prayer and devotions, and all of our material resources to the service of God. That implies that we need to spend out of what we earn in the way of God. One gets real happiness – that is one's virtue – by living for others. God's prophets came to disseminate their divine or spiritual knowledge to all, and they did this without any remuneration (6:90; 26:109, 127, 145, 164, 180; 34:47; 52:40; 68:46; etc.). When we spend on others in the form of direct distribution, we need to display the same spirit as shown by the prophets that is that we need to spend without expecting any return from the receivers of our wealth: by living for others. This is the *raison d'etre* of spending for others. Overall social uplift and maximization of mutual benefit to all critically depends not only on a widespread dissemination of spiritual, educational and technological knowledge, but also on an equitable distribution of material riches.

Spending thus works essentially like prayer, or can broadly be conceived as part of prayer itself. Indeed, as God warns us in the Quran, neglecting needed help and support to needy people renders one's prayer null and void (107:1-7). Spending in God's way is thus an essential component of righteousness (2: 177).

The Quran emphasizes spending in God's way as a greatly virtuous act:

90:12-8   Ah, what will convey unto thee (O Muhammad) *what the Ascent is!*
(It is) to set a slave free,
And to feed the hungry,
An orphan near of kin,
Or a poor person in misery,
Then he hath become one of believers who enjoin one another patience and kindness.
Those are the people on the right path.

159

> **2:261** The example of those who spend their wealth in God's way is like a grain that groweth seven ears, with a hundred grains in every ear. God giveth increase manifold to whomsoever He pleaseth.

It is only the wrong-headed people who dispute the case for spending for others:

> **36:47** When they are told: Spend of what God hath provided you, those who disbelieve say to those who believe: "Shall we feed those whom God could feed, if He so willed?" Ye are clearly misguided.

From even a purely economic point of view, a high concentration of income and wealth in fewer hands is counter-productive. Such a concentration adversely affects the development of human resources, and holds down effective demand, and holds back economic expansion. High inequality of income and wealth destroys social cohesion, peace and harmony, and breeds bitter feelings on the part of the poor and deprived people, and creates scope for social crimes, immorality and frustration. The have-nots at some time may feel so frustrated that they may even feel prompted to rise against the haves to pull them down. As Ahmad points out:

> That social order is wrong when one rolls in wealth and others fallow in gutters and squeeze themselves into garrets to starve unto physical and moral death.[141]

The Scope of Spending in God's Way: the Wider Meaning

Spending in God's way means much more than is conventionally being understood. A careful reading of the Quran does reveal that such spending should be from both income and wealth, that the amount we should spend should be a considerably higher proportion of our income and wealth than is currently being practiced, and that the purposes for which we should spend are much more varied than are usually thought.

The Quran urges us to spend out of our wealth and income or production (2:254; 6:141). Besides, we should use part of our income for our and our families' current consumption, and save and invest part of our income for our future consumption, but we should not keep it idle or

160

hoard it. Hoarding is bad for an economy. It deprives others; it curbs effective demand in the economy, and holds back economic expansion, and if the hoarding is done in goods, it creates artificial scarcities, and high prices of the hoarded goods. The Quran strongly condemns hoarding (3): 180).

Though everything prescribed in the Quran is *fard* or obligatory for us, God specifically mentions *sadaqa* as *fard* for us, and He mentions where such spending should go:

> **9:60** The alms (*sadaqa*) are for the poor, the needy, and those who administer them, and those whose hearts are to be reconciled (to truth), and to free the slaves and the debtors, and for the cause of God, and (for) the wayfarers; an obligatory duty (*fard*) imposed by God. God is Knower, Most Wise.

Such spending is for those who are needy, and for those who are deprived, or poor (70:25), for parents, near relatives, orphans, wayfarers, and for those who ask (2:177), and for other causes of God, including that for freeing of captives or slaves, and for necessary reconciliation or rehabilitation of new converts to religion (2:177, 215; 8:41; 9:60; 24:22). Spending is also for those who are in need of help, but being involved in the cause of God, are unable to move about in the land, and who do not beg importunately (2:273). Likewise, we need also to spend for other noble causes such as for relieving the burden of those who are heavily laden with debt (9:60), and for miscellaneous other noble purposes, which can be termed as causes of God. As for the spending for the new converts, the Quran speaks well of the God-loving believers during the Prophet's time, who were so generous to those who came to them for refuge that they gave preference to the refugees over themselves in helping them, even though they were poor (59:9).

God advises those of us who are affluent that we should not make such promises as not to help our relatives, poor people, and those who leave their homes for the cause of God; and we are urged to forgive them and ignore their faults (24:22). He loves those who spend not only when they are in affluence or ease, but also when they are in hardship (3:134). He admonishes us to give others what is good, and not what we regard as bad and do not want to receive for ourselves (2:267). God characterizes freeing of war captives or slaves, or marrying them as equal partners as

161

very important righteous deeds. Spending for such purposes is likewise a great virtue in the sight of God (2:177; 9:60).

Zakat in the sense of charity is also mentioned in the Quran:

> **30:39** *That which ye give in usury in order that it may increase people's property hath no increase with God, but that which ye give in charity (zakat), seeking God's pleasure, hath increase manifold.*

Although unlike in the case of *sadaqa*, the Quran nowhere mentions where the *zakat* should go, and by how much in relation to income or wealth, both *sadaqa* and *zakat* appear to mean the same thing in principle, and also in practice. The current practice of *zakat* at a low proportion ($2^1/_2$ percent) of one's wealth (which includes the value of most of one's assets with some exceptions such as the family house) appears inadequate in light of the Quran, especially for high-income people, as well as from the point of view of the demands of society for a multiplicity of beneficial works (for God's cause) on top of the provisions for the poor.

Concerning what to spend in God's way and how much, the Quran explicitly states:

> **2:267** O ye who believe! *Spend of the good things which ye have earned, and of what We bring forth from the earth for you,* and seek not the bad to spend thereof when ye would not take it for yourselves unless ye close your eyes.

> **2:219** They ask thee concerning what they should spend. Say: That which is in excess (of your needs). Thus God maketh clear (His) revelations that you may think.

> **25:67** And they, when they spend (in charity), are neither extravagant nor stingy; they keep a just (balance) between these (two limits).

In these verses, the Quran asks us to spend out of what we earn and produce (i.e., from our income and production), out of what we like for ourselves, and from that which is in excess of our needs. Our needs can be understood as those for our own consumption, including needs that accommodate provisions for savings and investments for our needed future consumption. "Need" is a subjective term, and hence can be interpreted variously. The same is true of the term "stinginess". In one of the above verses the Quran exhorts us not to be stingy in spending as well. When deciding about how much to spend in God's way, individuals concerned need to make their decisions according to what they feel or think about their own needs, and what they consider as stingy. Thus the amount of spending in God's way should be in excess of our needs, and a reasonable balance between extravagance and stinginess.

Two other verses of the Quran also shed more light on how much one should spend out of windfall income or wealth like the spoils of war and other gains:

> **8:1** They ask thee (O Muhammad) about the spoils of war. Say: The spoils of war are for God and the Messenger. So be careful of (your duty to) God, and settle matters of your difference, and obey God and His Messenger if ye do believe.

> **8:41** And know: Of anything ye gain, a fifth is for God and His Messenger, relatives, orphans, the needy, and the wayfarer, if ye do believe in God and in what We have revealed to Our servant.

The first of these verses relates to gains such as the war booties. Such gains wholly belong to "God and the Messenger", which means that such gains should be distributed entirely for God's cause – for meeting the needs of the poor and needy people and other welfare needs. The handling and distribution of these gains should be done and administered by the state, or by state-sponsored appropriate public or private sector organizations (modern-day NGOs, for example). There may be other gains of the nature of what economists call "windfall gains", the handling and distribution of which warrant similar treatment. Some examples of such gains are instant treasure troves found by some people, and real estates, bank deposits, and other assets left by deceased people who have no near relatives with any legitimate claim to such assets. Lottery earnings also fall in the category of windfall gains, which deserve to be heavily taxed by the state for welfare needs. Note, however, that the Quran strongly discourages us to indulge in games of chance (2:219;

5:90–91). Hence, in Muslim countries lotteries and gambling should not be allowed in the first place. However, if any citizens in these countries receive profits from lotteries overseas, such profits deserve to be highly taxed by the Muslim state.

The second verse (8:41) calls for spending or distribution of a fifth of other gains or income we earn for God's cause, and for near relatives, orphans, needy, wayfarers, etc. That implies that there should be a twenty percent tax on normal or regular gains or income for both the state and other welfare activities. These verses warrant drawing the following summarized implications concerning how much we should spend in God's way:

- First, we should spend in excess of our needs, and choose an appropriate balance between extravagance and stinginess;

- Second, the excess over needs implies a more than proportionate ability to spend in relation to income and wealth of a person suggesting a need for progressive taxation for welfare needs;

- Third. windfall gains such as war booties and other gains of the essentially same nature should be spent entirely in God's cause, and their distribution should be left at the discretion of the public authority, i.e. the state; and

- Fourth, we should spend in God's way one fifth of our normal gains – income or wealth, which are gains other than windfall gains of the nature of war booties. This entitles the state to tax people's normal income or wealth at the rate of 20 percent for meeting the welfare needs of the state.[142]

These directions of the Quran highlight that the proportion of our income, wealth or gains to be spent in God's way should normally be a considerably higher fraction than the 2½ percent (of wealth), which is generally believed as the *zakat* amount. Note that such spending should go not only to the destitute and the needy but also to a multiplicity of noble causes, which we can lump together as God's cause. A substantial chunk of such causes is best handled at the government level, while others may be left for private individuals. During our Prophet's time, considerable resources in the forms of believing men and goods were mobilized for conducting war against the invading infidels.

9:41   Go forth (O ye who believe), equipped with light
             arms and heavy arms, and strive with your wealth
             and your lives in God's cause. That is best for you if
             .ye only knew.

Resources mobilized in the forms of men and goods used for purposes of
defense are spending in God's cause. There are many such needs that
need to be met at the government or public sector level. The government
should cater to such needs, and *sadaqa* or appropriate taxation should
finance such needs. All those parts of government expenditure, which are
meant for social welfare – feeding and rehabilitation of destitute people,
provisions for unemployed workers, education, labor training, health and
hospital services, and similar spending directed especially to
amelioration of the conditions of the poor, and those which are meant for
making available what economists call "public goods" that are best
produced at the public sector level – are indeed instances of spending for
God's cause. Public goods are those goods and services, the production
of which, if left to the private sector alone, is grossly neglected, or
inadequately met. Public goods are similar to what Muslim scholars
recognize as acts or goods of public interest (*muslaha*), but they are not
exactly the same. Some examples of public goods are social peace and
security, defense against external aggression, administration of law and
justice, promotion of social, cultural, and spiritual development,
economic policymaking, and general public administration for
miscellaneous government functions. All such state functions should
count within the purview of God's cause. And in an impoverished
developing economy, the state has a special role to play in promoting
economic development, which indeed is the best answer to alleviation of
poverty for the poor. For promoting economic development, considerable
investment is needed in physical infrastructure (such as roads, highways,
railways, waterways, ports, telecommunications, power and energy,
information exchange, etc.) as well as in human skills and education,
technology and research. Promotion of such development is crucial for
expanding employment opportunities, and raising living standards, and in
the long run for dealing with the problem of the poor.

It is clear that spending in God's way covers a lot more things than are
currently being covered by the *zakat* or *sadaqa* system. It matters little
whether one calls it *zakat* or *sadaqa*. But this system is in need of major
reform in light of the directions given in the Quran, and in light of recent
developments in the conception of functions of a modern state. Spending

in God's way then of individuals will comprise both the taxes they pay for benevolent works of the government at the government level, and whatever they can afford to spend voluntarily at the private sector level on top of the taxes they pay. It should be recognized that what the government can or should do efficiently is inadequate to deal with the total problem of social inequity, and to promote overall social welfare; and there is much still left to be done at the private sector or individual level. But limiting such benevolent and humanitarian spending to just 2½ percent of one's wealth will be taking a very narrow view of spending in God's way in light of the Quran. Such spending should not be limited just to a proportion of wealth alone as is generally understood in the case of *zakat*. The verses (2:267; 6:141) cited above clearly point to spending from earning and production. Hence earning or production could also be used as a base for such spending. And the proportion should be a flexible one depending on how much one can afford neither being too generous nor too stingy as directed in verse (25:67) cited above, taking into account what he or she has already paid to the government in the form of taxes for God's cause.

The ultimate aim of the *zakat* or *sadaqa* system should be to eradicate poverty, and help people get work opportunities, and become self-reliant, and not to perpetuate a beggars' class in society, which is not only degrading for them but also a nuisance in society. To the extent possible and economically efficient, such spending should be handled at the state level. Many modern developed countries have well-planned public welfare, and social security systems embodying unemployment benefits, and certain medical benefits, and administered at the state level in conjunction with enterprise level retirement, lay-off and medical insurance benefits, and it is not left to the whims of individuals to cater to such welfare needs. Social security systems existing in some of the developed countries essentially exhibit the basic principles of the *sadaqa* system that the Quran propounds. Though there is some debate as to what developed countries are really doing for developing countries (they often take back what they give in different ways[143]), the concessional aid they give and what their sponsored multilateral development financing institutions give to the developing countries is also a kind of *sadaqa* at state level on the part of the rich countries to the poor ones. Such aid should also be counted in the calculation for how much more resources the government should mobilize domestically to cater to the needs of the poor, and for development and social welfare needs. The need for paying *sadaqa* at the individual level will last as long as the state cannot pay full attention to the problems of the helpless people. The state in many developing countries is almost invariably unable to take full care of the poor and the needy. Also considering that public sector welfare systems in developing countries are found to be almost always plagued by significant corruption as available evidence suggests, there remains considerable room for charities at the individual level. When a believing man or woman can afford to spend, and perceives the need for such spending, it becomes incumbent on him or her to do it. That is as good as his/her prayer for his/her own spiritual advancement. And a significant part of such spending should be given to reputable international charitable organizations, and international and domestic NGOs (non-governmental organizations), which engage in development and social welfare activities, and which are known to be more efficient and less corrupt than the relevant government departments.

Another point to be noted in this regard is that the scope of such spending should also embrace interest-free or concessional lending, which the Quran calls *qarz-hasana* (beautiful lending) (2:245; 57:11, 18; 64:17; 5:12; 73:20). In modern days, some of this concessional financing function is being performed in developing countries by developed country aid agencies, and multilateral development financing institutions. The Quranic message of interest-free loans is applicable only for disadvantaged borrowers, who deserve to be treated with a humanitarian approach. The Quran also encourages the lenders to remit interest on remaining loans, and postpone or write off the original loans in cases where the borrowers are in difficulty to repay them (2:278-280). In cases, which deserve humanitarian considerations, loans should indeed be extended free of interest, and where appropriate, such loans should be given as grants or alms, which is *sadaqa* in the Quranic terminology.

Conclusion

Spending in God's way should be understood in a much broader sense than the generally understood *zakat* system. It involves considerable spending on the part of a modern state for a variety of functions financed through a well-devised taxation system, besides charitable spending at the individual level. The best kind of spending in God's way is helping others stand on their own feet. To help another person in a way, which makes him or her look for help all the time, is inherently ill motivated, and is like that of those who like to be seen by men, and is of no intrinsic virtue to them (2:264). From this point of view, the modern state should

167

take appropriate measures to promote investment and development to increase opportunities for gainful employment of unemployed people, along with crafting a well-devised social welfare and security system. At the individual level, such efforts should include savings, investment and work that would help build infrastructure and industries for employment-generating development, along with their humanitarian spending in deserving cases.

VII. RIGHTEOUSNESS IN LIGHT OF THE QURAN: GETTING OUR *IMAN* RIGHT

O children of Adam! We have indeed inspired unto you (the need for) clothing to cover your shame, as well as for your adornment, *but the clothing of righteousness is what the best is.* – 7:26

And *whether ye make known what is in your minds or conceal it, God will bring you to account for it.* – 2:284

[H]uman beings, by changing the inner attitudes of their minds, can change the outer aspects of their lives. – William James

INTRODUCTION

Religion teaches us to be righteous. This is the singular theme that runs through the whole Quran. Righteousness is the key to one's real success or, to say the same thing, it is the only criterion that enables one to go to Heaven (2:25; 3:15; 4:57, 122; 5:35, 100; 22:77; 23:1-6; 59:9; 64:16; 91:7-9; 15:45; 18:107-108 and many more verses). It matters little if a person belongs in name to any religion, caste or creed, ethnic group or tribe. Regardless of race, religion or color, whatever good a person does will be duly recognized and rewarded by God (3:113-115). If he is righteous, he belongs to a distinguished group, and is assured of the promise of a progressive and rewarding life leading to success, happiness, and bliss of Heaven:

> **2:62** Surely, those who believe, and those who are Jews, and Christians, or Sabians (some Middle East groups traditionally recognized as having a monotheistic orientation), whoever believeth in God and the Last Day (or ultimate outcome), and do right deeds – surely their reward is with their Lord, and there shall no fear come upon them, nor shall they grieve. (See also 5:69)

The concept of righteousness according to the Quran encompasses ethical codes of conduct as well as religious beliefs and practices. As argued before, the moral and ethical codes are part and parcel of religion, and also derive from the same source, i.e., divine inspiration. God has

169

given us soul or conscience and that soul has essentially come to know what is conscionable and unconscionable (See 91:8-10 cited earlier).

The Prophet Muhammad did not say anything of religion out of his own desire (53:3). Righteousness cannot be determined by personal desires or opinions:

> **23:71** And if the Truth had followed their lusts (low desires), verily the heaven and the earth, and whoever is therein would have been corrupted. (See also 28:50)

> **13:37** Thus have We revealed it (the Quran), a true proclamation in Arabic; and *if thou shouldst follow their (low) desires after that which hath come unto thee of knowledge, then truly wouldst thou have from God no protecting friend nor defender.*

The Prophet David was also similarly advised by God not to fall prey to his own desires:

> **38:26** O David! We have indeed made thee a successor (*khalifa*) in the land; so judge aright between human beings, and *follow not thy own desire, lest it should divert thee from the path of God. ...*

The Prophet Muhammad was specifically exhorted by God to judge between people by the revealed Book, and not follow the personal desires or opinions of any people (4:105; 5:48-49). He was exhorted not to follow those who have no knowledge (45:18). He was urged not to follow the majority, as they follow nothing but conjecture without any knowledge, and do nothing but lie:

> **6:116** *Shouldst thou (O Muhammad) follow the most of those on earth, they would have led thee far astray from the path of God.* They follow naught but conjecture; and they do naught but lie.

The Quran further points out that many indeed mislead people with their personal opinions without knowledge (6:119). We thus cannot rely on opinion polls as a basis for judging what is right or wrong, unless such opinions are based on divine or transcendental knowledge. We should be wary of the advice or opinions of other people. Even though the great scientist Einstein said that he did not believe in God, he nevertheless recognized the moral principles or guidelines given by distinguished people of religion.[144] The point that needs emphasizing is that one cannot be truly religious without being morally righteous at the same time.

It is ironic that some recent acts of terrorism have been linked to people who happen to be nominal Muslims. This fact has tarnished the image of Islam, especially in the western world, where many think that Islam is a religion of intolerance and violence. In fact, the Islam that the Quran professes has nothing to do with violence or terrorism. In the Quran, God has clearly and strongly warned mankind against any act of wrongdoing, murder, corruption, or mischief in the land (5:32; 7:56, 74; 13:25; 26:151-152, 183; 27:48-49; 47:22-23). (More on this below) There is thus a need to know Islam in its true image, and understand what the Quran characterizes as true righteousness.

Even an atom's weight of good or bad deed will not go unnoticed (34:3-4; 99:6-7). In God's sight, only those are superior, whether male or female, who are superior in conduct.

> **49:13** O humankind! Verily We have created you of a male and a female, and have made you nations and tribes that ye may know one another. *Verily the most honorable in the sight of God is the one who is the most righteous.* Verily God is Knower, Most Aware.

The best provision one can make for oneself is to attain righteousness (2:197). One is more righteous the more sincere, serious or diligent one is in pursuit of righteousness or piety. God recognizes such efforts, and assures us that those who strive hard achieve a higher degree or rank of piety:

> **17:19** And whoever desireth the Hereafter (the future) and striveth for it with the due effort, being a believer, for such their efforts will surely be appreciated.

> **6:132** For all there are ranks according to their deeds. Thy Lord is not oblivious of what they do.

In this regard an important point to note is that God Himself represents the criterion by which we can judge righteousness. His is the most ideal nature. If a person aspires to be someone better than what he is at present, then he needs a standard or ideal to follow. He cannot limit himself to following a standard, which is surpassed by another standard. It is only God who represents the standard or ideal that is unsurpassable; and thus it is this Ideal alone that we need to worship or emulate. God is Unique (42:11). It is this Uniqueness of God, i.e., of His attributes or qualities, that is most worthy of our adoration and emulation. That is why we need to take our color from God:

> **2:138** (Say, we take our) color from God; and who can give a better color than God? It is He Whom alone we worship.

Effort in the direction of molding one's character on the model or pattern of God's own nature is effort for true righteousness or religion (30:30). God always stays on the right course (*sirat al mustaqim*) (11:56). Through emulation of God, when one reaches the stage – and this is indeed a very high stage – where one's actions are in line with God's Wishes, one really acts not of his or her own accord but according to the wishes or will of God, and his or her sayings or actions become aboveboard and unquestionable (53:3; 18:79-82). If one can reach such a stage, he or she can consider himself or herself very blessed indeed. The aim of every person should, therefore, be to spiritually evolve towards such a stage. Accordingly, whatever a person does should be in accord with the spirit of that spiritual pursuit, and such actions will be his or her righteous deeds.

God is All Transcendent, Infinite and also a blinding Light (*Nur*) of the Universe 24:35). That is why He is invisible. His visible or human servants whom we can follow as models are His prophets. As the Quran itself testifies, the Prophet Muhammad is an excellent example of a character or ideal that we should emulate (33:21; 68:4-6). He exemplified in his life many good qualities a person should possess. He was the living Quran. He was not simply God's emissary – a religious and spiritual preacher, educator and guide (62:2; 33:45-46), but simultaneously also an ideal in righteous conduct and piety (36:3-4; 43:43; 73:20), a man with great humanity and concern for fellow beings (9:128; 15:88; 33:6; 3:159, 47:19), a social reformer who brought social

172

egalitarianism (2:188; 17:34; 3:130; 2:278-280; 26:181-183; 90:12-18; 3:180; 2:177; 3:92; 92:17-21; 9:50), a distinguished judge (4:65, 105; 24:51; 42:15), a military leader and organizer 3:121-128, 153; 8:64-71; 33:16-20), and an astute statesman – the image of a leader and social transformer the like of which the world has never seen before, and will likely never see again. God describes him as one sent to mankind as a light-giving lamp (*munir* or *nur*) (33:46), and as a mercy of the universe (21:107). No doubt he was a "wonderful man" and "the saviour of humanity."[145] Being the last Prophet, Muhammad has come with the latest, most authentic and comprehensive message for all humankind, and this message is all contained in the Quran. Messages left by earlier prophets have been either lost or corrupted. If we thus follow the Quran carefully, we can get all the necessary guidance about how we can proceed in life to be truly righteous.

Whatever we do with our mind or body counts, and we are accountable for all such deeds (2:284). The first group of actions – beliefs, feelings and thoughts – shapes up our *iman* or mindset. We discuss below how to get the *iman* right. In the chapter following, we deal with the question of our other actions.

GETTING OUR *IMAN* RIGHT

The process of getting one's *iman* (mindset) right embraces the following elements:

- Having the right metaphysical beliefs – belief in God, His creatures, His revelations, and prophets who received them;
- Believing in the divine laws of cause and effect – shunning fanaticism and fatalism, and entertaining the right kind of predetermined destiny (*taqdir*);
- Embracing humility or modesty – shunning vanity and complacency, and increasing humility;
- Being honest with oneself – shunning pretension;
- Nurturing a positive attitude – getting rid of frustration, and increasing self-confidence;
- Being moderate and considerate – getting rid of greed;
- Being tolerant – forsaking prejudice, intolerance and violence;

173

- Being brave – getting rid of cowardice, fear and servile mentality; and

- Harboring other right feelings and good thoughts – avoiding other wrong feelings and evil thoughts, and developing the right attitude.

Having the right metaphysical beliefs – belief in God, His creatures, His revelations, and prophets who received them

A progressive outlook demands that we do not reject or brush aside something as false, simply because, with our current level of understanding, knowledge, or intuition, we do not see or perceive if that is really true. In the past, many people wrongly believed that the earth was flat, simply because their sight did not go far enough. It was science and round the world air or sea travels that enabled men to see with their eyes that the earth is really round. Though to date there has been enormous progress in scientific knowledge, science has yet to traverse a vast unknown territory. It still remains for science to explore and vindicate the truths that the prophets of religion have brought to mankind.

The religion of Islam requires us to believe in certain metaphysical aspects such as that God exists, that God has revealed messages to men who became His prophets, that man will have resurrection or afterlife, and that there are other creatures of God such as angels and Jinns. About the need for believing in God, the Quran states:

> **2:186**   When my servants ask thee (O Muhammad) concerning Me, then surely I am nigh (to them); I answer the prayer of every suppliant when he crieth unto Me. So let them heed My call, and *let them believe in Me, in order that they may be led aright.*

Belief in God is necessary to be rightly guided. "Without imbibing the God idea man can never really be good. You may be a scientist but your inventions will be more destructive than constructive. [...] Without God there is no nobility in any action, thing (71:13) or being."[146] A person can afford to be of dubious, or no good, character, of no conviction in any principles of conduct, or of no trustworthiness to others as well as to his own self, if he is an atheist, for he considers himself as accountable to

174

none, and does not have to care for any good or godly values in life. Those who have faith in moral or godly values or principles, but do not expressly believe in God, they are so to say half-believers in God. They need to be full believers to rise anywhere near to the status of God's most loved servants who are prophets or saints.

Atheism in the proper sense of the term rules out the existence of a Superior Being who is superior to all living creatures. It is symptomatic of a disbelief in the existence of a being that can be superior to the atheist. It amounts to a disbelief in a higher standard or ideal that can exist other than what he represents. Atheism thus symbolizes pride or arrogance, which is the root of downfall. Iblis, Pharaoh, Qarun or others like them thought that they had no god other than themselves to obey or submit to, and for that they had to embrace their downfall (7:11-13; 26:29-30; 23:45-48; 28:76-81). Their pride led them to disbelieve in possibilities of progressive evolution of a being. Disbelief in what is really possible or true leads one to be arrogant and defiant (38:2). Hence we need to believe in the unseen realities or truths, though we may not have grown mature, or spiritually advanced enough, to see or perceive such truths (2:2-3).

Faith in God has multifarious implications, which we need to be conscious of, if we want to proceed in a progressive manner. The most significant implication of this belief is that we accept, or submit to, all that God represents or stands for – truth, reason, justice, knowledge, guidance, power, and all that is good, beneficial, noble, and beautiful. Thus a righteous person must always be truthful, and must always stand for truth, and accordingly must always be mentally prepared to testify or judge truthfully, even if that testimony or judgment goes against himself, his parents, and his relatives 4:135). God has advised us to heed and obey sounder advice (36:21, 25; 64:16). Not accepting or properly listening to reason or sounder advice that one may hear from another amounts to arrogance or denial of more godly powers, and indirectly of God (16:22; 2:87, 206; 7:12-13, 36, 40, 76; 10:75). Those who turn a blind eye to such advice, and do not understand nor try to understand are indeed blind, deaf, or dumb (8:22-23; 25:43-44; 2:18; 7:179; 27:80-81; 30:52.

Belief in God (One God - *tawhid*) is the most basic part of one's right *iman*. Such a belief is essential and important – essential because without this belief no one is a true believer of God, and important because this is the most directly opposing and powerful message of Islam that came for the polytheists and idolaters among the existing pagans, the Jews, and the Christians. The Quran declared that the original founders of Judaism and Christianity, Abraham and Jesus respectively, were not polytheists and idolaters, but believed in only One Supreme God. The Christian concept of the Trinity and veneration of the Virgin Mary in Catholicism are departures from the straight path, or errors that Islam has corrected. The Prophet Muhammad was also a "human messenger of the Lord" and his message was also "against the divine intermediaries clothed in human form."[147] He also came with the powerful idea that "man was free of the corruption of (the) *original sin*[148] and only kept apart from truth and the right way by error and negligence – and on occasion by divine will."[149] Note also that the Quran also rejects the related idea professed in Christianity that the Prophet Jesus's sacrifice (crucifixion) made for atonement and redemption of humanity.

Along with a belief in (one) God, we also need to believe in His revelations and His prophets who received them, His creations such as angels and Jinn, and the Last Day or the Day of Resurrection. The Quran states:

> **3:179**   It is not for God to leave you in your present state until He separateth the bad from the good. And God canst not let you (all) know the unseen. But God chooseth of His Messengers whom He willeth (to receive such knowledge). So *believe in God and His Messengers. If ye believe and are righteous, yours will be a great reward.*

> **4:136**   O ye who believe! Believe in God and His Messenger and the Book, which He hath revealed unto His Messenger, and the Book, which he revealed aforetime. *Whoever disbelieveth in God, and His angels, and His Books, and His Messengers, and the Last Day, he verily hath wandered far astray.*

Verse (4:136) gives the required core beliefs or doctrines of Islam. Such beliefs are part and parcel of the righteousness that the Quran prescribes (2:177). The Prophet Muhammad himself was specifically urged not to doubt the divine revelations, which require such beliefs:

2:147 It (the Quran) is the Truth from thy Lord (O Muhammad), so *be not of those who waver.* (See also 3: 60).

10:94-5 *If thou (O Muhammad) art in doubt about what We have revealed unto thee, then ask those who read the Book (that was) before thee.* Verily the Truth from thy Lord hath come unto thee. So be not thou of the waverers. Nor be of those who reject the revelations of God, for then thou wouldst be of the losers.

Resurrection (*qiyamat*) into afterlife (*akhirat*) is destined to come in order that God can reward those who are righteous, and let those who do wrong get their proper recompense (10:4; 34:3-6). It has its rationale and logic in the very conception of the evolutionary or creative process that is at play throughout the Universe. Good deeds need to be appropriately appreciated, rewarded, and encouraged for the doers so that they can carry forward and perfect their deeds. If a man commits wrongs or follies in his life, and dies before he can correct his follies, he needs to be resurrected after death to do so, and complete the process of mending his follies in his afterlife.[150] One who doubts about resurrection and asks: 'When I am once dead, shall I truly be raised to life (again)?' (19:66) is reminded by God that man was created out of the void: "Doth not man remember that We created him before, when he was nothing?" (19:67). About the need for believing in resurrection, the Quran further points out that the inevitability of this resurrection is as real as the revival of the dead earth with plant life after rainfall (7:57; 22:5; 30:19, 50; 35:9; 41:39; 43:11; 50:11).

41:39 *Truly He Who reviveth the (dead) earth can surely revive who are dead;* for He hath power over all things.

Though the skeptics doubt if man can at all be brought back to life after it becomes dust or ashes, this is not impossible for God who can create by just a will. All He needs to do to carry out what He intends is just to say "'Be', and it is" (2:117; 3:47,59; 6:73; 16:40; 19:35; 36:82). Thus those who doubt about resurrection in fact disbelieve in God and His powers:

13:5 But if thou art amazed [at the marvels of God's creation], amazing, too, is their saying, "What! After we have become dust, shall we indeed be [restored to life] in a new act of creation?" These are they who (indeed) disbelieve in their Lord. ...

Believing in the Divine laws of cause and effect - shunning fanaticism and fatalism, and entertaining the right kind of predetermined destiny (*taqdir*)

Belief in God also implies belief in God's inexorable Laws, which means that we must believe in cause succeeded by commensurate effect. This is belief in a rational God, i.e., in reason. There is no room for fanaticism in religion. Thus the causal relationship does mean that what we get is according to what we earn or deserve. That is what the Quran explicitly and categorically points out (53:39; 20:15; 2:286). There is no flaw in God's creation or action (67:3-4), which means that He does not will or act arbitrarily. God thus does not favor anybody. He rewards only those who do right (12:22; 28;14). He does not do anything on His own to reward or punish man or any creature.

A popular myth that prevails among many Muslims and people of other religions is that everything that happens is due to fate, or is predestined by God, and unrelated to one's work, and that reliance on God means a blind dependence on Him. This myth needs to be exploded once and for all for the greater benefit and progress of mankind. The Quran does not encourage such a belief. It is rather wrong appreciation of the Quranic message, which has given rise to such misgivings. This is rather fatalism or fatalistic attitude that belies God's Laws or the logical system. Fatalism or blind dependence on God, which negates the relevance of man's own efforts is, therefore, not only a real obstacle for one's spiritual progress, but a great impediment to overall human progress, and should therefore be shunned.

At the same time we need to note that belief in God's Laws or the logical system also implies that we need to be mentally ready to accept, and readily accept what cannot be escaped or avoided. This is what really means accepting the given set of facts or factors, that have already been predetermined by factors, and which man must live with. The given set of predetermined facts or factors is so to say God-given or God-willed.

178

One needs to believe in this kind of *taqdir* or predetermined fate or destiny, and this is not fatalism or predestination. However much we may detest the idea, because of hereditary, environmental, and societal reasons, such fate or destiny does play a part in human life. There is some truth in the statement made by the German Philosopher Goethe that "Man supposes that he directs his life and governs his actions, when his existence is irretrievably under the control of destiny."[151] This should not, however, be taken to mean that man is utterly helpless, and has no independent will to exercise. The Quran categorically mentions that God has shown the way, and it is up to man to either accept it, or reject it and that an evil destiny awaits the rejecters (76:3-4). With determination and effort, man can change his destiny. History provides us innumerable examples of men who rose to great heights of achievement and success from very humble beginnings. The great saint Nizamuddin of India was once a great dacoit. It was indeed a momentous turning point in his life when he made a decisive shift from evil work, and turned whole-heartedly to God. It was a Mercy of God that he could turn decisively to God. God admonishes us never to despair of His Mercy, and even the gravest of a sinner can transform his life, and become righteous (39:53-54). Yet we need to grant that predetermining factors play some role in shaping our destiny. It is on the basis of such predetermining factors that God or His agents, including man, can predict and preannounce future events.[152]

Embracing humility or modesty - shunning vanity and complacency, and increasing humility

Getting one's *iman* right also requires that one should shun feelings of pride and complacency, another major stumbling block to human progress. Vanity makes one blind to perceive truth, reason, and all that can make things better and nobler. Self-conceit (or egotism) leads to self-destruction. The Quran documents how pride led to the downfall of Iblis, Pharaoh, Qarun, or others like them. Shunning pride and complacency, and increasing humility or modesty is an essential trait of righteousness, as well as a foremost condition for a man's pursuit of knowledge and spiritual progress. One need not be proud or complacent, since all pride or praise after all belongs to God. When God's help and victory came for the Prophet Muhammad, and he saw people embracing Islam in large numbers, he was advised by God only to celebrate His praises, and seek His forgiveness and mercy:

110:1-3 When cometh God's Help and Victory, and thou seest humankind entering the religion of God in troops, then hymn the praises of thy Lord, and seek His forgiveness; for He is (ever ready) to turn (in mercy).

There are several verses in the Quran that shed light on what pride is, and what harm it does to man, and advises man to shun boastful conduct:

7:146 I will turn away from My revelations those who are unjustly proud in the earth. ...

3:188 Think not that those who boast about what they have done, and love to be praised for what they have not really done – think not that they are safe from the punishment. A painful punishment awaiteth them. (See also 11:9-10)

57:23 That *ye may not grieve over what hath escaped you, nor exult at what hath been given*; and God loveth not any arrogant boaster.

31:18-9 *Turn not thy cheek scornfully to others, nor walk in the land with pride. Surely God loveth not any arrogant boaster. And be modest in thy conduct, and subdue thy voice,* for the harshest of the voices is without doubt the braying of the donkey. (See also 17:37)

Pride gives rise to bigotry or intolerance to others' views, and the tendency to dominate others without intrinsic superior qualities, which also blocks human progress. Pride makes one refrain from doing righteous deeds, and makes him or her commit various deeds of mischief in the land (3:188; 7:146; 16:22-23; 40:56, 60; 30:41). It was pride, pure and simple, that led the Muslims to embrace retreat in the battle of Hunain despite their great number (9:25).

Being honest with oneself – shunning pretension

Getting the *iman* right requires one to be thoroughly honest with oneself – in thinking and in expressing. Pretension is being dishonest with oneself or others. Pretension often springs from vanity and pride. The Quran condemns pretension or hypocrisy in strongest possible terms:

"Surely, the hypocrites are at the bottom of the fire" (4:145). Hypocrisy is a disease of the heart (47:29), and people of knowledge can identify the hypocrites by their marks (47:30). God renders the actions of the hypocrites vain (47:28). One needs to overcome all forms of pretension, including egotism and self-delusion in his or her feelings, thinking and expressions. One needs to shun pretension the way the celebrated eleventh/twelfth century Muslim thinker and philosopher al-Ghazali did. Once Ghazali suffered from his existential crisis because he was "'seeking leadership and fame' [...] [and] delighted in putting people down 'out of haughtiness and arrogance and being dazzled by his own endowment of skill in speech and thought and expression, and his quest of glory and high status.'" When he realized his pretensions, he shunned them and embarked on a spiritual course of self-rectification and self-purification.[153]

Pretension, hypocrisy, and treachery are similar vices. It is not for a prophet or a decent man to put up a false or unrealistic show, or behave like an imposter (38:86). Hypocrites show themselves as possessing two hearts, even though God did not endow anyone with two hearts (33:4). A hypocrite requires much greater effort to mend his conduct, and wash away his sin, as he deserves the worst of Hell fire (4:145-146). On treachery, God says that He does not love the treacherous (4:107; 22:38):

> **4:107**   And plead not on behalf of (those) who betray themselves. Verily God loveth not one who is treacherous and sinful.

Nurturing a positive attitude - getting rid of frustration, and increasing self-confidence

Recent surge of interest in the power of positive attitude and thinking, as evidenced by many books, lectures and courses on this subject, highlights the great importance that the nurturing of a positive attitude assumes. Such an attitude is conducive to one's progress and success in life. Its opposite – frustration – is a wrong attitude of mind – a blocking factor for progress. As noted in Chapter 2, frustration reflects an extreme form of dissatisfaction with one's own situation, performance, achievement or progress, but is a wrong way of looking at the result of one's own effort. Frustration is degrading to one's soul, as it implies complete lack of confidence in one's own self, i.e., in one's own capacity and power, and in one's potential, which, in other words, reflects lack of faith in God Himself. One needs, therefore, to get rid of frustration, and increase one's self-confidence. Frustration often results from one's indolence, ignorance, lack of work and effort, and lack of sufficient preparation for anything one needs to address or face. None needs to despair of better days ahead or of God's spirit (*ruh*) or mercy (39:53-54; 12:87). It is none but those who disbelieve in God despair of His mercy (12:87).

In this context, we need also to note that, as modern medical science has brought to our attention, frustration taking the form of depression may in many cases just be a medical condition – a mental disease. In such cases, mere advice does little to alleviate their problem. Like other illnesses, such depressive mental cases need to be medically treated with appropriate medicine coupled with other therapies, where necessary.[154]

Being moderate and considerate – getting rid of greed

One needs to be moderate in demeanor, and considerate to others. God commands moderation, not excesses (20:81). That means that one needs to avoid selfishness or greed. Greed is another wrong attitude that degrades the human soul. God characterizes greed as an ignoble trait of character of those who are on the wrong path (33:19; 68:13; 74:15). Man is ungrateful and too intense in love of wealth (100:6-8). This Quranic message about greed is conveyed also by what one writer said: "The lust of avarice has so totally seized upon mankind that their wealth seems rather to possess them, than they to possess wealth"[155]. It is this greed that man needs to get rid of. As mentioned before, the Quran cautions us against wrongfully craving others' property, against bribing judges to seek access to such property (2:188), and against approaching orphans' property except with the best of intentions (17): 34), and urges us to return their property, and not exchange the good for the bad, when they come to maturity (4:2).

> **4:2** And give unto orphans their wealth. Exchange not the good for the bad; nor devour their wealth (by mixing it up) into your wealth. For that would indeed be a great sin.

As noted earlier, the Quran strongly urges us to give right measure, condemns any form of cheating, and exploitation of others' property or labor (17:35; 26:181-183). Greed leads one to hoard wealth, and be stingy in spending in God's way. The Quran strongly condemns hoarding (3:180).

Indeed one need not only to shun greed, but also to spend in God's way out of what one earns. As noted in the preceding chapter, we need to submit ourselves completely to God, which means that we need to devote our body and mind, our thoughts, our prayer and devotions, and our material resources, if any, to the service of God. That implies that we need to spend out of what we earn in the way of God.[156]

Being tolerant – forsaking prejudice, intolerance and violence

The quality of being tolerant is part and parcel of the right *iman* and righteous conduct of a Muslim. The significance of tolerance should become evident, as we perceive the essential role of religion for man. As noted in Chapter 2, religion is for creation of an enabling and conducive environment for all men and women to pursue spiritual development, including supportive material development. In such an environment, there is a need for full respect for human dignity, and for equal treatment of all human beings irrespective of race, color, sex, language, religion, political or other opinion, national or social origin, property, birth or other similar status. In such a context, tolerance plays a very important role. It is various forms of prejudice and intolerance, religious or other, that lead to all kinds of discrimination – racism, racial discrimination, xenophobia, and related intolerance – in society, which in turn often manifests itself in, beside unjust discrimination, violent religious and ethnic conflicts, and inhuman and barbarous acts of oppression, murder and other atrocities.

Prejudice is a mean mentality. Prejudice is akin to – and leads to – intolerance. "To hate a man because he was born in another country, because he speaks a different language, or that he takes a different view on this subject or that, is a great folly."[157] Intolerance or prejudice based on race, color, sex, language, religion, political or other opinion, national or social origin, property, birth or other similar status does great harm to social harmony and development. Religion does not encourage prejudice. For example, it is wrong to say, as many seem to suggest, that Islam permits treating women as inferior to men. There is no basis for such thinking. Likewise, it can be concluded that there is no room for other kinds of prejudice in religion, since all that really matters for a man or a woman is righteousness (2:62; 5:69). Getting the *iman* right thus requires that one should get rid of all kinds of prejudice.

With the progress of human civilization and the end of the colonial era, man has made important advances towards tolerance. According to a recent United Nations report, the international community has made some notable progress in this direction in the recent past, including and starting from, the adoption of the Universal Declaration of Human Rights. Since then national and international laws have been enacted, and numerous international human rights instruments, including particularly a treaty to ban racial discrimination, have been adopted. Progress also includes the defeat of apartheid in South Africa.[158] Yet acts of intolerance, including acts of religious and ethnic violence, continue unabated, and slavery and slavery-like practices still exist in parts of the world. A further United Nations description of such problems is worth citing:

> Despite continuing efforts by the international community, racial discrimination, ethnic conflicts and widespread violence persist in various parts of the world. In recent years, the world has witnessed campaigns of 'ethnic cleansing'. Racial minorities, migrants, asylum seekers and indigenous peoples are persistent targets of intolerance. Millions of human beings continue to encounter discrimination solely due to the color of their skin or other factors that indicate the race to which they belong.[159]

The world remembers some dark episodes of history marked by appalling and barbarous acts of oppression, genocide and massive human displacements, which include the Christian Crusaders' massacre of unarmed Muslim men, women, and children, the Spanish inquisitors' torture and murder of non-Christians (mainly Muslims), the Christian settlers' systematic extermination of Native American peoples in North and South America, often aided by missionaries, and the twentieth century ghastly events of the Holocaust, the genocides in Turkey, Rwanda and Cambodia, and the ethnic cleansing in Bosnia, and this century's genocide and still continuing saga of human tragedies in the Darfur region of Sudan.[160] Also disconcertingly, religious intolerance manifesting itself in the emergence of hostile acts and violence against certain communities, notably against the Jewish, Muslim and Arab

184

communities, because of their religious beliefs and their racial or ethnic origin – outward expressions of what have nowadays come to be known as 'anti-Semitism' and 'Islamophobia' – is still continuing in various parts of the world, which in particular limit their right to freely practice their belief. As Akbar Ahmed notes, after September 11, there is evidence of a rising tide of Islamophobia in the West.[161] "Although the great civil rights battles of the 1960s ended segregation in the United States, the lot of black Americans is still a delicate and difficult issue."[162] One American Muslim writer notes that though Christianity has similar universal claims as those of Islam, and though segregation in the form of existence of churches exclusively for whites or blacks has been formally ended in America, "informal, habitual and perhaps ideological" segregation still persists, and "racial discrimination and segregation" on the basis of the color of the skin still remains to be completely eliminated.[163] Also, there are hate sites on the Internet promoting intolerance and xenophobia. All this is despite the fact that in recent years great awareness has been created, and some action-oriented measures have been taken at international and national levels to stem the tide of intolerance worldwide.[164]

Islam is a religion of peace, tolerance and compassion. Unfortunately, it is because of the activities of some extremist groups that Islam is being viewed by many as an intolerant and violent creed. All men and women are equal in the eyes of God; only virtuousness determines who is nearer to Him (3:195; 4:124; 16:97; 33:35). All the children of Adam – all men and women – deserve the same dignity:

> **17:70** And verily *We have bestowed honor on the children of Adam*; provided them with transport on land and sea; given them for sustenance things good and pure; and conferred on them special favors, above a great part of Our creation.

While racial discrimination, or that on the basis of color, has existed in its stark form well into the twentieth century in some parts of the world – notable examples: apartheid in South Africa, and segregation in the United States, and though some vestiges of such discrimination are still to be found, Islam never approved of such discrimination, and abolished it from its conception.

Although traditionally women have been treated as inferior to men among Muslims, Islam never approved of such discrimination. All are equal in the eyes of God; it is only virtuousness that counts – not sex (3:195; 49:13; 4:124; 16:97; 33:35). Also, man and woman can excel each other in various qualities (4:32).[165]

Nor is there any rationale for discrimination on the basis of any religion in name (2:62; 5:69). For that matter, no other reason, e.g., wealth or property, strength in manpower, or status or power in society, is of any value to God (9:55, 69; 10:58, 88-89; 28:76-81; 30:39; 34:37; 43:32-35; 111:2). Thus human rights abuses that are found to have been committed from time to time by governments or ethnic groups are objects that deserve strong condemnation from Islam. The Quran categorically forbids us to do any wrongs to others:

> **26:183** And wrong not men of their things (or rights), and act not corruptly in the earth, making mischief.

The Quran strongly exhorts us to uphold the cause of justice, if necessary by testifying against ourselves, parents, and relatives (4:135), and not to let the hatred (by implication, enmity or injustice) of others make us commit any injustice (5:8). This call for upholding justice is essentially a call for peace and tolerance as well. "When we achieve justice for all – women, men, black, white, yellow, brown, red, Muslim, non-Muslim – we make it possible to forge a lasting peace."[166] According to the Quran, human discrimination on the basis of wealth or manpower is also futile:

> **34:37** It is not your wealth, nor your sons, that will bring you nearer unto us in degree, but only those who believe and do good deeds.

The Quran unequivocally and emphatically proclaims that there must be no coercion in religion:

> **2:256** *There is no compulsion in religion. ...*
>
> **10:99** And had thy Lord willed, verily all who are on earth would have believed together. *Wouldst thou (O Muhammad) then force people until they become believers (muminin)?*

109:1-6   Say: 'O disbelievers! I serve neither which ye serve nor ye serve that which I serve. And I will not serve that which ye serve; nor will ye that which I serve. *Unto you your religion (din) and unto me my religion*

50:45   We are best aware of what they say, and *thou (O Muhammad) art in no way a compeller over them. ...* (See also 88:21-22)

Note also what the Prophet Noah said to his disbelieving people: "He said: O my people! What think ye? If I stand upon a clear sign from my Lord, and He hath given a mercy from Him, and it hath been obscured from you, *shall we compel you to it while ye are averse to it* (11:28)?" Thus "[r]eligion is, by definition, incompatible with coercion."[167]

Verse (10:99) above and other related verses in the Quran such as those at (49:13 cited earlier) that refer to the creation of mankind into diverse nations and tribes and at (5:48) that refers to different laws and ways being given by God to different peoples also explicitly recognize the diversity of people on earth and underscore the need for, and the importance of, inter-communal tolerance.

5:48   *For each of you We have prescribed a law and a way.* Had God willed, He could have made you one community, but that He may try you by that which He hath given you. So vie ye one with another in good deeds.

The Prophet Muhammad was advised by God to strictly maintain cordiality in his preaching; and he was advised not to revile those to whom other religious people pray beside God lest they should revile God through ignorance:

16:125   *Invite unto the Way of thy Lord with wisdom and fair exhortation; and argue with them in the best possible manner.* Thy Lord knoweth best who strayeth from His path, and He knoweth best who receiveth guidance. (See also 29:46)

73:10   And bear with (O Muhammad!) what they say, and *part from them in a nice manner.*

6:108   *Revile not those unto whom they pray beside God lest*
              they wrongfully revile God through ignorance.

Some Quranic verses explicitly exhort Muslims to turn way from those who are ignorant, disbelievers, or who engage in idle talks, wishing them *"salam"* or peace at the same time:

25:63   And the slaves of the Beneficent (God) are those who
              walk on the earth with modesty, and when the
              ignorant address them, *they say: Salam (Peace).*

28:55   And when they hear idle talk, they turn away from it
              and say: 'Unto us our deeds, and unto you yours;
              salam (peace) be on you; we seek not the ignorant'.

43:89   So turn away from them and *say: 'Salam (Peace)*, for
              they will (soon) come to know'.

Noted Islamic scholar Khaled Abou El Fadl points out that these verses "emphasize the need not just for interreligious tolerance, but for cooperative moral ventures that seek to achieve Godliness on earth."[168] The call for such cooperative moral ventures is also explicitly reflected in the following verse of the Quran:

3:64   Say: O People of the Book! *Come to an agreement*
              between us and you that we shall serve none but God;
              and (that) we shall associate no partners with Him;
              and (that) none of us shall take from among ourselves
              lords or patrons beside God. And if they turn away,
              then say: Bear witness that we are they who have
              submitted (unto Him).

The Prophet was urged to hold on to forgiveness and ignore the ignorant and thus to be tolerant to others even if they did not listen to his call (7:198-199). He was urged to grant refuge or protection to the Pagans, who were idolaters, if they sought such protection:

9:6   *If anyone amongst the Pagans asketh thee (O*
              Muhammad) for asylum, grant it to him, so that he
              may hear the Word of God, and then escort him to
              where he can be secure; that is because they are a
              folk who know not.

188

The Quran thus provides clear and unambiguous instructions to Muslims for tolerance of other faiths and views and advice to them to be helpful to non-Muslims in case they need help.

According to noted scholar on Islam John Esposito, "Despite the recent example of the Taliban in Afghanistan and sporadic conflicts between Muslims and Christians in Sudan, Nigeria, Pakistan, and Indonesia, theologically and historically Islam has a long record of tolerance." He further notes:

> Historically, while the early expansion and conquests spread Islamic rule, Muslims did not try to impose their religion on others or force them to convert. As "People of the Book," Jews and Christians were regarded as protected people (dhimmi), who were permitted to retain and practice their religions, be led by their own religious leaders, and be guided by their own religious laws and customs. For this protection, they paid a poll or head tax (zijya). While by modern standards this treatment amounted to second-class citizenship in premodern times, it was very advanced. No such tolerance existed in Christendom, where Jews, Muslims, and other Christians (those who did not accept the authority of the pope) were subjected to forced conversion, persecution, or expulsion. Although the Islamic ideal was not followed everywhere and at all times, it existed and flourished in many contexts.[169]

Also worthy of note, as many writers of Islam point out, is the historical example of the Prophet Muhammad setting a precedent of peaceful and cooperative inter-religious relations in Medina among Muslims, Christians and Jews.

This is, of course, not to deny or exonerate the regrettable history of internecine strife within the Muslim *ummah* (community) itself during Islam's early history after the Prophet's death, the multiple divisions that took place among Muslims despite the Quranic admonition against such divisions, and the continuing saga of intermittent clashes between Muslims on the one hand and Christians, Hindus and Jews on the other in various countries[170], and most importantly the heinous terrorist acts being conducted by extremist Muslim organizations such as the al Qaeda and other groups against innocent civilians in many countries. Esposito adds,

189

in recent years acts of intolerance among Muslim groups, and between Muslims and non-Muslim groups have rather increased due, in significant part, to a resurgence or revivalism of Islam [*albeit* in its orthodox form].[171] Minority religious groups in Muslim countries such as Christians in the Sudan, Pakistan and Nigeria, Christian Copts in Egypt, Hindus in Bangladesh, Bahais and Jews in Iran, and Ahmadiyas (followers of Ghulam Ahmad Qadiani) in Pakistan and Bangladesh are particularly vulnerable and are being subjected to humiliation, harassment, torture and killing. In Egypt, modern Muslim thinkers have been subjected to Wahhabi-instigated and often government-supported killing, torture, and harassment, including banning of their works. Recent notable examples are the stabbing and maiming of the Nobel Laureate Naguib Mahfouz, the assassination of the human rights defender Farag Foda, the arrest and incarceration of the Ibn Khaldun Center's head Saad Eddin Ibrahim, and of many of his colleagues, and the court ruling on the Cairo University Professor Nasr Abu Zayd as an apostate, which called for divorcing of his Muslim wife.[172] Al-Azhar University Professor Dr. Ahmad Mansour and his followers who follow the Quran only and reject the so-called Prophetic traditions also became victims of harassment, persecution, and torture at the hands of the Wahhabi followers in Egypt.[173] It is obvious the Quran strongly disapproves of such acts.

Also worthy of note is the fact that the tragic attacks of September 11, 2001 in the United States and subsequent terrorist acts of the extremist groups in several other countries such as Indonesia, Saudi Arabia, Turkey, Morocco, Spain, the United Kingdom, Egypt, Jordan, Iraq, India, Pakistan, Afghanistan, and Bangladesh have put the minority Muslims living in Western societies in a very delicate situation, which not only requires Muslims to revisit the tolerance issue in a new light, but which also puts a special responsibility on the shoulders of the governments of those societies to avoid intolerance and discriminatory treatment against Muslims. In the aftermath of the 9/11, there has been considerable backlash against Muslims in the United States and Europe. Contemporary American Muslim writer Muqtedar Khan notes that there have been "many nasty episodes" and surfacing of "large-scale anti-Muslim prejudice" in the United States, despite the call for tolerance by President George Bush and members of his staff.[174] Officially, Muslims, especially from the Arab and Muslim worlds, have been subjected to special scrutiny and discrimination at border crossings and airports. But such treatment may backfire. As one journalist writer has aptly commented, when members of a community are feeling they are being unfairly treated by the society they are part of, this has the inherent danger of engendering "resentment, alienation and, possibly antisocial conduct".[175] American Muslims are "vulnerable as never before."[176]

The Quran permits avenging any wrong done to a person in the like manner, but at the same time encourages patience and forgiveness in lieu of revenge, as forgiveness helps a person expiate his sin:

5:45   And We prescribed for them (the Children of Israel) therein (in the Torah): Life for life, and the eye for the eye, and the nose for the nose, and the ear for the ear, and the tooth for the tooth, and (like) retaliation for wounds; *but whoever forgoeth (forgiveth) it, it shall be expiation for him.* Whoever judge not by that which God hath revealed are wrongdoers.

42:40   *The recompense of an ill-deed is an ill the like thereof. But whoever forgiveth and mendeth (his own conduct), his reward is (ensured) from God;* verily (He) loveth not the wrongdoers.

16:126   If ye punish, then punish with the like of that wherewith ye were afflicted. *But if ye endure patiently, that is indeed the best for those who are patient.*

What could be a better appeal for tolerance? The Quran has urged similar patience, generosity, and forgiveness in several other verses (2:263; 3:134; 7:198-199; 42:43; 45:14). It is a well-known historical fact that the Prophet Muhammad set a glorious precedent of tolerance when he and the Muslims accompanying him triumphantly marched into Mecca in 630 A.D. without any significant bloodshed or harm to the inhabitants who had earlier fought with the Muslims. According to the Historian von Grunebaum, "The resistance of a small group of Quraish was quickly dispelled [...]. The revolution was effected remarkably leniently. [...] even the extremist leaders were shown mercy. Looting was forbidden [...]."[177] Such political and religious tolerance in the treatment of people who had been archenemies before has no parallel in history. It is indeed a great irony that we still find Sunnis and Shiites fighting and killing one another in countries inhabited by them, causing loss of many innocent lives and immense human misery and suffering.[178]

God considers human life sacred and forbids taking any life except by way of justice (6:151). He characterizes the killing of a human being without any legitimate reason as like the killing of all humankind, and the saving of a human being as like the saving of all humankind:

> **5:32** For that reason (because of the killing of one son of Adam by another for no good reason) We decreed for the Children of Israel that *whoever slayeth a soul for other than manslaughter or mischief in the land, it is as though he slayeth all humankind; and whoever saveth the life of one, it is as though he saveth the life of all humankind.*

Some misgivings about Islam are circulated by some circles, including those who engage in maligning Islam, citing some Quranic texts out of context. Some examples are as follows:

> **2:191** And slay them wherever ye find them.
>
> **9:5** When the sacred months have passed, slay the idolaters wherever you find them, and take them, and confine them, and lie in wait for them at every place of ambush.
>
> **9:29** Fight those who believe not in God or the Last Day, nor hold that forbidden which hath been forbidden by God and His Apostle, nor hold the religion of truth of the People of the Book.

However, if we take the full verses and the full context into account, it becomes quite clear that the Quran does not unnecessarily encourage violence and killing, and that such slaying or fighting is sensible only when Muslims are at war with a non-Muslim group. Look at the full verses along with the context in which they were revealed:

> **2: 190-3** Fight in the way of God against those who fight against you, but *initiate not aggression. Verily God loveth not aggressors.* And slay them wherever ye find them, and drive them out of the places

192

wherefrom they drove you out, for *persecution is worse than slaughter*. And fight not with them at the Sacred Mosque until they first attack you there, but if they attack you (there), then slay them. Such is the reward of disbelievers. *But if they desist, then verily God is Ever Forgiving, Most Merciful. And fight them until there is no more persecution, and religion is for God. But if they desist, let there be no hostility except against the wrongdoers.*

9:5 When the sacred months have passed, slay the idolaters wherever you find them, and take them, and confine them, and lie in wait for them at every place of ambush. *But if they repent and establish worship and pay the zakat, then leave their way fre*e, for God is Ever Forgiving and Most Merciful.

9:29 Fight those who believe not in God or the Last Day, nor hold that forbidden which hath been forbidden by God and His Apostle, nor hold the religion of truth of the People of the Book *until they pay zijya (the poll tax)* with willing submission, and feel themselves subdued.

These and similar verses require Muslims to incline towards peace and take no action against their opponents when they offer to make peace with the Muslims (See also 4:90; 8:61-62). While enjoining fighting on believers even though they may dislike it, and at the same time characterizing it as a grave evil during the forbidden month, the Quran still considers it necessary during that month if it is required to end oppression and injustice (2:216-217). However, the Quran never encourages aggressive wars, but allows fighting only for self-defense (2:190-193, 256; 4:91; and 60:8-9). Note also that the verse (9:5) is followed by another verse, which exhorts the Prophet Muhammad to provide protection or asylum to idolaters who seek such protection (9:6). The verse (9:29) is also followed by a statement that says "until they pay the poll tax." Critics point out, however, that the idea of a special poll tax to be paid by disbelievers living in a Muslim territory to the Muslim rulers is in itself a form of religious discrimination and intolerance. However, as Abou El Fadl points out, such a levy should be understood in a historical context when "it was common inside and outside of Arabia to levy poll taxes against alien groups." The tax was in return for protection of the disbelievers. He cites the example of a case of return of the poll tax by the second Caliph Umar to an Arab Christian tribe when it could not be protected from Byzantine aggression. During Umar's time, he allowed the Christian tribes to pay *zakah* instead of the *zijya* that they regarded as degrading. Abou El Fadl further notes that the Prophet Muhammad did not collect the poll tax from all non-Muslim tribes, and he in fact paid periodic sums of money or goods to many non-hostile non-Muslim tribes. "In short," he further notes, "there are various indicators that the poll tax is not a theologically mandated practice, but a functional solution that was adopted as a response to a particular set of historical circumstances. Only an entirely ahistorical reading of the text could conclude that it is an essential element in a divinely sanctioned program of subordinating the nonbeliever."[179]

Prominent Turkish-American scholar Edip Yuksel, in addition to the verses cited above (2:191; 9:5, 29), refers to also other verses of the Quran, which are abused by uninformed critics and enemies of Islam to portray Islam as a religion of violence, war, and terror: 3:28, 85; 5:10, 34; 9:28, 123; 14:17; 22:9; 25:52; 47:4 and 66:9. In his Reformist Translation of the Quran as well as in his new book *Peacemaker's Guide to Warmongers: Exposing Robert Spencer, David Horowitz, and Other Enemies of Peace*, he discusses these verses to effectively refute the contentions of the critics of Islam. He aptly notes:

> The Quran does not promote war; but encourages us to stand against aggressors on the side of justice. War is permitted only for self-defense (See 2:190, 192, 193, 256; 4:91; 5:32; 8:19; 60:7-9). We are encouraged to work hard to establish peace (47:35; 8:56-61; 2:208). The Quranic precept of promoting peace and justice is so fundamental that peace treaty with the enemy is preferred to religious ties (8:72).[180]

Also importantly, the above-mentioned verses should be understood only in the context of a war situation where Muslims are urged to fight only for defensive purposes, i.e., to fight against only those who fight with the Muslims, and not to initiate aggression, as God does not love the aggressors. Indeed, as Karen Armstrong aptly notes,

> During the ten years between the *hijra* and his death in 632 Muhammad and his first Muslims were engaged in a desperate

struggle for survival against his opponents in Medina and the Quraysh of Mecca, all of whom were ready to exterminate the *ummah*. In the West, Muhammad has often been presented as a warlord, who imposed Islam on a reluctant world by force of arms. *The reality was quite different; Muhammad was fighting for his life, was evolving a theology of the just war in the Koran with which most Christians would agree, and never forced anybody to convert to religion.* Indeed the Koran is clear that there is to be 'no compulsion in religion.' In the Koran war is held to be abhorrent; the only just war is a war of self-defense. Sometimes it is necessary to fight in order to preserve decent values, as Christians believed it necessary to fight against Hitler.[181]

In some verses, the Quran clearly advises the Muslims fighting non-Muslims to opt for peace when the enemies want peace, and not to worry about the possibility that the enemies may deceive them thereby:

8:61-2   And *if they (the enemies fighting you) incline to peace, then incline to it,* and trust in God, for verily He is Hearing, Knowing. And *if they intend to deceive you, then verily God is sufficient for you.* He it is Who strengthened you with His help and with the believers.

How clear are these verses! God forbids us to begin aggression, and exhorts the fighting Muslims to desist from fighting with the disbelievers when they cease hostilities and persecution, and seek peace. And the Quran strongly condemns persecution, as it characterizes persecution as worse than slaughter (2:217). Also note that God authorizes us to attack others in the like manner as the others attack (2:194; 22:60). As noted above, the Quran rather encourages us, where possible, to condone and forgive, which is considered still better (5:45; 7:198-199; 42:40, 43; 45:14, 73:10). Thus far from encouraging intolerance, the Quran clearly advocates peace, tolerance, and peaceful and compassionate co-existence.

Also note that, citing some Quranic verse, some allege that Islam discourages Muslims from making friends with the people of other religions. Again, this is another classic example of misgivings based on the citation of a Quranic verse out of context. The Quran does not

195

discourage making friends with the people of other religions unless such people can be identified as real foes. Note the following verses:

60:7-9 It may be that God will ordain love between you and those of them with whom ye are at enmity. God is All-Powerful, and God is Ever Forgiving, Most Merciful. God forbiddeth you not those who fought not against you on account of your religion, and drove you not out from your homes, that ye show them kindness and deal justly with them. Verily God loveth the just dealers. God forbiddeth you only those who fought against you on account of your religion and have driven you out from your homes and helped to drive you out, that ye make friends of them. Whoever maketh friends of them are wrongdoers.

These verses make it amply clear that making friendship with people of other religions is possible within Islam unless such people have proved themselves to be enemies of Muslims. Also, the Quran unequivocally forbids and denounces any acts of mischief, violence, or terrorism:

7:56 And do not make mischief in the earth, after it hath been set in order. ... (See also 7:74; and 13:25)

26:183 And wrong not humankind of their right things (of rights), and do no evil, making mischief in the earth. (See also 47:22-23)

From the foregoing discussion it is clear that, far from encouraging violence and terrorism, Islam advocates peace, tolerance, and peaceful co-existence with other religious communities. Hence being tolerant to others is an important part of righteousness. Note, however, that it is the Hadith literature that contains many texts, which misguide Muslims and lead them to commit violent and other acts of intolerance against other religious groups. However, a proper understanding of Islam must dismiss such Hadith texts as not representing Islam.[182]

Being brave - getting rid of cowardice, fear and servile mentality

Cowardice is a debilitating vice for a man. A coward compromises principles and undermines his soul, which retards his spiritual development. Confucius rightly said: "To see what is right, and not to do it is want of courage."[183] Shakespeare said:

> Cowards die many times before their death,
> The valiant never taste of death but once.[184]

To effectively handle many situations faced in life, one needs to have sufficient courage, or to get rid of undue fear. Fear is a great enemy of man. Undue fear cripples a man in his pursuit for progress, whether material or spiritual. British political thinker Edmund Burke said: "No passion so effectually robs the mind of all its powers of acting and reasoning as fear."[185] President Franklin D. Roosevelt of the United States once said: "Let me assert my firm belief that the only thing we have to fear is fear itself; nameless, unreasoning, unjustified terror which paralyzes needed efforts to convert retreat into advance."[186] True believers need not be cowards, as they have nothing to fear. God admonished the Prophet Moses not to fear Pharaoh's sorcerers, and he was assured that he would overcome the sorcerers: "Fear not, for thou hast indeed the upper hand" (20:68). God reprimanded those who did not leave their homes to join the Prophet and his people to fight against the attacking infidels; they were either cowards or wicked people (4:77-78; 48:11-12).

God-loving, well-meaning, righteous, and knowledgeable people have no reason to fear anything. They indeed live in the heavenly state, where no fear or grief afflicts them (2:38, 62, 112, 262, 274; 5:69; 6:48; 10:62; 43:68; 46:13). Fear comes from devilish thoughts and activities:

3:175   *It is only the devil (Satan) who would make (people) fear his partisans.* Fear them not; fear Me if ye are true believers.

3:73   Those (believers) unto whom the people said: *'Verily a great army (of men) has gathered against you; so fear them.' But this (only) increased their faith, and they said: 'God is sufficient for us!* And Most Excellent He is as Protector.'

197

42:22   *Thou seest the wrong-doers in fear on account of what they have earned, and it will indeed befall them.* But those who believe and do good deeds (will be) in the Meadows of the Gardens, and will have all that they wish from their Lord. This is the great grace.

God's prophets were the most dauntless advocates of His message to mankind in the face of stiff opposition by the established elite groups in society, and amid all kinds of obstructions, and trials and tribulations (33:39). They had to fearlessly confront those vested interest groups who were opposed to change for the better. A small army of King Saul fearlessly fought with, and routed, a large army of Goliath, who was killed by (the prophet-soldier and later king) David. God describes such incidents as repelling the bad elements by means of the good ones. This has been a divine process throughout history, and if this had not been the case, the world would have remained a corrupt place to live in.

2:251   And *if God had not repelled some men by others, the earth would have been corrupted.* But God is the Lord of Kindness to (His) creatures.

True believers of God do not have to fear the criticism of others (5:54). The Prophet Muhammad was admonished by God that he should fear Him rather than what people around him would think and say (33:37). God has warned us against fearing people rather than Him (4:77). In fact we need not fear anything. As noted earlier, it is neither the fear of Hell nor the lure of Heaven that should really drive us to do good deeds and strive for spiritual development, although as doers of right deeds we need to be conscious that the outcome of such deeds must in the end be good.

There are men who show that they are doing some good deeds just to be seen by other people, which is due to a kind of fear of men. Such men are not really righteous. For them neither the fear of men nor their doing of the seemingly good deeds is of any avail (107:4-7; 4:38, 108-109, 142; 8:47).

Being courageous also implies shunning a slavish or servile mentality. Exiled Egyptian writer Ahmed Mansour illustrates this by taking examples from his own country: servile mentality takes such forms as "flattering a tyrant, yielding to him, accepting his injustices, or putting up with his nonsense." It is a pity that it is because of a culture of servile mentality that tortures suffered by ordinary citizens and intellectual thinkers who are prisoners of conscience are often tolerated by the people. This in turn helps to perpetuate a culture of servile mentality in Egypt and the Middle East.[187] What Ahmed Mansour notes about his own country and the Middle East is also true of many other Muslim countries. There are copious examples of the voices of Muslims offering progressive ideas being gagged and suppressed, and their books prohibited in Muslim countries, and they are tortured and victimized in various ways. There are people in these countries who passively or actively support such torture and oppression, and they do it because of a servile mentality they suffer from. The sooner they can get rid of this culture of servile mentality the sooner these countries can get out of a vicious atmosphere of cultural and religious fanaticism, extremism and degradation. Muslims can think and write more freely in Western countries than in Muslim countries. This suggests that it is the Muslim countries that follow less the Islamic values and principles of tolerance, understanding and compassion than the Western world.

Harboring other right feelings and good thoughts – avoiding other wrong feelings and evil thoughts, and developing the right attitude

There are several other wrong feelings or attitudes of mind that one needs to avoid such as hatred or malice, jealousy, suspicion, anger, etc. We may touch on these attitudes below.

Having no hatred or malice. The Quran describes Heaven or the heavenly state as one where there is, among other things, no hatred or malice, but only feelings of brotherhood or love in the hearts of the dwellers (7:43, 15:47). The new converts to Islam removed from their heart their old hatred to the earlier believers (59:10). God warns us not to do injustice to any people out of hatred (5:2, 8):

> **5:8**　　And *let not the hatred of a people make you commit wrong and depart from justice.* Be just; that is nearer to piety.

God warns us not to take as friends those people who nurture hatred (3:118). The devil or devilish activities give rise to feelings of enmity and hatred (3:91). Feelings of enmity and hatred behoove only those people who neglect their right duties, and have gone astray (3:64; 10:90-91). It is they who grieve at others' fortune and rejoice at others' misfortune (3:120). Indeed our efforts to transform a hellish state into a heavenly one will succeed only when we remove feelings of hatred, malice, and animosity from our minds towards others. That means that we cannot make progress on the spiritual front unless we remove rancor and ill feelings toward others, and develop a feeling of goodwill and love towards others.

Having no jealousy. Envy or jealousy is akin to vanity or pride, and is in a way the other side of the same coin. Jealousy is one's unduly coveting the things in which God has made some to excel others, or one's feeling of discomfort at others' superiority or advantage in some respect. It thus includes ill will for others. The Quran states:

> **4:32**   And covet not the thing in which God hath made some of you excel others.

Instead of admiring, or taking inspiration from, another's superiority, the jealous person wishes ill of him, which is a wrong attitude. Such a person feels bad at others' fortune and good at others' misfortune. By being jealous, one blocks the door of spiritual progress for himself or herself. Jealousy in its naked form often leads one to commit wrong deeds and serious crimes. The Prophet Joseph's brothers did not like that he should be loved more by their father, and this jealousy led them to throw infant Joseph into a pit (12:8-9, 15). Jealousy makes one blind to see that another person can be superior, and can bring a higher truth. Such jealousy led many in the past to become disbelievers in a new religion brought by a prophet, or to differ on matters of religion, and be divided into different groups (45:17). It is also out of jealousy of one another that Muslims have also become divided into different sects, despite God's clear directive to the contrary (3:103, 105).

Not having too much suspicion. Suspecting something, which is not really true, is a manifestation of one's ignorance, meanness or malevolent attitude. Nothing could perhaps be more embarrassing to one than suspecting a friend to be a foe, or to misunderstand him. God has strongly warned us against too much suspicion, spying and backbiting. And suspicion taking the form of slander is a grave sin in the eye of God:

49:12   O ye who believe! *Avoid much suspicion; for verily suspicion in some cases is a sin.* And spy not; nor speak ill of one another behind their backs. Would one of you like to eat the flesh of your dead brother? Ye abhor that. So be careful of (your duty to) God.

24:23   Verily those who slander chaste believing women, (who are) careless, they are cursed in this world and the Hereafter. Theirs will be a terrible punishment.

God's curse for the slanderers is also mentioned in verse (104:1). Referring to a slander surrounding an incident involving one of the Prophet Muhammad's wives, the Quran described the slanderers as a party existing among humankind, and the slander as a grave sin, and scolded the believing men and women who did not properly respond to this slander ((24:11-18).

Restraining anger. Anger often leads one to forget sanity. It can damage a noble cause. "Anger is a sort of madness and the noblest causes have been damaged by advocates affected by temporary lunacy."[188] The Prophet Muhammad was of a very gentle nature. He was advised by God to be not too severe in conduct with men, a conduct that may encourage people to disperse from around him:

3:159   It is due to the Mercy of God that thou dost deal gently with them. Hadst thou been severe and hard-hearted, they would have dispersed from around thee. So pardon them and ask for forgiveness of them and consult with them on the conduct of affairs.

The Quran describes the righteous believers as those who restrain anger, and become generous and forgiving to mankind:

3:134   (Righteous are) those who spend (of that which God hath bestowed on them) in ease and in adversity, *those who restrain (their) anger, and are forgiving toward mankind*; God loveth the good.

An attitude of magnanimity towards others does help one control one's rage. God rewards those who depend on their Lord, keep away from great sins and indecencies, and forgive even when they feel angry (42:36-37). God removes rage from the hearts of the believers (9:14-15).

Other feelings or thoughts. There are still other good feelings or thoughts, or bad ones. Some of the good feelings include those of love, independence, contentment, and gratitude or appreciation. We may touch on these very briefly.

As explained in Chapter 4, developing *love* is critical to one's progress on the spiritual front. One needs to develop love and devotion to God. At the same time, however, love of God should translate into love of humanity. Serving God really means serving humanity in the same way as God serves humanity. So love and goodwill for others should be the hallmark of a good believer's *iman*. Spiritually developed people in turn are full of love for God, which translates into love for humanity. The Prophet Muhammad was full of love and concern for his people (9:128). He was closer to the believers than the believers themselves were to one another (33:6). He blessed the believers, as he was asked by God to pray for them (3:159, 47:19).

A man's goal in life should be *self-reliance* or *independence*, though at birth and during childhood and formative years, he needs to be brought up, supported, and nourished by others. Independence is a godly quality (35:15; 47:38; 3:97). It is hardly becoming of a man to seek others' help to do a thing, if he can do it himself. If a person is serious about his or her material or spiritual progress in life, he or she needs to cultivate an attitude of independence from others. This would amount to emulating God Who is independent. This should not, however, be interpreted to mean that we are not indirectly dependent on others' work and help all the time. This indirect dependence is unavoidable, as all in society are interdependent in some way or other. The independence we need is that from seeking unilateral help from others without a *quid pro quo*, i.e., which amounts to begging. Dependence in the form of begging is a curse, and degrading to human soul. A real seeker of spiritual enlightenment detests begging from others. A spirit of give and take best promotes human relationship as well as human dignity.

Indeed one's mission in life should be to give more rather than to take more. If everybody in society aims at doing, and sincerely tries to do, just that, society cannot remain poor, but becomes rich in all respects. It was prophets who neither craved, nor needed, any remuneration for the great contribution they made to humanity, for which humanity must remain deeply indebted to them for ever (6:90; 10:72; 11:29, 51; 12:104; 23:72; 25:57; 26:109, 127, 145, 164, 180; 34:47; 38:86; 42:23; 52:40; 68:46). In fact God wants us to follow only those who do not ask for any remuneration (36:21). If the prophets asked anything of the people, that asking was only for the people themselves (25:57; 34:47). At the same time, trying to be self-reliant should not be interpreted to mean that one should not try to benefit from others who are superior in knowledge and guidance, and who are always ready to share their knowledge and guidance.

Feelings of *contentment, gratitude* and *appreciation* are good virtues. One needs to be contented with what one has, or with one gets. Gratitude springs from contentment. Whoever is grateful to God for all that he gets or enjoys in life is grateful for his own soul, i.e., for his own spiritual benefit (31:12). God loves the grateful (39:7). He gives more to people who are grateful to Him (14:7). God does not like the unfaithful and the ungrateful (2:276; 22:38). This also does imply that a person needs to show proper recognition or appreciation of others' work, which is essentially expressing gratitude to God.

CONCLUSION

It should be apparent from the foregoing discussion that getting the *iman* right on a Muslim's part involves much more than just professing faith in God and His Messenger Muhammad, which the *ulama* seem to suggest. To become good Muslims, we need to have a good mindset, entertain the right kinds of metaphysical beliefs and attitudes that foster our spiritual and supportive material development. The Quran well expounds those qualities that a man needs to develop. It is indeed a pitiable sight that Muslims are found to engage in bitter internecine and sectarian suspicion, animosity, violence, and killing in various parts of the world. One shudders to think how Sunni and Shiite Muslims are killing one another on an alarming scale in Iraq! The brotherhood of amity and love that once characterized the Muslim *ummah* has long been found missing among Muslims. They have forgotten, and are not paying enough attention to, the clear, invaluable message of their Holy Book, the Quran.

VIII. RIGHTEOUSNESS IN LIGHT OF THE QURAN: GETTING OUR ACTIONS RIGHT

... Verily the most honorable in the sight of God is the most righteous. ... – 49:13

And *who is better in speech than he who invites (men) unto God, while he himself does right,* and says: 'I am surely of those who submit (to God)?' – 41:33

Verily, those who believe, and those who are Jews, and Christians, or Sabians (Middle East groups traditionally recognized as having a monotheistic orientation), *whoever believeth in God and the Last Day, and do right deeds – surely their reward is with their Lord, and there shall no fear come upon them, nor shall they grieve.* – 5:69

The Quran contains many verses describing what constitute righteous deeds. The following verse details some of such deeds:

2:177 It is not righteousness that ye turn your faces to the East or the West; but righteousness is that one should *believe in God and the Last Day and the angels and the Book and the Prophets,* and *give away wealth,* out of love of God, *to relatives and the orphans and the needy and the wayfarers and to those who ask, and to free slaves,* and *establish prayer* and pay the *zakat* (poor-due)115; and the *keepers of promise,* if they make one, and the *patient in distress and affliction and in times of conflicts.* These are they who are sincere and who are righteous.

Chapters 3-6 discussed various elements involved in spiritual evolution, and needed religious practices such as prayer, fasting, pilgrimage, and spending for poor and needy people and deserving causes. The preceding chapter dealt with desirable beliefs and attitudes. Here we concern ourselves mostly with the moral and ethical codes.

Being truthful, honest, just and kind

Islam teaches us the fundamental moral values of truthfulness, honesty, justice, and kindness. God represents the Truth (18:44; 24:25); and He always says what is true (4:87, 122). He does not make vain promises (2:80; 30:6); and none is more faithful to his promise than God is to His own (9:111). The true servants of God cannot but be truthful as well. They always keep their word (2:177; 3:17; 13:20; 33:23). God advises us to be correct or straightforward in our words (33:70), to establish and uphold justice, and not hesitate to testify truthfully even against ourselves, and our parents and relatives, whether they be rich or poor (4:135), and to never mix truth with falsehood, nor conceal the truth (2:26). God admonishes us to be with, or to stand for, those who are truthful (9:119). We need to make firm pledges of allegiance and support to those of us who want to do us some good, and God urges and blesses such pledges of allegiance and support (48:10, 18). He wants us to keep our firm pledges when we make them (16:91). He wants us to restore trusts to their owners, and judge justly between people (4:58). He curses those who, among other things, break their promise after confirming it, and make mischief in the land (13:25). Various verses containing these admonitions are worth citing:

4:135   O ye who believe! *Be ye staunch in justice; be witnesses for God, even though it (the testimony) be against yourselves or (your) parents or (your) near relatives, whether (the case be of) a rich man or a poor man.* God is nearer unto them both. So follow not (your) low desires, lest ye lapse (from truth) and if ye lapse or turn aside, then verily God is well aware of what ye do.

6:152   *When ye speak be just, even if it be (against) a relative*; and fulfill the covenant of God. This He hath commanded you that haply ye may remember.

33:70   O ye who believe! Guard your duty to God, and *speak straight to the point.*

2:26 *Mix not truth with falsehood, nor knowingly conceal the truth.*

9:119 O ye who believe! Be ye careful of (your duty to) God, and *be with the truthful.*

16:91 *Fulfill the covenant of God when ye have made a covenant, and break not your oaths when ye have made them firm;* ye have indeed made God your surety; for verily God knoweth all that ye do.

4:58 *Verily God commandeth you to restore trusts to their owners, and that when ye judge between people, ye judge justly.* Verily God admonisheth you with what is excellent. Verily God is Ever Hearer, Seer.

Only true words are meaningful. Indeed we really express or correctly represent ourselves when we are honest to ourselves, as God has not given us two hearts (33:4). By lying we not only deceive others, we also deceive ourselves. Thereby we undermine the value of our words, and lose our credibility. That way we degrade and lose our own self, and lose the right to command love and respect of others. Falsehood and dishonesty carry the germs of all kinds of injustice, mischief, and corruption. It is a great pity and travesty of religion that we find people galore who appear as religious, yet who do not even slightly hesitate to tell lies, who are not straightforward in their talk, and who are basically dishonest. They are obviously not truly religious. Dishonesty may manifest itself in various forms: insincere speech, insincere work, deliberate misinformation, deliberate improper judgment, and deception, and corruption of all kinds. Corruption has been rampant in many developing countries, including Muslim countries, and has in recent time been a subject of attention, since it has been a significant drag on the economic and social development of such countries.[189]

While we need generally to keep our promises, at the same time we should not make our unjust or unjustifiable promises a barrier for doing good, or make them for deceiving others. The Quran warns:

16:94 *Make not your oaths a device of deceit between you,* lest a foot should slip after being firmly planted; and ye should taste evil because ye debarred (men) from the path of God, and yours will be a grievous punishment.

At the same time we should note that words need to be not only true but also good. God likens a good word to a good tree with a firm root and good branches giving fruit in every season (14:24-25). A very good test of an honest, righteous person is whether or not he wrongfully and deliberately deprives others of their wealth, and whether he takes particular care of the property of an orphan or, by implication, of that of a disadvantaged person, and whether he returns that property fully, after just adjustment for maintenance costs if necessary for his trusteeship, to the orphan when he or she becomes a responsible adult, or attains maturity in understanding, or to the disadvantaged person when his or her disadvantage is gone. The Quran forbids wrongfully devouring others' property and willful bribing of judges in order to grab others' property (2:188). It condemns unjust grabbing of orphans' property in particularly strong terms, and likens this to swallowing of fire into one's bodies (4:10). It admonishes man not to go near to orphans' property except with good intentions (17:34), and to manage their property with fairness, and restore such property to them when they become adults or attain understanding (4:5-6). The Quran proclaims:

2:188   And *devour not each other's property among yourselves wrongfully*, nor seek to gain access to that by bribing judges so that you devour a part of the property of men wrongfully while ye know.

4:10   Those who devour the wealth of orphans wrongfully, verily they do but swallow fire into their own bodies, and they will (soon) enter a burning Fire. (See also 17:34)

4:5-6   And give not unto those (orphans) weak in understanding your (maintained) properties that God hath entrusted with you to maintain; but feed and clothe them from it, and speak to them kindly. And check the orphans for their puberty. And if ye find them of sound judgment, restore unto them their property. Devour it not extravagantly in a hurry, lest they should grow up. If the guardian is well-off, let him   refrain   generously   (from   taking   any remuneration from the orphans' property), but if he is poor, let him have thereof for himself what is just and reasonable. At the time ye return them their properties, call witnesses in their presence. And God sufficeth as a Reckoner.

4:2 And *give back unto the orphans their wealth. Substitute not (your) worthless things for (their) good ones, nor devour their property (by mixing up) with your property.* Verily that would be a great sin.

The Quran testifies that among the People of the Book (the Jews and the Christians), there are such honest people as can be trusted with a heap of treasure, while there are others who cannot be trusted even with a single coin; they will not return it unless one is after them. They do so mistakenly thinking that they have no duty to the gentiles. They have no such warrant from God, and they knowingly lie concerning God (3:75). This verse is a pointer to Muslims that there are good and honest people in other communities as well, and that Muslims also have no warrant from God to think that they have no duty to other communities, or to brand all people of other communities as untrustworthy.

God is Just (39:75; 40:20) and Beneficent, Merciful and Kind, and He enjoins upon humankind justice, fairness or equity, and kindness in all of our actions and behavior, including business deals (16:90, 76; 5:8; 42:41-42; 2:188; 17:34; 49:9; 4,127, 135; 58; 55:9; 60:8; 65:2). The Quran requires us to forget hatred that others may have for us (or, by implication, hatred that we may have for others) to dispense proper justice. God exhorts us to give the right measure, and not to deceive or exploit others. In short, in Islam we have the basic ingredients of a just, equitable and exploitation-free economic and social system.[190] A just and decent person cannot think of doing any harm to others. Deceiving others amounts to deceiving God and His believing servants; and the Quran characterizes such deceiving as deceiving one's own self (2:9). The hypocrites do not hesitate to commit perjury – lie or deceive even under oaths, but by doing so they surely incur a great evil for them (63:1-2).

16:90 Verily God *enjoineth (on you) the doing of justice, and the doing of good* (to others).

5:8 O ye who believe! *Be steadfast as witnesses for God with justice, and let not malice of any people (toward*

208

you) induce you to depart from justice. Deal justly, that is nearer to piety, and be careful (of your duty) to God. Verily God is aware of what ye do. (See also 26:181–183)

We also need to be kind, patient and forgiving (2:263; 3:134; 7:198-199; 42:43; 45:14). God wants us to be kind, generous, and forgiving as far as possible, even when we can legitimately take revenge for any wrongs done to us (5:45; 42:40). We need to be good and kind to our parents, relatives, orphans, the poor and the needy, the neighbors – whether relatives or strangers, fellow-travelers and the wayfarers, and the slaves (4:36; 6:151; 17:23-24; 2:83, 215; 4:36; 19:14, 32; 29:8; 31:14-15; 46:15; 71:28), and need to speak kindly to humankind (2:83). We have a special duty to our parents. Indeed God wants us not to say even "Fie" to them, or to show any indication of annoyance with them. Man generally gives preference to his own children over his parents. But the Quran says:

4:11   Your parent or your children: Ye know not which of them is nearer unto you in usefulness. (See also 46:15)

17:23-4   Thy Lord hath commanded that ye worship none but Him, (that ye show) kindness to your parents. If one of them or both attain old age in thy life, *say not 'Fie' unto them nor repulse them, but speak unto them a gracious word.* And lower your wing of humility unto them through mercy, and say: 'My Lord! Have mercy on them both as they did care for me while I was young.

Parents, however, must not be obeyed if they misguide, and insist on associating partners with God; yet we need to treat them – live with them - with kindness (31:15).

No piety without giving

This topic – spending in God's way – has been covered at some length in Chapter 6. Here some brief notes are in order.

In numerous places, the Quran emphasizes the virtues of spending in God's way, and characterizes the act of such spending as part-and-parcel of righteousness (See in particular 3:92 cited earlier, and 2:177 and 3:134). A spirit of give-and-take best promotes human relationship as well as human dignity. And our mission should be aimed at giving more rather than at taking more. God's Prophets gave more to humanity in the form of spiritual knowledge than they took from them in spiritual or material resources (6:90; 10:72 and many other verses). Indeed, society's progress can be best advanced not only with a widespread dissemination of spiritual, educational, and technological knowledge, but also with an equitable distribution of material resources. Indeed most often, a crucial test of whether a person is good or kind to another person is whether or not, and if so, to what extent, he is helping the other person in some material way. God is not kind to those who neglect spending for the poor and the helpless (107:1-7). The Quran emphasizes spending in God's way as a greatly virtuous act (See 90:12-18 and 2:261 cited earlier, and 2:265). God says that those who contend that they are not required to spend on others, and say "if God willed He could have provided for all", are in flagrant error (See 36:47 cited earlier). We need to spend on the poor and the needy, parents and near relatives, orphans, wayfarers, for relieving the burden of debt of heavily indebted persons (See 9:60 cited earlier), and for miscellaneous other noble purposes, which can be termed as causes of God. We need also to spend on those in need who are unable to move through the land, and who do not beg importunately.

God advises those of us who are affluent that we should not make promises not to help our relatives, poor people, and those who leave their homes for the cause of God; and we are urged to forgive them and ignore their faults (24:22). He loves those who spend not only when they are in affluence or ease, but also when they are in hardship (3:134). He admonishes us to give others what is good, and not what we regard as bad and do not want to receive for ourselves (2:267). The curse of God or dire punishment is in store for those who are stingy in spending (33:19; 92:8-10). At the same time, one needs to note that kind words and compassion are better than charity with an insult or injury; and a person should not nullify the virtues of his charitable actions by reminders or reproach or injury, or with a grudge (2:262-264; 9:54). There is virtue in one's spending in God's way, whether it is done publicly or secretly, but doing such charitable acts secretly is more virtuous than doing them publicly or with publicity; spending secretly atones for some of the giver's ill-deeds (2:271). On the other hand, God does not love the extravagant, i.e. those who spend on wasteful purposes (7:31; 6:141; 17:26-27). The extravagant are brothers of the devil (17:26-27). The Quran is forthright on these points:

2:271-3 If ye do deeds of charity (*sadaqa*) openly, it will be good; but if ye bestow it upon the needy in secret, it will be even better for you, and it will atone for some of your bad deeds. ... *Whatever good things ye spend is for the good of your self (nafs)*, when ye do it seeking God's countenance. Whatever you spend out of goodness will be retuned to you, and you will not be wronged. *It is for those in need, who are constrained in the cause of God, unable to move about in the land seeking (work or trade).* The ignorant think, because of their modesty, that they are free from want. Thou wilt know them by their mark; they beg not importunately from all and sundry. And whatever good ye give, verily God knoweth it well. (See also 3:134)

24:22 And *let not those among you who have dignity and abundance of means swear against helping their near kinsmen, and those in want, and those who have left their homes in the cause of God.* ...

47:38 Verily ye are those who are called upon to spend in the way of God; but among you are those who are miserly. *But any who are miserly are so at the expense of their own souls (nafs).* ...

17:26-7 And give unto the kinsfolk his due, and (to) the needy and the wayfarer; but *squander not (thy wealth) wastefully. Verily the squanderers are the brothers of the devil*; and the devil is ever ungrateful to God.

These verses relating to spending in God's way amply suggest that the Quranic admonitions are quite elaborate for the benefit of humankind! As mentioned in Chapter 6, the implications for spending in God's cause mean that the scope of such spending goes well beyond the confines of a narrowly defined and generally understood *zakat* or *sadaqa* (charity) system, and includes spending on a lot of the functions of a modern state, which are to be financed by a well-devised taxation system. In fact, the

211

modern state should take on its shoulders a lot of the share of the burden of providing for the basic needs of the poor and disadvantaged groups in society. Some of the highly developed countries have a well-devised social welfare system. However, even with a well-devised social welfare system crafted by the modern state, the need for charity at the individual level does still remain. Another point to be noted is that the scope of such spending should also embrace interest-free or concessional lending, which the Quran calls *qarz-hasana* (beautiful lending) (2:245; 57:11, 18; 64:17; 5:12; 73:20). In modern days, some of this concessional financing function is being performed in developing countries by developed country aid agencies and multilateral development financing institutions.

As emphasized in Chapter 6, the best motive for, or the best kind of, spending in God's way should be to help others stand on their own feet, not to keep them permanently in the beggars' seats. Indeed, to help another person in a way, which makes him to look for help all the time is inherently ill-motivated, and cannot be liked by God. Such spending is like that of those who like to be seen by men, and is of no intrinsic merit to them (2:264). From this point of view, the modern state should take appropriate measures to promote investment and development to increase opportunities for gainful employment of unemployed people. Such efforts also constitute spending in God's way. At the individual level, such efforts would be savings, investment and work that would help build infrastructure and industries for employment-generating development.[191]

Living morally

The Quran prescribes for man, along with religious practices, also strict moral principles. Living according to strict moral principles means living truthfully, honestly, justly, and with decent sexual conduct. As noted in Chapters 3 and 4, living morally is a crucial precondition for one's spiritual development. Along with honesty and integrity, a vital trait of character of a righteous person is decency in his sexual conduct. It is a major area deserving our attention, an area where man fails the most, and where he needs to be guided the most. Chastity, restraint in married life and learning to love without any touch of lewdness – these are the valuable lessons one can learn from the Quran as criteria or norms for sexual decency or righteousness: (See 17:32; 5:5; 79:40-41; 7:28). The Prophet Muhammad was strictly exhorted by God not to pay attention to that with which man enjoys worldly life (20:131). He was also urged by

God to give similar advice to his wives (33:28). Neither he nor his wives, who were like mothers to the believers, thus could be perceived to have cared much for worldly pleasures (20:131; 33:28-34; 60:12; 66:3-5).[192]

The Quran advises man to remain chaste as long as he cannot afford to get married (24:33). It asks believing men and women to lower their gaze, and guard their modesty (24:30-31). It urges believing women to put on proper dresses to cover their private parts and bosoms, except what is ordinarily apparent, and not to display their beauty and strike their feet in such a way as may look or sound like invitation to indecency (24:31; 33:59).[193] It urges sexual restraint in married life (5:5; 79:40-41). It wants us not to go near to acts of indecency, whether open or secret (6:151], and to avoid sin, whether open or hidden (6:120). If somebody commits a sin, and then blames it on the innocent, he carries the burden of both a false charge, and a flagrant sin (4:112).

24:33   And *let those who find not the means to marry keep chaste till God maketh them free from want* out of His Grace.

24:30-31 *Tell the believing men to lower their gaze and be modest.* That is purer for them. Verily God is Aware of what they do. *Tell the believing women to lower their gaze and be modest,* and to display of their beauty only that which is apparent, and to draw their veils over their breasts, and not display their beauty except to their own husbands, their fathers, their husbands' fathers, their sons, their husbands' sons, their brothers or their brothers' sons, or their sisters' sons, or their women, or their slaves they rightfully possess, or male servants free of sexual need, or children who have no knowledge of women's naked beauty; and let them not strike their feet in order to draw attention to their hidden beauty. And o ye believers! Turn unto God together, that ye may succeed.

17:32   And *come not nigh unto adultery (or fornication).* Verily it is an indecency and an evil way. (See also 6:151 and 120.)

> **7:28**   And when they commit some indecency, they say:
> We have found our fathers doing so, and God hath
> enjoined it on us. Say (O Muhammad): Verily God
> never enjoineth what is indecent. Say ye concerning
> God which ye know not? (See also 5:5 cited earlier.)

The Quran strongly condemns acts of indecency, which includes both homosexual, and premarital or extramarital heterosexual sexual acts. Religion cannot admit of any acts of indecency, as God wants to purify us of all impurities (33:33). Adultery or fornication (*zina*) is a great sin in the sight of God (17:32). The Quran makes such acts punishable in a stern manner (4:15-16; 24:2-4) unless the committers of such a sin repent sincerely and mend their conduct (4:16-17; 24:5). It is ironic that the laws in western countries enacted by legislatures do not consider consensual premarital relationship as punishable fornication, which the Quran does. It is reckless sexual behavior that is primarily responsible for the spread of the HIV[194], the virus that causes the AIDS[195] disease. This disease is a modern-day scourge in many countries – especially in Africa, where it has already turned into an alarming epidemic, not only causing a heavy toll of death and immense human suffering, including turning a huge number of children into orphans, but also having enormous adverse impact on overall economic and social development.[196]

Living in peace, decency, and harmony with others

Though there is some disillusionment and misgivings in certain quarters about the message of Islam on peace, there cannot be any question that Islam is a religion of peace and tolerance. This topic has been covered at some length in the last chapter. Here it seems in order to jot down some additional points.

Islam stands for peace by definition. The root word from which "Islam" is derived is "*salama*", which means "peace" as well as "to surrender". It symbolizes peace also because we serve, or surrender to, God Who stands for peace – one of Whose names or attributes is "Salam" or "Peace" (59:23). Islam is symbolized also by the salutation of peace (*salam*) with which Muslims are exhorted to always greet others (6:54), or to turn away from ignorant people in a decent manner, i.e., wishing them "peace" (25:63; 28:55; 49:9). God urges us to incline to peace when the enemies incline to peace (See 8:62-63 cited earlier), to make

214

peace between feuding parties with justice and fairness, and to fight for only establishing justice against the aggressors and wrongdoers.

> **49:9** If two parties among the Believers fall into a fight, make ye peace between them; but if one of them acts wrongfully against the other, then fight ye against the one that acts wrongfully until he complieth with the command of God; but if he complieth, then make peace between them with justice, and be fair; for God loveth those who are fair.

Islam does not go as far as saying that one should turn the other cheek also to the person who strikes him or her on one cheek, as in the Bible.[197] Always turning the other cheek also, after being hurt on one cheek, could not be a tenable proposition, as that would amount to encouraging injustice, which Islam does not approve of. The Quran allows or urges us to take arms against those who indulge in injustices, and religious intolerance and persecution, for persecution is worse than slaughter (2:191, 217); and it urges us to fight until persecution is no more (2:193; 8:39). But Islam also emphasizes the importance of forgiving, and exhorts believers to condone and forgive others' faults as far as possible, and that is deemed more righteous in the sight of God even when we can legitimately retaliate against any wrongs done to us (3:134; 5:45; 8:38; 16:126; 42:40). Three of the Quranic verses are strikingly similar to, but more reasonable than, the statements attributed to the Prophet Jesus cited in Endnote 197 (See 5:45, 42:40 and 16:126 cited earlier).

As mentioned in the previous chapter, the Quran strongly condemns any acts of mischief, violence, torture or persecution, and killing – the last except that which is required to dispense justice, or which is done in the course of legitimate fighting with others. God has strongly warned humankind against causing any injury or harm to others, and any act of wrongdoing, corruption, or mischief in the land (7:56, 74; 13:25; 26:151-152, 181-183; 27:48-49; 47:22-23).

The Quran forbids us to cause unnecessary bloodshed in society, and characterizes killing of any man without any valid reason as like killing all humankind, and saving one soul as like saving all humankind (5:32). God forbids killing of children for fear of poverty, and characterizes such killing as a great sin (17:31; 6:151). He forbids killing except for a just cause (4:29-30, 92-93; 6:151; 17:33). Those who kill without any legitimate reason will find themselves thrown into fire or Hell (4:29-30, 93).

> **17:33** *Take not a life that God hath forbidden except for a just cause* (See also 6:151 and 4:29).

Fighting is prescribed by the Quran as necessary for dealing with aggression, torture and persecution, and wrongdoing and injustice in society (2:190-193; 49:9). Such fighting was enjoined on reluctant believers.

> **2:216** *Fighting is enjoined upon you, and ye dislike it. And it may be that ye dislike a thing which is good for you, and it may be that you love a thing which is evil for you.* And God knoweth; ye know not. (See also 2:190-193 cited earlier)

Fighting and killing, though bad in general, are righteous deeds in a different context. This is for the sake of ensuring durable peace, security, justice, and harmony in society. However, contrary to misleading writings of some quarters, there is no room for aggressive *jihad* in Islam against other communities.[198]

How good and courteous should we be to others?

Doing any harm to others includes discourteous or harsh treatment, or doing any acts of mischief, violence, torture, injury and killing. These human crimes are manifestations of intolerance to man by man. Some references to these crimes and what the Quran says against such crimes were made in that context in the preceding chapter. Here we may provide some more references to what the Quran has to say about such misdeeds of mankind. Indeed the Quran is so detailed in its advice to humankind about what they should or should not do to promote their ethical and moral values, and ultimately to advance their spiritual goals that it does not forget to provide some of the minutest details of its admonitions relating to what many might consider as petty matters of etiquette. For example, the Quran teaches us to be duly polite to others in conversation and arguments (2:83; 16:125; 29:46), and to greet or salute others, or to return salutation (4:86; 24:27, 61; 25:63; 33:56), to be duly polite and respectful to those who are superior (2:104; 4:46; 24;62-63; 33:56-57; 58:11; 49:1-5], to enter a house not without the due permission and greeting of its inmates (24:27-29), to seek permission to enter rooms of couples at specified private times (24:58-59); not to ridicule, or mock at, others (49:11; 23:110); and not to back-bite one another of our own people (49:12; 104:1). Some of these verses are worth looking at:

2:83   *... Speak nicely to the people. ...*

31:19   *Be modest in thy going about, and lower thy voice*; for the harshest of voices without doubt is the braying of the ass.

6:54   And when those who believe in Our revelations come unto thee, say: 'Peace be upon you!'

4:86   *When ye are greeted with a greeting, greet with a (still) better (greeting) than it or return it.* Verily God taketh account of everything.

24:61   *When ye enter houses salute one another with a greeting of blessing and goodness from God*; thus God maketh clear the revelations to you that ye may understand.

God's direction to us that we should return the greeting of others with even a better greeting, or with a similar greeting in the least, conveys a deeper message calling for maintaining cordial human relationship that we need to foster among ourselves. Building such relationship in society is precisely the way we can create an environment of durable peace, friendship, and harmony in society.

We need to be polite in our conversations with others, say the best words, and argue in the best possible manner (2:83; 16:125; 17:53; 29:46). The model of our behavior with superiors is illustrated well by God's admonitions to the believers about how they should behave with the Prophet given in two verses (33:56-57 and 49:1-5) cited earlier. Also worthy of note is the following advice:

24:62   They only are *the true believers* who believe in God and His messenger and, when they are with him in some community meeting, they *do not leave until they have asked for his permission*; verily those who ask for the permission are those who believe in God and His Messenger.

In fact, we should duly respect those who command knowledge and legitimate authority, and should obey them. Indeed, a good measure of our respect to the superiors is whether we listen carefully to what they say and whether we sufficiently respond to their sound advice. We should not ask too many questions, which hardly make any sense or which, if answered, may cause trouble (5:101-102). God urges believers to honor and obey the Prophet thus:

4:59   O ye who believe! *Obey God and obey the Messenger, and those who command authority from among you; and if ye have any dispute concerning any matter, refer it to God and the Messenger if ye are believers in God and the Last Day.* That is better and more seemly in the end.

2:104   O ye who believe! *Say not (unto the Prophet): 'Listen to us', but say 'Look upon us', and be ye listeners.* For disbelievers there awaits a painful doom.

5:101-2   O ye who believe! *Ask not of things which, if made known unto you, would trouble you;* but if ye ask of them when the Quran is being revealed, they will be made known unto you...A folk before you asked (of such disclosures) and then disbelieved therein.

How we should behave when we enter houses whether inhabited or uninhabited is also mentioned in the Quran:

24:27-9   O ye who believe! Enter not houses other than your own, until ye have asked permission and greeted those in them. That is best for you, that ye may heed. And if ye find no one therein, still enter not until permission hath been given. And if ye are asked to go back, then go back. That is purer for you. God knoweth what ye do. (It is) no sin for you to enter uninhabited houses wherein (there is) use for you. God knoweth what ye reveal and what ye hide.

2:189   And it is not righteousness that ye go to houses by the backs thereof, but the righteous man is he who guardeth (against evil). And enter houses by the gates

218

thereof, and be careful (of your duty) to God, that ye may be successful.

God wants us not to make fun of others, nor to speak ill of our own people behind their backs. It is the disbelievers or mischievous people who find enjoyment in making fun of others. God curses the slanderers and the backbiters.

49:11-2   O ye who believe! *Let not people (among you) laugh at others,* who may be better than they (are); nor let women (among you) laugh at others, who may be better than they (are); *nor be sarcastic to one another, nor insult one another by nicknames.* Evil indeed is the name of wickedness after faith; and whoever turneth not in repentance after this is an evil-doer. O ye who believe! *Avoid much suspicion; for verily suspicion in some cases is a sin.* And spy not; *nor speak ill of one another behind their backs.* Would one of you like to eat the flesh of your dead brother? Ye abhor that. So be careful of (your duty to) God.

104:1   *Woe unto every slanderer, back-biter!*

The yardstick by which we can judge whether we are being rude or unfair to others is that of whether or not we are crossing or transgressing the limits of decency. A conscientious person can judge when he is transgressing the limits in his conduct. If he really transgresses the limits, he can feel it, and feels sorry for it. Thus, when the Prophet Moses in his youth wrongfully sided with a person of his own tribe in his quarrel and fight with another person, and accidentally killed that person, he could realize that he transgressed the limits, and became deeply repentant for his action, and asked for God's forgiveness, and vowed to never again side with a wrong person (28:15-17). The Prophet Muhammad possessed an excellent and extra-ordinary character, which is well worth emulating by all believers (33:21; 68:4-6). He could realize – get inspiration from God – if he had, by mistake, any lapse on his part in his conduct with others, which he rectified instantly, e.g., his lack of sufficient attention to a blind man (80:1-11), and his concealment of something in his mind for fear of men when he was trying to bring about a rapprochement in the marital relation of Zaid with Zainab (33:37), because of which he was inspired by God not to fear men, but fear God (33:37).

Other righteous deeds

The Quran advises all parties to maintain cordial relations with all other parties – how husbands should behave with their wives, how wives should behave with their husbands, how husbands should behave when they wish to part with, or divorce, their wives, what should be the status in which we should hold women, how we should treat war captives or slaves and orphans, how creditors should behave with poor debtors, etc. These questions except the last one are discussed in Chapter 9, while the last mentioned creditor-debtor relation is discussed in Chapter 10, and hence these questions are not discussed here. There are norms of good conduct in all human situations and relationships. The Quran leaves untouched hardly anything of importance to our well-being.

Among other righteous deeds which we need to be aware of and do when the context arises is the bequest that we should leave for our parents and near relatives when death approaches us. Leaving a written bequest or will before death to parents and near relatives according to reasonable usage is a solemn duty prescribed for us by the Quran (2:180-183, 240; 5:106-108). This provision for making a will before death provides a special opportunity for the dying person to make any special considerations for his near relatives who are poor and disadvantaged, or other poor people he may have in mind. The laws of inheritance at death prescribed by the Quran also provide for making a special accommodation for the needs of the poor, including poor relatives, in our property:

> **4:7-8**   Men shall have a share in what parents and kinsfolk leave behind, and women shall have a share in what parents and kinsfolk leave behind, whether it be little or much – a share ordained [by God]. And when at the time of distribution (of inheritance), relatives, orphans, and the needy are present, give them (out of the property), and speak to them kindly.

If some of the near relatives are poor relative to the others, this consideration should enable the poor ones, including the females, to receive a larger share of the property than the usual distribution rules prescribed in the Quran would warrant. The Quran urges us to make a will for distribution of inherited property in the following way:

> **2:180-2** It is decreed for you, when death approaches one of you, if he leaveth wealth, that he bequeath (i.e., make a will for distributing) unto parents and near relatives equitably. (This is) a duty (which is incumbent) upon the righteous. If anyone changeth the will after he hath heard (or seen) it, the sin thereof is only upon those who change it. Verily God is Hearer, Knower. But if one feareth partiality and wrongdoing on the part of the testator, and bringeth settlement among the parties (concerned), there is no blame on him. Verily God is Ever Forgiving, Most Merciful.

Making a will is a righteous or virtuous duty that God has prescribed for us. The rules of distribution of inherited property after death that the Quran prescribes in addition to the will apply really after consideration of the will, and after settlement of any debt lying outstanding against the deceased relative (4:11). The rules of distribution of any property left by a deceased person to his surviving close relatives as prescribed by the Quran also need to be followed by the believers as virtuous deeds. These are described in several verses of the Quran: (4:7-13, 33, 176).[199]

The Quran provides advice on still other things, which may be good or bad for us. Some of the bad things relate to intoxicants, gambling, sacrificing to stones or idols, and divining by arrows. The Quran states:

> **5:90-1** O ye who believe! Intoxicants and games of chance and (sacrificing to) stones and (divining by) arrows are only an abomination, the Satan's handiwork. So shun them that ye may succeed. Satan seeketh only to cast enmity and hatred among you by means of intoxicants and gambling, and to turn you from remembrance of God and from prayer. Will ye not then abstain (from such things)?

> **2:219** They ask thee about intoxicants and games of chance. Say: In both there is great sin, and (some) utility for men; but the sin of them is greater than their usefulness.

Drinks that cause intoxication, and trigger irrational and immoral behavior are admittedly not desirable by any norms of civility. Drunken driving is a source of accidents, and is prohibited by law in many countries. God advises us not to go near to prayer when we are intoxicated, and do not understand what we say (4:43). Going to prayer when one is out of one's mind makes no sense. The Quran states that there is some good in both intoxicants and games of chance, but the evil in them is greater than their good. Gambling is bad precisely because it often does irreparable damage, both material and mental or spiritual, to the persons who lose the stakes. The use of drugs for intoxication, or of that causes hallucinations or distortions of perceptions, currently so widespread in many countries, also falls in the same category as intoxicants, and hence needs to be avoided for both health – both physical and mental health – reasons and good behavior.

God also likes us to keep away from vain talks and activities (6:68; 23:3):

> **6:68**   When thou (O Muhammad) seest men engaged in vain discourse about Our revelations, turn away from them unless they turn to a different theme. If Satan ever maketh thee forget, then after recollection, sit not thou with the company of those who do wrong.

Good food is necessary for good health. We need to eat wholesome food, and avoid food that may cause us problems. The things God has forbidden us to eat include only meat of animals that die of themselves (carrion), blood, pork, and meat of animals that are sacrificed to other than God (2:172-173, 5:3; 6:3-5, 121, 145; 16:115-116; 22:30).[200] The reason given in the Quran for forbidding pork is that the swine is unclean (6:145). Dead animals, the meat (carrion) of which is forbidden, also include the dead through either strangling, beating, falling from a height, or the dead through goring by horns and partially devoured by wild animals (5:3).

> **6:145**   Say (O Muhammad): I find not in that which hath been revealed unto me anything forbidden to an eater to eat of except carrion, or blood poured forth, or swine flesh – for that verily is foul – or what is a transgression, (meat) on which a name other than

God's hath been invoked. But whoever is driven by necessity, neither craving nor transgressing (the limit), then verily your Lord I sever Forgiving, Most Merciful. (See also 2:172-173 and 5:3).

A message similar to those at (2:172-173; 6:145) is also repeated at (16:115). God wants us not to eat of animals on which His name is not mentioned (6:121). Note, however, that whoever is driven by necessity, for him eating the forbidden food is no sin, if he eats it not craving it, and not exceeding the limit. For those who go on a pilgrimage to the Holy Kabah, gaming of animals is forbidden during the pilgrimage; but gaming of the sea and its food are lawful (5:95-96). The Quran also mentions of animals with claws, or undivided hooves, and some specified fat of oxen and sheep that were prohibited particularly for the Jews. Such prohibitions were specially imposed on them as a measure of punishment to them on account of their rebellion (6:146).

The above verses make it quite clear that all other good things except the four mentioned in the Quran – namely carrion, blood, pork and that which is sacrificed to other than God – are lawful to us. God has warned men against forbidding food that was not forbidden by Him (5:87; 10:59; 16:116), and has advised us not to follow the desires or footsteps of the wrongdoers or the devil (6:142, 150). In the past some people unfairly prohibited some food without any divine authority (6:119, 138-139, 143-144). As in the past, despite the clear Quranic direction to the contrary, the Hadith literature mentions some additional foods as unlawful (*haram*) (e.g., the meat of domestic asses as in *Sahih Muslim*, Book 021, Number 4769 and 4772, meat of hedgehog as in *Sunan Abu Dawud*, Book 27, Number 3790, and uncooked garlic as in *Sunan Abu Dawud*, Book 27, Number 3819).

Providing for criminal justice

There can be little doubt that forgiveness to an extent contributes to an environment of peace and harmony in society, just as tolerance does. Forgiveness is akin to, and inter-related with, but not fully identical to, tolerance, a topic that we have already dealt with in Chapter 7. Tolerance and forgiveness reinforce each other. A tolerant attitude induces one to forgive, and a forgiving mentality encourages one to tolerate. Intolerance expresses itself outwardly in acts of hostility toward another person or group of people because of a different race, color, sex, language,

223

religion, political or other opinion, national or social origin, property, birth or other similar status. On the other hand, forgiveness relates to condoning of others' faults and crimes such as immoral activities, and social crimes, including mischief, violence, torture, persecution, slaughter, etc. The Quran provides for forgiveness of certain sins or crimes of those who repent, and mend their conduct, but at the same time it provides for stern punishment of those who persist in their sins or crimes. Forgiveness or tolerance must be understood in a proper perspective. Human behavior, which is inimical to decent human and moral values as prescribed by all religions and recognized by all decent people, cannot be allowed even a passive endorsement by society in the name of human rights. Tolerance and human rights must of necessity go with certain obligations on the part of men and women. For the sake of peace, morality, and justice, those who are persistent perpetrators of mischief, violence, tyranny, immorality, and injustice in society need to be dealt with harshly.

The righteous are those who live, and like to live, with peace, harmony, and decency with others in society, avoiding all kinds of mischief, violence, terror, and injustice. They cannot do so if there are miscreants in society destroying peace and harmony. This provides the rationale for dealing with the acts of mischief in an appropriate way to ensure peace, security, and harmony in society. The Quran provides for exemplary punishments when the criminals do not repent their sins or crimes, and mend their conduct.

One example of such punishments is for war crimes. Those who fight against God or godly values, and commit serious crimes like murder and persecution deserve to be dealt a harsh punishment – either killing or crucifixion, or cutting of their hands and feet on alternate sides, or expulsion from the land (or imprisonment) (5:33). Only those who can be exempted from such severe punishment are those who repent (and, by implication, desist from such crimes) before they fall into the hands of those against whom they were fighting (5:34). The traditional interpretation of another verse (5:38) provides another example of an exemplary punishment: cutting of the hands of a thief, whether male or female, for the crime of stealing. However, modern interpretation such as that of Edip Yuksel and others suggests that the punishment for stealing should be limb marking, not limb cutting, which would be a humiliating punishment for the thief.[201] Note however, whether limb cutting or limb marking, such a dire or mild punishment can be waived, and the culprit can be forgiven if he or she repents, and mends his or her conduct (5:39). Also, the Quran provides for retaliation by capital punishment for deliberate killing without any valid justification – retaliation by the successors of the killed or, by implication, by the judicial system, but it also states that if the successors of the killed make any remission, then a lighter punishment according to usage should be given, and compensation should be made to the aggrieved party (2:178-179). There is provision for still lighter punishments or expatiation in the case of accidental killings (4:92).

The Quranic law is thus quite flexible. It is not always necessary then – it is not a hard and fast rule – that a killer, a persecutor, or a mischief-monger, or a thief has to be given the extreme capital or corporal punishment. Those who are the custodians of justice in society need to judge whether the culprits are those who really regret their misdeeds, or whether they are confirmed miscreants in society. The Quran provides for a wide range of choice for them, which can shift from an extreme punishment to a very light one, or outright forgiveness. That means that the appropriateness of a particular punishment should be decided by not only the nature of the crime but also by the type of the criminal. This can be illustrated by the example of two boys, one of whom is naughtier than the other. For the same crime, the less naughty boy deserves a lighter punishment than the naughtier one. A simple word of rebuke may be a sufficient punishment for a certain crime for some people. On the other hand, a more responsible person doing a misdeed deserves a greater punishment than a less responsible one doing the same misdeed. That is the reason why the slaves or servants, or those who possess less intelligence or sense, need to be treated more generously, and punished less harshly (4:25). By the same token, the mentally ill or deficient persons need to be treated generously. At the same time, in a more civilized society, where crimes are less frequent, punishments can afford to be lighter than in another society, where crimes are more widespread. That is why more and more civilized societies can afford to move further and further away from crude and severe punishments. The criteria to judge which system of justice dispensation is appropriate are whether the punishments being applied are proportionate to the wrongs done, and whether such punishments are sufficient deterrents to future crimes. Interpreting Shah Wali Allah, Iqbal aptly notes, "The [particular] Sahri'ah values (*ahkam*) … (e.g., rules relating to penalties for crimes) are in a sense specific to [a particular] people; and since their observance is not an end in itself they cannot be strictly enforced to the case of future generations."[202] Eminent contemporary Muslim thinker and scholar of Islamic law Khaled Abou El Fadl notes:

> The law helps Muslims in the *quest* for Godliness, but Godliness cannot be equated to the law. The ultimate objective of the law is to achieve goodness, which includes justice, mercy, and compassion, and the technicalities of the law cannot be allowed to subvert the objectives of the law. Therefore, if the application of the law produces injustice, suffering, and misery, this means the law is not serving its purposes. In this situation, the law is corrupting the earth instead of civilizing it. In short, if the application of the law results in injustice, suffering, or misery, then the law must be reinterpreted, suspended, or reconstructed, depending on the law in question.[203]

Thus the particular forms applied of the Quranic principles can be flexible depending on particular circumstances. This is evident from the following verse of the Quran:

> **16:126** And if ye punish, *let your punishment be proportionate to the wrong that has been done to you; but if ye endure patiently, verily it is better for the patient.*

The rigid application of the so-called *shariah* law[204], which is found applied in some countries and regions of the world, does not, therefore, stand justified in light of the Quran. The Quran does not say that the thief's hands must always be cut off, or that the adulterer and the adulteress must necessarily or always be flogged, or that the killer must always be hanged. Though the Quran provides for flogging of the adulterer and the adulteress (24:2), this should be interpreted as an extreme punishment applicable in cases that do not deserve leniency under any consideration. In another place, the Quran clearly allows for either punishment or forgiveness in case the guilty persons repent and mend their conduct:

> **4:16** And as for the two of you who are guilty thereof (of indecency), *punish them both. But if they repent and make amends, then leave them alone*; for God is Ever Forgiving, Most Merciful.

226

Media reports covered sensational stories of *shariah hudud* punishments such as stoning of adulteresses and amputations of hands and feet in some countries such as Afghanistan under the Taliban, Saudi Arabia, Iran, Sudan and Nigeria in recent years. With the ousting of the Taliban regime, the situation in Afghanistan has now changed. Human rights activists denounced these punishments. Though such punishments are not applied in most modern Muslim states, with the rise of orthodox Islamic political tendency, they were reintroduced in the late twentieth century in Pakistan, Iran, Sudan, Afghanistan and Nigeria.[205] It is indeed regrettable that following the Hadith, the *shariah* courts in these countries, especially Nigeria and Iran, are rigidly applying, or are trying to apply, the punishment of "stoning to death" to those who are guilty of adultery, a punishment that is not in the Quran. Hadith supporters insist that there was a verse calling for this punishment in the Quran, which was inadvertently omitted. But this must be a preposterous claim. Also striking is the fact that such a barbarous, and brutal punishment is often meted out to the women involved in such a crime, as their crime is often easier to prove. Another example of a *shariah*-prescribed brutal punishment is killing for apostasy of a Muslim, i.e., of a Muslim converting to another religion, a punishment that is against the very spirit of the Quran, which guarantees full religious freedom and tolerance, and which emphatically proclaims that there must not be any compulsion in religion (See 18:29, 76:3, 2:256 and 10:99 cited earlier).

A recent case in point was that of Abdul Rahman in Afghanistan, who was declared by the *ulama* an apostate fit for killing, because he converted to Christianity. He was being tried by a court by Afghanistan's *shariah* law, even though, with US-led forces, the country was wrested from the Taliban rule. Under intense pressure of international outcry, his life was spared when the court dismissed his case on technical grounds that he was not mentally fit to stand trial. But the life of Abdul Rahman still remained under threat in Afghanistan. It was good that he got refuge in another country. Abdul Rahman's case highlights the point that it is some Muslim countries or societies where lamentably there is no full religious freedom. Needless to say, the sooner such anti-Quranic punishments are banished from society, the better for society and civilization.

As noted above, the Quran provides for some harsh exemplary punishments. Sometimes it may be necessary to apply some of these punishments – if these are deemed necessary to maintain peace, decency, and harmony in society. There is evidently need for introducing harsher, and more effective punishments in countries where corruption and indecency are found to be widespread. But such punishments need to be only selectively and cautiously applied in order not to exceed the extent, which proves sufficient to deter the crimes that we address to eliminate. What we always need to bear in mind is that religion is for us; we are not for religion. God has forbidden us to commit excesses in the name of religion (4:171; 5:77). God is not unduly harsh to humankind. He first sends lighter punishments to see if human beings return from their sins, and when such punishments prove ineffective, He sends the heavier ones (32:21).

Some concluding remarks

To become a truly righteous person, and a good Muslim, it is sufficient for us to live according to the guidance provided in the Quran, which is most reliable, elaborate, and detailed (2:2; 17:9; 10:57; 16:89). It is not necessary for religion to spell out everything – what we should or should not do always, and how we should behave with all. God has given us sense or conscience by which we can often judge what is conscionable, right, or decent, and what is unconscionable, wrong, or indecent. It is our responsibility to strive to clear our conscience, and purify it, and work according to it for our success, as the Quran itself proclaims (See 91:8-10 cited earlier).

Our understanding of what is good or bad depends also on the level of our knowledge and wisdom. Because of our inadequate knowledge, what we may sometimes like and consider as good for us may really turn out to be bad for us, and what we sometimes dislike and consider as bad for us may really be good for us (2:216; 24:11; 18:79-80). A hard knock or kick to a person from some quarters need not always be taken in bad light for him, but may indeed turn out to be a turning point or blessing in disguise for him.

Man is evidently in a state of loss, unless he establishes faith in, and rapport with, God (which essentially means faith in godly values), and leads a righteous life, and enjoins one another upholding of the truth, and urges patience and perseverance (103:2-3). God changes the evil deeds of righteous people into good deeds (25:70). Righteousness or goodness leads to further guidance or goodness (19:76; 42:23):

42:23 And *whoever earns any good, We add further good for him.* Verily God is Ever-Forgiving, Appreciative.

Ahmad beautifully expounds this idea:

> Body and mind generate feelings and also discrimination between what is good and what is evil. Now, every being is prone to good as well as evil. When one gives goodness the upper hand, the evil gradually loses its edge and sustains defeat after defeat and in the long run conceals itself within goodness itself to cut out the ignominy of defeat. Then its motive power rather contributes to the expansion of goodness itself... [Likewise,] when a person gives evil the upper hand, goodness in the long run hides itself in the folds of evil out of shame and even then from within, it warns lest the person turn too bad.[206]

Righteous or good deeds wipe out evil deeds (11:114); and the righteous people repel evil with good (28:54). Righteous are those who hasten in every good work, and are foremost in them (23:61). They are not boastful, but walk on earth in humility and, when addressed by others, they say "Peace" to them (25:63). They are the best of creatures (98:7). It is they who are worthy successors (*khalifas*), or inheritors of the earth (6:165; 21:105). And God has promised them the ruler-ship of the world, who will establish the rule of law (or religion), peace, and security (24:55). It is they who create Heaven in the earth, and their afterlife will be still better (See 16:30 cited earlier and 16:97).

God wants us to be as good to others as we are to ourselves (2:267). God wants us to save a man rather than kill him, and saving a man is like saving the whole of humankind (5:32). In accordance with this spirit, we need to serve humanity to save them from any danger and disadvantage – from death, disease, injury, deprivation, ignorance, misery, poverty and hunger. To be good and generous to fellow human beings, especially to those who are poor and disadvantaged, is a great virtue in the sight of God (90:12-18; 2:261, 265; 70:24-25). Serving God amounts to serving humanity in the same way as God serves them through His agents. This is real religion. The prophets of God came to serve humanity, and they brought them the good news, and message of hope, healing, and salvation (10:57; 16:102; 17:9, 82; 40:41). The Eastern saint Shah Aksaruddin Ahmad aptly notes:

Be in Love with God;
And go along the Path of the Messenger.

The Path of the Messenger is the Path of the Quran;
Find the Path in the Quran;
And serve God, your Lord.

Fear not Hell;
Crave not Heaven.
Being only His lover,
Care for Him alone; rely on Him alone.

To serve God is to serve humankind,
Be they disbelievers, polytheists, hypocrites,
Or be they even sinners.

Leave it to the Creator of creation to judge;
It's not your right to judge.

Seek your own salvation;
Seek just your own salvation.[207]

IX. MARRIAGE, DIVORCE, THE STATUS OF WOMEN AND THE TREATMENT OF SLAVES IN LIGHT OF THE QURAN

And among His (God's) Signs is that He created from among yourselves your mates that ye may find rest in them, and He placed love and mercy (in your hearts) between you. Verily in this are signs for those who reflect. – 30:21

The rationale for marriage

The Quran states that any living species, nay, everything that exists in the universe is in pairs (36:36; 51:49). It is in the nature of everything that it seeks companionship – the positive attracts the negative. It is ingrained in human nature that a man should seek a woman as his wife, and that a woman should seek a man as her husband.

Indeed, as people come of age, they generally develop a liking or love for another of the opposite sex, which develops into a deep longing for companionship. A true lover wants to express himself or herself through his or her consort, and wants to keep this love alive forever. If both husband and wife live together with such a feeling for each other, and can keep alive this feeling, such a living can become a source of constant delight and happiness for each other, and can also turn into a springboard for mutual progress. Every human being represents a precious gift of God. A husband needs to find in his spouse abundant good for him:

> **4:19** *Live with them (wives) with kindness, for if ye dislike them, it may be that ye dislike a thing wherein God hath placed abundant good.*

That should be true the other way round also. Marriage is necessary – and religion prescribes it – for formalizing this intimate union between a man and a woman. Animals do not need marriage. But man, a superior being, needs a matrimonial bond to make a mutually respectable, responsible, and durable family. The family in turn creates a sound basis for procreation of children, who need the loving care and support of a family for their proper upbringing. Such families in turn make the basic foundation of a civilized society, and the very bedrock of a sound and prosperous civilization. The Quran states:

231

16:72   God hath made for you spouses from among yourselves, and through them hath given you children and grandchildren, and hath made for you provisions of good things.

The intimate relationship between a man and a woman is based on the premise that it is mutually beneficial. For this reason, this relationship should not be turned into a light affair. A relationship based on cohabitation without marriage is very shaky. Reluctance to marry may simply mean that the couple wants to shirk the responsibilities of husband and wife. This relationship can, and is often found to, break up at any time without imposing any obligation on either party. The Quran does not approve of such a relationship. The Quran generally requires the husband to bear the task of financially supporting his wife, and if they decide to separate, the Quran requires the husband let his wife go with dignity and honor. (See below for the provisions on divorce.) The trend of cohabitation before marriage that is found especially in western developed countries is, indeed, lamentable. The proliferation of artificial birth control measures for use in contemptible premarital and extra-marital sexual activities – which is also encouraging contemptible promiscuity, the growing problem of single mothers, and the tendency of couples or women seeking abortion of unintended unborn children from relationships before marriage or outside marriage have indeed become familiar, but unseemly and disgraceful, outcomes of relationships outside wedlock.

The Quran describes spouses as garments for each other (2:187). Just as men and women need clothes to cover shame, for comfort, a shield against cold and heat, and for adornment, so husband and wife need each other to mutually complement themselves with protection, comfort, and support materially, intellectually, and spiritually. Indeed, a man and a woman are endowed with diverse qualities in which they excel each other, and their union culminates in a mingling of such qualities to enrich their living in diverse ways. God admonishes us not to be jealous of the gifts which God has bestowed on some of us, and which make them excel others:

4:32   And *covet not the grace that God hath bestowed on some to excel others*. To men is allotted what they earn, and to women is allotted what they earn. But implore God for His grace. For God knoweth all things.

7:189   He it is Who created you from a single soul, and from it created his mate, that he may find rest in her. (See also 30:21 cited at the top of this chapter.)

Normally, a man does not seem a full, responsible, and mature man until he gets married. A woman likewise does not seem a full woman until she gets married. And a woman's dream is often to become a mother. Besides, and also importantly, the male quality needs to be supplemented by the female one for procreation of progeny (42:11).

Verse 5:5 implies that both husband and wife need to mutually respect, and understand each other, and restrain their animal propensity. A relationship that grows out of love and respect for each other, and through appreciation of each other's intrinsic qualities, not out of lust, is a mature, durable and ideal one, which will result in not only enriching life in all possible ways, but also in giving birth to ideal children. God advises us to go to wives with the best of intentions doing something good beforehand (2:223). God invites us to the path of purification and mercy, while the devil invites to the path of lust and destruction (4:27). God loves those who turn to Him much and purify themselves (2:222).

The eligible and the ineligible for marriage

The Quran specifically mentions in various places men and women who are not eligible as one's husband or wife, and who are so eligible (33:50; 24:32; 4:3, 20-25; and 5:5). Some of these relevant verses are cited below:

4:22-4   And marry not women whom your fathers married, except what is past, it was indecent and abominable – an evil custom (indeed). Forbidden for you (for marriage) are your mothers, and your daughters, your sisters, and your father's sisters, and your mother's sisters, and your brother's daughters, and your sister's daughters, your foster mothers, and your foster sisters, and your wife's mothers, and your step daughters under your guardianship, born of your wives if ye have gone in – but if ye have not gone in unto them, then it is no sin for you (to marry their daughters), the wives of your sons (who are) from your own loins, and two sisters at one and the same time, except for what is past. God is Ever Forgiving, Most Merciful. Also (forbidden are) women already married, except those (prisoners of war) whom your right hands possess. Thus God hath ordained for you. Except for these, all others are lawful (for marriage) provided ye seek them with gifts of property desiring chastity, not lewdness. Then those from whom ye seek content, give unto them the dower as prescribed. And there is sin for you in what ye do by mutual agreement to the dower. Verily God is Knower, Most Wise.

Marriage is a very important matter to every man and woman. That is precisely the reason why a man or a woman needs to choose for his or her life partner someone of like nature and qualities. Good men or good women need to find respectively good women or men as their spouses. The Quran states:

9:71 And the believing men and women are protecting friends of one another; they enjoin what is right and forbid what is wrong.

That is why God ordains that believing and chaste men and women marry respectively from among believing and chaste women and men. Idolaters and adulterers, or idolatresses and adulteresses are not lawful respectively to the believing and chaste women or men; for a believing boy or girl, a believing slave girl or boy is better to marry than an unbelieving free girl or boy, even though the latter may be more attractive (2:221 and 24:3). This is because, as the Quran states:

24:26 Vile women are for vile men, and vile men are for vile women. Good women are for good men, and good men are for good women; such are innocent of that which people say. For them there is forgiveness and a bountiful provision.

If matches in marriages are done properly, wives become in a way reflections of their husbands, just as children are the reflections of their

234

parents. Wives of pious men can expect to have the same pleasant fate of their lives as their husbands (43:68-73)

Other prerequisites of ideal marriage relationship

The foregoing passages suggest that ideal marriage relationship is between a man and a woman, which makes an ideal family for upbringing of children. There has been a tendency in the modern world among some people to be homosexual, and to seek formal recognition in society of same-sex marriages. The Quran, however, decries such tendencies as an aberration, rather than normal or ideal behavior (7:80-84). Homosexual relationship destroys decent human values, relationships, and social harmony, and creates a bad family environment for children who need the love and warmth of both parents. The current trends of homosexual relationships being observed in different regions and countries, their official recognition in some of such regions, and the clamors for such recognition need therefore to be deplored.[208] It is a modern-day challenge for decent men and women in society to strongly rise and stand against such unseemly trends in human behavior.

Also, there is no room for premarital or extramarital sexual acts for any decent man or woman. Having premarital or extramarital sexual relation or incest (such relation with persons forbidden for marriage) is an act of indecency that religion strongly censures. As mentioned earlier, the Quran characterizes such acts as adultery or fornication (*zina*), and condemns such acts as a great sin (17:32), and makes such acts punishable in a stern manner (4:15-16; 24:2-4) unless the committers of such a sin repent sincerely, and mend their conduct (4:16-17; 24:5). It is ironic that the laws in western countries enacted by legislatures do not consider consensual premarital relationships as punishable fornication, which the Quran does.

No room for artificial birth control

If husband and wife do not want children, they should practice abstinence, not resort to artificial birth control measures. The Quran does not approve of artificial birth control. By the same token, nor does it approve of abortion of unintended growth of children in the wife's womb, unless it can be justified on legitimate grounds of the wife's health. The proliferation of birth control measures in society, which has been a modern-day trend, has been unhealthy for society and civilization at large. It has encouraged laxity in morals, and fostered promiscuity in society, and has thereby undermined both manhood and womanhood. Nowadays, artificial birth control measures are widely practiced everywhere, and are being advocated and extensively used as a way of controlling population growth. This is being done out of the Malthusian fear that population growth tends to outstrip food production in the world. Though Malthus has been proved wrong long ago, the practice of artificial birth control continues apace, mainly to improve the living standards of families, whether rich or poor. The Quran discourages us to kill children, or to take life without justice, out of fear of poverty (6:151). Abortion amounts to taking life in growth. In some regions of the world, especially in China and Northern India – in China encouraged in significant measure by a one-child state policy, wide-scale abortion of unborn baby girls has led to worrying levels of gender imbalance – males far exceeding females.[209]

Fear of poverty should prompt us to either remain single or, if married, work harder for bread rather than artificially control birth. But that does not mean that we should encourage population growth where it is not needed. In some countries, population growth is unduly decelerating, or population is declining in absolute terms, where birth control obviously does not make any sense. But where the need for checking high population growth is felt as in many poor developing countries, such control can be encouraged by encouraging abstinence on the part of couples, by encouraging late marriage, and by encouraging education and employment of women in dignified jobs. God has indeed urged those who cannot afford to marry because of financial reasons to postpone their marriage and remain chaste until their financial condition becomes affordable (24:33).

Who should bear the financial responsibility and pay the dower?

Since a man is generally responsible for financially supporting his wife, it is not becoming or manly for him to seek a dower from a woman to marry her. Rather, a man should give an appropriate dowry according to his means to his wife. According to verse (5:5) cited above as well as other verses of the Quran (4:4, 19-21; 2:236-237; 33:50), it is incumbent upon a man to give a dowry, according to his means, to his wife, and not the other way round. The practice of dowry-giving by a woman's family to her husband, which is found to be prevalent among some groups of people in some regions, is contrary to what the Quran prescribes. Such a practice is disgraceful, and has created enormous financial distress for many poor families.

The Quran makes a man squarely responsible for bearing the financial burden of his wife and children after they are born. If one cannot afford to marry a free (or, by implication, more expensive) woman, he should consider marrying a maid (or, by implication, less expensive woman), and failing even that he should remain unmarried and chaste until he becomes financially solvent to afford a wife. Thus the Quran says:

> **4:25** And *whoever among you who have not the means to marry free believing women, (they) may marry believing girls from among those whom your right hands possess* (captive slaves).

> **24:33** And *let those who find not the means to marry keep chaste till God maketh them free from want out of His Grace.*

That man takes responsibility for financially supporting his wife is also mentioned in verse (4:34). However, this should not be taken to mean that a wife should not be allowed to engage in a dignified paying job, should she find one, to supplement the family's income. Women can certainly play some role in making both ends meet, in making a comfortable living, and in shaping a financially better future for their family. Husbands should not stand on their wives' way to seek such roles, unless the work is undignified, and unless such work seriously interferes with family management, including the caring for their children. Both husband and wife should work shoulder to shoulder, if necessary, to make their life materially and spiritually more worthwhile and rewarding. And in modern times, it has been hard for many impoverished families in many, both poor and developed, regions of the world to provide nicely for their livelihood without both husband and wife working.

Polygamy? Yes, but in only restricted cases

Monogamy is the natural choice for a man in normal circumstances. The growth of the human race originated with only one man and one woman, call them, if you will, Adam and Eve. A woman has one womb, and for this very reason she cannot afford to have more than one husband at a time. Since the fruit of their union may be the birth of a child, it is to be preferred that the child has a single identifiable father. Having more than one husband at a time is prostitution for a woman. But should a man ever consider taking more than one wife at a time?

When a man seeks to marry more than one wife, it may, among other possible reasons, simply imply that he is not fully content with his present wife. Whatever the reason, a husband's attention becomes of necessity divided, when he takes more than one wife. Polygamy may lead to a discontented family relationship. It is not a normal, ideal, or desirable family relationship we should seek.

The Quran permits polygamy – taking of more than one wife at a time by one man, but only in some restricted cases. The restrictions are that the husband must be financially solvent enough to support the additional wife or wives, and that he should be able to do justice to more than one wife. Unless both conditions are satisfactorily met, one should refrain from considering taking more than one wife. The following verse deserves a close attention:

> **4:3** If ye fear that ye will not be able to deal justly with the orphans (in giving them their wealth), *marry of the women who seem good to you, two, three or four; and if ye fear that ye cannot do justice (to more than one), then just one*, or that (the slave girl or captive) whom your right hands possess. This will be more appropriate, that ye will not do injustice.

In another verse, the Quran states: Ye will not be able to do justice between (your) wives, however much ye wish (4:129). This verse underscores the point that it is indeed very hard to accord just treatment to multiple wives. Monogamy is, therefore, always the preferred option. It is striking that the Quran mentions marrying more than one wife only in the context of how we should treat orphans. The Quranic advice is clear. Polygamy is permissible, but only when we can do justice to more than one wife. Polygamy is, however, generally interpreted to extend to taking wives from general women, not simply from orphans, including prisoners of war or slave girls. God's law needs to accommodate possible situations in society, when women outnumber men, for example after warfare when men are killed in substantial numbers, and there remain a greater number of widows or unmarried women than that of unmarried

238

men. In such situations, it will be in the interest of social harmony and welfare to allow one man to take more than one wife. The mandatory restriction of one wife to one man as in some faiths such as Christianity as practiced will in such situations force some women to remain unmarried for life. That cannot be a just arrangement. Also, a mandatory monogamous requirement may also encourage divorcing of the current wife to take another wife, or encourage adulterous extra-marital behavior in society, which would also be an unhealthy outcome for society. Thus to encourage morals and harmony to prevail in society, it will be in the fitness of things that polygamy is allowed in society.

One need not be too concerned about polygamous behavior of men, as such behavior is generally looked down upon in a modern Muslim society, and its practice is found to be waning with more education, greater urbanization, and greater mobility of people within countries and across countries. Some Muslim countries, notably Turkey, Tunisia, and Iran under the late Shah, in effect outlawed polygamy, which was rather too radical. In many other Muslim states, polygamy "has been hemmed in by legal restrictions, and has become socially unacceptable in the urban middle and upper classes, as well as economically impractical for the urban lower classes. Polygamy is now very rare outside the Arabian peninsula, where men have the means and the opportunity."[210] In any event, there should remain a provision that allows men to consider marrying more than one wife. It follows also that God desires us to do justice to women we marry, and that if we are unable to do justice to more than one wife, we should be content with marrying just one.

Some misperception entertained by certain quarters surrounding the Prophet's multiple marriages needs to be dispelled here. We need to note that he married Khadijah, a rich merchant's widow, who was some fifteen years older at the time of marriage. The Prophet lived with her alone for twenty-four years, which was the prime time of his youth, until her death, when he was forty-nine. His other marriages took place during his later years of life. It was a confluence of special circumstances that led him to take many wives. Several of his wives included aged war widows of his friends who left many children, some being past the age of sexual behavior. Two of his wives were Aisha and Hafsah who were daughters respectively of his close associates Abu Bakr and Umar. The marriage of Zainab with the Prophet's adopted son Zaid was not going well, which culminated in a divorce. Both of them were very devoted to God and the Prophet. The Prophet first hesitated but later decided to marry Zainab, when he was assured by divine inspiration that he should fear God rather than fear what men around him would think and say about it (33:37). To suggest that the Prophet took so many wives in order to satisfy his physical need would indeed be a grievous mistake, and would amount to estimating the Prophet far below what he deserves.[211] As discussed in Chapter 3, in order to rise to the spiritual height that he did, which earned him prophethood and nearness to God (53:1-8), the qualification of a great character (68;4-6), and the status of an ideal deserving to be emulated by all God-loving people (33:21), he could not afford to care for the mundane pleasures.

The Quran explicitly exhorted the Prophet Muhammad not to pay any attention to enjoyment of worldly life (20:131). Also the Prophet was urged by God to admonish his wives not to seek this worldly life, and if they had done so, he would have gladly bidden them goodbye (33:28). His wives had to live up to his standard (33:28-34; 60:12; 66:3-5), and could be conceived to have had a good deal of spiritual enlightenment through their close association with the Prophet. The objective of getting spiritual enlightenment from close association with the Prophet appears to have been a special reason that led Zainab to marry the Prophet. The Quran testifies that the Prophet's wives were not like other women (33:32). It is a rare case that a prophet's wife is left much behind in spiritual enlightenment.[212] Indeed the Quran has urged all Muslims to regard the Prophet's wives as their mothers (33:6), and it is for this reason that they were not lawful as wives to any Muslims after the Prophet's death (33:53).

Let there be no mistake about the fact that the Prophet remains an ideal and an inspiration for all men and women. Each and every Muslim and non-Muslim needs to ponder hard how he rose to spiritual eminence to receive the Great Book of Divine revelation, the Holy Quran, and how he became a mercy (*rahmat*) for the whole universe, and a light-giving lamp (*munir*) to all humankind (33:46). Evidently, a personality that earned this unique honor could not be other than one who had conquered his animal nature. After all, prophets and God's devout servants are the human models to project before humanity a pattern of life that is modeled on the divine image. God is always on the straight path (11:56), and asexual – neither male nor female, with no consort (6:101; 72:3). So it was incumbent upon the Prophet Muhammad to project this ideal to all humanity – a responsibility that he could be conceived to have dutifully and beautifully carried out.

Marriage is not essential; nor is bachelorhood mandatory

Normally a man or a woman feels the need for marriage, and if this is the case they should marry. Marriage is preferable to debauchery and prostitution going on in society. And that is why marriage of unmarried people is encouraged in the Quran:

> **24:32** And *marry (i.e., cause to get married) those among you who are single, and virtuous ones from among your slaves, male or female.* If they are in poverty, God will provide them of His grace. And God is Ample-Giving, Knower of Things.

Also, the Quran notes that the monasticism that the followers of the Prophet Jesus invented was not approved of by God, even though they did this practice only for seeking God's pleasure, since they did not really observe it with the right observance (57:27). God did not prescribe celibacy for them; they impose it on themselves but all of them do not observe the limits. In religion, celibacy is not essential; nor is marriage. Note that neither Jesus nor his mother Mary married, as they never felt the need for marriage. While marriage is not essential, it does not follow that religion should make it mandatory for any to remain a male bachelor or a female celibate for all his or her life. Scandalous acts of sexual abuse that have come to light in recent time with numerous Catholic priests involved are a stark pointer to us. God did not debar them from getting married. Why should the Papacy deny the priests the right to marry? Religion should not seek to impose something often found hard to observe. The Catholic Church is trying to do something well nigh impossible – it wants its priests to live beyond their normal capacity. But God does not task a soul beyond its capacity (2:285; 6:152; 7:42; 65:7). At the same time we should also note that the very system of priesthood that the Christian Church is continuing is questionable. Religion does not approve of any system of priesthood. No one needs a priest in order to be religious – to get one's salvation. One, of course, does benefit from a good religious teacher or guide. One needs, and it definitely helps one, to listen to a good religious teacher, but one should be wary of wrong teachers, gurus or *pirs* who mislead people. Another point to note is that good religious teachers, priests, gurus or *pirs* can only inspire us to be religious, and give us guidance and knowledge, but they cannot themselves give us salvation, or make us evolve spiritually (72:21). That can happen only when we ourselves put in required efforts.

Divorce

The Quran provides clear guidance on how a husband should proceed with divorcing his wife, should it be deemed necessary when the relationship between husband and wife becomes too sour to continue. It also provides guidance on how a wife can seek justice when she has grievances against her husband. If one follows the Quran's advice regarding divorce very carefully, it should become crystal clear that God wants us to proceed very gradually if we decide on separation and divorce. First of all, we should note that a mere uttering by a husband that he has divorced his wife, if he has not really meant it seriously, is no true word of divorce. In anger, a husband may say that he has divorced his wife. But this should not be considered as a real word of divorce, if he does not stick to it when he cools down. It is indeed very unfortunate that in our society, because of wrong teachings from religious teachers around them, there have been instances of instantaneous happenings of divorces just on the basis of uttering of the divorce word three times at a time. But the Quran says that God does not hold us responsible for the mere utterance of oaths or words:

> **2:225** *God will not take you to task for what is unintentional in your oaths (words), but He will take you to task for what your hearts have meant.* God is Ever Forgiving, Most Forbearing.

The first stage to proceed on the course towards a divorce is waiting for four months. This waiting is required for the husband if he is determined or serious about divorcing his wife. This is what the Quran states:

> **2:226** *Those who forswear (definitely intend to divorce) their wives should wait four months, if then they change their mind (and return), God is Ever Forgiving, Most Merciful.*

If after this waiting, a husband firmly decides on a divorce, he can proceed with the divorce. After this divorce, the wife is required to wait three (monthly) courses (the period of *iddat*). A clear message of the Quran is that the husband would be justified to take back his divorced wife in case she is pregnant, and if both agree to this effect. They are required not to conceal if the wife is pregnant. Both husband and wife have similar rights over each other. Look at the verse below:

> **2:228** Divorced women shall wait, keeping themselves apart, three (monthly) courses. And it is not lawful for them that they should conceal that which God hath created in their wombs if they are believers in God and the Last Day. *And their husbands have the right to take them back in that case if they desire reconciliation. And they (wives) have rights similar to those (of men) over them in kindness. ...*

For those women who do not expect to have menstrual courses, or for those who are not having courses, the period of waiting (*iddat*) for the divorced wife is three months. And for those women, who know they are pregnant, the waiting period for the divorced wife is till the birth of the child (65:4). God exhorts those who intend to divorce their wives to do so keeping an eye on the waiting period. God advises them not to drive their wives out of their houses, unless they commit flagrant indecency:

> **65:1-2** O Prophet! *When ye intend to divorce your wives, put them away for divorce for their (prescribed) period, and count the period, and be careful (of your duty) to God, your Lord. Drive them not out of their houses, nor should they themselves leave unless they commit open indecency.* Such are the limits (imposed by) God. And whoever transgresseth God's limits, he verily wrongeth his soul. Thou knowest not; it may be that God will afterward bring some new thing to you. *Then when they have reached their term, take them back with kindness, or part with them with kindness, and take for witness two just men among you, and establish right evidence for God. ...*

The Quran requires that the word of divorce should be pronounced twice, and after that the husband is free either to retain the divorced wife or release her in kindness (2:229, 231), and it is not lawful for the husband to retain his divorced wife to her hurt (2:231).

Verse 230 of Surah Baqarah speaks about the remarrying of the divorced wife by her former husband, if she has married another husband, and states that the remarrying is not lawful unless the second husband has divorced her. The verse reads as follows:

2:230 And *if he hath divorced her, she is not lawful unto him thereafter until another husband she hath married (after the divorce) hath divorced her.* (In that case) it is no blame for both of them if they return to each other, and if they think they can keep within the limits (imposed by) God. And these are the limits ordained by God, which He maketh plain for a people who know.

The meaning of the verse is clear. If the divorced wife marries another husband, it is quite sensible that she cannot remarry her former husband until and unless her second husband divorces her. This is common sense, and stands perfectly to reason. The verse should not be read to imply that the divorced wife has to marry another person, and that that person needs to divorce her to make it possible for the original husband to get her back. Unfortunately, the verse has been translated and interpreted in this latter wrong sense, which represents a glaring example of how some of the verses of the Quran have been grossly misrepresented by our learned religious scholars (*ulama*), who have been influenced by traditional interpretations offered by the Hadith. According to them, the remarriage of husband and wife is not possible unless the divorced wife has married another person, and until that person has divorced her. That precludes the remarriage of husband and wife, if the divorced wife does not, or refuses to, marry another person. That means that the question of remarrying will arise only when the divorced wife marries another husband, and when that husband divorces her. The remarrying of former husband and wife has thus been made conditional upon, first, marrying of the divorced wife to another husband, and second, on the break-up of that marriage. It is the so-called infamous *hilla* system, which has caused great harm in our society by imprudently leading to break-up of many happy marriages, and destruction of many happy lives! The Quran clearly admonishes those who divorce their wives not to force them out of their houses before their term expires, and to make a choice between taking their divorced wives back or parting with them when the term expires, as in verse (65:2) cited above.

The Quran also specifically and explicitly warns and exhorts us not to create any obstacles on the way of remarrying of the divorced wife with her husband:

> **2:232** And *when ye have divorced women, and they have reached their term (iddat), place no difficulties on the way of their remarrying of their husbands, if it is agreed between them in kindness.* This is an admonition for him who believeth in God and the Last Day. That is more virtuous for you, and cleaner. God knoweth and ye know not.

How clear these Quranic admonitions are! No difficulties should be created on the wives' remarriage with their former husbands, if this is mutually agreed. This means that such remarriage and reunion should not be made subject to any additional condition. Yet, it is unfortunate that our learned *ulama*, influenced by traditions, have chosen to mislead Muslims. Does it not ever occur to our common sense that we should not force a divorced wife to marry another husband against her will? Only in case if she willingly marries another person, she cannot be lawful to her former husband unless her current husband divorces her. And why should one ever anticipate that a person would marry the divorced wife of another person just for the sake of divorcing her? All this looks ludicrous. Yet, such a reprehensible practice is found to exist in some places, notably in the Iranian city of Qom where "there are men who make a living as 'one-night husbands': they marry thrice-divorced women, consummate the marriage, and divorce them the next day, so that the women can now lawfully go back to their families."[213]

The Quran has repeatedly urged us to reflect on the verses and apply our sense. Also, importantly, God urges the husband, after he has divorced his wife and the wife has reached her waiting period, to either live together with his divorced wife in kindness or to part from her in kindness, and not to treat lightly the divine advice:

> **2:231** And when ye divorce women and they reach their waiting term, either retain them in a fair manner or let them go in a fair manner. But do not retain them against their will in order to hurt [them] so that ye transgress the limits: for he who doeth so indeed wrongeth himself. And *make not the revelations of*

God a laughing-stock (by your behavior), but remember God's Grace upon you, and that which He hath revealed unto you of the Book and wisdom, whereby He exhorteth you. ...

Even though the current marriage laws in some countries have largely, if not wholly, taken care of the Quranic instructions,[214] yet the vested interest groups try hard to re-impose the notorious *hilla* system. The conscious people in society should firmly stand against such monstrous attempts.

The Quran cautions those who divorce their wives that they should treat their wives in a just and humane manner – that husbands should either retain their divorced wives with kindness, or release them with kindness; that they should not take back anything they have given their divorced wives; that they should bear the living expenses of the divorced wives if they are pregnant and, after delivery of their children, bear the expenses of the suckling of their children (2:231; 4:19-21; 65:6; and 2:233).

At the same time, the grievances of wives who are mistreated by their husbands need also to be appropriately addressed. The Quran urges us to take appropriate measures to address such cases of grievances and in case a dispute occurs between husband and wife in the following manner:

4:128   And if a woman feareth mistreatment from her husband, or desertion, it is no blame on them both if they make an amicable settlement between themselves. Such settlement is better. But greed occupieth (men's) minds. If ye do good and keep from evil, (for such of you), verily God is Ever Aware of what ye do.

4:35   And if ye fear a breach between the two (husband and wife), appoint an arbiter from his folk and an arbiter from her folk. If they desire reconciliation, God will make them of one mind. Verily God is Knower, All-Aware.

It needs also to be noted that the verse (2:228), which gives women rights over men similar to those of men over women, guarantees that

246

women have similar rights of divorce of their husbands as husbands enjoy over wives. In Muslim societies, men are often found to initiate divorce, and women's rights to divorce their husbands are practically limited. Such discrimination, however, goes against the very spirit of the Quran's message in the above verse.

The status of women - women are to be treated with dignity and honor, not as inferior to men

Contrary to the traditional interpretation, and perceived notion in many quarters that Islam has given women a subordinate status to that of men, it has rather accorded full dignity to women, and raised their status to a practically equal level with that of men. God is gender-neutral. So the status of women should not be subordinated to that of men. The Quran is a great vehicle for women's empowerment for all time. It gave them "legal rights of inheritance and divorce; most Western women had nothing comparable until the nineteenth century."[215] Bestowing upon women their proper rights and privileges was nothing short of a revolution in the prevailing social milieu of the time. The changes that the revelation of Islam brought about include prohibition of female infanticide, abolition of women's status as property, establishment of women's legal rights to inheritance, changing marriage from a proprietary to a contractual relationship with women's rights to a dowry, allowing women to retain control over their own property, granting women financial maintenance from their husbands, and controlling the husband's free ability to divorce.

Unlike the Biblical notion that Eve was created out of Adam's rib (Genesis 2:21-24), the Quran does not suggest that Eve was created from Adam. The Quran rather reminds us that we all originate from the same source – the same *nafs* or soul or cell, and that our mates are created of the same kind so that we may incline to them:

4:1 O humankind! Be careful of your duty to *your Lord Who created you from a single nafs, and from it created its mate*, and from them twain hath spread abroad a multitude of men and women.

7:189 *He it is Who did create you from a single nafs, and from it did create his mate that he might incline unto her.*

247

Thus being of the same source, man and woman are on a par with one another. Also, the Quranic expressions that everything has been created in pairs (36:36; 51:49; 53:45) and that a man and a woman are just parts of the same pair also illustrate and underscore the necessary complementary and equal nature of the relationship between a man and a woman.

The Quran has accorded women rights over men similar to those of men over women:

> **2:228**   … And *they (women) have rights similar to those (of men) over them* with justness, and the men are a degree above them. And God is Almighty and Most Wise.

Husband and wife should enjoy similar rights over each other. The above verse and another verse at (4:34) give some edge to men over women. The latter verse cites the reasons why men have some edge over women, which are that men are responsible for maintaining, protecting, and financially supporting the other. Contemporary Muslim scholars have observed that "the edge" referred to in verses 2:228 and 4:34 just reflects "men's socio-economic responsibilities for women", and does not indicate any superiority of men over women in general. They point out that the Quran itself distinguishes between two types of messages: those that are "universal principles" and those that respond "to specific social and cultural contexts or questions [that] were subject to interpretation (3:7). They believe that those verses that assign greater rights to men … reflect a patriarchal context in which men were dominant and solely responsible for supporting women."[216] Noted Islamic scholar Khaled Abou El Fadl very aptly puts it, "men and women equally qualify for God's grace and reward. The authority given to men over women is not because they are men but because, in a particular historical context, men financially provided for women. But if the circumstances change, and women share financial responsibility with men, authority must be equally shared between the two as well."[217]

There is nothing inherent in a man or a woman that makes one superior to the other. In God's sight, the most virtuous person, whether male or female, is the most honored person; and that a woman may indeed excel a man in that respect (49:13) as well as in various qualities (4:32). As mentioned earlier, men and women are gifted with diverse talents and qualities.

In our male-dominated society, women are often treated as inferior to men. Even in the work place, men often discriminate against women. Note, however, that God never discriminates between a man and a woman, and He does not do the least of injustice to any, whether male or female. The Quran emphatically proclaims:

> **3:195** And their Lord hath heard their prayer (and saith): Never do I cause the work of any to be lost, *be ye male or female* – ye are one from another. (See also 4:124; 16:97)

God's message of the equality of sexes is well emphasized also in another place:

> **33:35** Verily for men who surrender (to God), and women who surrender (to God);
> (For) men who believe, and women who believe;
> (For) men who obey, and women who obey;
> (For) men who are truthful, and women who are truthful;
> (For) men who are patient, and women who are patient;
> (For) men who are humble, and women who are humble;
> (For) men who spend in charity, and women who spend in charity;
> (For) men who fast, and women who fast;
> (For) men who guard their chastity, and women who guard their chastity;
> (For) men who remember God much, and women who remember God much;
> (For them all) God hath forgiveness and a great reward.

Men should observe the same spirit and should not discriminate against women. The expression *"ye are one from another or members of one another"* in verse (3:195), which recurs in another place of the Quran (4:25), is also a reminder to men that women are of the same human status as themselves. Further, the verses (30:21 and 2:187) underscores that it is love and mercy that should characterize the relationship between husband and wife. The verse (9:71) describes believing men and women as protecting friends or supporters of one another in virtuous deeds, who

249

enjoin what is just and forbid what is bad. All these verses depict the ideal vision of the relationship between men and women – one of equality and complementarity.

A man need not claim any superiority to his wife. Pharaoh's wife was a pious woman – an example to others, and far superior to Pharaoh in foresight and work (28:9; 66:11). In God's sight, only those are superior, whether male or female, who are superior in righteous conduct and accomplishment (See 49:13 cited earlier).

Men should be chivalrous enough to be able to liberate women from the stranglehold of their domination over them. As husband and wife are in need of each other, they need to respect each other in a similar way. Husbands should be conscious of their obligations to their wives, and responsive to their needs (2:233, 240-241; 4:19-21). Likewise, wives should also be conscious of their obligations to their husbands, and responsive to their needs (60:12).

Also, it is important that wives are conscious of their rights over their husbands. As noted above, if wives fear mistreatment or desertion from their husbands, the Quran provides that they should have a mutual marriage settlement or agreement as a cushion against such possible mistreatment, and such an agreement is a best guarantor of their rights (4:128). The way women can best understand and protect their rights over, and understand their obligations towards, their husbands is through letting them get proper and sufficient education. The opportunities and access to education should be equally available to both boys and girls. It is ironic that in Muslim communities in particular in many regions and countries, female education is grossly neglected, and the existing education facilities are not equally available to boys and girls. As a result the literacy rate among the females is deplorably low in some of these countries. This situation needs to be remedied with great urgency and utmost effort.

It should not be forgotten that mothers play a crucial role in shaping the future of children. An educated mother can guide her children better than an educated father because the father may not find enough time to attend to his children. There is much truth in the adage that "the hand that rocks the cradle rules the world". Indeed, in countries and various regions of the world where the education of girls is neglected, the overall progress of society is hampered relative to those countries and regions where proper emphasis is placed on the education of girls along with that of boys. The relative neglect of the education of girls in Muslim countries goes against the Quran's emphasis on the importance of the acquisition of knowledge and wisdom that only can properly guide every human being, male or female, and empower women to get their rightful place in society. In addition to giving girls equal access to education facilities, another important and practical way Muslim women's status can be lifted would be to empower them economically by supporting them with opportunities to earn income independently, and to enable them to become business entrepreneurs. One good way would be to provide them access to micro-credit facilities along the model of the Grameen Bank of Bangladesh.[218]

God exhorts men to treat women with dignity and honor. This is what the Quran says:

> **4:19-21** O ye who believe! It is not lawful for you to inherit the women against their will, nor should ye treat them with such strain that ye may take back part of that which ye have given them (as dower) unless they commit flagrant indecency. *But live with them with kindness, for if ye dislike them, it may be that ye dislike a thing wherein God hath placed abundant good.* And if ye decide to take one wife in place of another, and even if ye have given one a treasure (of dower), take not back anything from it. Would ye take it back by slandering and a manifest sin? And how could ye take back, when ye have gone in unto each other, and they have taken from you a solemn pledge?

Even at the time when a man divorces his wife, God urges him to take care so as not to cause any injury to his divorced wife (2:231). And the Quran makes the husband fully responsible for financially supporting his divorced wife during pregnancy, and both her and their child during the two years of nursing the baby (2:233).

In still another verse, the Quran explicitly mentions that the virtuous are those who, among other things, wish to see their spouses and their children as a source of comfort for them, and pray to God for such an effect:

> **25:74** And (virtuous are) those who say: Our Lord! Grant us from our wives and children comfort to our eyes, and make us models of those who are upright.

The virtuous men's wives need to be, or are in general, virtuous as well (33:28-34); they go to Heaven along with their husbands (43:68-70). The respectable men's wives are respectable also with rare exceptions. The Prophet's wives are like mothers to all of his followers (33:6). The purport of all this is that women are not to be treated as inferior to men, and their status and rights should be regarded as similar to those of men.

A wrong impression about how husbands should treat their wives, and that the beating of wives by husbands has been made permissible by the Quran has apparently been created by Verse 34 of Surah Nisa (4), which reads as follows:

> **4:34** Men are supporters of women, because God hath given the one more than the other, and because they spend of their means. So good women are *obedient* (*quanitat*) guarding in secret that which God would have them guard. As for those from whom ye fear rebellion, admonish them, leave them apart in beds, or *beat* (?) *them* (*adribu-hunna*). But if they obey you, seek not a way against them.

This verse has been traditionally interpreted as giving husbands the authority to beat or scourge their wives in case of open rebellion (as a matter of last resort after trying the methods of admonishing them first, and then of leaving them alone in bed). However, many modern Muslim scholars point out that the expression "*adribu-hunna*" in the verse does not necessarily mean "strike or scourge them". Amina Wadud points out, "According to *Lisan 'al-Arab*, and *Lanes's Lexicon*, *daraba* does not necessarily indicate force or violence."[219] According to Reza Aslan, the expression "*adribu-hunna*" (which is an extension of *daraba* including the object "them") can also mean "turn away from them," "go along with them," and remarkably, even "have consensual intercourse with them."[220] Edip Yuksel and his colleagues, in their *Quran: A Reformist Translation* have translated this particular text as "separate them" and not as "beat them."[221] According to Jeffrey Lang, "From a purely rational standpoint this alternative interpretation ['turn away from them"] seems preferable to the traditional one ["beat them"], for with regard to the latter it is hard to see how inflicting physical punishment on the wife would lessen her resentment of her husband. If anything, one would think that beating her would accomplish just the opposite. ... This [alternative] interpretation of *udribu* also fits with the non-violent character of all the other recommendations [of 4:34-35], including the fourth step of bringing in family conciliators."[222] The usual interpretation of this verse marks the influence of traditions. However, if we grant that women have just rights over men as men have over women as the Quran demands (2:228), and if we are to maintain propriety and dignity in our mutual behavior, as implied by the Quranic verse: "Live with them in a manner that is dignified" (4:19), the verse above should be interpreted along more compassionate lines. Scourging or beating is undignified and inconsistent with the broader message of the Quran.

Also, one needs to carefully observe the next verse in the Quran, which makes it clear that this guidance of the Quran is directed to mankind in general, rather than to any particular husband, and is for guidance of the judicial process of society. It does not give any authority to husbands to take law in their own hands, especially to resort to the extreme measure of violence against their wives. The next verse of the Quran reads as follows:

4:35   And *if ye fear any breach between the two, appoint an arbiter from his folk and an arbiter from her folk.* If they both desire reconciliation, God will make them of one mind. Verily God is Knower, All-Aware.

This suggests that if a dispute occurs between a man and his wife, it should be settled through the judicial process of society, and should not rest on the husband taking the law in his own hand. Indeed, it is beneath good taste, and it hardly befits a decent man, that he should hurt, injure, or torture his wife in any way, as the Quran explicitly forbids one to injure his wife even when he decides to divorce her, as we have seen in the verse cited above at (2:231). In the admonition particularly given to the Prophet Muhammad in Verse (33:28), God exhorts him to bid goodbye to his wives in a fair manner, if they choose this worldly life. There is no talk of punishing them in other ways. Look at the verse below:

33:28 O Prophet! Say unto thy wives: If ye desire the life of this world and its glitter, then come! I will provide for your enjoyment, and set you free in a fair manner.

Evidently, no harshness to wives is prescribed in the Quran. It rather explicitly urges men to treat them and live with them with kindness (2:231, (4:19-21), not to hate them but regard them as a source of abundant good (4:19-21), and as a source of comfort (25:74). And the Quran also declares that women have rights over men similar to those of men over women (2:228).

The other term used in the verse (4:34) is *quanitat* that has been usually rendered as "obedient" (to the husband). Regarding this the remarks of Amina Wadud are significant:

> [T]he word *quanitat* used here to describe 'good' women is too often falsely translated to mean 'obedient', and then assumed to mean 'obedient to the husband'. In the context of the whole Qur'an, this word is used with regard to both males (2:238, 3:17, 33:35)) and females (4:34, 33:34, 66:5. 66:12).[223] It describes a characteristic or personality trait of believers towards Allah. They are inclined to be co-operative with one another and subservient before Allah.[224]

Also note that the verses (2:228; 4:34) have been interpreted by many Muslim scholars to denote general superiority of men over women. As Amina Wadud rightly points out, this interpretation is mistaken since the preference of men over women in this context is because of the particular conditions of men having larger financial ability and responsibility to support women; it is not an unconditional preference and hence it cannot be construed as indicating any general superiority of men over women.[225] Wadud further notes that the Quranic *tafasir* (exegetical works) done mostly by men reflect their own prejudices towards women and do not display the overall *Weltanschauung* or worldview of the Quran in terms of "emulating certain key principles of human development: justice, equity, harmony, moral responsibility, spiritual awareness, and development. [...] The Quran clearly rejects any [...] notion of the 'inherent' evil of woman. It explicitly demands respect for her 'inherent' good as potential child-bearer (and primary nurturer). It places her on absolute par with man in terms of the spiritual potential (to know and serve Allah) and the potential to attain Paradise."[226]

Indeed, God is unforgiving to those who, among other things, make an unfair discrimination between husband and wife:

> **6:139** And they say: That which is in the bellies of such cattle is reserved for our males, and is forbidden to our wives; but if it is still-born, then they (all) have shares therein. He (God) will punish them for such (false) attribution (to Him). Verily God is Wise, Knower.

The Quran does, however, make some exceptions to the treatment of men and women in a few cases such as in the case of distribution of inherited property from deceased parents, children or other relatives, and in the case of taking them as witnesses for dispensation of judicial justice in business dealings. But such exceptions cannot be considered as real discrimination between men and women, as these are required to maintain proper balance and equity between men and women in property ownership and use, and to ensure justice in business dealings in a social context where men, and not women, shoulder full financial responsibility, and where women do not have the same level of business knowledge as men. The Quran requires that when parents leave behind property at death, a son should get twice as much as a daughter by way of inheritance (4:11); the surviving father gets twice as much as the surviving mother (4:12); and the deceased parent's parents, if they are still living, also get according to the rule that the father gets twice as much as the mother (4:11). Such distinction prescribed in the Quran for distribution of property between men and women is made precisely due to the fact that for the most part, when a daughter gets married, she gets financial support mainly from her husband, and when a son gets married, he needs to take full responsibility for supporting his wife and children, including sometimes supporting the surviving parent. In such circumstances, it should be logical that the male gets a higher share of the inherited property from relatives. But "the rules of law that apply to women", as Abou El Fadl aptly notes, should not be regarded as "static and unchanging. The Islamic law has to keep changing forward to achieve the moral objectives expressed in the Qur'an. To achieve justice, there has to be a constant effort to achieve a more authentic proportionality between the duties and rights of Muslim women. So, for instance, if within the social dynamics of time, women carry a financial responsibility equal to [that of] men, it is more consistent with Shari'a to allow women an equal share to men in inheritance."[227]

One important thing that we need to carefully note in the context of distribution of inherited property is that we do need to accommodate any special needs of the relatives who are poor and other poor people who may be present or perceived during such distribution of inherited property from deceased relatives (See 4:7-8 cited earlier). This consideration plus the fact that we have been exhorted by God to make a will for distribution of our property at the time when death approaches us, i.e. before death, suggest that a special consideration should be applied for accommodation of the needs of the poor, including poor relatives, in our property. If some of the near relatives are poor relative to the others, this consideration should allow the poor ones, including the females, to receive a larger share of the property than the usual distribution rules prescribed in the Quran would imply.

Apart from the inheritance case, the other case where the Quran makes some distinction between men and women is where testimony is taken for making contracts for financial transactions. The Quran requires two men as witnesses, and in case two men are not found, one man and two women can substitute for two men as witnesses (2:282). It is only in the case of financial transactions that the Quran makes this distinction for making testimonies. Contemporary scholars think that such discrimination is in order in a context when women are less informed than men in financial matters. Thus the Quran states that two females are required because if one of them forgets, the other may remind her (2:282). "Some contemporary female [Muslim] scholars have argued that the requirement of two female witnesses demonstrates the need for women to have access to education, both secular and religious, in order to receive the training and experience to be equal to men in a business environment – something that has not been prohibited by the Quran. In light of the right of the women to own property and make their investments, this interpretation is in keeping with broader Quranic values."[228]

A first significant effort for Muslim family law reform covering marriage, divorce and inheritance through reinterpretation of the Quran, and to liberate women advocating their rights, education and access to social life and the professions was made by Qasim Amin, an Egyptian and a disciple of Muhammad Abduh, through his remarkable book in

Arabic titled *The Liberation of Woman* published in 1899. The book, translated in Turkish and other languages, "evoked a very strong reaction from the traditionalist establishment in Egypt and elsewhere ... [but] had a considerable impact, more especially on the rising generation of women."[229] Qasim Amin's efforts in Egypt were paralleled by similar efforts by Mumtaz Ali, a disciple of Sir Sayyid Ahmad Khan, in India. As Esposito notes:

> Both focused on the plight of Muslim women as a primary cause of the deterioration of the family and society. [...] Qasim Amin criticized lack of education, child marriages, arranged marriages, polygamy, and easy male-dominated divorce as causes of the bondage of Muslim women. Ali took a similar position. Ali refuted the antifeminist Quranic exegesis of some classical legal scholars, maintaining that their interpretations did not reflect the meaning of Quranic texts but the customs and mores of the exegetes' own times. Fundamental reforms were required. These ideas informed the positions of the feminist movements and political elites a generation later in the 1920s and 1930s.[230]

As noted earlier, in recent years notable reforms have been made in Muslim marriage and divorce laws in a number of countries (See endnote 213). Yet the plight of Muslim women still remains deplorable in many parts of the world. As Aslan notes, a feminist movement is currently under way throughout the Muslim world in trying to regain their equal status in light of the Quran:

> [...] a whole new generation of contemporary female textual scholars is reengaging the Quran from a perspective that has been sorely lacking in Islamic scholarship. Beginning with the notion that it is not the moral teachings of Islam but the social conditions of seventh century Arabia and the rampant misogyny of male Quranic exegetes that has been responsible for their inferior status in Muslim society, these women are approaching the Quran free from the confines of traditional gender boundaries. Amina Wadud's instructive book *Quran and Woman: Reading the Sacred Text from a Woman's Perspective* provides the template for this movement, though Wadud is by no means alone in her endeavor. Muslim feminists throughout the world have been laboring toward a gender-

neutral interpretation of the Quran and a more balanced application of Islamic law while at the same time struggling to inject their political and religious views into the male-dominated, conservative societies in which they live. Muslim feminists do not perceive their cause as a mere social reform movement, they consider it as a religious obligation. As Shirin Ebadi proudly declared while accepting the 2003 Nobel Peace Prize for her tireless work for defending the rights of women in Iran, "God created us all as equals. [...] By fighting for equal status, we are doing what God *wants* us to do.[231]

In the early Islamic community in Medina, women played important roles. Aslan adds, "The so-called Muslim women's movement is predicated on the idea that Muslim men, not Islam, have been responsible for the suppression of women's rights. For this reason, Muslim feminists are advocating a return to the society Muhammad originally envisioned for his followers. Despite differences in culture, nationalities, and beliefs, these women believe that the lesson to be learned from Muhammad in Medina is that Islam is above all an egalitarian religion. Their Medina is a society in which Muhammad designated women like Umm Waraka as spiritual guides for the Ummah; in which the Prophet himself was sometimes rebuked by his wives; in which women prayed and fought alongside the men; in which women like Aisha and Umm Salamah acted not only as religious but also as political – and on at least one occasion military – leaders; and in which the call to gather for prayer, bellowed from the rooftop of Muhammad's house, brought men and women together to kneel side by side and be blessed as a single undivided community."[232] As Esposito notes, women in this early Islamic community not only fought in battles but also "nursed the wounded during the time of the Prophet. They were consulted about who should succeed Muhammad after his death. Women also contributed to the collection and compilation of the Quran[, ...] owned and sold property, engaged in commercial transactions, and were encouraged to seek and provide educational instruction[. ...] The second Caliph, Umar Ibn al-Khattab, appointed women to serve as officials in the marketplace of Medina."[233]

The way women are required to dress in some Muslim societies is often seen as a reflection of men controlling women - "a symbol of women's inferior status"[234]. The veil (*burqa*), the headscarf (*hijab*) or *chadar,* which many Muslims wear has become a subject of intense religious and

258

political debate in recent time. Many Muslims view the recent ban on *hijab* wearing by Muslim girls in schools in France and parts of Germany as an infringement on human rights, while the governments imposing the ban argue that this goes against their secular tradition. Many Muslims view it as part of the modesty requirements stipulated by the Quran (24:31), and in line with the directions made to the Prophet's and believers' wives and daughters (33:59). Note also that the Quran stipulates modesty requirements also for men (24:30). Wearing a veil was not a general practice of Muslim women during the Prophet's time. In fact veiling did not become a widespread vogue in the Muslim world until three to four generations after the Prophet's death.[235] What the Quran directs, and what is really important, is that Muslim women should wear decent and dignified dresses so as not to evoke men's invitation to indecency (33:32-33). The Quran allows leaving parts of the body uncovered that are normally apparent such as head, face, hands and feet. It specifically mentions the private parts and bosoms for covering by the dress; it does not mention head, face, hands and feet for covering by the dress (24:31). Guarding modesty requires believers to maintain purity of attitude in mind, and decency of behavior with persons of the opposite sex. This is obviously more important than using a veil (*burqa* or *hijab*), which is not always found to be a good reflector of one's decency of behavior with persons of the opposite sex. Veiling thus should not be viewed as an essential Islamic dress.

Since women have the same rights over men as men have over them (2:228), women should be allowed to exercise the same rights as men in all decision making processes, including the political process. That means that they should have the same political and voting rights as men, and that they have similar rights to govern as men, if they are equally qualified to do the job. The Quran approvingly refers to the Queen of Sheba as a head of state, which illustrates the point that women have the necessary capacity, judgment and expertise to take on important state responsibilities. It is encouraging to see that several countries in the contemporary Muslim world (Pakistan, Turkey, Indonesia and Bangladesh) have had or have women Presidents or Prime Ministers.

Islamic religion as prescribed by the Quran does not undermine the status of women *vis-à-vis* that of men. The Quran rather gloriously upholds the dignity and status of women, coming at a time when, and in a society where, women were being treated in a far degrading manner. It is, however, the so-called Hadith, which with its misleading messages, has confounded and misguided Muslims. Look at just a few of the individual Hadith narrations below, which are sufficient to demonstrate how great a damage the Hadith has done to the understanding of the status of women by most Muslims.

> Narrated Usama: The Prophet said: I stood at the gate of Paradise and saw that the majority of the people who entered it were the poor, while the wealthy were stopped at the gate. But the people destined for the Fire were ordered to be taken to the Fire. Then I stood at the gate of the Fire and saw that the majority of those who entered it were women. (Sahih Bukhari, Volume 7, Book 62, Number 124)

> Narrated Usama bin Zaid: The Prophet said: After me I have not left any affliction more harmful to men than women (Sahih Bukhari, Volume 7, Book 62, Number 33).

> Narrated Ibn 'Umar: Evil omen was mentioned before the Prophet: The Prophet said: If there is evil omen in anything, it is in the house, the woman and the horse (Sahih Bukhari, Volume 7, Book 62, Number 31).

It is indeed surprising how these Hadiths, which are clear lies and clearly contradictory to the Quran, are attributed to the Prophet Muhammad! Yet another virulent Hadith against women narrated by Abu Said al-Khudri depicts them as deficient in intelligence and religion *(Sahih Bukhari,* Vol. 1, Book 6, # 301). In regard to this Hadith, Aslan remarks that many have considered Abu Said al-Khudri's memory as "unchallenged, despite the fact that Muhammad's biographers present him as repeatedly asking for and following the advice of his wives, even in military matters".[236] One wonders how a man of the stature of a prophet could speak so lightly of women and, most importantly, against the very spirit of the message of the Quran. The fact of the matter is that all such Hadith texts are fabricated – fabrications made in a male-dominated and misogynic society, and are misleading to humankind. It is ironic that Muslim fundamentalists or puritans display a particularly demeaning attitude toward women, treating them "as a constant source of danger, and vulnerability for Islam," and going "as far as branding women as the main source of corruption and evil."[237] Indeed, as Bernard Lewis points out, the emancipation of women in Muslim countries has been a most problematic challenge in the face of a strong resistance from traditional conservatives and radical fundamentalists, who view such liberation as mere Westernization, distinguished from modernization, and "a betrayal of Islamic values".[238] No doubt, as Lewis identifies, the degrading way women are being treated in many Muslim countries and regions – their rights of access to education and work in public place being suppressed, their social and political rights being curbed and their personal freedom being curtailed relatively to the rights and privileges enjoyed by the males – has been a major cultural factor holding back modernization and development of these countries.[239] But this cultural snag is not a fault line with Islam if understood in light of the Quran alone; it is due to the misleading influence that has come from the Hadith.

The treatment of slaves: free or marry slaves, not enjoy them in captivity

In the context of marriage, it is not simply the issue of the status and rights of women *vis-à-vis* those of men that is relevant, but the issues of whether a human being should be a slave, and how slaves are to be treated in marriage relationships are also important matters to consider. The institution of slavery is strongly discouraged by the Quran. With the progress of civilization, stark and large-scale forms of slavery have been largely abolished from the earth. However, slavery and slavery-like practices still exist today in parts of the world. If slavery exists or persists in society, the Quran strongly urges the believers to free the slaves as a matter of virtuousness. Indeed it is not for the righteous to have captives or slaves with them unless as free members of their family, since God has ordained freeing of slaves as an integral part of righteousness (See 90:12-18 cited earlier.)

The Quran thus condemns slavery and extols the virtues of freeing slaves in unequivocal terms. The Prophet Muhammad himself set a noble example by freeing his slave Zaid, and making him his own adopted son. In fact, the duty incumbent upon those who seek real virtuousness is to free slaves, not to enjoy them in captivity. The Quran makes it amply clear that those who earnestly seek righteousness do not themselves indulge in keeping any as slaves rather than as part of the same family, as the Prophet himself demonstrated by making Zaid his adopted son.

Slavery has existed in human society from time immemorial. Moses' people were slaves, and victims of torture perpetrated on them by Pharaoh's folks, and it was Moses who liberated them from Pharaohs' folks. Even though the Quran, revealed in the seventh century, came with a clarion call for freeing slaves, slavery has significantly existed in Saudi Arabia and much of the Muslim world well into the twentieth century until it was officially abolished[240], and has been widely practiced in the developed countries such as the United States even in the nineteenth century. In 1830, there were more than 2 million African-American slaves in the United States. The 1865 Emancipation Proclamation (1863) and Union victory (1865) freed almost 4 million slaves.[241] The United Kingdom abolished it in its empire at the beginning of the nineteenth century, and treated slave trading as an international crime. It took up to the late twentieth century for slavery to be abolished in the Middle East, with rare local exceptions.[242] In one form or another, slavery still persists in various countries including developed countries. News reports suggest existence of clandestine or overt human trafficking in women and children from less developed or impoverished to more developed or rich regions of the world. The long-running troubles in the Darfur region of Sudan have led to a spate in slave trade.[243]

Slavery is a most cruel and dehumanizing institution. It does not advance the cause of overall human evolution. The full potential for the human race cannot be achieved if human beings enslave and suppress other human beings. A good Muslim will never enslave a person, but will rather free him or her, or keep him or her as an equal member of his family. Social egalitarianism is a hallmark of Islam. This is the only way we evolve and elevate all men and women, and help develop their latent talents and bring about all round progress in society.

In Verse (4:25), God provides a clear direction that one should consider marrying from among slave girls, should he find it difficult to marry a free woman. In some other verses also, the Quran clearly states that one needs to marry slave girls or free them to get married, not to own and enjoy them in captivity without marriage. The full verse at (4:25) along with other related verses are reproduced below:

> **4:25** And whoever among you who have not the means to afford to marry free believing women, (they) *may marry believing girls from among those whom your right hands possess* (slave girls, including girls among prisoners of war); and God knoweth best your faith. Ye are one from another. Marry them obtaining permission from their guardians, and give them their dowries according to what is just; they should be

chaste, not committing indecency, and nor having (them) as paramours in secret (or concubines). After marriage if they commit indecency, their punishment will be half of that for free women. This is for those among you who fear falling into evil; and that ye abstain is better for you; and God is Ever Forgiving, Most Merciful.

24:32-3   And *marry (cause to get married) those who are single, and the virtuous among your male or female slaves.* If they are poor, God will give them means out of His Grace. And God is Ample-Giving, and Knower of All Things. Let those who have not the means to marry, keep themselves chaste till God giveth them means out of HIs Grace. *If any of your slaves ask for a deed in writing (for freedom from slavery), give them such a deed if ye know of any good in them; give them of the means that God hath given you. But force not your maids to prostitution that ye may seek enjoyment of this worldly life, when they desire chastity.* ... (See also 4:3 cited earlier)

In verse (33:50), which does not explicitly mention the requirement of prior marriage, the Quran mentions slave girls (prisoners of war) as lawful to the Prophet in the same way as his cousins and other believing women, which suggests that slaves deserve similar treatment, i.e., they need to be married prior to being lawful, like cousins and other believing women. The Quran also exhorts us not to take any as paramours or concubines (4:25; 5:5). It speaks of marrying orphans (4:3), not enslaving them. It urges believers to give deeds of emancipation to those slaves who ask for such a writing if they know any good in them, and give them out of their riches, and not to compel them to prostitution (24:33). So it follows that the Quran strongly encourages us to set slaves free, and marry them, rather than take them as legal partners in conjugal life without marrying them, even though in some other verses, the Quran appears to give the sense that slave girls are lawful without prior marriage (4:24; 23:5-6; and 70:29-30).

One is also likely to get the impression from the last part of Verse (24:33) that God is lenient or forgiving to those who force slave girls to prostitution. However, such an interpretation of the verse would appear to be rash and inappropriate, since to think that God is forgiving to those who violate His advice is wrong. We have already cited above some verses (4:25; 24:32), where the Quran has explicitly advised us to marry slave girls. Also note that the verse at (24:33) clearly mentions that those who force slave girls to prostitution seek this worldly life. God cannot be kind and forgiving to those who seek worldly gain. God cannot approve of beast-like behavior. Such people, who are driven by lewdness, and who forsake chastity, are not eligible for God's forgiveness unless they are truly repentant, and unless they mend their conduct. It is far beneath the taste of decent, righteous people that they should enjoy girls in captivity, let alone compel any of them to prostitution, especially since the Quran specifically mentions freeing of slaves as part and parcel of righteousness. The duty of those who earnestly wish to be virtuous cannot have any slaves with them, since they will free them in accordance with God's wishes, or retain them as free members of their own families in the way the Prophet Muhammad did.

One thing we need to carefully observe is what God says He wishes for us:

> **5:6** God wisheth not to place any burden (or difficulty) on you. But *He wisheth to purify you, and to perfect His niamat (grace) for you*, that ye may be grateful.

If we sincerely wish to move in the direction of purification and piety, we cannot be bogged down with the mundane pleasures of this world, and cannot think of enslaving human beings against God's clear advice to free slaves.

X. SOME IMPLICATIONS OF THE QURANIC MESSAGE FOR THE ECONOMIC SYSTEM

(O humankind!) *Give full measure; and be not of those who give less. And weigh with right scales. And wrong not men of their things (or rights), and act not corruptly in the earth, making mischief.* – 26:181-183

Introduction

Some might wonder if economics or economic system has anything to do with religion. Yet, it is instructive to see if religion in general – and Islam in particular – has anything to offer in this regard. Religion provides normative guidance and inspiration to man to be true and honest in all respects, to be good to others, and to do justice in all of his dealings, including economic dealings. We do need to translate the concept of justice as proclaimed by religion in the conduct of ourselves in all affairs, including economic activities and transactions. And, for maintaining equity, and ensuring special humanitarian treatment of disadvantaged groups, Islam in particular offers not only inspiration but also specific guidelines. Overall, we get broad guidelines from Islam for conducting our economic affairs. God repeatedly exhorts us in the Quran to reflect on His message, and apply our sense (38:29; 10:24; 47:24; 39:27; 59:21). This highlights the need for efforts to interpret the Quranic message carefully and appropriately to work out its implications in various areas.

A vibrant and prosperous economic system is built upon the bedrock of certain core human values, which are values of any religion including Islam – values of truthfulness and honesty, fairness and justice and rule of law, respect for human dignity, and freedom and human rights. In such an economy, some preconditions that need to be fulfilled include social harmony, and political peace and stability, decent living conditions for the labor force, a supportive government with a good legal system and efficient and corruption-free service providers, and freedom for all men and women to uninterruptedly pursue their economic goals. Religion in a proper sense embraces all elements of modernity that make things better, fairer and more just for all people with proper checks against any bad elements. Islam, properly understood, embraces the elements of modernity that define the western economic system – the ideas of liberty, competition, free enterprise, integrity and business ethics, etc. Religious groups like Muslims have lagged behind because of

265

their obsession with wrong traditions. The wrong fatalistic attitudes fostered and cultivated among Muslims, which are not part of Islam but wrongly attributed to it, are largely to blame for their lack of initiative and drive for their own development. The Quran makes it amply clear that "Man has only that for which he makes effort" (See 53:39 cited earlier and 20:15), and that "God does not change the condition of a people until they change their own *nafs* or soul" (13:11 cited earlier). Thus, to come out of their economic doldrums, the first thing Muslims need to do is to shun and change their fatalistic attitudes, and come to believe that they can expect rewards or results to follow according to, and proportionately to, what they actually do, and try to get done.

The Quranic guidelines and some implications for the economic system

A careful study of the relevant Quranic guidelines points to some broad and important implications for the economic system as follows:

- Islam favors neither pure capitalism nor pure socialism, but a capitalist system with a socialistic overtone to care for the basic needs and welfare concerns of the poor and disadvantaged groups in society;
- Islam is for an equitable economic system where economic inequalities are not stark;
- Islam allows trading, and endorses a free market system with appropriate qualifications; and
- Islam condemns and forbids all kinds of exploitation, including market manipulation.

One theme that runs through the Quran is that we must be fully alive to the need for ensuring distributive justice in society, and should not neglect the needs of the poor and the deprived. The Prophet Muhammad himself was an orphan and a needy person, and when he found shelter and became free of want he was strongly urged by God not to be oblivious of the needs of the orphans and the needy (93:6-10). The Quran thus emphasizes distribution; but at the same time it lays down certain broad guidelines that point to the need for an efficient production and marketing system in the economy to support what we might say is the most important objective of human endeavor, i.e., moral and spiritual uplifting of all men and women in society.

266

According to the Quran, some of the essential elements or principles of an ideal economic system would include the following:

- Respect for private property;
- Respect for individual economic freedom, initiative and enterprise;
- Requirement of recording of loan and debt dealings, and respect for contractual obligations, and requirement of returning of trusted properties;
- Recognition that everything belongs to God, which calls for an equitable distribution of wealth, and allowance for social security, social welfare and common good;
- Condemnation of exploitation or monopoly power, and promotion of sufficient market competition;
- Allowing free play of economic forces, i.e., freedom of work, initiative and enterprise, freedom of production, free movement of factors of production, and goods and services with some exceptions (See below); and
- Promotion of an environment conducive to both spiritual development and supportive material development, i.e., social and economic development.

The Quran recognizes the sanctity of private property, but not of ill-gotten property that should be confiscated by the state, and properly redistributed among the poor, deserving citizens, or for other beneficial social causes. The recognition of private property rights along with the related stipulation that none should encroach upon others' property is clear from the verse "devour not each other's property among yourselves wrongfully (2:188), and another verse that advises us to approach orphans' property only with good intentions, and not with an intention of grabbing such property (17:34).

On the other hand, the Quran advises the custodians of orphans' property not to return it to them if the orphans are found weak in understanding, which implies, if they are unable to manage their property themselves:

> **4:5-6** And *give not unto those (orphans) weak in understanding the properties that God hath entrusted with you to maintain; but feed and clothe them from it, and speak to them kindly. And check the orphans*

for their puberty. And if ye find them of sound judgment, restore unto them their property. Devour it not extravagantly in a hurry, lest they should grow up. If the guardian is well-off, let him refrain generously (from taking any remuneration from the orphans' property), but if he is poor, let him have thereof for himself what is just and reasonable. When ye return them their properties call witnesses in their presence. And God sufficeth as a Reckoner.

Though these verses refer to orphans' property, the substance of the message contained in these verses is equally applicable to any property, the owners of which are found to be unable to manage, or manage properly or efficiently, for some reason. According to this message, in cases where some valuable national property is found to be mismanaged by its owner(s), the state has a right to entrust its management to others who are more efficient, while giving the owners their due after deduction of the reasonable management fees.

Note that some of the above verses urging well-off custodians to refrain from taking any remuneration for managing the property, and the poor custodians to take reasonable remunerations point to the need for avoiding any form of exploitation of others' property, and the need for observing restraint on sharing poor men's wealth on the part of rich men managing their assets.

The Quran encourages recording of loan and debt operations, and urges honoring of contractual obligations, and returning of trusted properties:

2:282   *O ye who believe! When ye contract a debt for a fixed term, record it in writing.* Let a scribe record it in writing between you with equity... And be not averse to writing down (the contract) whether it be small or large, with (record of) the term thereof. That is more equitable in the sight of God, and more accurate for testimony, and the best way to avoid doubt among you, except only in the case of ready merchandise which ye trade from hand to hand.

2:283   *If ye be on a journey, and cannot find a scribe, then a pledge in hand (shall suffice).* And if one of you entrusteth (something) to another, *let him who is trusted deliver up that which is entrusted to him*, and let him be careful (of his duty) to God. Hide not testimony. He who hideth it, verily his heart is sinful. God is aware of what ye do.

4:58   *Verily God commandeth you to restore trusts to their owners*, and if ye judge between mankind, judge justly.

These verses underscore the importance of recording of all economic deals, where such deals involve a time element, and honoring of all contractual obligations. Indeed an economy cannot function well and prosper unless these norms of behavior are meticulously followed. One of the reasons why developed countries in the world are more developed than the less developed countries is precisely the fact that business ethics is much more strictly observed in the former countries than in the latter. Corruption is generally widespread in developing countries, including Muslim countries, and it significantly affects their economic development.[244]

Since hoarding is often resorted to by unscrupulous businessmen to artificially raise prices of the hoarded goods in the market, such hoarding is both economically and socially unjustified. Hoarding is a device for gaining market (or monopoly) power, and thus for cheating or exploiting consumers. As mentioned in Chapter 6, hoarding hurts an economy by creating artificial scarcities and high prices of the hoarded goods. Hoarding of monetary assets leads to curbing of effective demand in the economy. The Quran strongly condemns hoarding:

3:180   And *let not those who hoard up that which God hath bestowed upon them out of His grace think that it is better for them. Nay, it is worse for them.* That which they hoard will be tied to their necks like a collar on the Day of Resurrection. God's is the heritage of the heavens and the earth; and God is aware of what ye do.

The Quran rules out any kind of human injustice, exploitation or cheating of any kind, whether it is individual, societal, religious, sectarian, political or economic (16:90; 5:8; and 26:181-183 cited earlier; and

269

17:35). When it comes to economic matters, economic policies, activities, or transactions that cannot be justified by the norm of justice should be considered as not permitted by Islam. A just and exploitation-free economy conceived by Islam has far-reaching implications. Some are as follows:

- There should be competition in economic dealings – in trading (selling or buying) of anything (goods, services and factors of production such as capital, land and labor), and appropriate measures should be taken to curb monopolistic behavior and elements found in any such dealings;

- There should be no hurdles or obstructions to the free production, and free flow and movement of goods and services and factors of production, including capital, labor, and knowledge and technology within a country as well as across the borders of countries, excepting for some goods that can be restricted on religious and health grounds or for strategic reasons;

- Work in the work place should be judged by quality or efficiency of work alone, and there should be no discrimination according to sex, creed, color, or geographical origin. If concessions are to be made for disadvantaged groups, these should be made in a policy-neutral way that does not affect the production system or the allocation of resources. This would require that the social safety net or subsidization programs, if undertaken by the state, should be financed by the state general budget from general government tax revenue, not by taxes on or subsidies for specific economic activities; [245]

- From the point of view of creating equitable opportunities for access to resources for all men and women, and from the point of view of making maximum possible contribution to the production and welfare potential of an economy, where existing distribution of land and other resources is found grossly unequal, a redistribution of such resources should be carried out;[246] and

- Economic policies should be directed to ameliorating the material and spiritual conditions, and facilitating such pursuits of all men and women, and to removing distortions in all economic activities, and creating an environment conducive to private enterprise, growth and development.

270

Since it will take us much beyond the confines of this chapter to elaborate on these implications, it may suffice here to make some brief observations as follows:

- Islam advocates an appropriate synthesis of both capitalistic and socialistic systems. The socialistic features that need to be incorporated in a predominantly capitalistic system are appropriate social security and safety net measures, embodying the charity system and social welfare programs that the Quran prescribes. (See Chapter 6 on Spending in God's Way).

- Islamic principles call for abolition of all controls and taxes on production and trade of all goods and services except for goods that qualify for a prohibition on religious, medical or strategic defense grounds. Controls and licensing create vested interests and artificial scarcities, and scope for corruption and exploitation. Production or trade-specific direct controls and taxes cause distortions in the allocation of resources that is consistent with natural efficiency in each line of production. Since production or trade subsidies also distort the allocation of resources by artificially encouraging such production or trade, these subsidies are also not permissible from the point of view of economic or social justice that Islam endorses.

- By the same token, there should be no direct restrictions, tariffs or subsidies on imports and exports of any country. Modern economic theory and also available empirical evidence on the effects of trade liberalization and other globalization measures worldwide suggest that free trade fosters maximum economic growth and welfare of all countries, including developing countries. The world will be a much better place if existing protectionist practices and tendencies both in developed and developing countries are significantly reduced and phased out as quickly as possible. This calls for co-operation and support on the part of all countries for multilateral trade reform programs being conducted through the auspices of the World Trade Organization (WTO). Opposition to free trade and globalization that comes from certain quarters on fears of losses of jobs in previously protected industries to foreign countries, and less growth of developing countries is largely misperceived. However, any adverse effects on employment that may follow

271

from a free trade situation can be effectively tackled by additional safety measures, as recent and ongoing donor-supported policies and practices of developing countries suggest. The fear of any loss of economic growth is simply misplaced, since it is protection that causes a net loss of economic growth.

- The state should take appropriate effective measures to curb monopolistic practices of both suppliers or sellers and buyers of any goods and services, as well as of factors of production such as labor, land and capital. That means that the government should endeavor to ensure competitive pricing of the following prices:

  - Prices of all goods and services;
  - Wages of labor;
  - Rent on land; and
  - Interest or return on borrowed and lent capital.

  Note that competition in such prices can be encouraged by curbing of monopolistic practices, not by any direct price controls. Direct controls on prices are counter-productive: they distort the allocation of resources. (For more, see below.)

- And the state should also take the responsibility of putting in place appropriate economic policies and measures to ensure an environment that is conducive to economic development with reasonable price stability. The State should also make use of pro-active policies to promote and accelerate economic development to alleviate poverty and create employment for the unemployed. Inflation is a hidden and regressive tax on the poor; and deflation is damaging to development. The state needs to ensure a reasonable price stability to avoid too much price increase, which is unjust to the poor, and at the same time the state should not allow price inflation to go below a certain level that may trigger deflation, recession or depression, which is more damaging to an economy.

Islamic principles are thus basically oriented to promotion of a free market competitive economy. The idea that Islam really promotes the capitalistic orientation of the economy rather than a heavily socialistic

272

one is also shared by Turkish journalist Mustafa Akyol. He provides an interesting, critical review of the positions generally taken by Muslim scholars on the issues of interest (See below for his position on the interest issue) and capitalistic *versus* socialistic orientation of the economy – positions that, according to Akyol, are harming the interests of Muslims. They mostly lean toward a socialistic structure of the economy, while, Akyol argues, Islam is really compatible with a free capitalistic economy, not socialism. "It is true that the Koran has a strong emphasis on social justice and this has led some modern Muslim intellectuals to sympathize with socialism and its promise of a 'classless society.' A careful reading of the Koran would work against such 'Islamo-socialism'", he writes.[247]

Indeed the Quran urges us to compete one with another in all good work:

5:48 … So *vie ye one with another in good work*. Unto God is your goal. …

By implication, competition in good work should be extended to all economic activities. The best or most effective way to eliminate monopolistic behavior or exploitation is to ensure competition in all economic activities and transactions. Note, however, that competition must be a fair one in the sense that it must not be cutthroat competition at below cost price, which is sometimes resorted to by unscrupulous businessmen to gain monopolistic control of the market. This cannot be approved of by religion. The state should assume the responsibility to enforce sound and effective competition rules for the market.

But at the same time Islam requires a well-devised safety-net or social welfare program to safeguard the interests of, and cater to the basic needs of, the poor and disadvantaged groups in society. It also requires state promotion of economic and social development to effectively solve the problem of the poor and the unemployed. If the distribution of economic resources is grossly unequal, Islam requires some appropriate redistribution of such resources, especially of land. These points need some further elaboration.

As already explained in Chapter 6, high inequality of income and wealth not only hurts healthy economic and social development but also destroys social cohesion, peace and harmony, and breeds bitter feelings on the part of the poor and deprived people, and creates scope for social crimes, immorality and frustration. After all, everything belongs to God:

22:64   *Unto Him belongeth all that is in the heavens and all that is in the earth.* Verily God is Rich (Self-Sufficient), Praiseworthy.

So, in nations where stark inequality of resources, especially land, is found as in many countries, it will be advisable to carry out appropriate redistributive land reform in such countries (see also Endnote 245). There is also a need for the state to shoulder a major part of the required spending for welfare or benevolent activities for the poor and disadvantaged groups in society, which is *sadaqa* in the Quranic terms. There is a well-devised social security system in many developed countries. Such a system should be replicated in all countries, including developing countries, and the required fiscal (appropriate taxation and expenditure) implications and responsibilities should be worked out and borne by the respective states. Also the state needs to take a great deal of responsibility to devise an appropriate tax and expenditure system to cater to the needs of public goods and services, which if left to the private sector alone will risk being grossly neglected or inadequately met.[248] All such state functions should count within the purview of God's cause. And, as already mentioned in Chapter 6, in an impoverished developing economy, the state has a special role to play in promoting economic development, which indeed is the best answer to alleviation of poverty for the poor.

Monopoly in production, selling or buying of any goods and services and factors of production leads to an undue constriction in their production and supplies causing monopolistic pricing of such goods and services. That demands abolition of all existing controls or barriers that impede competition in such activities, e.g., existing barriers or difficulties to, and controls on, new entry to business by aspiring entrepreneurs. However, in the case of production, even with full removal of existing controls and barriers to production, the very nature of the scale of production can create monopolies, both at individual and state levels. In such situations of what are known as natural monopolies, the government needs to resort to effective taxation measures to siphon off monopoly profits with some qualification. The qualification relates to the need for retention of a sufficient incentive to technological innovation. Technological innovation plays a very significant role in fostering growth, and in reducing costs of production, in reducing prices that consumers pay, and thus in improving the living standards of man. A proper synthesis or compromise needs to be struck between mopping up excess profits from the production and distribution system and retaining a sufficient incentive for those who innovate.

Monopolistic sellers charge higher than normal prices; monopolistic buyers (monopsonists) cause the sellers to sell at lower than normal prices. Both such sellers and buyers cause exploitation, which needs to be tackled by appropriate policy response, but not through direct price control or regulation. Price regulation has been proven to be an inappropriate policy instrument because of its possible adverse effects on the allocation of resources. Economists advocate appropriate taxation in the case of both monopolies and monopsonies, which does not artificially affect production on specific lines.

In sum, the implications of the Quranic guidelines as analyzed above profess an economic system that is ideal in all respects: which has a distribution of productive resources that is not grossly unequal in the first place, which ensures as much equality of opportunities for all as possible; which ensures maximum possible protection from human exploitation; which ensures maximum possible economic liberalization and competition, while trying at the same time to reward private initiative and enterprise, and technological innovation; which ensures basic needs of all disadvantaged groups by humanitarian safety-net programs; and which promotes economic, social and spiritual development.

The Quran prohibits interest charged to the poor and disadvantaged, not interest *per se*

A careful reading of the Quranic advice on interest or usury (*riba*) clearly suggests that its prohibition really relates to interest on loans that are extended to poor and disadvantaged people, who deserve humanitarian treatment or charity (*sadaqa*). This is evident from the following verses:

2:275-6 Those who devour usury cannot rise except as one who riseth whom the devil hath prostrated by touch. That is because they say: 'Trading is just like usury'; but *God hath permitted trading and forbidden usury. ... God blesseth not usury; but He causeth charitable* *deeds (sadaqa) to prosper.* He loveth not an ungrateful sinner.

3:130 O ye who believe! *Devour not usury, doubling and quadrupling*; and be careful of (your duty to) God, that ye may succeed. (See also 30:39 cited earlier)

2:278-80O ye who believe! Be careful of (your duty to) God, and *give up what remaineth of usury*, if ye are (true) believers. And if ye do not, then be warned of war (against you) from God and His messenger. And if ye repent, then you have your principal. Wrong not and ye shall not be wronged. And *if the debtor is in straitened circumstances, then postpone (the debt repayment) till it is easy for him to repay. But if ye remit it by way of charity (sadaqa), that is best for you if ye only knew.*

Some points of these verses deserve close attention:

- Interest or usury is not comparable to trade. This is suggestive of the practice of interest during the period of revelation, when interest was indeed not comparable to profits in trading. Trading is between two commercial groups, but interest was charged on loans extended generally to people who did not engage in commercial trading or production.

- Charging of interest to people who deserve *sadaqa* or *zakat* is unethical, and hence cannot be permitted. The kind of interest or usury that God forbade was really the kind which was being charged to people who deserved rather charity or compassionate treatment, not business-like treatment. The individual lenders in the past usually did not consider the plight of the people whom they lent money, and they used to lend money at exorbitant rates exploiting the monopolistic situation they enjoyed, which enabled them to double and quadruple the interest on the lent capital as evidenced by the verse at (3:130). This was a practice, which indeed deserved to be condemned not only by religion, but is worth condemnation also from the point of view of good economics.

276

- The lenders should consider the circumstances of the borrowers, and if they are found in financially straitened conditions, the lenders should remit interest altogether, postpone the loan repayment and, still better, write off the loans as *sadaqa*.

These verses do not categorically prove that interest *per se* is to be condemned. Interest has become an integral part of a modern economy where it is being universally used for lending and borrowing for commercial purposes, and also as a monetary policy instrument, and as an essential device for efficient allocation of productive resources (See below for elaboration). The Quran mandates that we strictly maintain justice in all of our dealings. We will see below that abolition of nominal interest on loans extended to businessmen will rather result in inflicting injustice on the lenders who comprise the relatively poor people keeping their deposits in banks. Also, doing away with nominal interest does not eliminate the involvement of a "real" interest, i.e., interest in real prices (See below for explanation).

It is ironic that Muslim jurists have always equated interest, however small, with usury (*riba*), which the Quran prohibits. Imam Feisal Abdul Rauf rightly points out that the invention and use of interest was one of the pillars of capitalism, which, together with the development of limited liability corporate businesses and the growth of liberalism, was instrumental in dramatically changing the economic fortunes of the Western world, while the Muslim world lagged far behind. "The strict prohibition on charging interest still prevails in the Muslim world and has largely prevented it from robustly developing the financial market's institutions of banking, capital markets, and stock exchanges, the foundations of capitalism. Neither could the Muslim nations effectively control their own monetary policies, since raising and lowering interest rates is the chief way a nation's central bank controls inflation and the amount of money in circulation."[249] Another scholar, Mustafa Akyol, by quoting Imad-ad-Dean Ahmad of the Minaret of Freedom Institute, contends that the term '*riba*' "actually means any unconscionable overcharging, whether on an interest rate or a spot price. Charging a market rate of interest, he holds, does not constitute *riba*." Akyol then shows how, among all Muslim countries, only Turkey most developed and modernized its economy by shunning the orthodox Muslim thought that Qutb and Mawdudi promoted.[250]

There has been a surge of so-called Islamic or interest-free banking institutions in many countries around the world, and such banks are working side by side with conventional interest-bearing banking system. However, the basic question that may be raised in this context is whether the Quran really forbids interest *per se*, or it forbids interest or usury charged to people who could not really bear it. That means that the Quran forbids interest or usury that could be conceived as extortionate or exploitative. In the pre-Islamic Arabic practice, interest was being charged at an extortionate rate – it was doubled at the first instance of default of loan repayment, and quadrupled at the second default. This practice was indeed reprehensible, and the Quran forbade it (3:130).

Note also that God has permitted trading, but not exploitative trading, where the seller can dictate the price (seller's market), and where the buyer can dictate the price (the buyer's market). Exploitative or monopolistic trading gives rise to excessive or extortionate profit, which the Quran certainly does not approve of. Extortionate interest or usury is analogous to extortionate profit. Both deserve the same condemnation. So trading that is not comparable to exploitative usury is trading that is free from any exploitation element. If exploitation elements are stripped from both trading and usury, they should stand on the same footing. So it follows that interest, which can be conceived as exploitation-free is not really disapproved of by the Quran.

Now let us analyze a little closely whether or not we can really get rid of interest in an economy. Interest is usually understood in the context of borrowing of money from the borrower's point of view, or in the context of lending of money from the lender's point of view. Such a transaction necessarily involves some time element, as the money is lent or borrowed for some period of time. Now let us say a lender lends some money at a zero (nominal) interest. After a year the borrower gives back that money without any interest. It will be understood that no interest has been involved here. But is this really correct? This is correct in only nominal terms. If there is no inflation or deflation in the economy in the year, no interest will be involved also in real terms, i.e., interest in real prices, as opposed to nominal prices. But some real positive or negative interest (i.e., interest in real prices) will accrue to either the borrower or the lender depending on whether there is some inflation or deflation in the economy in the year. In the case of inflation, it will be the borrower who gains, and the lender loses. In the case of deflation, it is the other way round: the lender gains and the borrower loses. In reality, almost no economy has a zero inflation or zero deflation situation, and usually economies undergo an inflationary situation. It is then realistic to think that money lending or borrowing almost invariably involves some interest element in real terms, even if no nominal interest is charged on the loan. One may call it interest due to inflation or deflation reason, but interest nevertheless.

Now think of lending or borrowing not in money but in real goods. Will there be any interest involved here? Most will probably say: No. But is this correct? The answer will depend on whether the relative prices of goods change or remain unchanged over the time. If the relative prices of the goods concerned that are lent, i.e., the prices of such goods relative to the prices of other goods rise over time, the borrower will lose in real terms in repaying the loan in the same amount of the same goods, and the lender will gain. If their relative prices fall, the exactly opposite will be the gainer and loser situation. None will gain or lose if the relative prices remain the same. But the real world situation almost always involves some change in relative prices. Interest in real terms is thus almost inevitably involved. We cannot get rid of interest in most cases, even when we have a barter system in the economy, and deal in real goods for lending or borrowing purposes.

It can thus be seen that however hard we try, it is almost always the case that some interest gets involved in the lending (or borrowing) transaction, whether the lending transaction is in money or real goods, in view of the usual real world changes in prices.

It should be recognized that interest could arise also because of other factors such as time preference and the occurrence of a return or profit on capital invested in any economic activity such as trading, production, etc. People value a thing at the present moment more than at a future date. This is time preference. If for example, a person would like to exchange $100 today for $110 a year after, his rate of time preference would be 10 percent. Interest plays an essential vital role in helping individuals allocate his income into present consumption and future consumption (i.e., saving) by bringing individuals' time preference at the margin into equilibrium with the interest rate.[251] The higher is individuals' time preference, the higher will be the interest rate that will be in equilibrium with time preference, which means that the interest incentive will need to be higher for one to save for the future. Or which means the same thing, an individual will go on saving his present income up to the point at the margin, i.e., up to the last dollar of his saving, where he finds his time preference for this last dollar of saving equal to the prevailing interest rate. Interest has an essential link also to profit or return on capital. A producer would like to borrow money to use in his enterprise so long as he earns a return at the margin higher than, or at least equal to, the rate of interest he pays on borrowed capital. The higher is the return on capital, the higher will have to be the interest rate to be in equilibrium with the rate of return situation.[252] In both cases, it can thus be seen that interest plays a vital role in allocating resources – in the first case between consumption and saving, and in the second case, between different uses of capital. In the second case, interest also plays the role of a rationing device, rationing uses of resources to the limit of the available resources. The scarcer the available amount of capital, the higher is the interest rate that will serve as an appropriate rationing device.[253]

In an equilibrium situation, the prevailing rate of interest is equal not only to marginal rate of time preference, but also to the marginal rate of return on capital. That means that interest that is paid to depositors of a bank must be closely linked to, and must mirror, the actual profitability situation on the ground. Interest here is a substitute for the profit that can be actually earned with the money. So, this interest cannot be termed as exploitative, and is not disapproved of by the Quran.

In a modern economy interest plays a central role in many kinds of economic decision-making. In both developed and developing economies, interest is a vital instrument used for directing appropriate monetary policy for achieving sustained economic growth with reasonable price stability. Countries' commercial and other banks adjust their interest rates on loans and deposits to the central rate that is governed by the central bank. Interest influences, among other things, money supply and demand in the economy, economic project planning, selection and evaluation, inventory planning and management, and a myriad of other economic decisions. Interest represents the opportunity cost of capital. Unless a producer is conscious of such a cost, it is likely that he will engage in inefficient lines of production, use inefficient methods of production, and end up producing the wrong products, which are uneconomic or unprofitable. Indeed the role of interest in economic decision-making of various kinds is so deeply entrenched that the efficient working of a modern economy is not conceivable without interest. This is interest that plays a very useful and beneficial role in the economy. It is not exploitative interest or usury that the Quran prohibits.

In so-called interest-free (i.e., with zero nominal interest) banking system, the following two types of concepts are used and practiced:

- In the first concept, depositors entrust their money with banks only for safekeeping; they are neither paid any interest (in nominal terms) nor any profit (in nominal terms). Their capital (in nominal terms) is guaranteed. Banks lend on behalf of the depositors to the borrowers, and charge a fee for their services. In this practice, the depositors derive no income from their savings, though the borrowers do business with their own money, and generate profits and income for themselves.

- A second concept used in such interest-free banking allows for sharing of profits and income among the depositors, banks, and borrowers in what is called participatory banking, where the bank, using the money entrusted to it by depositors, participates in an enterprise. It is a partnership between the entrepreneur, the bank, and the depositor, in which all risks are shared among them. The funds invested come from depositors' time deposits in the banks in so-called "investment accounts", which bear no interest, nor are such deposits guaranteed.

Under the first concept, it is obvious that the depositors are deprived, and the borrowers who do business with the money are given an unfair advantage. The borrowers are mostly traders, or other business concerns, or individual entrepreneurs, who make money at the expense of the depositors. This practice is not only unjust and inequitable, it is not defensible also from the point of view of good economics, since such use of scarce capital could be a diversion from its most efficient or productive use, and thus could result in its misallocation. It cannot be conceived that the Quran approves of this kind of inequitable banking.

The second concept of participatory banking can make sense, and be appropriate only if a good synchronization can be achieved between the depositors, the banks, and the investors in all of the activities where the money gets invested. However, as a review by Jan Mark Berk (Berk 1998[254]) of two recent books written by Gafoor on Islamic banking shows, such synchronization is difficult to achieve. The problems and drawbacks with such banking, as outlined by Berk, are that:

- The intermediary role played by the banks implies that these institutions need to have considerable expertise and experience in project selection and evaluation, and assumes that the bank knows as much about the business in question as the entrepreneur does. If not, there is asymmetry in information which could make the banks averse to such participations.

- Moreover, participatory financing seems applicable only to certain types of projects, i.e., entrepreneurs investing in new enterprises. The failure to recognize the latter drawback is, according to the author (Gafoor), the main reason for the problems currently faced by the Islamic banks. The latter applied the concept of participatory financing to projects for which conventional financing through lending from their deposit accounts would be appropriate.

- Also, they used funds from other accounts than the investment account for financing the participations. This caused problems as the guarantee of capital is (in the absence of interest) the sole reason for holding these other accounts (i.e. time and savings deposits), and capital is not guaranteed under participatory financing.[255]

Thus the second concept of so-called Islamic banking cannot be appropriately applied to businesses other than new enterprises. This is a serious limitation of such banking. The attempt to apply these banks to other areas has landed them into insurmountable problems emanating from internally contradictory rules of participation. It is far from clear why depositors should be subjected to taking risks of losses in projects where their money is invested. Banks can and should take on full risks on depositors' behalf, as under the conventional interest-bearing system, as this makes them more responsible in investing money.

It thus appears that the attempt to go without interest in banking activities is genuinely problematic, economically inefficient, unjust to the depositors, and is not so useful in a modern economy. The problems of so-called Islamic banks are compounded also by the fact that they operate side by side with, and are still in need of the economic functions performed by, the "Western-style" interest-bearing banking system.

Note that a substantial part of bank deposits belongs to the poor and middle-income groups of people, and that the relatively rich people employ such deposits for business investment purposes. In such a situation, if the depositors are deprived of any return on their deposits, or if, in the case of participatory financing, even their original capital is not guaranteed, then will this not be a highly inequitable, discriminatory treatment meted out to the relatively poorer people? Can we think that this is what the Quran approves of? The answer should be unequivocally: No. It is obvious that such a system exposes the depositors to great risks of losses, risks that they can avoid from the conventional interest-bearing banking system. At the same time they are also deprived of even a minimum return on their deposits, which they can earn from the conventional banking system in the same country or abroad.

Thus the so-called Islamic or interest-free banking is a misnomer – a deviation from the true spirit of the Quranic message. The Quranic message of interest-free loans is applicable only for disadvantaged borrowers, who deserve to be treated with a humanitarian approach. The kind of interest that the Quran prohibits is usury or interest that is charged to people who deserve to be given an interest-free loan on humanitarian grounds. This is *qarz-hasana* or a beautiful loan that the Quran talks about in several verses (2:245; 57:11, 18; 64:17; 5:12; 73:20). This is a loan without interest or any gain to deserving people on humanitarian grounds. The question of interest cannot arise in such cases. The Quran even encourages the lenders to write off the original loans in cases where the borrowers are in difficulty to repay them (2:278-280 cited earlier).

> **2:245**   *Who is it that will lend unto God a beautiful loan,* so that He will increase it manifold? God straiteneth and enlargeth. Unto Him ye will return. (See also 2:278-280 cited earlier.)

It is clear from these verses that in cases, which deserve humanitarian considerations, loans should indeed be extended free of interest, and where appropriate, such loans should be given as grants or alms (which is *sadaqa* in Quranic terminology). But when loans are extended for business purposes, taking no interest as a substitute for potential profits, which borrowers can make on such loans, is clearly unjust to the lenders, and cannot thus be disapproved of by the Quran. In a Muslim country like Iran, banks charge what they call "an estimated or provisional profit" on loans extended to traders and enterprises, and provide "an estimated or provisional profit" on bank deposits. This is nothing but interest in the guise of profit. Co-operative banks in the USA provide what they call "dividends" on their members' deposits. But this is nothing but interest. Where capital or money is used for profitable purposes, it is only just that that the profit the borrower earns on it be distributed between the borrower and the lender. The return the lender gets is profit-linked but essentially interest in nature.

The Quran in fact encourages and approves what is just and equitable. And whether any nominal interest is charged or not in any lending-borrowing transaction, some interest in real terms is almost always involved in view of the real world situation where prices of goods and services almost invariably change. However hard we try to do it, we generally cannot go without interest. And the working of the modern economy in an efficient manner is inconceivable without interest playing a central positive and beneficial role. This is not what the Quran forbids.

We need also to take into account the fact that side-by-side with the institutional credit market served by banks, an informal credit market also exists and operates in many countries. The informal credit market operates precisely because the formal banks do not serve the needs of all willing borrowers. Banks operate by lending against collateral. However, small businesses and poorer borrowers often lack such collateral, and accordingly they have little or no access to bank credit. The informal market serves such borrowers, and usually the interest rate charged on such loans is considerably higher than that charged by banks. It is most likely that lenders in this market charge exorbitantly high interest rates that deserve to be condemned. Taking advantage of the unusual character of the informal market, even a reputable institution such as the Grameen Bank of Bangladesh, which lends to the destitute people, charges very high interest rates. In such a situation, it should be the duty of the government to bring such interest rates into line with the rates charged by the regular banks by subsidizing the Grameen Bank in an interim period, and by introducing pro-active policies that allow more credit institutions of the same type to come into existence and operate like the Grameen Bank. Currently the Grameen Bank is in a position to charge a high interest rate precisely because of its monopolistic situation. Having said this, it should, however, be recognized that despite the high interest rate, the very availability of credit for the poor has been serving a very noble cause, in recognition of which the Grameen Bank and its founder Dr.

Muhammad Yunus were awarded the Nobel Prize for Peace in 2006. But a change of the current situation into one where the poorer people get access to credit at rates comparable to, or even lower than, those charged by banks will be highly desirable. There is clearly a need for benevolent people who should come forward to extend interest free loans or even grants to needy and deserving people, in the way the Quran dictates.

Finally, we also need to point out that an excessive interest rate hurts both investors and consumers, and hurts growth and development of an economy. At the same time too low a rate encourages excessive credit expansion in the economy, too much investment and consumption, leading to an overheating of an economy and inflation. On the other hand, a high inflation in the economy requires a high nominal interest rate to be maintained to control inflation. An excessive budget deficit causes inflationary pressure in an economy, which in turn causes the nominal long-term interest rate to rise. The interest rates maintained by different countries also influence their inter-country capital flows, and thereby also influence their exchange rates. On the other hand, a country's investment and thus growth may be influenced by external capital flows, which in turn can influence the interest rate. An increase in the real rate of growth in an economy raises the real interest rate, and *pari passu* raises the nominal interest rate as well. Thus interest in an economy is interlinked with many economic variables. The central bank of any economy needs to carefully weigh all such relevant variables to set its central interest rate at an appropriate level, around which all other interest rates in the economy are adjusted.

Conclusion

The Quran calls for a free and exploitation-free egalitarian economic system. Strict observance of justice and fairness necessarily implies ensuring a system that has the least distortions in economic activities (production, trade, etc.) and prices (prices of goods and services, of capital, etc.) that come from controls, restrictions, and monopolistic practices, etc. While there should be recognition of private initiative and enterprise, and hence of private property and ownership, this should be subject to an understanding that all things ultimately belong to God. One important implication of the Quranic directions is that there should be an equitable distribution of economic resources, especially land, if these are found to be starkly unequal in a society. An important message of Islam is that none should fully enjoy his own fruits of labor but share them with his fellow beings through an appropriate distribution system. Such a system must necessarily encompass public welfare and development expenditures. Contrary to what is generally believed among Muslims, the Quran does not really condemn interest *per se* that is being universally used for lending and borrowing purposes, and also as a monetary policy instrument, and an essential device for efficient allocation of productive resources. What it condemns is interest that is charged to people who deserve humanitarian treatment. So-called Islamic interest-free banking is a misnomer, an unsound institution, and a drag on the development of Muslim countries.

XI. REEVALUATING THE HADITH

Survey of Earlier Hadith Criticism, and Theological and Historical Tests of Hadith Authenticity

(Say, O Muhammad!) *'Shall I seek for judge (or law) other than God, when He it is Who hath revealed unto thee the Book explained in detail?' –6:114*

So *admonish (thou O Muhammad) with the QURAN* those who care about My warning. –50:45

These are God's signs (or revelations) that We recite unto thee (O Muhammad) with truth. *Then in which HADITH (story), after God and His revelations, will they believe?* –45:6

INTRODUCTION

The Holy Quran is unquestionably the Divine Book of Islam. However, most Muslims regard the Hadith as Islam's second essential source. Though the Quran uses the term *"hadith"*[256] in a number of its verses, we use it here in its popular sense to refer to traditions attributed to the Prophet Muhammad, which are defined to include his sayings and practices – accounts of what he said, what he did, or what he refrained from doing, and what he approved silently. The term *'sunnah'*[257] is used to mean 'the example of the Prophet' embodied in his statements, actions, and overt or tacit approvals or disapprovals. The terms *'sunnah'* and 'Hadith' are often used synonymously, but they are not exactly the same. The Hadith literature is the vehicle through which the Prophetic *sunnah* is believed to be reported. The Hadith and related literature[258] has greatly influenced Muslim beliefs and practices. However, all Muslims should dispassionately ask themselves this critically important question: Is the Hadith a reliable religious guide? It is time this question was settled decisively for all of us, for if there is some doubt about the authenticity and credibility of the Hadith, the influence it exerts on Muslim beliefs and practices cannot be regarded as wholly welcome, if not totally unwelcome.

Indeed many Muslim and non-Muslim scholars have questioned, and in contemporary times, are questioning, the historicity and authenticity of the Hadith. All Muslims should pay attention to what they have said or are saying. No doubt they represent the minority voice, most often due to

287

the suppression of their views in the existing politico-religious conditions in Muslim countries. But the opinion of the majority is not always true. In fact, our Prophet was exhorted not to follow those who have no knowledge (45:18), and he was specifically urged not to follow the majority, as they follow nothing but conjecture without any knowledge, and do nothing but lie:

6:116   *If thou (O Muhammad) obeyst most of those on earth, they would lead thee astray from the path of God. They follow naught but conjecture; and they do naught but falsely guess.*

The reader may ask a Muslim: Exactly when and how did the Hadith come? The usual answer is most likely to be: "I do not know." The time when the Hadith compilations surfaced – particularly those in which Muslims have come to believe – is an important factor to be reckoned with, as it should have important implications for its religious significance for Muslims. It is striking that the compilations that Muslims believe in appeared with a long time gap after the demise of the Prophet Muhammad – mostly during the ninth and tenth centuries C.E. (third and fourth centuries Hijrah or A.H.), i.e., between 220 and 270 years after the Prophet's death. The Sunnis who are the majority sect of Muslims generally consider the compilations done by Bukhari (who died in 256 Hijrah/870 C.E.), Muslim (d. 261/875), Abu Dawud (d. 275/888), Tirmidhi (d. 279/892), Ibn Majah (d. 273/886) and Nasa'i (d. 303/915) as six *sahih* (authentic or true) Hadith, but that done by Bukhari is regarded as the most authentic, while Muslim's compilation is put in the second place. The Shiites believe in an entirely separate body of Hadith such as those by al-Kulaini (d. 328 or 329 A.H.), Ibn Babuwayh (d. 381 A.H.), Jaafar Muhammad al-Tusi (d. 411 A.H.) and al-Murtada (d. 436 A.H.).

The long time gap and other factors (see below) inevitably give rise to the question whether the Hadith literature is reliable enough. All Muslims, even including those who champion the Hadith, accept the fact that after the death of the Prophet Muhammad, false Hadith reports about or attributed to the Prophet Muhammad "mushroomed" into hundreds of thousands. The compilations that were made more than two centuries after the Prophet's death were done after sorting through mountainous piles of individual Hadith reports. Bukhari, for example, made a selection of some seven thousand traditions (including repeated ones) out of reportedly six hundred thousand he found in circulation – roughly one out of every one hundred. That means that he discarded all but a tiny fraction of the Hadith in circulation as false. This factor alone leaves open the question whether his selection has been foolproof. A similar question is true of the other compilers, too. It is time the Hadith was properly reevaluated in terms of its trustworthiness.

Generally, those who portray Islam in a good light do so by tapping its "best traditions."[259] The issue, however, is not really about choosing between good and bad traditions; the issue is really about whether we can still afford to continue with traditions that often misguide us. A religious book needs to be completely holy to command compliance. It is time that all Muslims take a dispassionate look at the reliability of the Hadith. Regrettably, Islam is perceived in terms of both the Quran and the Hadith, and therefore generates a mixed message. The position presented here is that the Hadith is "more a detractor of the Quran and the Prophet than a real guide."[260] It has held back the adoption and growth of the progressive outlook of Islam that the Quran so beautifully professes. The Hadith can be subjected to criticism from the perspectives of all conceivable criteria: theological, historical, and objective as follows:

- **Theological:** The Hadith has no theological sanction or authority – the Quran does not validate the Hadith.

- **Historical:** The Hadith does not stand the test of historicity either. Available historical evidence strongly suggests that the Prophet Muhammad himself and all the four Caliphs after him disapproved of the recording, collection and compilation of any Hadith. Other historical questions surrounding the timing, preservation, transmission, collection, and compilation of any Hadith material also point to compelling evidence that the Hadith is no reliable religious guidance.

- **Objective:** The Hadith fails also the objectivity test. It contains texts that either contradict or negate the very message of the Quran, or do not stand to scientific truth or reason, or give conflicting messages, and contribute only to confusion. Or at its best, the Hadith diverts one's attention from things that are substantive to those that are not of much substance. We prove these points by examining a sample of the so-called *sahih* Hadith.[261]

Since the topic is too wide to deal with adequately in the normal size of a chapter, it is divided into two chapters. Analysis of the objective test is taken up in the next chapter. Here in this chapter we consider the theological and historical tests, along with a survey of earlier criticism of the Hadith.

SURVEY OF EARLIER HADITH CRITICISM

Any efforts to record, collect, and compile Hadith reports were, in a sense, liable to, and became subjected to, criticism from the very beginning of the process of their recording and collection. From early times on, many distinguished Muslim scholars were critical of the Hadith. During the time of al-Shafii (d. 204 A.H.), who was the founder of one of the four known Sunni divisions (*madhhabs*), and a champion of the Hadith (*sunnah*) holding it as divinely inspired, there was an Ahl al-Kalam group who rejected the authority of the Hadith altogether. Their principal argument was that the Hadith does not accurately reflect the Prophetic example, as the transmission of Hadith reports was not reliable. The Prophetic example, they argued, "has to be found elsewhere – first and foremost in following the Qur'an". And according to them, "the corpus of hadith is filled with contradictory, blasphemous, and absurd traditions."[262] As we shall see, we find echoes of such arguments in modern criticisms of the Hadith. Mutazilites, who represented one of the earliest rationalist Muslim theological schools, and are the later Ahl al-Kalam, also viewed the transmission of the Prophetic *sunnah* as not sufficiently reliable.[263] The Hadith, according to them, was mere "guesswork and conjecture … [and] the Quran was complete and perfect, and did not require the hadith or any other book to supplement or complement it."[264] After Mutazilites, as Azami notes, many early Muslim writers criticized Bukhari's work concerning 80 narrators and 110 individual accounts of Hadith. Of these critics, he mentioned the names of two fourteenth century scholars: Abdur Rahman b. Abu Bakr Suyuti (author of *Tadrib ar-Rawi*, ed. by A. R. Latif, Cairo, 1379) and Ibn Hajar (author of *Hadyal-Sari*, Cairo 1383).[265] However, such early Hadith criticism became suppressed and drowned under opposition by the established *ulama* and their supporters, often with state support.

Strikingly though, the work of subjecting the Hadith to more vocal scrutiny is a relatively modern phenomenon – begun in earnest in the late nineteenth century in the Indian sub-continent as part of a reformist program in Islam. The first such major challenge to the Hadith came from Sir Sayyid Ahmad Khan (1817-1898). He viewed the Hadith as an obstacle to reform and "questioned the historicity and authenticity of many, if not most, traditions, much as the noted scholars Ignaz Goldziher and Joseph Schacht would later do."[266] According to him, the transmitters of Hadith (*rawis*) often engaged in transmitting Hadith according to the sense rather than the exact words of the Prophet. This widespread practice resulted in textual variations among traditions on the same subject, "differences that go well beyond the wording and affect the meaning. As a result, he contends, *one can be sure in very few instances that traditions accurately portray the Prophet's words and actions, even if they can be shown to have originated during his lifetime.*"[267] About Hadith compilers' capacity to judge the character of Hadith transmitters of several past generations involved in oral Hadith transmission, Sayyid Ahmad Khan further notes, "*it is difficult enough to judge the character of living people, let alone long dead.* The *muhaddithun* [hadith scholars/transmitters] did the best they could, but their task was almost impossible."[268]

In Egypt Muhammad Tawfiq Sidqi (d. 1920) and Mahmud Abu Rayya, whose book on the Hadith was published in Cairo in 1958, viewed the Hadith as unreliable.[269] "Sidqi held that nothing of the hadith was recorded until after enough time had elapsed to allow the infiltration of numerous absurd or corrupt traditions."[270] At the theological level, he argued that the Quran was sufficient as guidance: "'what is obligatory for man does not go beyond God's Book.' Thus the Qur'an explains itself as 'the book which explains all things' (16:89), and God Himself bears witness that He has 'omitted nothing from the Book' (6:38) [...] obedience to the Prophet [...] Muhammad's authority [...] is strictly limited to implementing the Quran."[271] "If anything other than the Qur'an had been necessary for religion," Sidqi further notes, "the Prophet would have commanded its registration in writing, and God would have guaranteed its preservation."[272] Abu Rayya regarded the absence of recording of Hadith in written form in more than one hundred years after the Prophet's death as a major obstacle to the authenticity of the Hadith.[273]

It is also worth noting that in the early twentieth century, in the generation following Sayyid Ahmad Khan (in India) and Muhammad Abduh (in Egypt), there emerged a self-designated Ahl-i-Quran group who argued along Sidqi's theological lines. They "came to view adherence to hadith as the cause of Islam's misfortunes;" and "argued

291

that pure and unadulterated Islam is to be found only in the Qur'an," which alone is "a reliable basis for religious belief and action."[274] This movement was represented by Abd Allah Chakralawi (d. 1930), Mistri Muhammad Ramadan (1875-1940), Khwaja Ahmad Din Amritsari (1861-1936), and Muhammad Aslam Jayrajpuri (1881-1955).[275] In Bangladesh, Maulana Akram Khan (1869-1968)[276], a noted journalist and biographer of the Prophet Muhammad, taking examples from *Bukhari* and *Muslim*, showed that Hadith texts (*matn*) could be incorrect or unacceptable, even if the chain of transmission (*isnad*) was regarded as sound.[277] He sampled nearly a hundred Hadith texts from *Bukhari* and proved them to be false or contradictory to the Quran.[278]

Ghulam Ahmed Parwez (1903-1985) of Pakistan (originally of the East Punjab, India)[279] was one of the first major Hadith critics of modern time. According to him, the treatment of the Hadith or *sunnah* as a divinely inspired source in Islam was fundamentally wrong. He refuted Shaffi's contention that the expression "*hikmah*" in the Quran (2: 129) referred to the Prophet's *sunnah* by contending that this expression is used in a general sense of "wisdom".[280] If the Hadith was divine revelation (*wahy*), Parwez argues, then why was it not preserved in the same way as the Quran? In sharp contrast to the case of the Quran, he notes, "No steps were taken by the Prophet or by his immediate followers to preserve the integrity of hadith."[281] He also contended that unreliability of Hadith transmission "undermines its validity."[282] Thus, according to him, there could not be any *shariah* (or *sunnah*) aside from the Quran. This contention has been termed as heresy by Mawdudi's Jamaat-i Islami group, even though Mawdudi himself is regarded by some as a critic of the Hadith in some way. Regarded as the founder of the anti-Hadith movement in the Indo-Pak sub-continent[283], Parwez was declared an infidel (*kafir*) by the *ulama*. Another Muslim scholar, a contemporary of Parwez, who did not accept the unquestioned authority of the Hadith was Ghulam Jilani Barq[284] who contended that only such Hadith was acceptable which did not conflict with the Quran and which did 'not repudiate morality or human experience.'[285]

Another notable work in this direction in recent years is that of an Egyptian-American scholar Rashad Khalifa (1935-1990).[286] Some of his earlier work on Islam such as that on a mathematical miracle about the Quran along with his admirable, easy-to-understand English translation of the Quran[287] drew international acclaim from the Muslim world, which he soon lost with his anti-Hadith stance. Using mainly theological arguments, his fundamental thesis was that it is the Quran alone that fully defines Islam. The Quran is complete, fully detailed and explained, and also the best and only legitimate Hadith. The Prophet's job was simply to deliver the Quran, and nothing else. He was forbidden even to explain it. "Obeying the Prophet" means obeying the Quran. Following the so-called Hadith amounts to following the Hadith of those who collected and compiled them; it does not mean following that of the Prophet. Following the so-called Hadith has led Muslims to insult as well as idolize the Prophet. A progressive deterioration of the Muslim *ummah* began with the appearance of the Hadith.[288] Rashad Khalifa, however, complicated his position by declaring himself as a Messenger of God, even though he maintained that the Quran is the final Message from God brought by the Prophet Muhammad. An assembly of *ulama* in Saudi Arabia declared him an apostate, which apparently led to his assassination in 1990. However, the movement triggered by him did not end with his assassination, but got rather reinvigorated. Some of his followers or admirers, notably Edip Yuksel and Layth Saleh al-Shaiban, are playing key roles in an ongoing Quran-only movement (See below for some elaboration).

Little-known devout Muslim saint of Bangladesh Shah Aksaruddin Ahmad (d. 1956) was trying in the 1950's to write a critique of the Hadith. However, even before he could finish and publish his work, on the basis of a legal complaint lodged by the *ulama*, he received a court injunction preventing publication of his works.[289] In his unfinished, unpublished work, he notes that following the Prophet essentially means following his advice, and also the divine advice, to follow the Quran. The Quran is sufficiently detailed, self-explained, and easy to follow. The Prophet followed God's advice and emulated His Ways or *Sunnah*, which never changes (17:77), and the Prophet's *sunnah* should not be construed as separate from God's *Sunnah* or the teachings embodied in the Quran. He further notes, because of the long lapse of time after the Prophet's death with which the Hadith appeared, it has inevitably become corrupted. The compilers themselves discarded an overwhelming bulk of Hadith as false, which gives an impression of deeper problems with the entire body of Hadith, and raises questions of reliability also for the ones selected by them. Also, there was not much unanimity in their collections or compilations – what one compiler chose as true, the other compiler discarded as false. He further points out, if one reads the Hadith, even so-called *Sahih Bukhari*, one can find some ludicrous accounts of the marital life of the Prophet and his wives, and other filthy

293

material beyond any acceptable norms of propriety, which goes against the very advice of God in the Quran. Any sensible reader should shudder to think how such absurd stories could find place in the so-called *sahih* Hadith. He notes that the Hadith was recorded and compiled despite the Prophet's explicit prohibition on this, and despite the burning of the Hadith collected and recorded at that time by his companions Abu Bakr and Umar, and their discouragement for further Hadith collection and recording. It is the Umayyads who encouraged Hadith writing to serve their royal ambitions. It is the following of the Hadith that has led to the division of Muslims into several sects despite God's explicit advice to the contrary.

In his stirring treatise on *marefat* (study of knowledge leading to the understanding of God) *"Creator and Creation"*, Panaullah Ahmad, a close student of Shah Aksaruddin Ahmad, made some terse and forthright comments on the Hadith scattered in his book,[290] which encapsulate a powerful case for dismissing the Hadith effectively as not of any real religious worth. According to him, the "chequered history" of Hadith recording, collection and compilation "due to bribery, sabotage", and a long lapse of time from the Prophet's death points to its "grave shortcomings." Islam does not entertain "monarchical imperialism and any state or even priestly interference" with the Divine code, but examples of such interference abound in the Hadith. This has resulted in numerous Hadith texts that give up or negate "parts or key points of the Quran [...] or clouding of the real issues." In the process, the Hadith has become "more a detractor of the Quran and the Prophet than a real guide [...] *Non-compilation by the Prophet's contemporaries during his lifetime, non-systematization for about two centuries, concoction and ingenious forging of reports by pseudo-enemies and faulty transmission – all contributed to a spurt of spurious Hadith* that led to clouding of the real issues and so practice of religious principles affected by this inimical process tended towards rigidity rather than elasticity so beautifully inherent in God's revelation [...] [This] has contributed to regimentation of thoughts and ideas." The Hadith gives conflicting interpretations and *shan-i-nazul* (genesis), which fail to satisfactorily explain even such intricate questions as *miraj* (ascension), *wahy* (revelation), and the Prophet's marital life. Being "more or less confined to the ritual aspect of Islam", it "tended towards regimentation not only in thought but also in habits". It has painted the Prophet and some of his illustrious wives in ways that go beyond the "bounds of propriety. [...] It has given four schools of thought, which stultify the Quran itself (II-176 Baqra, VI-159 An'am)."[291]

Another notable recent piece of work along this line is that of Kassim Ahmad[292] of Malaysia. His work rejected the Hadith as a basis for theology and law, and states that "*the Hadith are 'sectarian, anti-science, anti-reason and anti-women'.*"[293] He contends that the Prophet brought only one book, the Quran, not two books. He raises the pertinent questions: why it took 250-350 years for the Hadith to be compiled, and why the Sunnis have collections different from the Shi'ites. He analyzes the factors such as power struggles and theological disputes that led to Hadith compilation, and draws a close parallel between the appearance of and reliance on the Hadith and the decline and backwardness of Muslims?[294] According to him, "the purging of this harmful ideology and with it other foreign modern ideologies, from the Muslim community, and their return to the original ideology brought by Muhammad in the Quran is the *sine qua non* for the regeneration of the Muslim community and for a new Muslim Renaissance."[295] The Malaysian government proscribed Ahmad's book in 1986, and the country's established *ulama* have declared him as "the enemy of Islam".

M. Jamilul Bashar of Bangladesh made a critique of the Hadith a major topic in a book in Bengali titled "Reformation",[296] which is along the same lines as Shah Aksaruddin Ahmad. According to him, the appearance of such spurious religious writings after a divine book has come is not unique to Islam, but was also found in the case of earlier religions. He catalogues a good number of so-called Sahih Hadith texts, and shows them to be untrue in light of the Quran. He also notes the strict prohibition of the Prophet on Hadith writing, and the burning and discouragement of such writings during the four Caliphs. He is also sharply critical of the historical process of Hadith compilation, and of the criteria used to judge its authenticity. However, under street protests staged by the *ulama*-supported groups, and a complaint lodged with the Bangladesh government, the book was officially banned in 2003.

It is worth noting that a growing number of Muslims are questioning the religious authority of the Hadith. New Hadith critics among Muslims include M. A. Malek[297], Ibrahim Mustafa[298] and Mesbah Uddin[299]. In a recently published book, Jeffrey Lang notes that "numerous converts and second generation Muslims [in America] have shared their doubts with me about the Hadith literature, but it appears that skepticism among

Muslim youth about the trustworthiness of this material may be growing worldwide."[300]

A vigorous ongoing movement to reform Islam along the teachings of the Quran alone is being led by Edip Yuksel. As a first key step, he along with his colleagues Layth Saleh al-Shaiban and Martha Shulte-Nafeh came out in 2007 with their "Quran: A Reformist Translation" – second, to my knowledge, after Rashad Khalifa's – which is a landmark contribution toward getting an understanding of the Quran free from the undue influence of the Hadith literature and the sectarian teachings of traditional Muslim clerics. Their commentary in this translation powerfully demonstrates why we should trash all the Hadith books. It also contains a manifesto for Islamic reform along the Quranic lines alone. Yuksel, a dedicated activist, has been engaging in debates with Muslim sectarian scholars as well as with some uninformed critics and enemies of Islam, and organizing and addressing seminars and conferences in various parts of the world to spread the word about this movement. A new compilation of contributions from many contemporary reform-minded Muslim scholars, *Critical Thinkers for Islamic Reform*, organized and published by Yuksel in 2009, is a first major effort at group level to spearhead this ongoing movement. It is also being importantly aided, in this Internet age, by numerous website writings, and blog and forum discussions, and email communications among Islamic scholars focusing on the Quranic message alone. These and other recent developments such as the negative stereotyping of Islam amid the recurrence of violence and terrorism orchestrated by Muslim extremists have spurred what appears to be an unprecedented surge in interest and curiosity among both Muslims and non-Muslims to know what Islam genuinely represents in light of the Quran and reason. It is evident that the Quran-only movement is showing new signs of life, and gaining a new momentum.[301]

It is also in order here to mention that the Islamic reformist or modernist ideas – Islamic modernism – that emerged in the late nineteenth and early twentieth centuries through such outstanding figures as Jamal al-Din al-Afghani (1838-1897) and his disciple Muhammad Abduh (1849-1905) in the Middle East, and Sir Sayyid Ahmad Khan (1817-1898) and Muhammad Iqbal (1875-1938) in South Asia stressed the role of *ijtihad* (independent reasoning or reinterpretation) in Islam to respond to the demands of modernity, and to revive the inner dynamic and creative character of Islam.[302] These writers-reformers maintain that Muslims need to reassert their right to *ijtihad*, the door of which was closed by the tenth century.[303] The closing of the door of *ijtihad*, according to the Indian Poet-Philosopher Iqbal, put Islam in "'a dogmatic slumber' that resulted in five hundred years of immobility due to the blind following of the tradition."[304] Thus this call for modernism in Islam, which has been joined by many modern Muslim writers especially in America and Europe, including some notable names such as Abdulaziz Sachedina of the University of Virginia, Fathi Osman, an independent extensive writer on the Quran, and Islamic reform, M. A. Muqtedar Khan of the University of Delaware, and Tariq Ramadan of Oxford University, is a call for rejection of *taqlid* or blind imitation of the past, and is essentially a call for rejection of the unquestioned authority of the Prophetic traditions.

Non-Muslim modern Western scholars have also seriously questioned the historicity and authenticity of the Hadith, which became a legitimate source that undermined Islam in their eyes. They maintain, "the bulk of traditions attributed to the Prophet Muhammad were actually written much later."[305] Noted among these Hadith critics are Sir William Muir[306], Alois Sprenger[307], Ignaz Goldziher[308], Joseph Schacht[309] and G.H.A. Juynboll[310]. Muir and Sprenger were the first Western scholars to question the reliability of the Hadith literature as a historical source.[311] Muir contended that "the Qur'an alone represents a reliable source for Muhammad's biography", and it accurately portrays "his own thought":

> The Coran [Quran] becomes the groundwork and the test of all inquiries into the origin of Islam and the character of its founder. Here we have a store-house of Mahomet's own words recorded during his life, extending over the whole course of his public career, and illustrating his religious views, his public acts, and his domestic character.[312]

He regarded the Hadith literature as "plagued with corruptions and of limited value as a source for the earliest history of Islam. Muir completely discounted the value of classical hadith criticism based on an examination of the chain of transmission, the *isnad*. He insisted that the text of the tradition itself, the *matn*, 'must stand or fall upon its own merits.'"[313]

The Hungarian scholar Goldziher pointed out that there were many contradictory Hadith texts supported by *isnads* (chains of narrators) "that could not represent authentic Prophetic discourse; he suggested that they were fabricated either by various political and religious factions in their efforts to legitimate themselves and discredit their rivals, or indiscreet attempts to provide answers for specific religious issues that were in need of clarification."[314] He "has documented numerous hadith the transmitters of which claimed were derived from Muhammad but which were in reality verses from the Torah and Gospels, bits of rabbinic sayings, ancient Persian maxims, passages of Greek philosophy, Indian proverbs, and an almost word-for-word reproduction of the Lord's Prayer."[315]

Schacht, "the most influential modern Western authority on Islamic law [...] on the basis of his research, [...] found no evidence of legal traditions before 722 [C.E.], one hundred years after the death of Muhammad. Thus he concluded that the Sunna of the Prophet is not the words and deeds of the Prophet, but apocryphal material originating from customary practice that was projected back to the eighth century to more authoritative sources – first the Successors, then the Companions, and finally the Prophet."[316]

Juynboll's work is a powerful critique not only of the authenticity of Hadith, but also of scholarly works which have attempted to support notions of the authenticity of Hadith. In criticizing the *isnad*s he quite bluntly states:

> I am skeptical as to whether we will ever be able to prove beyond a shadow of a doubt that what we have in the way of 'sound prophetic traditions' is indeed just what it purports to be.[317]

Juynboll cites numerous Hadiths with which persons such as Sa'id ibn al Musayyab (died 93 A.H./711 C.E.) and Hasan al Basri (died 110 A.H./728 C.E.) and several other companions and successors of the Prophet could be rightfully credited, but which "he contends later evolved into prophetic traditions that can be found among the Six Books."[318]

Eminent French physician Maurice Buccaille, whose work earned some praise from Muslim scholars for his documentation of remarkable consistency of a number of Quranic observations with modern scientific

298

knowledge, showed the Hadith as inconsistent with scientific truths.[319] He commented:

> The difference is in fact quite staggering between the accuracy of the data contained in the Quran, when compared with modern scientific knowledge, and the highly questionable character of certain statements in the hadith on subjects whose tenor is essentially scientific [...] In view of the fact that only a limited number of hadith may be considered to express the Prophet's thought with certainty, the others must contain the thoughts of men of his times, in particular with regard to the subjects referred to here. When these dubious or inauthentic hadith are compared to the text of the Quran, we can measure the extent to which they differ. This comparison highlights [...] the striking difference between the writings of this period, which are riddled with scientifically inaccurate statements, and the Quran, the Book of Written Revelation, that is free from errors of this kind.[320]

Many regard the Hadith as an indispensable source of Islamic law. "Yet, further study compels one to face the fact that there are some complexities involved in the use of the hadith as a basis for Islamic law and practice."[321] Certainly difficulties arose because of the proliferation of the Hadith reports. "By the ninth century, the number of traditions had mushroomed into the hundreds of thousands. They included pious fabrications by those who believed that their practices were in conformity with Islam and forgeries by factions involved in political and theological disputes."[322] As already noted above, many modern Islamic scholars, who have not completely rejected the traditions, recognize that there is "a powerful need to reexamine Islamic traditions and the Islamic message in the light of our present existential conditions", and that there is a need for *ijtihad* (independent thinking and interpretation); and they call for discarding "the present rigid and inflexible approach to Islamic legal opinions of the past" in favor of "a more open and compassionate understanding of Islam".[323] According to distinguished contemporary scholar Khaled Abou El Fadl, the current practice of Islamic or *shariah* law suffers from the deficiencies of both "a lack of competency [on the part of those who apply it] in the usage of legal objectives and methodologies [of *shariah*]" and the non-development of such objectives and methodologies "to meet contemporary advances in epistemology, hermeneutics, or social theory. In the contemporary age, Muslims end up with a rather ironic and painfully nonsensical paradigm."[324]

Although the Hadith scholars claim that a scientific approach was applied to screen out fake Hadith, the fact remains that this approach was inherently deficient and flawed, and could not, and did not, succeed in giving us an unquestionably authentic corpus of Hadith literature (see below for a scrutiny of the criteria used to select authentic Hadith).

THE THEOLOGICAL TEST

Since the Hadith is known among Muslims as the words of the Prophet Muhammad and accounts of his deeds, it is quite natural that it would have a special sentimental value and appeal to them, especially to those who are unwary and unsuspecting believers. Unfortunately, however, those who deliberately wanted to mislead Muslim believers have abused this sentimental value by cooking up or distorting reports about the Prophet. The Hadith has been given the status of quasi-revelation or revelation from God. A selection of Hadith texts is actually viewed as Hadith Qudsi, i.e., the Hadith that has been received through divine revelation. The *ulama* present various arguments in support of Hadith authenticity. These arguments could be grouped as follows:

- God advises us to obey His Messenger and follow his example;

- The Hadith is also some kind of revelation from God, which the Prophet followed;

- Our Prophet has brought us something new, which is contained in the Hadith; and

- The Quran is not sufficient for us; it does not explain everything; e.g., *salat* is not explained fully by the Quran; and the Hadith makes it easier to understand the Quran.

Do these arguments really stand up under scrutiny? We appraise these arguments below.

300

The argument: God advises us to obey his Messenger and follow his example

This most cited argument, the *ulama* insist, has support in various verses of the Quran, some of which are as follows:

3:31-2   Say (O Muhammad): '*If ye do love God, then follow me; God will love you and forgive your faults*, and God is Ever Forgiving, Most Merciful.' Say: '*Obey God and the Messenger*; but if they turn away, then verily God loveth not those who disbelieve.' (See also 4:59)

4:80   He who obeyeth the Messenger indeed obeyeth God.
           …

8:20   O ye who believe! *Obey God and His Messenger; and turn not away from him while ye hear.*

33:21   *Indeed in the Messenger of God ye have an excellent example for him who looketh unto God and the Final Day*, and remembereth God much.

The Hadith scholars and supporters have interpreted these verses to mean that we should follow the Quran to follow God, and follow the Hadith to follow the Prophet. They have thus interpreted following God and following the Prophet as two different things. However, the verses (3:31-32; 33:21) noted above clearly imply that we should love and follow the Prophet as a way of loving and following God. Following the Prophet should not, therefore, be construed as separate or different from following God. This is evident also from the verses where God refers to sayings of the Prophet as nothing different from those revealed as the Quran. The following verses make this amply clear:

69:40-3   *It is the SAYING of an Honored Messenger.*
                It is not the saying of a poet; little it is that ye believe.
                Nor is it the saying of a soothsayer; little it is that ye heed.
                It is a Message revealed from the Lord of the Universe.

These verses clearly identify the sayings or utterances of the Prophet as the Words of God Himself as revealed to him, and contained in the Quran. If we love God, we need indeed to love and follow the Prophet,

301

and heed his sayings that are nothing but the message contained in the Quran. Indeed, for those of us who are not in his midst, the most meaningful message of the verses urging us to follow the Prophet is that we heed his inspiring sayings (and practices) that are inspired from God, and that are all in the Quran. Will it not be the best justice we do, and the most devotion we show, to the Prophet by heeding to his clarion call that we believe in, and follow, precisely the divine revelations, which he has brought us? His sayings relevant for us were nothing other than the revelations he received, and recited to people around him (62:2; 75:16-19), which are all in the Quran.

The Prophet, of course, also said things to his people around him, which were not just recitations from the Quran. During his lifetime, it was incumbent upon the Muslims living around him that they respond to what he said to them and obey him closely, as evident from the verse at (8:20), where God urges believers who hear the Prophet not to turn away from him. Only those around him could hear him. For us and other people of succeeding generations who are not around him, the only meaningful way for responding to him, and not turning away from him, would be to carefully follow the revelations that he has brought, and that have been passed on to us.

Other responses to the above argument, which are applicable for both his contemporaries and later generations, are as follows:

- The Prophet followed nothing except what was revealed to him, which is all in the Quran (6:50; 46:9); and God advised him and us to do the same (6:155; 45:6). So if we just follow the Quran, we really follow him as well.

- The argument that we need to follow his *sunnah* tacitly assumes that the *sunnah* reflected in the sayings and actions of the Prophet is separate from the *sunnah* reflected in the sayings and actions of, or approved by, God. He has been asked to emulate God's nature (30:30), which really means that the Prophet's *sunnah* should not be separated from that of God, which He has spelled out in the Quran. In fact, God has characterized the content of the Quran as the most consistent and best Hadith (39:23). Thus if we follow the Quran, we also follow both God's and the Prophet's *sunnah*.

302

- And the fact that there was not much compiled Hadith during over two centuries after the Prophet's death, which the Prophet's companions and other Muslims during that long period of history could follow, also highlights the point that the Hadith is after all not of much religious utility or significance to Muslims.

Some of the relevant verses of the Quran reflecting these points are as follows:

6:50   Say (O Muhammad): I say not unto you that I have the treasures of God; nor that I know the unseen; nor do I say to you that am an angel. *I follow not aught except what is revealed unto me.* (See also 46:9 cited earlier.)

30:30   *So set thy purpose truly (O Muhammad) for religion as a man by nature upright, the nature (made) of God,* in which He hath created man. *There is no change in the way God createth.* That is the right religion, but most men know not.

45:6   These are God's signs (or revelations) that We recite unto thee (O Muhammad) with truth. *Then in which Hadith (Message), after God and His revelations,* will they believe?

17:77   (Such was Our) WAY (*Sunnah*) with the Messengers We sent before thee (O Muhammad); and *thou wilt find no change in Our WAY (Sunnah)*.

The fourth verse noted at (45:6) cautions us about believing in anything other than God's revelations, which are all in the Quran. Thus, as these verses clearly say, if the Prophet followed nothing but the Quran, and if he emulated God's Nature or Way, which never changes, it is hard to establish the thesis that the Hadith represents his *sunnah*. He was obligated to follow and profess only God's Way or *Sunnah*. There was no scope for the Prophet to introduce a *sunnah* of his own. This is further corroborated by the Quranic verse at (53:3), which says that the Prophet did not say anything of religion of his own desire. The Prophet was asked to admonish his people only with the Quran:

50:45   … So *admonish (thou O Muhammad) with the Quran*
those who care about My warning.

And we have been exhorted to follow only what has been revealed from
God or the Quran alone, and not any other guardians beside Him: *"And
this (the Quran) is a Book that We have revealed as a Blessing. So follow
it, and become upright, that ye may find mercy"* (6:155). … *"(O
Humankind!) Follow that which hath been revealed from your Lord. And
follow not guardians beside Him. Little it is that ye heed"* (7:3). The
Prophet was specifically urged by God to judge only by the Quran, and
not follow any personal desires (6:114; 4:105; 5:48-49). We have also
been urged to seek no source other than the revealed book for deciding
legal cases: *"(Say, O Muhammad!) 'Shall I seek for judge (or law) other
than God, when He it is Who hath revealed unto thee the Book explained
in detail?'"* (6:114). And the Quran also unequivocally proclaims that
those who do not judge by what has been revealed from God are
disbelievers (*kafirs*) (5:44), wrongdoers (*jalims*) (5:45), or rebellious
(*fasiqs*) (5:49).

Even accepting, for argument's sake, that there are still things the
Prophet did outside what was advised in the Quran, the question arises:
What are the things about the Prophet that we need to know for our own
benefit? This is the same question as to ask: To what extent do we need
to follow the Prophet? In responding to this question, we can say that it is
the Quran that best mirrors his conduct, which we need to emulate. The
Quran provides all kinds of advice for the Prophet and us to go along the
sirat al mustaqim or the straight or right path.[325] Besides providing
advice for all believers, which the Prophet also followed, the Quran also
gives particular references to what the Prophet was, and what he did.
Note also that he was advised by God to preach and teach only with the
Quran (50:45); and judge only with the Quran (4:105; 5:48-49). In
addition, there are particular references in the Quran about what he
personally believed (2:285; 42:15); how he prayed (26:218-219; 52:48-
49; 73:2-8, 20); and about his actions that God disapproved of (80:1-11;
33:37; 66:1, 93:7), which he, of course, corrected. The Prophet did not
want to impress people with any miracles, even though they were curious
to know if he had any as proof of his prophethood, as miracles did little
in the past to attract people to God's path. God says that the Quran itself
is the greatest miracle sent for the people (29:50-51; 74:35-37). Still how
he rose to the status of a Prophet that enabled him to receive God's
revelations and his *miraj* (Ascension) (17:1, 53:5-18) point to things that

304

men of understanding who have aspiration to attain spiritual progress need to ponder. There are references in the Quran about the Prophet's wives too (33:32-34; 33: 28-34; 60:12; 66:3-5). In a way the whole Quran is a reflection of, or about, what the Prophet did and said in his life, and about how he conducted himself in various situations. Also importantly, God proclaims in the Quran that the Prophet's sole duty was to deliver this Book to humankind (5:67, 92, 99; 13:40 and more verses): *"But if ye turn away, then know that Our Messenger's duty is only to deliver (the Message)"* (5:92). What else do we need for our guidance? Do we need another book in addition to the Quran? Indeed God has made following the Quran binding (*fard*) on us (28:85). It is rather the Prophet who lamented to God that his people have treated the Quran as a forsaken thing: *"The Messenger said: O my Lord! Surely my own people have treated this Quran as a forsaken thing"* (25:30).

Do we need to know more about the Prophet than what we know about him from the Quran? The answer should not be "yes". This is for two reasons: first, the fact that the reports about the Prophet that we get in the Hadith do not have much credibility; and second, even given that there may be some truth in some of such reports, we need not try to imitate or follow all such actions since they may not be of much relevance or significance to our own efforts for religious piety. We need to understand that all that the Prophet did, or said, or approved, or disapproved were in the context of his own circumstances, and the particular physical and socio-economic environment, in which he lived and worked. All of such actions may not carry religious significance for other contexts. For example, what he did with his beard or hair; how he cleaned his teeth; what dress he put on; how he slept; what particular foods except the forbidden ones he liked and ate; what forms of transport he used; whether or not he used scent and when; and similar other questions are not matters that others need to imitate. Indeed trying to follow everything that the Prophet did or said without trying to explore and understand the underlying reasons of such deeds or sayings has no real meaning for us. Blind imitation of a person, or of the past (i.e., without understanding), is *"taqlid"*, which has been rejected by many Islamic scholars. Imitating a person without trying to see the reasons of his actions is like idolizing him like a god. Such idolizing is what God has strictly forbidden us (3:79-80). Indeed the Quran does not want us to follow everything the Prophet did, since he also made mistakes (9:43; 80:1-10; 33:37; 66:1), which he, of course, corrected. Furthermore, when particular physical and socio-economic environments differ, human needs and things that suit them best also differ. Even human body needs, and accordingly food needs, differ from person to person, and from time to time as well as in different health conditions for the same person. The same food may not suit everybody; many are found to be allergic to specific foods (e.g., even normal milk that contains lactose is unsuitable to those who are not lactose-tolerant). The Quran itself recognizes the diversity of nations and tribes (49:13; 2:60). For every one of us God has established a law and an open way; if God had willed He could have made us one nation, but He will try us in what He has given us (5:48). Thus even if the Hadith could succeed in giving us the real Prophet, it still would not have validated the need to follow him in every bit of detail. So an attempt to sanctify everything the Prophet did or said as *sunnah* for us cannot be considered as relevant or appropriate. As Kassim Ahmad remarks:

> It is unreasonable and unthinkable that God would ask the Muslims to follow the prophet's personal mode of behavior, because a person's mode of behavior is determined by many different factors, such as customs, his education, personal upbringing and personal inclinations. The prophet's mode of eating, of dress and indeed of general behavior cannot be different from that of other Arabs, including Jews and Christians, of that time, except regarding matters which Islam prohibited. If the Prophet had been born a Malay, he would have dressed and eaten like a Malay. This is a cultural and a personal trait which has nothing to do with one's religion.[326]

From whatever point of view one likes to consider, the need for the Hadith has no legitimate basis. Beside the Quran we have really no good Hadith. The Quran declares itself as the best Hadith:

39:23   *God hath revealed the best message (HADITH), a Book consistent, paired (with information on both ways, good and bad), whereat doth tremble the skin of those who fear or reverence their Lord, so that their skin and their hearts soften to remembrance of God. Such is God's guidance wherewith He guideth whom He will.*

Indeed the Prophet's utterances or commonly understood Hadith were at their best when they were nothing less or more than the divine inspirations themselves. Thus outside the Quran we have really no

Hadith of the Prophet, which is worth heeding by us. All the verses of the Quran noted in this context clearly rule out canonical authority for any Hadith other than the Quran.

The argument: the Hadith is also some kind of revelation from God

The origins of this argument can be traced to Muhammad b. Idris al-Shafii (d. 204 A.H./819 C.E.), a founder of one of the four schools of Muslim jurisprudence. Shafii argued that the expression "*hikmah*" (wisdom) in the Quranic verse where reference is made to the Prophet's teaching of the Book and wisdom (62:2) points to his Hadith.[327] We have noted above the rebuttal of this argument that Ghulam Ahmad Parwez made, which is that "*hikmah* or wisdom" is meant in a general sense, and cannot be characterized as specifically meaning the Prophet's Hadith. This contention has support in the fact that all prophets essentially undergo spiritual transformation, and they all bring to humankind wisdom and insight into religion and spirituality. Their revealed book is the main vehicle of such wisdom. But apart from that it is also true that their followers and associates during their lifetime did have an extra advantage to have some access to such wisdom (62:2). Note also that this verse refers specifically to the inhabitants of Mecca, who were in clear error, to whom the Prophet came. That the expression "the Book and the *hikmah*" used in the Quran need not specifically mean the Prophet's Hadith is supported by the fact that the same expression is found to have been used also in the case of other prophets, Jesus, the house of Abraham and John (3:48, 79, 81; 5:110, 4:54; 19:12). Also note that God characterizes the Quran itself as a Book of wisdom (10:1; 31:2; 36:2; 43:4). So it cannot be held with certainty that the expression "*hikmah*" at verse (62:2) unequivocally refers to the Prophet's Hadith. Rather all these verses reinforce the idea that "wisdom" refers to general "spiritual or religious knowledge and insight" that prophets are usually endowed with, and those who came in close association with such persons benefited the most from such wisdom. But this does not necessarily lend support to any Hadith hypothesis.

The Quranic verse at (53:3), which says that the Prophet did not say anything of his own desire, is also taken to mean that everything he said was divinely inspired. So whatever he said outside the Quran is meant as referring to his Hadith. This argument is also flawed, since this verse could and should be interpreted to precisely mean that he has not uttered anything of religious significance that is not in the divinely inspired

307

Book, the Quran, as supported by the verse (69:40-43) cited above. It further begs the question at the very outset: if the Hadith is also some kind of revelation from God, how is it that it is not included in the Quran, or even not compiled by his close associates? "The absence of written records brings into question the revealed status of *sunna*; if *sunna* was *wahy* [revelation] it certainly would have been recorded in writing. [...] neither the Prophet, nor his Companions, nor the early Caliphs considered anything to be revelation except the Qur'an."[328] The question also arises of why it took well more than one hundred years after the Prophet's death to discover this perceived truth that *sunnah* is also divine revelation.

As mentioned above, the Prophet was exhorted by God to advise people with the Quran alone (50:45). He was specifically urged by God not to move his tongue while receiving revelation, but just to follow it and read it to others, and not try to explain it to others; the explanation was the responsibility of God Himself:

> **75:16-9** Move not (O Muhammad) thy tongue herewith (with the Quran) to make haste with it. Lo! It is for Us to put it together and read it. And *when We have read it, just follow thou the reading. Then lo! It is upon Us to explain it.*

In fact the Quran affirms that it is the disbelieving or wrongdoing people who used to fabricate sayings in God's name even during the Prophet's lifetime:

> **3:78** *And verily there is a party among them who distort the Book with their tongues, that ye may think that it is of the Book, but it is not of the Book. And they say: It is from God; but it is not from God. And they invent a lie against God, while they know it.*

And during the Prophet's time there were also illiterate people who did not know the Quran except from hearsay, and those who used to write with their own hands and say that those writings were from God (2:78-79). These verses and the verse at (3:78) strongly indicate that the tendency to fabricate sayings in God's name or, by implication, in the Prophet's name has been there ever since the Prophet's lifetime. These verses lend strong support to the point that the Hadith that came long after the Prophet's demise can claim little credibility, let alone claim the status of divine revelation.

The argument: our Prophet has brought us something new, which is contained in the Hadith

This argument, which is sometimes made, goes against the very grain of the divine message, which the Quran says always remains the same. The Quran emphasizes that the Prophet Muhammad was not new among God's Messengers (See 46:9 cited earlier) and that he did not bring or say anything new (See 41:43, 42:13 and 22:78 cited before).

There is no change in God's Words or Way (See 10:64; 35:43 cited earlier), and true religion (*deen*) with God has always been Islam (3:19), though in some sense the latest Book of revelation, the Quran brings the most comprehensive message to humanity, as it takes account of all past notable human errors. When one religion was corrupted or lost by men in a habitation, it needed to be re-discovered or re-revealed. The latest religion of Islam came with the revelations of the Quran, and was perfected by the Quran alone. God says in the Quran:

> **5:3** *...This day have We perfected your religion (deen) for you*, and completed My favor unto you, and chosen for you as religion 'al Islam'. ... (See also 6:115 cited earlier)

Thus if the Prophet Muhammad did not bring or say anything new, if what he brought is all contained in the Quran, if God's religion was perfected by the Quran, and most importantly if he advised Muslims only with the Quran, then there is then nothing else left of his task except to simply deliver the Quran:

> **5:99** *Nothing is (incumbent) on the Messenger but only to deliver (the Message).* God knoweth what ye proclaim and what ye hide.

This then conclusively precludes any Hadith for us to follow.

Some might still insist that though the fundamentals of religion have always remained the same, the Prophet brought new details, which had not been there before, and that these details can be found in the Hadith.

However this argument also holds no water in light of the Quran. This argument assumes that the Quran does not provide all the details that are necessary for us to know to be guided aright. However, this assumption is unwarranted and contradictory to the Quran itself, which claims that it is fully detailed and sufficient for us as guidance. (For elaboration, see below)

The argument: the Quran is not sufficient and easy; it does not explain everything

It is indeed ironic that it is Muslims, who are influenced by the Hadith, who think that the Quran is not sufficient or easy for us as guidance. The *ulama* usually employ this argument in favor of the Hadith. But by so doing they do in effect doubt or contradict the Quranic claims that it *explains everything* (See 12:111 cited earlier; 6:114; and 16:89), and that it has been made sufficiently *easy to follow* (54:17**, 22, 32, 40**).

> **6:114** Say (O Muhammad!): Shall I seek for judge other than God, when He it is Who hath revealed unto thee (this) *Book, explained in detail*?

> **16:89** *And We have revealed unto thee (O Muhammad) the Book explaining everything,* a guidance and a mercy and good news for those who have surrendered (to God, i.e., became Muslims).

> **54:17** *And We have indeed made the Quran easy to learn;* then is there any that will learn? (See also 54:22, 32, 40.)

The revealed Word of God is, as it has been meant to be, clear, accessible, and readily comprehensible. The Quran is self-contained, and must be understood by its internal logic, and interpreted by its own verses, without any external aid. Inayat Allah Khan Mashriqi, the founder of the radical Khaksar movement in India, notes:

> The correct and the only meaning of the Qur'an lies, and is preserved, within itself, and a perfect and detailed exegesis of its words is within its own pages. One part of the Qur'an explains the other; it needs neither philosophy, nor wit, nor lexicography, nor even hadith.[329]

The Quran is comprehensive; and all the requirements for belief and practice in religion are contained in it. It is a fully sufficient guidance for humankind:

> **17:9** *Surely this Quran guideth unto that which is most right*, and giveth good news to those who believe and do good work that theirs will be a great reward.

Thus if God says He has made the Quran easy enough to learn or understand, it is incomprehensible why our *ulama* should dispute it. On the other hand, it is also true that the Quran is a Book of wisdom, and that how far one succeeds in deciphering the wisdom of the Quran depends on one's capacity to understand, which, in turn, is a function of one's level of intelligence, knowledge, and wisdom. What turns out to be the real beauty of the Quran is that as one gets wiser and wiser, one can find and extract deeper and deeper meanings from the Quranic message. As mentioned in Chapter 1, there are some verses in the Quran, which are allegorical and not easily comprehended by all. Only those who are grounded well in knowledge, i.e., spiritually advanced, understand them. The fact that there are some verses in the Quran, which are not understood or well understood by some readers, does not warrant them to take recourse to the Hadith. Is there any evidence that the Hadith has made clearer those verses of the Quran, which are not easy to understand? Rather on the contrary, the available evidence suggests that the Hadith has made confusion more confounded (see the next chapter).

Indeed, the Quran has been revealed with so much clarity and elaboration and, in many cases, with repetitions of the same verses, that it hardly needs any explanation from an external source. To become a good and wise Muslim, one does not need any other document, just as Muslims during the two centuries after the Prophet's death did not need any.

The contention, or concerns, of the *ulama* that the Quran does not give sufficient details of the *salat* system that Muslims practice have been addressed in Chapter 5. What we need to realize is that whatever has not been categorically mentioned in the Quran concerning anything should not be regarded as essential elements of Islam. Whatever religious practices God wants us to follow are adequately and lucidly described, and explained in the Quran. Even minute details of admonitions have not been left untouched. Rather, the Hadith has corrupted the *salat* practice, as discussed in Chapter 5, as other practices (See also the next chapter).

We should learn to do the *salat* according to what the Quran wants us to do. We do not need another book for this.

Also, as some commentators have argued, certain religious rituals such as *salat* and *hajj* were already there, and have come down to us from generation to generation through our fathers and forefathers. They were copied and carried forward from the time of the Prophet Abraham (21:73), whom the Prophet Muhammad followed (3:95; 2:135; 4:125; 16:123). Such practices or *sunnah* do not require any reference to the Hadith.[330]

THE HISTORICAL TEST

The historical basis of the Hadith is at best tenuous. Some of the historical points such as (1) the prohibition of the Prophet himself on Hadith writing, and honoring of the same position by his immediate followers, (2) the long gap between the Quran and the Hadith, and the accompanying lack of proper records of the deeds and sayings of the Prophet, and (3) flawed oral transmission due to weakness of the human sources, including their imperfect memories add well to effectively dismiss the Hadith altogether. To this list one may add (4) the influence of the ruling regimes, of people with wealth and power of the time, and of the disputing theologians on Hadith collection, recording, selection and compilation, and finally (5) the weakness of the criteria used to judge authenticity of individual Hadith texts.

The position of the Prophet and his immediate followers

Historical evidence, if there is any, appears to be that the Prophet himself was against the reporting of his own sayings and practices; and his four close companions who became Caliphs after him upheld the same position. Kassim Ahmad notes: "Notwithstanding the conflicting versions of hadith that say otherwise, historical facts [...] prove beyond any shadow of doubt that there were no hadith collections existing at the time of the Prophet's death. History also proves that the early caliphs prevented the recording and dissemination of hadith."[331]

The *ulama* take it for granted that the Prophet gave his blessing to the collection and writing of his Hadith. Mazhar Kazi reports that in his farewell address the Prophet declared, "Convey to others even if it is a single verse from me."[332] This is taken as a go-ahead for Hadith

312

dissemination. However, the statement here more meaningfully appears rather to point to the revealed Quranic verses, not his own words, since he was the messenger of God's message, and mercy for the whole universe (68:52; 21:107); and his message, which was nothing but the Quran, needed to be conveyed to all humankind.

The available evidence is rather compelling that the Prophet forbade collection and writing of his own words except the Quran, and left clear direction that if anyone has collected and recorded such statements, these should be erased. This is evident from one Hadith narration included in *Muslim* that reads as follows:

> Abu Sa'id Khudri reported that Allah's Messenger (may peace be upon him) said: *Do not take down anything from me, and he who took down anything from me except the Quran, he should erase that* and narrate from me, for there is no harm in it and he who attributed any falsehood to me – and Hammam said: I think he also said: "deliberately" – he should in fact find his abode in the Hell-Fire (*Sahih Muslim*, Book 042, Chapter 17, Number 7147).[333]

There are similar other Hadith reports, e.g., one from *Abu Dawud*, and another from *Taqyid* by al-Baghdadi confirming the Prophet's prohibition on Hadith writing, and direction for erasure of any Hadith.[334] The *ulama* recognize and accept the Prophet's prohibition on Hadith recording, but brush aside this prohibition by expressing the view that it was applicable for an initial period when the Quran was being revealed to avoid a possible mix-up of the Quranic verses with the Hadith. However, this sort of reasoning is unconvincing, since the Prophet did not explicitly mention this, and since there is no evidence that the Prophet ever withdrew or cancelled his earlier discouragement of the Hadith. Evidently, the Prophet was aware of the dangers of writing down Prophetic traditions beside the words of God and, as Guillaume reports, the Prophet did caution against Hadith writing as such writings led people astray before.[335]

Some may point out that taking recourse to the Hadith to prove that the Prophet gave no authority for the Hadith and that he rather discouraged it could be considered as circular reasoning. Yet it does give the message that if the Hadith about the Prophet's prohibition on Hadith writing is true, as it seemingly was, there remains no genuine basis for the rest of the Hadith literature to stand validated.

Whatever historical reports we seem to have about the position of the Khulafai-Rashidun (the Righteous Caliphs) on the Hadith suggest that they also discouraged its compilation. According to one report, the first Caliph Abu Bakr burned his own notes of Hadith (said to be some 500), after being very uneasy about these notes.[336] "According to Jayrajpuri, because the Companions (of the Prophet) so often disagreed with one another Abu Bakr forbade the collection of hadith."[337] Caliph Umar cancelled his initial plan to compile Hadith, apprehending its possible adverse impact in the form of neglect of the Book of God – the Quran.[338] During his caliphate, "the problem of hadith forgery was so serious that he prohibited Hadith transmission altogether."[339] Umar reportedly also arranged for burning of all available Hadith. The position of Uthman and Ali also appears to have been lack of any overt effort to collect any Hadith for dissemination purposes.

The fact remains that there were no written records of Hadith during the lifetime of the Prophet as well as during the rule of the four Caliphs, hazy or conflicting historical reports about the early period of Islam notwithstanding. This is despite the fact that "several documents of the Prophet, such as the Medina Charter or Constitution, his treaties and letters, had been written on his orders."[340] This amply proves the point that if the Prophet had wished, he could have made arrangements for recording of his Hadith as a separate religious document, just as he did in the case of the Quran. The stark fact is that he did not wish such recording, and his discouragement of Hadith recording was honored by the four Caliphs, and remained in force apparently for some thirty years after the Prophet's death, but was ignored later. According to one report, a Hadith in *Abu Dawud*, the Ummayad ruler Muawiya wanted a Hadith to be written in the presence of one of the Prophet's most noted scribes Zayd ibn Thabit, but when Zayd ibn Thabit reminded him of the Prophet's prohibition on Hadith writing, he (Muawiya) erased it.

As Iqbal notes in his seminal work *The Reconstruction of Religious Thought in Islam*, even Abu Hanifah, regarded as "one of the greatest exponents of Muhammedan Law in Sunni Islam [...] made practically no use of [...] traditions", even though there were collections available at that time made by other people no less than thirty years before his death. Nor did he collect any Hadith for his use, unlike his peers Malik and

Ahmad Ibn Hanbal. Thus, according to Iqbal, "if modern Liberalism considers it safer not to make any indiscriminate use of them [traditions] as a source of law, it will be only following [the example of Abu Hanifah]."[341] "In reaction to a situation [where huge numbers of forged hadith reports were in circulation] that was virtually out of control, Abu Hanifah approached hadith with the assumption that very few could be proved *sahih* [authentic]."[342]

The long time gap, and the lack of proper records

We already noted that the Hadith surfaced more than two centuries after the Prophet's death, which *de facto* means a long time gap between the Quran and the Hadith. This long time gap raises questions of reliability for the Hadith that can never be satisfactorily resolved. Muslim and non-Muslim historians and scholars all point out that there were no written records of the Prophet's sayings and deeds during the first century after his death, and not much Hadith writing – and not any Hadith book that gained respectability later on by the Muslim community at large – during the long two centuries after the Prophet's death.[343] The Hadith literature that gained recognition such as that collected and compiled by Bukhari, Muslim, etc., came more than two hundred years after the Prophet's death, and they were all based on *oral transmission from generation to generation through chains of transmitters (isnads) numbering seven to even one hundred in the chain*. A Herculean feat! Isn't it? But hold your breath. Even written records of the past traditions were not good enough. As the historian MacDonald notes that one danger in written records "was evidently real ... the unhappy character of the Arabic script, especially when written without diacritical points, often made it hard if not practically impossible, to understand such short, contextless texts as the traditions."[344] "There was fierce opposition to the written records of traditions *for a long time* also on the theological ground that this would lead to too much honoring of the traditions and neglect of the Quran, a fear that was justified to a certain extent by the event."[345]

The scholars of Hadith (the *muhaddithun*), "no matter how dedicated, were simply too distant from the time of the Prophet, and forgery had become too rampant for authentic hadith to be recovered."[346] Some anecdotes of the *muhaddithun* suggest that they could not prevent forged Hadith from being circulated even in their own names.[347] It is also worth noting that there were enemies of Islam and pseudo-Muslims who wanted to sabotage the propagation of true Islam by attributing false statements or reports either to God, or to His Prophet, right from the Prophet's lifetime. Evidence that there were such people who directed their efforts to diverting attention from the mainstream Islam, and to causing dissension and divisions in the Muslim *ummah* even during the Prophet's lifetime is provided by the Quran itself:

> **9:106-7** And *there are those who put up a mosque by way of mischief and disbelief, and in order to cause dissension among the believers, and as an outpost for those who fought against God and His messenger before.* They will indeed swear: 'Our intention is nothing but good'; but God beareth witness that they are certainly liars. Never stand there (to pray). A mosque whose foundation was laid from the first day on piety is more worthy of your standing therein, wherein are men who love to purify themselves. God loveth those who purify themselves.

Here it refers to some people who put up a mosque to cause dissension among Muslims. Such people were evidently not well-meaning Muslims. Thus, forgers had been active even during the Prophet's lifetime. Forgery had been rampant during the caliphate of the Prophet's immediate successors, and it "only increased under the Umayyads[348], who considered Hadith a means of propping up their rule and actively circulated traditions against Ali, and in favor of Muawiya. The Abbasids[349] followed the same pattern, circulating Prophetic Hadith, which predicted the reign of each successive ruler. Moreover, religious and ethnic conflicts further contributed to the forgery of Hadith."[350]

It was during the rule of the Abbasids that Hadith compilation making a mark for the later Muslims was done in earnest. The first such compilation in the third century Hijrah was by al-Bukhari, who died in 257 A.H., whose book, as already mentioned, contains a selection of some seven thousand traditions (including repeated ones) out of reportedly six hundred thousand he found in circulation. Another contemporary compilation was by Muslim (d. 261 A.H.), which contains some four thousand selections out of some three hundred thousand. Other four compilations included in the so-called authentic six and written more or less towards the end of the third century Hijrah are by Abu Dawud as-Sistani (d. 275 A.H), Ibn Maja (d. 303 A.H), at-Tirmidhi (d. 279 A.H) and an-Nasa'i (d. 303 A.H), which "deal almost entirely

316

with legal traditions, those that tell what is permitted and what is forbidden, and do not convey information on religious and theological subjects."[351] The compilations accepted by the Shiites came even later.

The big question is: Why did the compilations come after such an inordinately long lapse of historical time after the Prophet's death? Kassim Ahmad legitimately asks: "Why was the official compilation not made earlier, especially during the time of the righteous caliphs when the first reporters, i.e., the eye witnesses, were still alive and could be examined?"[352] Because of the long time lag one can hardly be sure that the accounts are genuinely those of the Prophet Muhammad. How can one be so certain that the chain of narrators through the oral transmission has been successful in transmitting the same message *ad verbatim* from generation to generation, when even in the same generation, or say, even in the same year or month or day, people are often found unable to exactly reproduce one's utterances? Even in the current electronic age, news reporters often find it hard, without proper recording, to reproduce the exact texts of what speakers say in their speeches. Even today, sometimes there are conflicting news reports of the same event, which may not be intentional lies on the part of the reporters. Note also that noticeable differences can be found in the compilations done by the different compilers – a factor that can also raise a question of credibility of the compilations.

Flawed oral transmission due to weakness of the human sources, including their imperfect memories

Thus the manner in which Hadith was preserved and transmitted raises a lot of questions. Since the Hadith was preserved and transmitted primarily orally, both by default and design, the transmission process was as good as the human sources involved in the process. (The oral transmission was preferred to written records by the Hadith scholars, because written records to be credible required to be directly attested to by living transmitters of Hadith who could vouch for their credibility.) The question is: Was this transmission process reliable enough to give assurance that what we get as words or reports of deeds of the Prophet are genuinely those of the Prophet?

Also note that Hadith reports originating from all narrators do not command the same credibility. Hadith reports that are reported to have originated from two of the companions of the Prophet, Anas b. Malik and

317

Abu Huraira are especially suspect. Anas lived long (about hundred years), because of which it was convenient for Hadith forgers to list him as an originator.[353] "Aisha criticized Anas for transmitting traditions although he was only a child during the life of the Prophet."[354] Aisha was reported to have criticized also Abu Huraira, and she was joined in this criticism by Ibn Abbas.[355] Abu Huraira was originator of a very large number of Hadith texts (more than 5000), even though he converted to Islam in less than three years before the Prophet's death. According to some reports, the second Caliph "Umar called Abu Huraira a liar,"[356] and reprimanded him for his questionable conduct. During Muawiya's rule, he reportedly lived in his palace in Syria.[357] His memory was poor, but the Bukhari compilation provides reference to his poor memory being miraculously cured by the Prophet (*Sahih Bukhari*, Vol. 1, Book 3, # 119, also repeated at Vol. 4, Book 56, Number 841, also repeated by another narrator with a somewhat different text at Vol. 1, Book 3, # 120), a claim that looks rather suspicious. And legitimately, a question also arises: how sure can one be that the later transmitters (who are known as *rawis*, some of whom were *tabiun*, i.e., companions of the companions of the Prophet, or *tabi-tabiun*, i.e., companions of the *tabiun*) in the chain of narrators (*isnad*) attributed Hadith texts to the original companion of the Prophet accurately without any mistake, even with full good intentions? Any mistake made by anyone of the narrators of any Hadith in the chain (*isnad*) involved would necessarily make its transmission flawed, and its accurate attribution to the Prophet difficult.

There are even some Hadith texts in *Bukhari* that suggest that even the Prophet used to forget things *(Sahih Bukhari,* Volume 1, Book 5, Number 274, also Vol. 1, Book 8, # 394)! Surely the less reliable human agents involved in Hadith transmission were more likely to forget and make mistakes. Is not the Hadith transmission a reflection of too much dependence on human memory and that also covering several generations? The authenticity of Hadith breaks down on this count alone. The Hadith definitely relies on too many unproven assumptions, and thus can hardly claim authority.

Critics have also pointed out that the compilers of the so-called authentic six Hadith books were all non-Arabs, originating from Iran or other places. One may legitimately think that this may also suggest some foul play or conspiracy by some interest groups to divert Muslims' attention away from the Quran, and to create dissension among them, which is proved by the course of subsequent events.

The influence of power struggles and theological rivalries on Hadith writing

Hadith writing was actively promoted by the Umayyad and Abbasid rulers. According to a historical tradition, Ibn Shihab al-Zuhri (d. 742 C.E.) was the first individual to record (in writing) the Hadith, but under duress – under orders from Caliph Hisham, "who became the first traditionist to violate the Prophet's prohibition on recording Hadith in writing. Al-Zuhri is reported to have said: 'We disapproved of recording knowledge until these rulers forced us to do so. After that we saw no reason to forbid Muslims to do so.'"[358]

About the power struggles and theological rivalries that led to forging of Hadith in circulation, MacDonald notes:

> [T]he Umayyads, who reigned from A.H. 41 to A.H. 132 [and who cared little for religion], for reasons of state, [...] encouraged and spread—also freely forged and encouraged others to forge—such traditions as were favorable to their plans and to their rule generally. This was necessary if they were to carry the body of the people with them. But they regarded themselves as kings and not as the heads of the Muslim people. This same device has been used after them by all the contending factions of Islam. Each party has sought sanction for its views by representing them in traditions from the Prophet, and the thing has gone so far that on almost every disputed point there are absolutely conflicting prophetic utterances in circulation. It has even been held, and with some justification, that the entire body of *normative* tradition at present in existence was forged for a purpose.[359]

One example of Hadith fabrication given by Goldziher is that by Ummayad caliph Abd al-Malik also known as Malik b. Anas[360] who was an important collector of Hadith is as follows:

> When the Umayyad caliph 'Abd al-Malik wished to stop the pilgrimages to Mecca because he was worried lest his rival 'Abd Allah b. Zubayr should force the Syrians journeying to the holy places in Hijaz to pay him homage, he had recourse to the expedient of the doctrine of the vicarious hajj to the Qubbat al-Sakhra in Jerusalem. He decreed that obligatory circumambulation (tawaf) could take place at the sacred place in Jerusalem with the same validity as that around the Ka'ba ordained in Islamic law. The pious theologian al-Zuhri was given the task of justifying this politically motivated reform of religious life by making up and spreading a saying traced back to the Prophet, according to which there are three mosques to which people may take pilgrimages: those in Mecca, Medina, and Jerusalem. .. An addition which, apparently, belonged to its original form but was later neglected by leveling orthodoxy in this and related sayings: 'and a prayer in the Bayt al-Maqdis of Jerusalem is better than a thousand prayers in other holy places,' i.e. even Mecca or Medina. Later, too, 'Abd al-Malik is quoted when the pilgrimage to Jerusalem is to be equated with that to Mecca.[361]

Contemporary Muslim scholar Jeffrey Lang cites another example of a politically motivated Hadith. The following Hadith report in *Sahih Bukhari*, "which so succinctly exonerates the first three Caliphs [after the Prophet's death] in the precise order of their reigns, certainly sounds like it was invented to refute their detractors."[362]

> On the authority of Abu Musa: the Prophet entered a garden and bade me guard its gate. Then a man came and asked leave to enter. And [the Prophet] said: Let him enter, and announce to him [that he will gain] Paradise. – And lo, it was Abu Bakr. Thereafter another man came and asked leave to enter. And [the Prophet] said: Let him enter, and announce to him [that he will gain] Paradise. – And lo, it was 'Umar. Thereafter another man came and asked leave to enter. And [the Prophet] remained silent for a while; then he said: Let him enter, and announce to him [that he will gain] Paradise after a calamity

that is to befall him. – And lo, it was 'Uthman ibn 'Affan.[363]
(Similar texts in *Sahih Bukhari*, Vol. 5, Book 57, # 42, 44)

Lang provides two examples of Hadith fabrication in the area of theological disputes. One point of contention is that "[…] the legitimacy of *ijma* (consensus) as a source of Islamic Law was much debated during Imam al Shafi'i's time, who defends it in his *Risala, Yet al Shafi'i, a leader in the hadith party, was apparently unaware of the famous statement of the Prophet, "my community will never agree on an error"* (*al Tirmidhi*), *which establishes its validity.* Another point of contention among al Shafi'i's colleagues is whether prophetic *sunnahs* on issues unmentioned in the Qur'an are binding. This time, however, al Shafi'i is able to call upon a *made-to-order hadith* (emphasis mine):

> Narrated Abu Rafi: The prophet said: 'Let me not find any one of you reclining in his couch and saying when a command reaches him, "I do not know. We shall follow [only] what we find in the Book of God." (*Abu Dawud*)[364]

Lang also cites the example of the stoning of married adulterers introduced by the Hadith, but which conflicts with the Quran, and which did not go unchallenged in early Islam. He further notes:

> There are numerous examples like these in the tradition literature of seemingly made-to-order hadiths that provide unequivocal proof for the correctness of various juridical stances that were taken in long-standing legal debates. If these traditions are genuine, it is surprising that these debates persisted so long – often into the late second and third Islamic centuries – and that these extremely convenient traditions are not cited in earlier works that discuss the topics they address.[365]

> The *rijal* and other *Hadith* related literature describe […] motivations behind *hadith* fabrication. Political, sectarian, partisan, prejudicial, and self-aggrandizing aims were frequently behind *hadith* deception. Most often *hadiths* were manufactured and manipulated to lend prophetic authority to customs, opinions, doctrines, or party planks that were unconnected to his [the Prophet's] teachings and behaviors.[366]

About questionable Hadith authentication, contemporary Iranian-American scholar Reza Aslan comments as follows:

> By the ninth century, when the Islamic law was being fashioned, there were so many false hadith circulating through the community that Muslim legal scholars somewhat whimsically classified them into two categories: lies told for material gain and lies told for theological advantage. In the ninth and tenth centuries, a concerted effort was made to sift through the massive accumulation in order to separate the reliable from the rest. Nevertheless, for hundreds of years, anyone who had the power and wealth necessary to influence public opinion on a particular issue – and who wanted to justify about, say, the role of women in society – had only to refer to a hadith which he had heard from someone, who had heard it from someone else, who had heard from a Companion, who had heard it from the Prophet.[367]

Thus according to Aslan, one basic reason behind the distorted Prophetic traditions was that those who took upon themselves the task of projecting Islam – "men who were, coincidentally, among the most powerful and wealthy members of the *ummah* – were not nearly as concerned with the accuracy of their reports or the objectivity of their exegesis as they were in regaining the financial and social dominance that the Prophet's reforms had taken from them."[368]

The novel criteria used to judge authenticity of the Hadith

The Hadith believers boast of certain criteria that were used by the compilers to screen out fake Hadith and select authentic Hadith (listed in annex to this chapter). Euphemistically, they have labeled such criteria as "the science of the Hadith" (*ilm al-Hadith* or, *ilm al-Jarh wa al-Ta'dil* – the science of accepting and rejecting narrations). Unfortunately however, on close scrutiny, the criteria used could never prove to be foolproof to establish undisputed authenticity of the Hadith texts. This is evident from the very fact that even after such screening, numerous false Hadith texts still remain in so-called *Sahih Bukhari* and other Sahih Hadith books – texts that are "vulgar, absurd, theologically objectionable, or morally repugnant"[369] (See the next chapter for illustrations). These criteria, as an anonymous writer remarks, are:

[A] system of guidelines which numerous scholars, both Muslim and non-Muslim alike, have clearly shown to be seriously inadequate - if not a complete farce, as these standards are broken on numerous occasions in even the 'best' collections of hadith. This of course makes the authenticity of the hadith dubious at best – a situation with serious ramifications for the Islamic *sharia*, and the religion of Islam as a whole [when, of course, understood in terms of the Quran and the Hadith together].[370]

The criteria relate to *isnad* or the chain of Hadith narrators and *matn* or Hadith text. However good such criteria look on paper, they are grossly inadequate for the following reasons:

- Presence of subjective elements involved – most obviously, subjective judgments by the individual Hadith compilers about the character of the numerous narrators, which cannot be vouched as infallible;

- The multiplicity of narrators involved and the huge number of Hadith texts involved running into hundreds of thousands, which raise the feasibility question of how it was possible to undertake such a massive exercise of meticulously flawless screening for both the narrators of the contemporary period (contemporary with the Hadith compilers) and narrators of past several generations, and for the Hadith texts;

- Possibility of human error committed by the narrators involved due to memory or other problems;

- Observed biases of the compilers in their choice of narrators and choice of texts; and

- Flaws in the criteria themselves.

The basic question that needs to be judged first is that it is the compiler like Bukhari, Muslim, etc., who is judging the character and qualifications of the narrators, and his judgment could easily go wrong. It is beyond anybody's comprehension how it was possible for one to ascertain with full accuracy that a narrator had not lied, or not made any unintentional mistake in stating things, even if he was known to be pious or virtuous by some traditional standards. As Jayrajpuri aptly notes, "Honesty and dishonesty are internal qualities which cannot be known with any certainty by observers. As a result, *ilm al-rijal* [the science of men] is only an approximate *qiyasi* [science], and one can never be absolutely certain that one's judgment about a transmitter is correct."[371] Also, as already noted earlier citing Sayyid Ahmad Khan, judging the character of contemporary people is difficult enough; accurately judging that of the transmitters of earlier generations must have been very hard indeed, if not totally impossible, especially when the transmitters involved were so numerous and the period covered was so large. As contemporary Muslim scholar Jeffrey Lang aptly notes, "All things considered, it seems that a major drawback of classical Hadith studies is that judgments on the veracity of one set of data – the *Hadith* reports - are based on a second set of data – the *rijal* reports – that we have no compelling reason to believe is more reliable than the first, quite the opposite."[372]

The criteria of classical Hadith judgment are subject also to criticism that there was always the possibility of forging of the *isnad* (the chain of transmitters), and such forging, according to some reports, took place on just as large a scale as the forging of contents. For forgers, there was always a great incentive to attribute reports to most trustworthy authorities.[373] It appears that *isnad* tampering occurred in various ways: *isnad* invention and theft and, most frequently, *isnad* manipulation, which involved "'tampering with *isnads* in order to make them appear more reliable than they are in reality.'[374] It consisted either of interpolating the name of a trustworthy transmitter or eliminating the name or names of discreditable transmitters from the *isnad*, or both of these."[375] This practice of what is called *tadlis* was widespread; and it consisted of *ihala* (transfer) of traditions from a dubious to a reliable *isnad*, *wasl* or *tawsil* (connecting) of missing links in the *isnad* by interpolating some names of authorities, and *raf* (raising) a tradition to the level of a more prestigious authority, mostly the Prophet, by supplying the necessary links."[376] As Jeffrey Lang points out, "we know from *rijal* and other *Hadith* related literature that besides *matn* fabrication, *isnad* theft, invention, and tampering had also occurred on an enormous scale, so that the focal point of *hadith* evaluation had also suffered from extensive corruption. Yet if the main evidence of *hadith* criticism had often been manipulated, then we have every right to wonder how well suited was *isnad* criticism to detecting corrupted chains of transmission."[377] Lang further notes, "Another weak point of classical *isnad* appraisal is that systematic *rijal* criticism upon which it depends did not commence until around 130 A.H./747 C.E., nearly a century after the origins of the *isnad* system. Hence we find ourselves in a serious predicament: the assessment of the reliability of hadith reports is based on information that is in nature less reliable than the material we are supposed to judge. This is all the more disconcerting since we have every reason to believe that *tadlis* (*isnad* tampering) occurred on as massive a scale as *matn* fabrication."[378]

And how could one be fully certain that the narrator fully remembered what he had heard from another narrator and that any of the narrators involved in the chain had not made even the slightest mistake in communication, and there was absolutely no communication gap between the narrator who narrated a certain story and the narrator who heard the story? There was almost always the possibility for human error, even assuming that the narrators had all the good qualifications and good intentions? As we know from the experience of extensive scientific experimentation carried out in the field of modern information science, it is a proven fact that we find most people not able to exactly reproduce statements made by others – sayings change swiftly from one set of ears to another set. We also know that the compilers had biases in their choice of narrators and both the compilers and the narrators had biases in their choice of Hadith texts, motivated by political and theological grounds. One critic cites that a Hadith originating from Abdullah bin Umar was rejected by Bukhari, although the basically same Hadith narrated by Abu Huraira was accepted, and although many other Hadith texts from Abdullah bin Umar were accepted by Bukhari.[379] In a nutshell, there were too many unknowns and uncertainties as well as biases involved in the selection process of so-called authentic Hadith, which it could not be humanly possible to resolve fully satisfactorily by people like Bukhari. Kassim Ahmad notes:

> However accurate the methodology of the isnad, the scholars first started talking about it and started writing it down only about 150 - 200 years after the deaths of the very last *tabi`i tabi`in*. This means that when the research to establish the *isnad* got started, none of the Companions, the succeeding generation or the generation coming after them [was] available to provide any kind of guidance, confirmation or rebuttal. Therefore, the authenticity of the statements cannot be vouched for at all.

325

It is not our intention to say that Bukhari, Muslim and others were fabricators. However, even students of elementary psychology or communication will testify that a simple message of, say, 15 words will get distorted after passing through only about five messengers. (Our readers are welcome to try out this experiment). Keep in mind that the hadith contains thousands of detailed and complex narrations – everything from ablution to jurisprudence. These narrations passed through hundreds of narrators who were spread out over thousands of miles of desert, and spanned over two to three hundred years of history. All this at a time when news traveled at the speed of a camel gait, recorded on pieces of leather or bone or scrolls in a land that had neither paper nor the abundance of scribes to write anything down![380]

Kassim Ahmad continues: "It stands to reason that the hadith writers depended on much story-telling to fill in the blanks. Many `authentic' narrators whom the hadith writers allude to in their chains of isnad were wholly fabricated names."[381] It was "preposterous and impossible" for Bukhari to have meticulously considered over six hundred thousand hadith texts to pick his authentic 7,275 Hadith texts in his lifetime in an age when the camel journey was the only available means to cover long desert distances.[382]

Some of the *matn* criteria that were used are flawed or too weak on grounds as follows:

1. One criterion is that a text should not be inconsistent with other texts of Hadith. This criterion is weak as even if a text is not inconsistent with other Hadith texts, all such texts could be simultaneously wrong. Also, this criterion is found to have been violated by Hadith texts included in the so-called *sahih* category that are either self-conflicting or conflicting with one another (The next chapter provides some examples).

2. Texts prescribing heavy punishments for minor sins or exceptionally large rewards for small virtues were rejected. But this involves value judgments of what are too heavy and what are too large. And it is the compiler's judgment! There are serious instances of violation of this criterion (one

326

glaring example is Hadith-suggested punishment for apostasy by killing, though the Quran allows full religious freedom. See the next chapter for more examples).

3. Texts referring to actions that should have been commonly known and practiced by others but were not known and practiced were rejected. This criterion is flawed; it does not guarantee the veracity of the text about the Prophet.

4. Most importantly, the criterion such as that the Hadith texts should not be contrary to the Quran, and reason or logic is found to have been flagrantly flouted in numerous cases. Many scholars have demonstrated that numerous Hadith texts do in fact contradict the Quran, or do not stand to reason or logic, or scientific truths. Illustrations of such inconsistencies are provided in the next chapter.

As Hadith critics have pointed out, the Hadith scholars were mostly concerned with the *isnad* criteria, and in the process they neglected the *matn* criteria. Otherwise, how could they compile traditions that were clearly absurd or simply unacceptable from the point of view of the Quran? Khaled Abou El Fadl points out:

[T]he methodologies of the field [of *'ilal al-matn*, i.e., the field within the science of hadith related to the defects of Prophetic reports] were elusive, and the judgment reached was fairly subjective. Furthermore, most of the efforts of past scholars of *hadith* were directed at authenticating the *isnad* of *hadith*. *Matn* analysis remained undeveloped and under-utilized. Even more, the science of *hadith* did not correlate the authenticity of *hadith* with its theological and social ramifications. The scholars of *hadith* did not demand a higher standard of authenticity for a *hadith* that could have sweeping theological and social ramifications. Additionally, […] *hadith* scholars did not engage in historical evaluation of *hadith* or examine its logical coherence or social impact. Consequently, *hadith* scholars often accepted the authenticity of *hadith* with problematic theological and social implications.[383]

Thus the so-called criteria used to authenticate Hadiths are flawed and simply inadequate to the massive task. They rather mask or camouflage the real character of the Hadith, and thus mislead unsuspecting Muslims.

ANNEX TO CHAPTER XI

CRITERIA USED FOR HADITH EVALUATION

Cannons for the Evaluation of Ahadith[1]

A *hadith* consists of two parts: its text, called *matn,* and its chain of narrators, called *isnad.* Comprehensive and strict criteria were separately developed for the evaluation of *matn* and *isnad.* The former is regarded as the internal test of *ahadith,* and the latter is considered the external test. *A hadith* was accepted as authentic and recorded into text only when it met both of these criteria independently.

Criteria for the Evaluation of *Isnad*

The unblemished and undisputed character of the narrator, called *rawi,* was the most important consideration for the acceptance of a *hadith.* As stated earlier, a new branch of *'ilm al-hadith* known as *asma' ar-rijal* was developed to evaluate the credibility of narrators. The following are a few of the criteria utilized for this purpose:

1. The name, nickname, title, parentage and occupation of the narrator should be known.

2. The original narrator should have stated that he heard the hadith directly from the Prophet.

3. If a narrator referred his hadith to another narrator, the two should have lived in the same period and have had the possibility of meeting each other.

4. At the time of hearing and transmitting the hadith, the narrator should have been physically and mentally capable of understanding and remembering it.

5. The narrator should have been known as a pious and virtuous person.

---

[1] Kazi, *op. cit.,* pp. 12-14. All information in this annex has been taken from Kazi's work and shows the orthodox Muslim view of the criteria used to 'authenticate' hadith. Also cited in, Anonymous author, *Hadith Authenticity: A Survey of Perspectives,* at website: http://www.rim.org/muslim/hadith.htm, or at http://www.rim.org/muslim/islam.htm, pp. 9-10.

6. The narrator should not have been accused of having lied, given false evidence or committed a crime.

6. The narrator should not have spoken against other reliable people.

7. The narrator's religious beliefs and practices should have been known to be correct.

8. The narrator should not have carried out and practiced peculiar religious beliefs of his own.

Criteria for the Evaluation of *Matn*

1. The text should have been stated in plain and simple language.

2. A text in non-Arabic or couched in indecent language was rejected.

3. A text prescribing heavy punishment for minor sins or exceptionally large reward for small virtues was rejected.

4. A text which referred to actions that should have been commonly known and practiced by others but were not known and practiced was rejected.

5. A text contrary to the basic teachings of the Qur'an was rejected.

6. A text contrary to other *ahadith* was rejected.

7. A text contrary to basic reason, logic and the known principles of human society was rejected.

8. A text inconsistent with historical facts was rejected.

9. Extreme care was taken to ensure the text was the original narration of the Prophet and not the sense of . what the narrator heard. The meaning of the *hadith* was accepted only when the narrator was well known for his piety and integrity of character.

10. A text derogatory to the Prophet, members of his family or his companions was rejected.

11. A text by an obscure narrator, which was not known during the age of *sahabah* [the Prophet's companions] or

the tabi'een [those who inherited the knowledge of the *sahabah*], was rejected.

Along with these generally accepted criteria, each scholar then developed and practiced his own set of specific criteria to further ensure the authenticity of each hadith. For instance, Imam al-Bukhari would not accept a hadith unless it clearly stated that narrator A had heard it from narrator B. He would not accept the general statement that A narrated through B. On this basis he did not accept a single hadith narrated through 'Uthman, even though Hasan al-Basri always stayed very close to 'Ali. Additionally, it is stated that Imam Ahmad bin Hanbal practiced each hadith before recording it in his Musnad [book or collection of hadith].

XII. REEVALUATING THE HADITH
THE OBJECTIVE TEST OF HADITH AUTHENTICITY

And *among men are those who purchase idle tales (Hadith) without knowledge to mislead (men) from the Path of God, and make a mockery of it* (God's Path). For them there awaiteth a humiliating punishment. – 31:6

Follow not that of which thou hast no knowledge (or verification); verily the hearing, the sight and the mind, all of these will be questioned about that. – 17:36

Introduction

It is very important for all believers to know for certain whether Hadith texts attributed to the Prophet Muhammad are genuinely his sayings and deeds. We have seen in the preceding chapter that the *isnad* and *matn* criteria used to authenticate Hadith texts are not sound or adequate enough to ensure their unquestionable reliability and authority. And, also importantly, even if the *isnad* is sound, it does not automatically guarantee that the *matn* would be true or authentic.

In sharp contrast to the well-corroborated coherent text of the Quran, the reader can find numerous examples of fabrication and inconsistency in the corpus of Hadith literature, including the so-called Sahih Hadith. One can even find Hadith reports that apparently look innocuous or pious but the inherent message of which is misleading. Its texts are open to question on various counts:

- Inconsistency with the basic message of the Quran;
- Inconsistency with basic reason or scientific or historical truth;
- Internal incongruities, and confusing messages; and
- Inclusion of fragmentary, evanescent, and insubstantial details or idle tales, which have little or no religious or spiritual significance.

Inconsistency of some texts of the so-called Sahih Hadith with the Quran or basic reason should suffice to open one's eyes to its unreliability as religious guidance. Some suggest that if some Hadith texts are found to conflict with the Quran or reason, one is entitled to discard them; but one should not discard the whole body of the Hadith. This sort of argument is, however, unconvincing and unacceptable from a theological point of view. To claim respectability and compliance, a theological book needs to be completely holy or true. Inconsistency or absurdity of even some Hadith texts should suffice to make the entire body of Hadith suspect and unworthy of following. It would be a sheer waste of time for one to try to separate the grain from the chaff of the vast Hadith literature. One should rather sincerely strive to study the Quran, which is comprehensive and revealing to the true seeker of knowledge. Also, for everybody it is not an easy task to see which Hadith is, or which Hadith is not, consistent with the Quran, or with basic reason or established scientific truth. Hence it is better to discard the entire body of the Hadith as unreliable. Hadith texts that either contradict the Quran or do not stand to reason are, of course, numerous, as many Hadith critics have shown. Below we try to provide a good sample of such Hadith texts.

Our main purpose here will be to demonstrate that the Hadith gives a distorted view of religion, which is fundamentally opposed to and different from what one can get from the Quran. The Hadith misleads believers and deflects their attention from the true path of the Quran. Contrary to the generally held belief that the Hadith complements the Quran and explains it, it does precisely the opposite – it negates the Quran and confounds it.

What the Hadith does to religion can be summarized as follows:

- The Hadith muddles the very conception of God, and encourages fatalism;
- It presents a misleading image of the Prophet Muhammad and his wives;
- It explicitly negates parts of the Quran, and claims omission of certain verses in the Quran in addition to being anti-Quran in an overall way;
- It misguides on the conception of a Muslim, and on religious practices, sayings, and rituals – on prayer, fasting, and pilgrimage;
- It denigrates women's status;
- It misguides on marriage;
- It misleads on *jihad* (fighting in God's cause);
- It is against progress and modernity, and conflicts with scientific

truth and reason;

- It encourages religious intolerance, violence and terror;
- It encourages cruel punishments;
- It justifies slavery and slavery-like practices;
- It favors supporting ruling regimes;
- It clouds rather than clarifies the Quranic message;
- It provides unsatisfactory *shan-i-nazul* (context or genesis) of revelations;
- It makes bizarre predictions; and
- It makes much ado about nothing, and sends inconsistent and confusing messages, and narrates idle tales of little or no religious significance.

These points are documented below.

The Hadith muddles the very conception of God, and encourages fatalism

Admittedly, it is not an easy task to have a proper understanding of the conception of God. Trying to understand God and how He acts is a major challenge for all believers, and this is indeed a core purpose of religion. By a close study of the Quran and/or through prayer and contemplative meditation, one can gain some good understanding of God. If, on the other hand, one reads Bukhari's Book 77 of Vol. 8, which is devoted to the subject of "divine will or *qadar*"[384], one can find statements that misrepresent God by saying that He decides man's fate beforehand. Two relevant Hadith texts are worthy of quote:

> Narrated Anas bin Malik: The Prophet said: Allah puts an angel in charge of the uterus and the angel says, 'O Lord, (it is) semen! O Lord, (it is now) a clot! O Lord, (it is now) a piece of flesh.' And then, if Allah wishes to complete its creation, the angel asks, 'O Lord, (will it be) a male or a female? A wretched (an evil doer) or a blessed (doer of good)? How much will his provisions be? What will his age be?' *So all that is written while the creature is still in the mother's womb. (Sahih Bukhari*, Vol. 8, Book 77, # 59).

> Narrated Imran bin Husain: A man said, "O Allah's Apostle! Can the people of Paradise be known (differentiated) from the people of the Fire; The Prophet replied, "Yes." The man said,

"Why do people (try to) do (good) deeds?" The Prophet said, *"Everyone will do the deeds for which he has been created to do or he will do those deeds which will be made easy for him to do.* (i.e., everybody will find easy to do such deeds as will lead him to his destined place for which he has been created)." (*Sahih Bukhari*, Vol. 8, Book 77, # 595).

These Hadith texts imply that man is like a programmed robot. If a man's fate is written in the mother's womb, and who will do what to go to Heaven or Hell is already decided beforehand, then is there a role of religious guidance for man? Such Hadith texts are clearly at odds with the Quranic ideas that man has been given freedom of choice to choose between good and evil (76:3; and that he is rewarded or punished according to what he does (53:39; 20:15; 28:84). The Hadith thus advocates the doctrine of predestination, and encourages fatalism among men.[385]

Look at another Hadith giving some idea of how God thinks of Himself:

Narrated Abdullah bin Mas'ud: Allah's Apostle said: None has more sense of ghira (intense feeling of self-respect) than Allah, and for this He has forbidden shameful sins whether committed openly or secretly, and none loves to be praised more than Allah does, and this is why He Praises Himself. (*Sahih Bukhari*, Vol. 6, Book 60, # 162, also at #158)

To say that God praises Himself because He loves most to be praised is at odds with the idea that God declares Himself as Independent, and can go without anybody praising Him (35:15; 51:56-58; 47:38). He does not need to care about whether anybody praises Him or not, as the Quran says "If any rejects faith, God stands in no need of any of His creatures" (3:97). God is no doubt Most Worthy of Praise, but it is we who need to praise Him for our own sake.

The Hadith misrepresents God by also asserting that He forgives the sins of believers just on the asking. As explained in Chapters 1 and 3, a close reading of the Quran does give the message that though God is Forgiving, He does not forgive a person unless he sincerely repents, and mends his conduct, and if he does not knowingly repeat the misdeeds (6:54; 3:135). The Hadith on the other hand gives the message that one can get forgiveness of one's sins from God even with repeated misdeeds. The following Hadith illustrates this:

> Narration by Abu Huraira: I heard the Prophet saying, "If somebody commits a sin and then says, 'O my Lord! I have sinned, please forgive me!' and his Lord says, 'My slave has known that he has a Lord who forgives sins and punishes for it, I therefore have forgiven my slave (his sins).' Then he remains without committing any sin for a while and then again commits another sin and says, 'O my Lord, I have committed another sin, please forgive me,' and Allah says, 'My slave has known that he has a Lord who forgives sins and punishes for it, I therefore have forgiven my slave (his sin). Then he remains without committing any sin for a while and then commits another sin (for the third time) and says, 'O my Lord, I have committed another sin, please forgive me,' and Allah says, 'My slave has known that he has a Lord Who forgives sins and punishes for it I therefore have forgiven My slave (his sin), he can do whatever he likes." (*Sahih Bukhari,* Vol. 9, Book 93, # 598).

It is obvious that such Hadith texts can encourage believers to commit mistakes or misdeeds over and over again. There are many other Hadith texts that give the believer the impression that he can get forgiveness for all of his past sins regardless of the kind and degree of sins committed, or that going to Paradise is ensured for him if he just utters certain words of belief, or recites certain verses of the Quran, or does some religious rituals! For example, a narration by Itban bin Malik states that the Prophet reportedly said: Allah has forbidden the (Hell) fire for those who say, 'None has the right to be worshipped but Allah' for Allah's sake only. (*Sahih Bukhari,* Vol. 1, Book 8, # 417). Another Hadith narrated by Abu Huraira says: Allah's Apostle said: Whoever says, 'Subhan Allah wa bihamdihi,' (God is Magnificent and all praise is His) one hundred times a day, will be forgiven all his sins even if they were as much as the foam of the sea (*Sahih Bukhari,* Vol. 8, Book 75, # 414). Likewise, the Hadith is replete with sayings that performance of certain rituals such as prayer at certain special times, e.g., during the nights of the Ramadan (*Sahih Bukhari,* Vol. 1, Book 2, # 36) and in the night of the *qadar* (*Sahih Bukhari,* Vol. 1, Book 2, # 34; Vol. 3, Book 31, # 125), observance of fasts during the Ramadan (*Sahih Bukhari,* Vol. 1, Book 2, # 37; Vol. 3, Book 31, # 125), and utterances of certain words a certain number of times (*Sahih Bukhari,* Vol. 4, Book 54, # 514), etc., will entitle one to complete remission of all past sins. A Hadith especially worth noting is reproduced below:

> Narrated Anas: The Prophet said: Whoever said "None has the right to be worshipped but Allah and has in his heart good (faith) equal to the weight of a barley grain will be taken out of Hell. And whoever said: "None has the right to be worshipped but Allah and has in his heart good (faith) equal to the weight of a wheat grain will be taken out of Hell. And whoever said, "None has the right to be worshipped but Allah and has in his heart good (faith) equal to the weight of an atom will be taken out of Hell" (*Sahih Bukhari,* Vol. 1, Book 2, # 42).

Such examples are legion. Clearly, such Hadith texts not only exaggerate the virtues of beliefs, sayings, or rituals but also by so doing also give a perverted conception of God. Such texts are clearly against the spirit of the Quran's message. Prayer and fasting are striving for self-purification and self-development. Unless the striving is successful, just a one-night prayer or a one-month fast may not erase one's past sins, regardless of the level of sins. And just believing or saying that there is no god but God to be worshipped, or uttering certain words of praise of God may not entitle one to go to Heaven. Also, as explained in some detail in Chapters 1, 3 and 5, getting forgiveness is not a painless process; it cannot be expected just on the asking. Forgiveness does not come unless one fully atones and repents for one's misdeeds, and mends one's conduct, and when one does not repeat the misdeeds (11:3; 3:135; 16:119; 4:17-18). The Hadith misrepresents the concept of forgiveness, and thus misleads.

The Hadith misrepresents God also by portraying Him as One Who accepts intercession from only the Prophet Muhammad, and on whose request persons even with a little faith are taken out from Hell [*Sahih Bukhari,* Vol. 6, Book 60, # 3, 236, 242; Vol. 9, Book 93, # 507; Vol. 9, Book 93, # 532v; Vol. 9, Book 93, # 532s; Vol. 9, Book 93, # 60, etc.]. God, however, cautions that neither prophets nor other believers should plead for forgiveness for people, even if they are near relatives, after it has become clear that they are destined to go to Hell (9:113). God rebuked the Prophet Noah for pleading for his drowning son, and He rebuked the Prophet Abraham for pleading for his father (9:114; 11:45-46; 9:80).

According to the Quran, one idea about God is that He is the Foremost and the Last (57:3). However, the Hadith identifies God with Time. In trying to emphasize the value of time for man, it makes the absurd statement that God is Time:

> Narrated Abu Huraira: Allah's Apostle said: Allah said, 'The son of Adam hurts me for he abuses Time though *I AM TIME*' (*Sahih Bukhari*, Vol. 6, Book 60, # 351).

The Hadith presents a misleading image of the Prophet Muhammad and his wives

The Hadith has greatly distorted the image of the Prophet Muhammad first, by tarnishing his character, and second by eulogizing him beyond all bounds.

The Hadith maligns and insults the Prophet Muhammad and his wives

The Hadith makes a fanfare of the Prophet's multiple marriages, and greatly taints his sex life. It is a "monstrous reading", as Ahmad puts it.[386] One can find a lot of such awful stuff about the Prophet and his wives' private lives in Vol. 1, Books 5 and 6 and other parts of *Sahih Bukhari* (translation by M. Muhsin Khan).[387] One may wonder how a good believer can believe that the Prophet's companions would go beyond the generally accepted norms of propriety to ask the Prophet's wives, who were like their mothers (33:6), about their private lives. And is it believable that some of the Prophet's wives would come forward to talk about such things? Look in particular at the following text in Bukhari:

> Narrated Qatada: Anas bin Malik said, 'The Prophet used to visit all his wives in a round, during the day and night and they were eleven in number.' I asked Anas, 'Had the Prophet the strength for it?' Anas replied, 'We used to say that the Prophet was given the strength of thirty (men).' And Sa'id said on the

authority of Qatada that Anas had told him about nine wives only (not eleven). (*Sahih Bukhari,* Vol. 1, Book 5, # 268)

Another Hadith at (*Sahih Bukhari,* Vol. 1, Book 4, # 229) attributed to the Prophet's wife Aisha speaks of her washing the Prophet's clothes with stains of semen. Similar and related awful texts are at (*Sahih Bukhari,* Vol. 1, Book 5; # 270; # 274; # 282; and Vol. 7, Book 62, # 6). Texts are also in *Muslim,* which are reported to have originated from Aisha that state that she used to perfume the Prophet, and he used to go round his wives after that (*Sahih Muslim,* Book 007, # 2698-2700). Bukhari also compiled texts in his Vol. 1 and Book 6 suggesting that the Prophet used to fondle his wives while they were menstruating, and that at one time he and one of his wives took a bath required for purification, while his wife was menstruating, suggesting that they became impure by intimate union, even though the Quran explicitly directs us not to touch wives during such times (2:222). One of these Hadith texts reads as follows:

> Narrated 'Aisha: The Prophet and I used to take a bath from a single pot while we were *junub* [impure]. During the menses, he used to order me to put on an Izar (dress worn below the waist) and used to fondle me *(Sahih Bukhari,* Vol. 1, Book 6, # 298, similar texts also repeated at # 299 and 300)

There are also other Hadith texts that say that the Prophet used to kiss and embrace his wives while they were fasting (*Sahih Bukhari,* Vol. 1, Book 6, # 319, also Vol. 3, Book 31, # 149). One Hadith, a narration by Abu Huraira, says that the Prophet once left his *musalla* (prayer rug or place) after coming there for taking a bath because he remembered at that time that he was *junub* (impure after sexual activity), and after taking the bath he returned to his *musalla* for prayer (*Sahih Bukhari,* Vol. 1, Book 5, # 274).

What a slight on the character of the Prophet! The Hadith has razed his position to the ground! What kind of message do all these Hadith reports convey to the believers? Is all this not a direct contradiction of what the Quran says of the Prophet and his near companions? The Quran states that they used to spend one-third to two thirds of the night in prayer and meditation, and study of the Quran (26:218-219; 52:48-49; 73:2-8, 20)? God has cautioned us in the Quran not to make mockery of religion (31:6); but this is precisely what the so-called Sahih Hadith has done to religion. The Hadith has made a mockery of the Prophet's multiple marriages, and thus misleads mankind, turning their attention to enjoyment of worldly life instead of turning to God. As explained in Chapters 3 and 5, God urges us to seek the way of approach to Him and strive for this with due effort (5:35), which implies that we cannot afford to care much for worldly or carnal pleasures. Both the Prophet and his wives were admonished not to pay much attention to worldly pleasures (20:131; 33:28). The Hadith paints the Prophet Muhammad's character in a way that is not only distasteful, but totally reprehensible, which is clearly against the spirit of the Quranic message. Chapter 9 explained the circumstances that led to his multiple marriages. The Hadith has done a great damage to the reputation of his character.

One Hadith narrated by Abdul Aziz who heard it from Anas states that after the Khaibar battle, one of his companions named Dihya requested the Prophet for a captive girl, and on his orders that he (Dihya) could take any of the captive girls, he took Safiya bint Huyai for his wife. However, when a companion pointed out to the Prophet that she was the chief mistress of the tribes of Quraiza and an-Nadir, and that she befitted none other than the Prophet, the Prophet changed his mind, and asked Dihya to hand over Safiya to him, and he married her. (*Sahih Bukhari,* Vol. 1, Book 8, # 367) Can the reader notice a defamation of the Prophet's character in a subtle way here? Can a good Muslim ever think that the Prophet could behave in this undignified manner – first letting one of his companions take her, and then later telling him to spare her for his own marriage? The Prophet, of course, married Safiya, but it was definitely not in this undignified manner. The Hadith must have been a fabricated one to imply that the Prophet was inclined to worldly things, even though the Quran explicitly states otherwise (20:131; 3:152). Also, it was unbecoming and improper on the part of any of his companions to ask for such things, except leaving it to the good discretion of the Prophet (8:1). The Hadith is a clear slur on the Prophet.

There are still other Hadith texts such as those narrated by Jabir bin Abdullah that encourage marriages with young virgins and fondling them (*Sahih Bukhari,* Vol. 7, Book 62, #s 16-17, also repeated at # 172 and 174). It is inconceivable that the Prophet could ever engage in such light and irresponsible discourse. Another Hadith states that the Prophet used to visit a lady named Haram bint Milhan who was the wife of 'Ubada bin As-Samit, and that one day when the Prophet visited her, he allowed her to look for lice in his head (*Sahih Bukhari,* Vol. 9, Book 87, # 130). Is it believable that the Prophet could ever allow himself to be so closely treated by the wife of another person?

The approach of the Hadith is thus fundamentally different from that of the Quran, wrong, and misleading. The above Hadith texts should suffice to open the believers' eyes to the havoc that the Hadith has done to Islam.

The Hadith has also projected the Prophet as one who was very cruel. One can find several texts in Vol. 8 and Book 82 of *Sahih Bukhari*, which are narrated by Anas bin Malik, that show the Prophet as having pronounced very harsh judgments for a group of people who came to Medina from another place and embraced Islam, but who later committed criminal offences of killing of livestock and theft. The punishments included cutting off the hands and feet without cauterization, and at the same time branding the eyes with red-hot iron; these people were thrown at a place, and when they asked for water, they were not given it (*Sahih Bukhari*, Vol. 8, Book 82, # 794-797, a similar Hadith is narrated by Abu Qilaba at Vol. 1, Book 4, #234, also at Vol. 4, Book 52, # 261). Another Hadith text narrated by Ibn Umar reports that the Prophet burned the garden of date-palms of Bani an-Nadir (*Sahih Bukhari*, Vol. 4, Book 52, # 263). Still another Hadith states that the Prophet sent a group of people to kill Abu-Raffi in his house (*Sahih Bukhari*, Vol. 4, Book 52, # 264). There are even reports that the Prophet did not forgive the Jewish tribe Bani al-Qurayza, whose necks were struck, and whose children were made slaves, and whose members estimated between 400 and 900 were killed.[388]

Such Hadith reports cannot be but malicious lies against the gentle-natured Prophet, whose tolerance and kind-heartedness is historically known and applauded. His forgiveness of the arch-enemies of Islam during his triumphant march into Mecca was a classic and monumental example of tolerance that is rarely found in history. The Quran itself is witness to the fact that he was of a gentle nature and not harsh-hearted:

> **3:159** It was by the Mercy of God that thou (O Muhammad) wast gentle to them; hadst thou been harsh and hard-hearted, they would have dispersed from around thee. So pardon them, and ask forgiveness for them, and take counsel with them in the conduct of affairs; and

when thou art resolved, put thy trust in God. Verily
God loveth those who put their trust (in Him)..[389]

The Hadith has portrayed the Prophet also as a person who did not
hesitate to speak ill of the Prophet Abraham. In one Hadith the Prophet
Muhammad is reported to have said that the Prophet Abraham lied on
three occasions (*Sahih Bukhari*, Vol. 7, Book 62, # 21). Can one ever
conceive that the Prophet Muhammad could ever make this derogatory
remark about the Prophet Abraham? Is this the ideal of the Prophet
Abraham, which God has advised him (the Prophet Muhammad) and all
of us to follow (60:4-6}, when God wants us always to speak the truth
(33:70), never mix up truth with falsehood, nor conceal the truth (2:26),
and never hesitate to testify truthfully even if it goes against ourselves
and our parents and relatives (4:135)? The Hadith makes telling lies a
light matter, while this is a very serious matter in the sight of God. The
Hadith thus misleads.

The Hadith also states that magic was worked on the Prophet by some
people, because of the effect of which he began to fancy that he was
doing a thing which he was not actually doing, a thing that was cured by
God (*Sahih Bukhari*, Volume 4, Book 54, #490). This Hadith, a slight on
the Prophet, is clearly contradictory to the Quran and misleading. The
Quran states that the Prophet never became possessed (81:22), and no
magic could work on God's true believers, let alone God's prophets who
possessed extraordinary character, personality and exceptional powers
(2:102).

Also worth noting are the related defamatory stories about some of the
Prophet's illustrious wives. According to one Hadith allegedly reported
by Aisha, she was once accused by a slave girl of stealing a red leather
scarf decorated with precious stones, and that, because of that, her body,
including her private parts, was thoroughly searched for this scarf; but
the scarf was later found dropped by a kite (*Sahih Bukhari*, Vol. 1, Book
8, # 430). Can a good Muslim ever believe that anybody, and of all
persons a slave girl, could dare to suspect one of the Prophet's wives as a
thief, especially when his wives were like mothers to all believers (33:6)?
This Hadith must be a figment of imagination, a classic example of
fabricated tales.

Another Hadith states that some of them played tricks with the Prophet
by telling him lies to dissuade him from taking honey syrup ((*Sahih

Bukhari, Vol. 7, Book 63, # 192, 193). This is not the character of the Prophet's wives that is becoming of them. The Hadith spreads calumny over them.

The Hadith idolizes the Prophet Muhammad at the same time

According to one Hadith narrated by Jabir bin Abdullah, the Prophet reportedly boasted of five things God gave him but not given to earlier prophets, which included sending him for all humankind, while earlier prophets were sent to their own nations, and his exclusive privilege of intercession with God for all people (*Sahih Bukhari*, Vol. 1, Book 7, # 331). The claim that, unlike in the case of earlier prophets, God has endowed the Prophet Muhammad with the exclusive authority of intercession for all believers is also reported in a number of other Hadith texts at (*Sahih Bukhari*, Vol. 6, Book 60, # 3; Vol. 9, Book 93, # 507, 532v, 601 and 607). The Hadith texts at (*Sahih Bukhari*, Vol. 1, Book 2, # 42; Vol. 9, Book 93, # 600) speak of the Prophet as being the savior on the Day of Resurrection for those who will have had even a little faith. Still another Hadith at (*Sahih Bukhari*, Vol. 1, Book 3, # 98) states that the Prophet reportedly said that he would intercede for one who says from the bottom of his heart: "None has the right to be worshipped but Allah" and that he would be the luckiest person.

But the Quran does not support all this. It is inconceivable that the Prophet Muhammad could ever make such boastful claims about his own position *vis-à-vis* that of the earlier Prophets, when the Quran says that some of the messengers excelled others – some spoke to God, and Jesus was given special powers of miracle (2:253), when it is forbidden for believers to make any distinction between His messengers (2:285), and when Abraham, Moses, Jesus – all earlier prophets were sent for all humankind, and we have been advised to take lessons from their histories (12:110-111), and when the Prophet Muhammad was, and by implication we have been, especially advised to follow the faith of Abraham (16:123), and follow him as an excellent example (60:4-6). The Quran warns us against a Day when there would be no bargaining, nor friendship, *nor intercession* (2:254); and it says that none can intercede with God except with His permission (2:255). Also, the Hadith gives the impression that a little faith is enough for one to qualify for going to Heaven, when in the Quran God urges us to strive with the right striving (91:9-10; 79:40-41; 17:19; 5:35; 2:148; 94:7-8). The Hadith diverts attention from the basic and more fundamental teachings of the Quran, and thus misleads.

The Hadith explicitly negates parts of the Quran, and claims omission of certain verses in the Quran

A Hadith narrated by Nafi, who heard it from Ibn Umar at (*Sahih Bukhari*, Vol. 6, Book 60, # 33) abrogates the Quranic verse (2:184) that states that one who cannot fast should feed a poor man by way of expiation. Another Hadith at (*Sahih Bukhari*, Vol. 6, Book 60, # 32) narrated by Ata who heard it from Ibn Umar implies that this verse is abrogated for persons other than old men and women. Still another Hadith, which ostensibly clarifies it further, is as follows:

> Narrated Salama: When the Divine Revelation: "For those who can fast, they have a choice either to fast, or feed a poor person for every day," (2.184) was revealed, it was permissible for one to give a ransom and give up fasting, till the verse succeeding it was revealed and abrogated it. (*Sahih Bukhari*, Vol. 6, Book 60, # 34)

But this sort of abrogation of a verse or part of a verse by the Hadith is untenable, as God cautions against disbelief in parts of the Quran (2:85). The verse (2:184) states that one should fast a certain number of days, and if he is sick or on a journey, he can fast other days, or those who find it difficult to fast, and can afford it, they should pay a ransom in feeding poor persons; and it states clearly that fasting is better. The verse at (2:185) advises believers to fast during the Ramadan, and repeats the statement that if one is sick or on a journey, he or she can fast other days. This verse does not repeat the earlier statement that one could pay a ransom in the event that he or she cannot fast. This does not mean that the earlier verse message about the ransom has been abrogated. The Hadith misinterprets the Quran.

Another Hadith narrated by Ibn Abbas at (*Sahih Bukhari*, Vol. 6, Book 60, # 68, 69) states that the verse "Whether you show what is in your minds or conceal it" (2:284) is abrogated by the following verse (the following verse is not mentioned). The full verse at (2:284) gives a very important message that whether we make known what is in our minds or conceal it, we will have to account for it to God. The Hadith negates this very important message of God, which is not only anti-Quran but it also

343

does not stand to reason. Still another Hadith narrated by Al-Qasim bin Abi Bazza who asked Said bin Jubair at (*Sahih Bukhari*, Vol. 6, Book 60, # 285) states that the verse revealed in Mecca: "Nor kill such life as God has forbidden except for a just cause" in (6:151) was abrogated by another verse revealed later in Medina, which is at (4:93) that says that whoever intentionally kills a believer is destined for Hell. Both verses convey important messages. The Hadith has no authority to nullify parts of the Quran. God never changes His Words (10:64).

Contemporary Muslim scholar Jeffrey Lang notes that some Hadiths claim that some verses were revealed to the Prophet but were omitted from the Quran. These include the Hadith prescribing stoning to death of married adulterers, which is in *Muwatta* of Imam Malik and a shorter version in *Sahih Bukhari* (Vol. 8, Book 82, # 816-817). In another Hadith, Anas reports that they used to recite regarding the martyrs in the battle of Bir Mauna a Quranic verse "Inform our people that we have met our Lord. He is pleased with us and He has made us pleased", but this verse was retracted later on (*Bukhari,* Volume 4, Book 52, Number 69; also *Muslim*). "This and the stoning verse tradition indicate that at least two verses of the Qu'ran have been eliminated from the text. Other sound traditions indicate that much larger sections were withdrawn."[390] These Hadiths suggest that the present Quran is not complete, a contention that is hardly tenable in light of the verse (15:9) that clearly assures protection of the Quran from any corruption. Such an assertion of the Hadith can easily turn out to be a Pandora's Box.

The Hadith misguides on the conception of a Muslim, and on religious practices, sayings and rituals

The Hadith defines a Muslim in a fragmentary way

The Hadith defines a Muslim in terms of a person who believes in, and worships, God alone; offers prayers to Him; pays *zakat*; and fasts during the Ramadan (*Sahih Bukhari*, Vol. 1, Book 2, # 7, 44, and 47). As additional qualifications for being a Muslim, some Hadith also includes believing in Muhammad as God's Messenger (*Sahih Bukhari*, Vol. 1, Book 2, # 50; Vol. 1, Book 3, # 87); some Hadith includes pilgrimage to Mecca (*Sahih Bukhari*, Vol. 1, Book 2, # 7); some includes not harming, or being true to, other Muslims (*Sahih Bukhari*, Vol. 1, Book 2, # 9, 54, 55); and some includes feeding the poor and greeting others (*Sahih Bukhari*, Vol. 1, Book 2, # 11, 27). Another Hadith narrated by Anas bin

Malik defines a Muslim in terms of whether a person prays, faces the same *qiblah*, and eats of the same slaughtered animals like the Prophet's men (*Sahih Bukhari*, Vol. 1, # 386 and 387); the Hadith at # 387 adds: and he believes 'None has the right to be worshipped but Allah.').

The Hadith provides fragmentary advice. But according to the Quran, a Muslim is one who has fully surrendered to God, and is righteous in all respects – in religious beliefs and practices as well as in moral and ethical conduct. Neglecting required right deeds disqualifies one to be a true Muslim. Just note how God curses the worshipers who mistreat the orphans, neglect spending for the poor, and refuse acts of kindness (107:1-7), let alone do other misdeeds. Just observance of some religious practices does not make one a Muslim.

The Hadith misleads on beliefs and sayings

As already cited in the context of the conception of God wrongly portrayed by the Hadith, a Hadith narrated by Itban bin Malik attributed to the Prophet qualifies a person to be exempted from Hell fire just on his or her saying that none has the right to be worshipped but Allah (*Sahih Bukhari*, Vol. 1, Book 8, # 417). This Hadith misleads by grossly exaggerating the virtue of a statement of belief. Such claims of the Hadith are clearly against the Quranic message, which requires not only right beliefs but also righteous deeds for one to qualify for exemption from Hell fire.

A narration from Abu Huraira says that whoever utters certain words of glorification such as "Sub-han-al-lah", "Alhamdu-lillah" and "Allahu Akbar" (God is pure - above all, All praise be to God and God is great) thirty three times after every prayer could catch up with or overtake others in virtuous work except those who did the same (*Sahih Bukhari*, Vol. 1, Book 12, # 804). But this kind of assertion is counter to the Quranic message that merit results from striving with due effort (53:39; 20:15; 17:19).

Another misleading Hadith text is as follows:

> Narrated Abu Mas'ud: The Prophet said: If somebody recited the last two verses of Surat Al-Baqara at night, that will be sufficient for him (for that night) (*Sahih Bukhari*, Vol. 6, Book 61, # 560, 571).

A statement that reciting certain verses of the Quran is "sufficient" can hardly make any sense. Another such misleading Hadith narration from Abu Said al-Khudri states that the Prophet reportedly said that Surah Ikhlas # 112 was equivalent to one third of the whole Quran (*Sahih Bukhari*, Vol. 6, Book 61, 533, 534). It is unthinkable that the Prophet could ever make such statements, which amount to an untenable shortcut to studying the Quran. The Hadith has other similar texts. Such Hadith texts are a clever way of misleading the believers away from the harder path of studying the Quran, and following the straight and righteous path that is well described in the Quran.

The Hadith misleads on salat

This topic has been covered in detail in Chapter 5. Here we briefly note the following points:

- The Hadith focuses attention almost wholly on the ritual aspects or forms of *salat*, and offers little on its substance;

- It talks about recitation of the Quran in *salat* regardless of its relevance to *salat*;

- It lays too much emphasis on observing the times of prayer rather than on establishing prayer itself, which requires one to work consistently with prayer;

- It falsely assigns great virtues to performing the formal *salat* ritual, or doing the number of *rakahs* (cycles) of *salat* without any qualification; and

- It focuses the attention of the worshipers on petty things.

We have noted in Chapter 5 that the very conception that *salat* needs to be performed five times every day is based on questionable, inconsistent versions of a Hadith, which misjudges and demeans both God and the Prophet.[391]

The Hadith misleads by laying too much emphasis on forms, while the Quran says that forms without sincere devotion do not really matter (2:177; 22:37). It does great harm by projecting the idea that *salat* is a place for recitation of the Quran, even though the *surahs* of the Quran, or selected verses, may be quite irrelevant to the context of prayer. Using certain verses of the Quran that are quite in line with the spirit of prayer is, of course, quite appropriate. However, giving a blanket authorization to use any Quranic verses in *salat* regardless of their relevance to *salat* cannot be appropriate. Also, while addressing God in *salat*, recitation *per se* cannot make any sense. *Salat* is a place where the worshiper should rather speak his mind to God. Also the Hadith falsely assigns virtues to the number of *rakahs* of prayer, and greatly exaggerates the virtues of some utterances or recitations, or exaggerates the performance of specific *salat* or *salat* on a specific night, claiming that such praying may erase all of one's past sins regardless of the kind and degree of sins.

One Hadith extolling the virtues of ablution and prayer is as follows:

> Narrated Humran: I saw 'Uthman performing ablution; he [...] said: I saw Allah's Apostle performing ablution similar to my present ablution, and then he said: Whoever performs ablution like my present ablution and then offers two Rakat in which he does not think of worldly things, all his previous sins will be forgiven. (*Sahih Bukhari*, Vol. 3, Book 31, # 155, also repeated at Vol. 1, Book 4, # 161 and 165).

This is an absurd claim attributed to the Prophet. Just performing ablution and offering two *rakahs* of prayer cannot wipe out all of one's past sins, regardless of the type and level of sins committed. The Hadith misleads by giving a misleading message that just seeking forgiveness through prayer results in forgiveness regardless of whether one repents and mends one's conduct or not. This is against the Quranic message that none receives forgiveness unless one sufficiently repents and mends one's conduct, and does not knowingly repeat the sins (3:135; 16:119; 4:17-18).

Another Hadith illustrating too much importance to forms such as *rakahs* is as follows:

> Narrated Abu Huraira: The Prophet said, "When the call for the prayer is pronounced, Satan takes to his heels, passing wind with noise. When the call for the prayer is finished, he comes back. And when the Iqama is pronounced, he again takes to his heels, and after its completion, he returns again to interfere

347

between the (praying) person and his heart, saying to him. 'Remember this or that thing.' till the person forgets whether he has offered three or four Rakat: so if one forgets whether he has prayed three or four Rakat, he should perform two prostrations of Sahu (i.e. forgetfulness)." (*Sahih Bukhari,* Vol. 4, Book 54, # 505)

This Hadith is also vulgar and wrong about how Satan behaves and works on man. Suggesting that with the call of prayer or *iqama*, Satan takes flight having no effect whatsoever on man is saying something that can be found to be empirically incorrect. Satan is with us all the time, and resides in our hearts and minds and in those of others. The *iqama* or not, Satan can work on us the moment we listen to, and welcome, his evil whispers in our hearts or minds (114:4-6).

Such examples of Hadith texts giving too much importance to forms of prayer, to *rakahs* of prayer, or to special prayers or recitations, etc., could be multiplied. Look at still another text giving too much importance to extraneous things:

Narrated Abu Said Al-Khudri: The Prophet said: If while you are praying, somebody intends to pass in front of you, prevent him; and should he insist, prevent him again; and if he insists again, fight with him (i.e. prevent him violently e.g. pushing him violently), because such a person is (like) a devil. (*Sahih Bukhari,* Vol. 4, Book 54, # 495).

One might legitimately ask what kind of prayer this is where the worshiper's attention is diverted to extraneous things, and he can engage in even violent acts against a person passing before him when praying!

Also, in the *tashahud* (words of invoking blessings upon the Prophet and the believers) taken from the Hadith that is recited in the sitting position in the currently practiced *salat*, the worshiper addresses the Prophet.[392] But this is not in accord with the requirement of prayer that one should address God alone.

348

The Hadith misleads on fasting

The Hadith prescribes a very harsh punishment for one who breaks a fast, engaging in a sexual act while fasting, during the Ramadan: two months' fasting or, in lieu of that, feeding sixty poor people, or freeing of a slave as atonement for breaking just one day's fast. The Hadith also speaks lightly of fasting, and suggests that one can engage in sexual activity during fasting, and get away clean with just some charity, thus negating the very spirit of the Quranic message:

> Narrated 'Aisha: A man came to the Prophet and said that he had been burnt (ruined). The Prophet asked him: what was the matter. He replied, "I had sexual intercourse with my wife in Ramadan (while I was fasting)." Then a basket full of dates was brought to the Prophet and he asked, 'Where is the burnt (ruined) man?' He replied, 'I am present.' The Prophet told him to give that basket in charity (as expiation). (*Sahih Bukhari*, Vol. 3, Book 31, # 156)

Note that this Hadith is not fully consistent with other Hadith texts, where the Prophet is alleged to have suggested freeing of a slave, or fasting for two successive months, or feeding sixty poor people as atonement for sexual activity during fasting, and failing that, charity to a poorer person with a basket of dates brought before him, and failing that feeding his family with that basket (*Sahih Bukhari*, Vol. 3, Book 31, #s 157-158; similar text also in *Sahih Muslim*). It is inconceivable that the Prophet would ever engage in religious discourse in such a light manner, without reminding him of the straightforward Quranic admonitions for repentance and atonement.

Look at another Hadith:

> Narrated 'Aisha: The Prophet used to kiss and embrace (his wives) while he was fasting, and he had more power to control his desires than any of you. Said Jabir: The person who gets discharge after casting a look (on his wife) should complete his fast. (*Sahih Bukhari*, Vol. 3, Book 31, # 149)

This Hadith not only undermines the Prophet's character, it condones one's lewd feelings leading to discharge of semen. The Hadith says that the Prophet could control his sexual impulses, but such action could

349

easily induce such feelings with the wives. This is against the very spirit of fasting enjoined on us by the Quran.

The Quran enjoins fasting on believers as a better option, but at the same time says that those who are not able to fast, and who can financially afford, should expiate in the form of feeding poor people (2:184). But, as noted above, strangely and audaciously enough, the Hadith says that this verse stands abrogated for people other than old people and women by the next verse where the redemption by feeding of poor people is not mentioned. That means that the redemption by feeding poor people instead of fasting is not applicable for people other than old men and women. This is misguidance by the Hadith.

Other examples of misleading Hadith texts on fasting, which exaggerate the virtues of fasting and prayer on a night of Ramadan, are as follows:

> Narrated Abu Huraira: Allah's Apostle said: Whoever observes fasts during the month of Ramadan out of sincere faith, and hoping to attain Allah's rewards, then all his past sins will be forgiven. (*Sahih Bukhari,* Vol. 1, Book 2, # 37)

> Narrated Abu Huraira: Allah's Apostle said: When the month of Ramadan starts, the gates of the heaven are opened and the gates of Hell are closed and the devils are chained. (*Sahih Bukhari,* Vol. 3, Book 31, # 120, 123, repeated at Vol. 4, Book 54, # 497)

> Narrated Abu Huraira: I heard Allah's Apostle saying regarding Ramadan: Whoever prayed at night in it (the month of Ramadan) out of sincere Faith and hoping for a reward from Allah, then all his previous sins will be forgiven. (Sahih Bukhari, *Volume 3, Book 32, Number 226)*

> Narrated Abu Huraira: Allah's Apostle said: Whoever establishes the prayers on the night of Qadr out of sincere faith and hoping to attain Allah's rewards (not to show off) then all his past sins will be forgiven. (*Sahih Bukhari,* Vol. 1, Book 2, #34, 36; also Vol. 3, Book 31, # 125; Vol. 3, Book 32, # 231)

As noted above, prayer and fasting are striving for self-purification and self-development. Unless the striving is successful, just a one-night prayer or a one-month fasting may not erase one's past sins, regardless of the level of sins.

There are two Hadith texts reportedly narrated by Aisha or Ibn Abbas, which suggest that one can fast on another's behalf who is dead to fill the dead person's missed days of fasting (*Sahih Bukhari,* Vol. 3, Book 31, # 173-174).

What a fabrication! The Quran clearly says: one's efforts/actions count for one's own self, not for another self (29:6).

Note also that even the conception and date of the night of power (*shab al qadar*) given by the Hadith has a dubious basis. There are several Hadith texts narrated by various people suggesting the possible date of the night, which do not fully agree with one another, One Hadith narrated by Ibn Umar states that the Prophet said that Muslims should search for this night in the last seven nights of the Ramadan, and that also he said on the basis of the dreams of some of his companions (*Sahih Bukhari,* Vol. 3, Book 32, # 232). There are several other texts narrated by Abu Salama, Aisha, Abu Said Al-Khudri or Ibn Abbas, which state that the Prophet suggested that this night should be searched in odd nights of the last ten nights of the Ramadan (*Sahih Bukhari,* Vol. 3, Book 32, # 233-239). The following Hadith suggests that this night should be searched on the odd nights – 25th to 29th – of the last five nights of the Ramadan:

> Narrated 'Ubada bin As-Samit: The Prophet came out to inform us about the Night of Qadr but two Muslims were quarreling with each other. So, the Prophet said: I came out to inform you about the Night of Qadr but such-and-such persons were quarreling, so the news (knowledge) about it had been taken away; yet that might be for your own good, so search for it on the 29th, 27th and 25th (of Ramadan). (*Sahih Bukhari,* Vol. 3, Book 32, # 240)

This Hadith is a classic example of fabrication. Is it conceivable that the Prophet's knowledge about this night was snatched away because of the quarrelling of two Muslims? Note also, some of the Hadith texts referred to above also state that the Prophet was informed of the date, but he forgot it. All these texts are inconsistent with one another. It is inconceivable that the Prophet would speak about a night, which is perceived to be so important by Muslims, on such a fragile basis, and

351

with such a level of uncertainty? The Hadith is a well of conjecture. The Quran cautions us against conjecture (6:116, 148; 10:36; 53: 28; etc.): "They follow naught but conjecture, but conjecture is of no avail against the truth at all" (53:28). The glorious night the Quran talks about was a night when the Quran was revealed. If it was a definite date, it could be celebrated. Such a date could not be based on a conjecture. Also, a particular date could be very significant and glorious for a devout Muslim when he can experience the divine in a special way in his sincere spiritual endeavor. This could have some inspiration for other Muslims. But for them to commemorate it with due solemnity, such a date needs to be known with certainty.

The Hadith misleads on pilgrimage

In Chapter 3, we mentioned how the *hajj* institution has been corrupted by traditional practices such as kissing of a black stone in the Kabah, and stone-throwing at an imaginary devil at another place. The stone-throwing practice each year results in too much crowding of pilgrims at one place, and often in unnecessary stampedes and human death.

A Hadith narrated by Abu Qatada states that he along with some other companions of the Prophet who were in a state of *ihram* (i.e., in the state of *hajj* or pilgrimage mission), though Abu Qatada himself was not in that state, were traveling to Mecca and on the way saw an onager (wild fast running ass). Abu Qatada killed that animal, and all the companions ate of its meat. The Prophet, when he heard about it, reportedly approved of the eating of this killed game, and asked if there was some of it left for him to eat. (*Sahih Bukhari*, Vol. 4, Book 52, # 163, a similar Hadith at # 106) This Hadith must be a fabrication, as hunting of animals during the pilgrimage is forbidden by the Quran (5:95).

Another Hadith exaggerates the virtues of pilgrimage:

> Narrated Abu Huraira: Allah's Apostle said, "Whoever performs Hajj to this House (Kaba) and does not approach his wife for sexual relations nor commits sins (while performing Hajj), he will come out as sinless as a newly-born child." (*Sahih Bukhari*, Vol. 3, Book 28, # 45 and 46)

Like prayer and fasting, pilgrimage helps one attain some piety, but it cannot be claimed that it erases one's past sins regardless of the level of sins, and without adequate remorse for the sins on the part of the pilgrim. If performing *hajj* makes one sinless as a now-born child, it is hard to explain why we often find people who have completed the *hajj* not changing their earlier evil actions.

The Hadith denigrates women's status

In the backdrop of cultural prejudices in the seventh-century Arabia, it was nothing short of a "revolutionary social egalitarianism"[393] introduced by the Quran that women should be treated on a par with men. This revolutionary idea was effectively translated into practice in a society where women were being treated little better than slaves, when they had virtually no rights and privileges, but mainly indignity and neglect, and when female infanticide was common. In Chapter 9, we have seen that the Quran gloriously lifts the status of women. The Hadith has, on the other hand, relegated their position to one not only inferior to that of men, but also to one that is far degrading and disgraceful.

The Quran emphasizes the relationship between men and women as one of love, compassion, and complementarity (30:21; 2:187; 9:71). The Quran also describes spouses as garments of each other (2:187). The wives of pious people generally do qualify to go to Heaven along with their husbands:

> **43:70** (Ye) who have believed Our revelations and surrendered (unto God)! *Enter ye the Garden, ye and your wives, (and) rejoice.*

The exceptions that wives of pious men are not pious are rare.[394] Women should not be considered as inferior to men, since one has similar rights over the other (2:228); and since both a man and a woman are one from another (3:195). God never discriminates between men and women (3:195; 4:124; 16:97; 33:35). The Quran urges men to consider their spouses as source of abundant good (4:19), and source of comfort to their eyes (25:74). Even women can excel men in virtuousness (49:13) and in some qualities (4:32).

In sharp contrast to all this, as cited in Chapter 9, the Hadith says that the majority of the inhabitants of Hell will be women; that there is no greater affliction left after the Prophet than women; and that women are among the bad omens (References cited in Chapter 9 from Bukhari). Similar texts are also in *Muslim, Tirmidhi* and *Nasa'i*. There are, of course, some Hadith texts that display respect for women. However, these are overwhelmingly overshadowed by the negative texts against them. Look at some more of them:

> Narrated 'Abdullah bin Abbas: ... 'Then I *(the Prophet) saw the (Hell) Fire*, and I have never before, seen such a horrible sight as that, and *I saw that the majority of its dwellers were women.*' The people asked, 'O Allah's Apostle! What is the reason for that?' He replied, 'Because of their ungratefulness.' It was said. 'Do they disbelieve in Allah (are they ungrateful to Allah)?' He replied, 'they are not thankful to their husbands and are ungrateful for the favors done to them. Even if you do good to one of them all your life, when she seems some harshness from you, she will say, 'I have never seen any good from you.' *(Sahih Bukhari,* Vol. 7, Book 62, # 125; a similar Hadith at Vol. 1, Book 2, # 28)

> Narrated Abu Huraira: Allah's Apostle said: If a husband calls his wife to his bed (i.e. to have sexual relation) and she refuses and causes him to sleep in anger, the angels will curse her till morning. *(Sahih Bukhari,* Vol. 4, Book 54, # 460)

Yet another virulent Hadith against women narrated by Abu Said al-Khudri depicts them as deficient in intelligence and religion *(Sahih Bukhari,* Vol. 1, Book 6, # 301). Similar texts portraying women as destined for Hell in greater number than men due to poorer faith and inferior intelligence are also available in *Muslim, Tirmidhi* and *Nasa'i*. In regard to this Hadith depicting women as more deficient in intelligence and religion, Reza Aslan remarks that many have considered Abu Said al-Khudri's memory as "unchallenged, despite the fact that Muhammad's biographers present him as repeatedly asking for and following the advice of his wives, even in military matters".[395] One wonders how a man of the stature of a prophet could speak so lightly of women and, most importantly, against the very spirit of the message of the Quran. The fact of the matter is that all such Hadith texts are fabricated – fabrications made in a male-dominated, misogynic society, and are misleading to mankind. Look at another Hadith showing women as not fit for running the affairs of a country:

Narrated Abu Bakra: During the battle of Al-Jamal, Allah benefited me with a Word (I heard from the Prophet). When the Prophet heard the news that the people of the Persia had made the daughter of Khosrau their Queen (ruler), he said: Never will succeed such a nation as makes a woman their ruler. (*Sahih Bukhari*, Vol. 9, Book 88, # 219)

Those who fabricated this Hadith were oblivious to the fact that a woman was a ruler of Sheba, whose reference has been given in the Quran. In contemporary times also, Muslim countries such as Turkey, Pakistan, Indonesia, and Bangladesh have had or now have female heads of state.

Other similar Hadith texts subordinating women's status *vis-à-vis* that of men include those, all narrated by Abu Huraira, that say that it is not lawful for a wife to fast without her husband's permission if he is at home *(Sahih Bukhari,* Vol. 7, Book 62, # 120 and 123); and that angels curse wives who refuse to sleep with their husbands *(Sahih Bukhari,* Vol. 7, Book 62, # 121-122); and that a wife should not allow anyone to enter the house without his permission *(Sahih Bukhari,* Vol. 7, Book 62, # 123); and that if a wife spends of her husband's wealth for charitable purposes without being ordered by him, he will get half of the reward *(Sahih Bukhari,* Vol. 7, Book 62, # 123).

Khaled Abou El Fadl cites several Hadith reports that make wives virtually slaves to their husbands, which are unreliable and problematic, since they ignore the overall moral teachings of Islam.[396] Included in these reports are:

- Hadiths that say that if the Prophet allowed prostration of a human before another, he would have allowed a wife to prostrate before her husband (reported by Abu Huraira in *Tirmidhi*; also similar reports in *Abu Dawud, Ibn Majah, Nasai, Musnad* of Ahmad ibn Hanbal and Ibn Hibban*)*;

- A Hadith saying that a woman cannot fulfill her obligations to God until she fulfills her obligations to her husband (*Ibn Majah*);

- A Hadith that says that a woman would not fulfill her husband's rights even if she licks an ulcer excreting puss from his feet to the top of his head (*Musnad*);

- A Hadith that says: "Any woman who dies while her husband is pleased with her enters Heaven" (*Abu Dawud, Tirmidhi, Ibn Majah*, etc.);

- A Hadith that says: "If a woman prays five (times a day), fasts Ramadan, obeys her husband, and guards her chastity, she enters Heaven" (reported by Anas b. Malik and narrated by Ahmad b. Hanbal, Ibn Hibban and al-Tabari).

- A Hadith that says: "Any woman who asks her husband for a divorce without suffering hardship will not enter Heaven" (*Abu Dawud, Tirmidhi, Ibn Majah*, etc.)

With respect to these Hadith texts, some of the comments made by Abou El Fadl himself are worth citing:

> The difficulty with this genre of traditions is that they promote a formalistic obligation of obedience to husbands while ignoring all competing moral values in Islam. [...] it makes God's pleasure contingent on the husband's pleasure. [...] Furthermore, these traditions are not consistent with the Qur'anic conception of the marital relationship. [...] The Qur'anic conception of marriage is not based on servitude but on compassion and cooperation, and the Qur'anic conception of virtue is not conditioned on the pleasure of another human being, but on piety and obedience to God.[397]

Abou El Fadl adds that these Hadiths have terrible theological and social implications. Obviously, all such Hadith texts, apart from conflicting with the Quranic conception of the marital relationship, also cast aspersions on the chivalrous and good-natured character of the Prophet.

The Hadith misguides on marriage

As explained in Chapter 9, the Quran allows polygamy to respond to exceptional circumstances, e.g., to take care of orphan girls, or in situations of female preponderance, e.g., after a war when men are killed, and more women are left single than men. The Quran allows polygamy, but subject to certain restrictions, the most important of which is that one must do justice to all wives. It was also mentioned in that chapter that special circumstances led the Prophet Muhammad to have multiple wives, which was after the death of his first wife Khadijah when he was forty-nine years old. He married several women who were widows of his friends, and beyond the age of sex life. Yet the Hadith has made a fanfare of his multiple marriages. Look at the following Hadith text:

> Narrated Said bin Jubair: Ibn 'Abbas asked me: Are you married? I replied: No. He said: Marry, for the best person of this (Muslim) nation (i.e., Muhammad) of all other Muslims, had the largest number of wives. (*Sahih Bukhari,* Vol. 7, Book 62, # 7)

A slanderous Hadith on the Prophet Solomon is as follows:

> Narrated Abu Huraira: Allah's Apostle said: Once Solomon, son of David said, '(By Allah) Tonight I will have sexual intercourse with one hundred (or ninety-nine) women each of whom will give birth to a knight who will fight in Allah's Cause.' On that a (i.e. if Allah wills) but he did not say 'Allah willing.' Therefore only one of those women conceived and gave birth to a half-man. By Him in Whose Hands Muhammad's life is, if he had said 'Allah willing', (he would have begotten sons) all of whom would have been knights striving in Allah's Cause. (*Sahih Bukhari,* Vol. 4, Book 52, # 74i)

This as well as the earlier cited Hadiths are an indirect incitement to polygamy and sexual activity. The latter Hadith is also an exaggeration of the virtue of uttering, or of the vice of not uttering, a certain expression. The Prophet could never say such a preposterous thing about the Prophet Solomon, who has been presented as a much honored and spiritually powerful Messenger of God in the Quran.

One Hadith narrated by Abu Huraira, which also undermines the status of women, and indirectly encourages polygamy, is as follows:

> The Prophet said: It is not lawful for a woman (at the time of wedding) to ask for the divorce of her sister (i.e. the other wife of her would-be husband) in order to have everything for herself, for she will take only what has been written for her. (*Sahih Bukhari,* Vol. 7, Book 62, # 82).

The Prophet could not have made such a ridiculous suggestion, which is against the Quranic assertion that a woman has rights over a man similar to those of a man over a woman (2:228). A dignified woman has a legitimate right to ask a would-be husband who asks her to marry him, to divorce her other wife, if the former does not wish to marry a man who wants to retain his existing wife.

Note that the above Hadith narrated by Abu Huraira directly conflicts with another Hadith narrated by Al-Miswar bin Makhrama, where the Prophet is shown to have disapproved of the idea that Ali should be allowed to take another wife without divorcing his current wife who was the daughter of the Prophet:

> I heard Allah's Apostle who was on the pulpit, saying: Banu Hisham bin Al-Mughira have requested me to allow them to marry their daughter to Ali bin Abu Talib, but I don't give permission, and will not give permission unless 'Ali bin Abu Talib divorces my daughter in order to marry their daughter, because Fatima is a part of my body, and I hate what she hates to see, and what hurts her, hurts me. (*Sahih Bukhari*, Vol. 7, Book 62, # 157)

The above two Hadith texts show that the Hadith is self-contradictory.

There are two Hadith texts narrated respectively by Abdullah and Abu Jamra in Bukhari, which say that the Prophet permitted *muta* marriage, i.e., marriage with a temporary contract (*Sahih Bukhari*, Vol. 7, Book 62, #s 13o and 51). One self-conflicting Hadith narrated by Jabir bin 'Abdullah and Salama bin Al-Akwa says both that *muta* marriage was permissible, and also not permissible (*Sahih Bukhari*, Vol. 7, Book 62, #s 52). There is another Hadith narrated by Ali that says that the Prophet forbade such marriage during the battle of Khaibar (*Sahih Bukhari*, Vol. 7, Book 62, # 50). However, it is unthinkable that the Prophet could ever permit *muta* marriage, which is clearly adultery (*zina*), and simple prostitution according to the Quran.

Yet another example of an irresponsible Hadith narrated by Anas bin Malik is at *Sahih Bukhari*, Vol. 7, Book 62, # 10, where the Prophet is alleged to have suggested to one Abdur Rahman bin Auf who went to Medina from Mecca to share one of two wives, and half of the property of one Sad bin Ar-Rabi' Al-Ansari. It is unthinkable that the Prophet could ever suggest that a believer should spare one of his wives to another believer, without considering the point that a husband cannot unilaterally decide to divorce his wife to let her marry another man, without taking into account her own wishes. This Hadith also treats women in an undignified manner.

In one Hadith narrated by Sahl bin Sad As-Sa'idi, the Prophet is reported to have advised one believer, who knew just some *surahs* (chapters) of the Quran but who was so poor that he practically did not have anything to offer by way of dowry, to marry a woman (*Sahih Bukhari,* Vol. 7, Book 62, # 24, also repeated at #s 54, 58, 63, 66, 72 and 79 of the same Vol. and book, also repeated at Vol. 6, Book 61, # 548). Another similar Hadith narrated by Sahl bin Sad suggests that the Prophet reportedly authorized marriage even with an iron ring, regardless of his financial standing (*Sahih Bukhari,* Vol. 7, Book 62, # 80; also Vol. 6, Book 61, # 547). It is unthinkable that the Prophet should give the irresponsible advice that one should marry while unable financially to support his wife, which is clearly against the Quran that says that one should rather wait until one is financially solvent (24:33).

An example of a weird Hadith narrated by Abu Huraira is worth citing:

> I said: O Allah's Apostle! I am a young man and I am afraid that I may commit illegal sexual intercourse and I cannot afford to marry. He kept silent, and then repeated my question once again, but he kept silent. I said the same (for the third time) and he remained silent. Then repeated my question (for the fourth time), and only then the Prophet said: O Abu Huraira! The pen has dried after writing what you are going to confront. So (it does not matter whether you) get yourself castrated or not. (*Sahih Bukhari,* Vol. 7, Book 62, # 13h)

This Hadith is an example of a bad taste and a bad reflection on the character of Abu Huraira. Shouldn't a good Muslim remain fully chaste until marriage, as the Quran advises? God has indeed urged those who cannot afford to marry because of financial reasons to postpone their marriage, and remain chaste until their financial condition sufficiently improves. And how could one dare to speak to the Prophet in this manner? It is unthinkable that the Prophet would entertain such an irresponsible discourse from any of his followers.

Should silence of a bride be always taken to mean consent for marriage with a bridegroom? Probably no; girls can best vouch on this. There are occasions when a bride may not actually like to marry the particular bridegroom, but remains silent under duress. But the Hadith at *Sahih Bukhari*, Vol. 7, Book 62, # 67 and 68 passes off silence as indicating consent for marriage.

The Hadith also gives wrong advice on the remarriage of a divorced wife with her former husband. One Hadith reportedly narrated by Aisha states that a divorced wife who has married another person, who was then found to be impotent, was barred by the Prophet from returning to her original husband until she consummated her present marriage with the current husband (*Sahih Bukhari*, Vol. 7, Book 63, # 186, 187, 190, 238). The idea "no divorce before consummation of marriage" is also in *Ibn Majah*. The Prophet, however, could not give such advice as it is in direct conflict with the Quran. The Quran allows married couples to divorce without any consummation (2:236). Another Hadith states that a divorced wife cannot go back to, or remarry, her husband until she marries another person, and until that person divorces her (*Sahih Bukhari*, Vol. 7, Book 63, # 249). The Hadith is then the source of the notorious *hilla* system, which misinterprets the Quranic advice (2:230). This Quranic verse should rather be interpreted as meaning that if a divorced wife marries another person, she is not lawful to her former husband until her present husband divorces her, which is quite reasonable and logical.[398] Also note the Quran clearly cautions against barring divorced wives from remarrying their former husbands (2:232). Note also that there is a Hadith, which upheld this Quranic advice, and allowed a divorced wife to remarry her husband without requiring her to marry another person (*Sahih Bukhari*, Vol. 7, Book 63, # 248).

The Hadith misleads on *jihad*

God has enjoined *jihad* or fighting on us to deal with aggression against those who fight against us, and has cautioned against any hostility except against wrongdoers (2:190-193), and has advised us to desist from fighting when the enemies cease fighting (2:193; 8:62-63). The Quran advises gentle persuasion in religious preaching (16:125; 29:46), and no coercion (2:256). However, the Hadith suggests that there should be *jihad* or fighting against other communities until they accept certain principles of Islam. In some Hadith texts, the Prophet is reported to have said that he has been ordered to fight against people until they accept that none except God is to be worshipped (*Sahih Bukhari*, Vol. 4, Book 52, # 196), and until they accept that Muhammad is His Messenger, and until they pray and offer *zakat* (*Sahih Bukhari*, Vol. 1, Book 2, # 24). In one Hadith narrated by Khalid bin Madan, the Prophet is reported to have said: The first army amongst my followers who will invade Caesar's City will be forgiven their sins (*Sahih Bukhari*, Vol. 4, Book 52, # 175). Thus the approach of the Hadith on *jihad* or fighting is fundamentally opposed to that proclaimed by the Quran, which never endorses any aggressive *jihad*. The Hadith texts that are attributed to the Prophet cannot be but fabrications. The military expeditions and territorial expansion carried out by many Muslim rulers did not therefore have the religious sanction that the Quran approves. In fact, as history amply proves, most, if not all, of the Muslim rulers after the Khulafai Rashidun assumed political power in an un-Islamic way, and they did not rule according to the Quranic standards.

Some Hadith texts also mislead on *jihad* by making confusing distinction between *jihad* in God's cause or just fighting on one hand, and other virtuous deeds on the other hand, though the Quran emphatically projects *jihad* as part and parcel of righteousness. The following Hadith text in particular is worth citing:

> A narration from Abu Huraira reports that the Prophet allegedly said: Whoever believes in Allah and His Apostle, offers prayer perfectly and fasts the month of Ramadan, will rightfully be granted Paradise by Allah, no matter whether he fights in Allah's Cause or remains in the land where he is born. (Sahih Bukhari, Vol. 4, book 52, #48)

This Hadith is counter to the Quranic message that fighting in God's way is part and parcel of one's religious and righteous deeds (61:11-12), that the rank of those who fight in God's cause with their possessions and persons is higher than that of those who sit at home (4:95), and that none who can and should fight in God's cause should remain in the land fearing death (3:168).

The Hadith is against progress and modernity, and conflicts with scientific truth and reason

As noted above the Hadith encourages fatalism, and by so doing it stunts the very spirit of striving and enterprise, which the Quran so forcefully extols and presents to humankind. The Quran also sends the message that it is not material progress and manpower, which are of real help to humankind in terms of their piety and salvation (26:88-89; 34:37). Quite sensibly, the Quran stresses spiritual piety in preference to material prosperity. At the same time the Quranic conception of the *sirat al-mustaqim* (the straight path of God's *niamat* or abundance) does not rule out material prosperity alongside spiritual progress. Indeed, God has made available and subjected everything on earth and in the heavens to the disposal and service of humankind (31:20; 45:13; 16:12-14). God is free of want (independent or self-reliant). If we want to emulate God, we also need to be self-reliant. The inherent purpose of the *sadaqa* or *zakat* or distribution system in society should also be aimed at making every body self-reliant or rich enough to obviate the necessity of any such *zakat* in the future. This will be real welcome progress in society.

Against the backdrop of this Quranic perspective, the Hadith erroneously propagates the idea that impoverishment is better than affluence, and by so doing it has contributed to the holding back of Muslims' progress on earth. Look at some of the examples of Hadith texts that have misled the Muslim *ummah*. There are Hadith texts which say that the poor are better people than the rich. One Hadith (*Sahih Bukhari*, Vol. 7, Book 62, # 124, a similar text also at Vol. 7, Book 62, # 126) says that it is the women and the wealthy people who enter Hell in greater number, while the poor people enter Paradise in greater number. Another Bukhari Hadith narrated by Sahl at (Vol. 7, Book 62, # 28) suggests that it is the poor who are better than others living on earth. There is a Hadith text that says that one of the signs of the last days before the Last Hour of the world is an increase in material abundance, and construction of high-rise buildings (Sahih Bukhari, Vol. 9, Book 88, # 237). Another Hadith suggests that men owning sheep are better than those who have horses and camels (*Bukhari,* Vol. 4, Book 54, # 520). Still another Hadith suggests that a time will come when the best property of Muslims will be some sheep (*Sahih Bukhari,* Vol. 1, Book 2, # 18). Is there any logical connection between one's poverty and virtue? Are those who beg better than others? The Hadith suggests that they are; but the Quran says that it is the devil that makes one fear and experience poverty, while God promises one bounty (2:268). God also says that He *gives sustenance* to whomever He likes *without measure, or beyond one's expectation* (3:27). How can He at the same time condemn them to Hell? One may rightly wonder whether it is the Hadith that has influenced Muslims to remain relatively backward and poverty-stricken on earth.

A very long Hadith, even much longer than the one at (*Sahih Bukhari*, Vol. 7, Book 62, # 117) (in 74 lines of translated text) narrated by Ibn Abbas who reported what Umar bin al-Khattab reportedly told him is at (*Sahih Bukhari*, Vol. 7, Book 62, # 119). In the Hadith, in a nutshell, there are references to two wives of the Prophet about whom the revelations at (66:4) came; to the poor way in which the Prophet lived; and to a question Umar asked and the Prophet's reply about why his followers were not rich like the Persians and Romans who were not believers; and to the Prophet's living aside from his wives for twenty-nine days; etc. To the question Umar asked, the Prophet reportedly replied, they (the Persians and the Romans) are the people who received the results of their good deeds in this world, implying that they will be denied good results in the Hereafter.

One should wonder how Bukhari's team of Hadith transmitters remembered this very long Hadith. The Hadith does not shed any more light on the issue of rebellion of some of the Prophet's wives than what the Quran says in (66:3-5). The Hadith rather clouds the issue further. Also note this Hadith contradicts the Hadith at (*Sahih Bukhari*, Vol. 7, Book 62, # 117), which compared the Prophet with a rich person. And also importantly, it further suggests that Muslims need not mind their poverty in this world, as they can expect their rewards in the Hereafter. No wonder why Muslims remain content with their relative poverty even today. But this Hadith goes against the spirit of the Quran, which says that those who do good deeds enjoy good results both in this world and the Hereafter (16:30), and that the dwellers of Heaven would say that they are enjoying the same fruits as they were enjoying also before (2:25). The Quran also states that it is His righteous servants who are established as inheritors and rulers of the earth (21:05; 24:55), and that might and honor belongs to them (63:8). Thus this is another anti-Quran, anti-progress Hadith.

In a Hadith allegedly reported by Aisha suggests that, among other things, the Prophet used to seek God's refuge or help in remaining free from debt, and that he reportedly said: A person in debt tells lies whenever he speaks, and breaks promises whenever he makes (them) (*Sahih Bukhari*, Vol. 1, Book 12, # 795). While one could legitimately wish to remain debt-free, it is unthinkable that the Prophet could ever make an irresponsible statement that a person in debt tells lies and breaks promises. If lending is good, and could be *qarz-hasana* (beautiful loan) according to the Quran, why is being in debt so bad? It is also an anti-progress and anti-modernity statement, since a modern economy could not thrive, or even survive, without having lending and borrowing operations in place.

The Hadith also conflicts with science and reason. Below we give some examples.

A Hadith narrated by Abu Dhar (*Sahih Bukhari*, Vol. 4, Book 54, # 421) interprets one Quranic verse as follows:

> The sun [...] goes (i.e. travels) till it prostrates Itself underneath the Throne and takes the permission to rise again, and it is permitted and then (a time will come when) it will be about to prostrate itself but its prostration will not be accepted, and it will ask permission to go on its course but it will not be permitted, but it will be ordered to return whence it has come and so it will rise in the west. And that is the interpretation of the Statement of Allah: And the sun runs its fixed course for a term (decreed). That is the Decree of (Allah) the Exalted in Might, the All-Knowing (36:38).

We know from science that it is rather the earth which moves round the sun, and that no heavenly bodies, including the earth, are stationary, but move in space. Also, can a reader make head or tail of this interpretation of the concerned Quranic verse? The Hadith rather makes for confusion. The relevant verses of the Quran read as follows:

> **36:38-40** The sun runneth (in its course or orbit) for an appointed term. Such is the design of the Mighty, the All-Knowing. And as for the moon, We have ordained it to appear in stages until it reverteth to an old thin palm leaf. It is not for the sun to overtake the moon, nor doth the night outstrip the day. Each floateth in its own orbit.

Note that many translators have interpreted the first verse as the sun running to a fixed resting place on the basis of the Hadith, thus compounding the confusion.

One Hadith narrated by Abu Huraira and attributed to the Prophet Muhammad is as follows:

> If a house fly falls in the drink of anyone of you, he should dip it (in the drink), for one of its wings has a disease and the other has the cure for the disease. (*Sahih Bukhari,* Vol. 4, Book 54, # 537)

One should ask a microbiologist whether it is safe to have such a drink.

One Hadith narrated by Abu Huraira states that Allah's Apostle said: Five are regarded as martyrs: They are those who die because of plague, abdominal disease, drowning or a falling building etc., and the martyrs in Allah's Cause (*Sahih Bukhari,* Vol. 4, Book 52, # 82). The question of how those who die of plague, abdominal disease, drowning and who die from a falling building qualify as martyrs is not only unreasonable, but also contradictory to the spirit of the Quranic message.

Still another Hadith narrated by Abu Huraira states that Allah's Apostle said: The (Hell) Fire complained to its Lord saying, 'O my Lord! My different parts eat up each other.' So, He allowed it to take two breaths, one in the winter and the other in summer, and this is the reason for the severe heat and the bitter cold you find (in weather). (*Sahih Bukhari,* Vol. 4, Book 54, # 482) Severe heat or bitter cold are due to some scientific reasons such as relative distance from the sun (note that when there is summer in the northern hemisphere, there is winter in the southern hemisphere of the earth), the condition of the ozone layer (the upper atmospheric layer) through which the sun rays pass, variation in atmospheric pressure, formation of clouds, winds, storms, etc. The Hadith provides an imaginary reason.

Another Hadith narrated by Abu Said al-Khudri reads as follows:

> Some women requested the Prophet to fix a day for them as the men were taking all his time. On that he promised them one day for religious lessons and commandments. Once during such a lesson the Prophet said, "A woman whose three children die will be shielded by them from the Hell fire." On that a woman asked, "If only two die?" He replied, "Even two (will shield her from the Hell-fire)." (*Sahih Bukhari,* Vol. 1, Book 3,

101, 102 - this latter Hadith qualifies the earlier one by saying that the children die at an age when they are sinless i.e., below the age of puberty).

Is this Hadith believable? Could the Prophet ever say that a woman whose three or two children died is shielded from Hell fire, which is against the spirit of the Quranic message that only righteous deeds can save one from Hell fire?

There are numerous other Hadith texts that are against progress and modernity, and conflict with science and reason. Some more examples are as follows:

1. According to one Hadith narrated by Al-Bara bin Azib, the Prophet approved seven things and forbade seven things. Among the seven forbidden things are included gold rings, silver plates, Mayathir (cushions of silk stuffed with cotton and placed under the rider on the saddle), the Qasiyya (linen clothes containing silk brought from an Egyptian town), the Istibraq (thick silk) and the Dibaj (another kind of silk). (Similar Hadith also at #. 539 and 753).

    Comment: It is unthinkable that the Prophet could forbid things, which are not forbidden by the Quran.

2. Another Hadith narrated by Salim's father claims that angels do not enter a house that contains a picture or a dog (*Sahih Bukhari*, Vol. 4, Book 54, # 450). There are other Hadith texts that suggest the Prophet reportedly disliked pictures.

    Comment: What is wrong with pictures? This would preclude modern movie pictures and TV pictures as well.

3. According one Hadith narrated by Humaid bin Hilal a swirling cloud of dust in a lane was caused by the procession of angel Gabriel (*Sahih Bukhari,* Vol. 4, Book 54, # 437).

    Comment: This is a fanciful claim.

4. Narrated Abu Said Al-Khudri: The Prophet said to his companions, "Is it difficult for any of you to recite one third of the Quran in one night?" This suggestion was difficult for

them so they said, "Who among us has the power to do so, O Allah's Apostle?" Allah Apostle replied: "Allah (the) One, the Self-Sufficient Master Whom all creatures need.' (Surat Al-Ikhlas 112.1 to the end) is equal to one third of the Quran." (*Sahih Bukhari,* Vol. 6, Book 61, # 534).

Comment: Equating one small *surah* to one third of the Quran could not be reasonable –it is, rather, an easy shortcut invented by Hadith lovers.

5. According to one Hadith narrated by Abu Huraira, the Prophet is reported to have said that he who refuses an invitation (to a banquet) disobeys God and the Prophet (*Sahih Bukhari,* Vol. 7, Book 62, # 106).

Comment: There can be various genuine reasons for one to refuse an invitation. How can it be equated to not obeying God and the Prophet?

The Hadith discourages any inquisitive thought about God (*Sahih Bukhari,* Vol. 6, Book 61, # 496). The Quran advises us not to doubt God and His revelations (2:186; 2:147; 3:60; 10:94-95), but does not discourage thinking about Who is really God, as evidenced by the inquisitive search of God by the Prophet Abraham (6:75-79).

The Hadith encourages religious intolerance, violence and terror

As noted in some detail in Chapter 7, the Quran proclaims a message of tolerance to other religious groups. As noted above, despite the clear Quranic advice to the contrary, the Hadith encourages offensive wars, intolerance, violence, and terror.

There are several Hadith texts originating from Abdullah bin Abi Aufa that show Paradise as being under the shades of swords (*Sahih Bukhari,* Vol. 4, Book 52, # 73, 210, 266l). Such a statement may not be particularly objectionable if it is specifically meant for, and addressed to, fighters fighting a just war, but as a general statement it sounds rather belligerent, a sentiment which apparently has played, and is still playing, a role in encouraging aggressive campaigns by Muslims against other communities. Some Hadith texts preach particularly anti-Semitic sentiment, where Muslims are urged to fight and kill the Jews wherever they are. The Hadith below is worth citing:

Narrated Abu Huraira: "Allah's Apostle said, 'You (i.e. Muslims) will fight with the Jews till some of them will hide behind stones. The stones will (betray them) saying, 'O 'Abdullah (i.e. slave of Allah)! There is a Jew hiding behind me; so kill him.' " (*Sahih Bukhari*, Volume 4, Book 52, Number 176)

A similar Hadith at *Sahih Bukhari*, Vol. 4, Book 52, # 177 says that the Hour (the eventual hour of *qiyamat*) will not be established until the Muslims fight with the Jews and they kill the Jew hiding behind a stone. There is a similar Hadith also against the Turks (*Sahih Bukhari*, Vol. 4, Book 52, # 179).

Still other Hadith texts show that the Prophet ordered atrocities and violence against his enemies. The Hadith text narrated by Ibn Umar at Sahih Bukhari, Vol. 4, Book 52, # 263 states that the Prophet burned the date-palms of Bani an-Nadir. Another Hadith narrated by Al-Bara bin Azib states that the Prophet sent a group of men to kill Abu-Raffi, a merchant of Hijaz; Abdullah bin Atik entered his house at night, and killed him while he was sleeping (Sahih Bukhari, Vol. 4, Book 52, # 264, 265). Look at another venomous Hadith text:

Narrated 'Ikrima: Some Zanadiqa (atheists) were brought to 'Ali and he burnt them. The news of this event, reached Ibn 'Abbas who said, "If I had been in his place, I would not have burnt them, as Allah's Apostle forbade it, saying, 'Do not punish anybody with Allah's punishment (fire).' I would have killed them according to the statement of Allah's Apostle, '*Whoever changed his Islamic religion, then kill him.*'" (*Sahih Bukhari*, Vol. 9, Book 84, # 57; a similar text also at Vol. 4, Book 52, # 260)

Is it believable that a highly pious companion and son-in-law of the Prophet such as Ali could burn people? How is it believable that the Prophet said that if a Muslim discards his religion he could be killed? Such Hadith texts must be utter lies attributed to the Prophet and his close associates. The Quran nowhere speaks of punishing the renegades or apostates in such a manner; it clearly proclaims that there is no coercion in religion.

A narration attributed to Ali states that he heard the Prophet saying, "In the last days (of the world) there will appear young people with foolish thoughts and ideas. They will give good talks, but they will go out of Islam as an arrow goes out of its game, their faith will not exceed their throats. So, *wherever you find them, kill them*, for there will be a reward for their killers on the Day of Resurrection." (*Sahih Bukhari*, Vol. 6, Book 61, # 577; repeated at Vol. 9, Book 84, # 64) Needless to say, this is a highly reprehensible, provocative statement falsely attributed to the good name of Ali that goes against the Quran.

Still another narration from Abu Burda recounts the story of a Jew being killed, because he converted to Islam and then reverted to Judaism (*Sahih Bukhari*, Vol. 9, Book 84, # 58). Still another Hadith suggests that Ali killed some people among those to whom the Prophet was distributing alms, but who were accusing the Prophet as unjust (*Sahih Bukhari*, Vol. 9, Book 84, # 67)

Such Hadith texts could not be those of the Prophet. They clearly encourage religious intolerance, violence and terror. Not surprisingly, it is from such Hadith texts that the extremist groups among Muslims get their inspiration for committing intolerant, violent, and terrorist acts against other communities in various parts of the world.

The Hadith encourages cruel punishments

As noted by some Hadith critics, the Hadith prescribes a much more brutal punishment – *rajam* or stoning to death – for adultery than what the Quran prescribes – a maximum of hundred lashes. There are some Hadith texts in Bukhari narrated by various people, which suggest that the Prophet and his companions applied punishment by stoning to death to those who were found guilty of adultery (*Sahih Bukhari*, Vol. 6, Book 60, # 79; Vol. 8, Book 82, # 803-810, 813-817, 821, 824-826, 842). Some texts suggest that a man, who was not married, accused of such a criminal offence was given one hundred lashes and exile for a year, instead of stoning to death. In some of these texts, the statement that a verse prescribing stoning to death for adultery was revealed to the Prophet is attributed to Caliph Umar. However, such Hadith claims cannot be credible. If stoning to death was a punishment prescribed by God, a verse to that effect would surely be found in the Quran. The Quran prescribes punishment for adultery in the following ways:

24:2-3   If a married wife is found and confirmed guilty of such a criminal offence, which requires to be confirmed by four witnesses, she should be punished with confinement to a house until death or until a way (of exit) is found for her (4:15). The way of exit from confinement to a house until death for a woman of this character would be flogging by a hundred lashes and, if she wishes, being married to a man of similar character, or to an idolater. (See also 24:26.)

4:15   The adulterer and the adulteress should be both punished after confirmation. The confirmation should be by four witnesses. The maximum punishment prescribed is one hundred lashes for each (24:2). But if they repent and mend their conduct, then they could be left alone without such punishment.

The Quranic punishment for adultery is thus a choice or variation between a maximum of hundred lashes for both the adulterer and the adulteress, confinement to house for the wife guilty of adultery, or outright forgiveness for both. Society needs to decide which punishment would serve as a sufficient or effective deterrent to such a crime.[399] It is not right to maintain, as the *ulama* would have us believe, that the verse (24:2) abrogates the verse (4:15). It is the Hadith that erroneously misleads believers by saying that some verses are abrogated or replaced by others in the Quran.[400]

The Hadith justifies slavery and slavery-like practices

The Hadith is ambiguous on slavery and slavery-like practices. While there are texts extolling the virtues of freeing slaves, these are undermined by other texts that justify continuing these practices. Look at an ambiguous text below:

Narrated Abu Dhar: I asked the Prophet, "What is the best deed?" He replied, "To believe in Allah and to fight for His Cause." I then asked, "What is the best kind of manumission (of slaves)?" He replied, "The manumission of the most expensive slave and the most beloved by his master." I said, "If I cannot afford to do that?" He said, "Help the weak or do good for a person who cannot work for himself." I said, "If I cannot do that?" He said, "Refrain from harming others for this will be regarded as a charitable deed for your own good." (*Sahih Bukhari*, Vol. 3, Book 46, # 694)

Indirect but strong justification of slavery by the Hadith is embodied in texts that strongly encourage slaves to be loyal to their masters. One such text is as follows:

Narrated 'Abdullah: The Prophet said, "*If a slave serves his Saiyid (i.e. master) sincerely and worships his Lord (Allah) perfectly, he will get a double reward*" (*Sahih Bukhari*, Vol. 3, Book 46, # 726, similar texts also at # 727 and 722).

The Hadith sanctifies keeping female captives as concubines, texts that nullify its other advice that slaves should be freed. As mentioned in Chapter 9, the Quran has clear, categorical directions against forcing slaves to serve as concubines, and for freeing them, and marrying them.

The Hadith favors supporting ruling regimes

There are several Hadith texts that lend unqualified support to the ruling regimes (*Sahih Bukhari*, Vol. 9, Book 88, # 175-179). Two of such texts are worth citing:

Narrated Ibn Abbas: The Prophet said, "Whoever disapproves of something done by his ruler then he should be patient, for *whoever disobeys the ruler even a little (little = a span) will die as those who died in the Pre-Islamic Period of Ignorance*. (i.e., as rebellious sinners (*Sahih Bukhari*, Vol. 9, Book 88, # 176).

Narrated Junada bin Abi Umaiya: We entered upon 'Ubada bin As-Samit while he was sick. We said, "May Allah make you healthy. Will you tell us a Hadith you heard from the Prophet and by which Allah may make you benefit?" He said, "The Prophet called us and we gave him the Pledge of allegiance for Islam, and among the conditions on which he took the Pledge from us, was that we were to listen and obey (the orders) both at the time when we were active and at the time when we were tired, and at our difficult time and at our ease and *to be obedient to the ruler and give him his right even if he did not*

371

*give us our right, and not to fight against him unless we noticed
him having open Kufr (disbelief) for which we would have a
proof with us from Allah." (Sahih Bukhari,* Vol. 9, Book 88, #
178)

Such Hadith texts can be presumed to have been politically motivated.
Another Hadith narration by Al-Ahnaf bin Qais states that the Prophet
reportedly said that when two Muslims fight with each other and one is
killed by another, both will go to Hell-fire (*Sahih Bukhari,* Vol. 1, Book
2, # 30). It can be seen that this is also a politically motivated Hadith to
discourage fighting against the Muslim rulers.

Another apparently politically motivated, classic example of a Hadith,
which not only directly preaches a message of despondency and gloom
for the future but also provides an indirect support to the current corrupt
regime, is as follows:

Narrated Az-Zubair bin 'Adi: We went to Anas bin Malik and
complained about the wrong we were suffering at the hand of
Al-Hajjaj. Anas bin Malik said, "Be patient till you meet your
Lord, for no time will come upon you but the time following it
will be worse than it. I heard that from the Prophet" (*Sahih
Bukhari,* Vol. 9, Book 88, # 188).

Such Hadith texts amply prove that the Hadith recording and compilation
were influenced by the ruling regimes.

The Hadith clouds rather than clarifies the Quranic message

Ahmad remarks that the Hadith "contributed towards giving up parts or
key points of the Quran or negation of the same by means of many
traditions, or even clouding of the real issues by a never ending ocean of
traditions"[401]

According to one Hadith narrated by Abu Said Al-Khudri, the
explanation of the Quranic verse "Thus We have made you a just nation
that ye may be witnesses over mankind and the Messenger (Muhammad)
will be a witness over yourselves" (2.143) is:

Noah will be called on the Day of Resurrection and he will say, 'Labbaik and Sa'daik, O my Lord!' Allah will say, 'Did you convey the Message?' Noah will say, 'Yes.' His nation will then be asked, 'Did he convey the Message to you?' They will say, 'No Warner came to us.' Then Allah will say (to Noah), 'Who will bear witness in your favor?' He will say, 'Muhammad and his followers. So they (i.e. Muslims) will testify that he conveyed the Message. And the Apostle (Muhammad) will be a witness over yourselves, and that is what is meant by the Statement of Allah (2.143) (*Sahih Bukhari,* Vol. 6, Book 60, # 14).

Does this Hadith explanation make any reasonable sense to the reader? Does it clarify the Quranic verse or cloud it? Why should Muslims who are followers of the Prophet Muhammad, and who are not Noah's own people be there to testify in favor of Noah? Is it worthy of any credence? The Quranic verse that Muslims will be witnesses over humankind can sensibly refer to only contemporary humankind.

More examples of how the Hadith has rather confounded the Quranic message are as follows:

1. According to a Hadith narrated by Ziyad bin Jubair, who went to Umar, Umar said regarding the vow of a man to fast on a day that happened to be Eid, "Allah orders vows to be fulfilled and the Prophet forbade the fasting on this day (i.e., Eid)" (*Sahih Bukhari,* Vol. 3, Book 31, # 214).

    Comment: Umar could not have said this. The Prophet could not tell a person to go against the commandment of God. Fulfilling a vow is the first incumbent duty (2:177; 3:17; 33:23). Vows or promises should be cancelled only when they are unjust or unjustifiable, made for deceiving others (16:94).

2. A Hadith narrated by Abu Huraira states that the Prophet allegedly said that if someone eats or drinks by mistake during fasting, he should complete his fasting, but adds that the eating and drinking by mistake was from God (*Sahih Bukhari,* Vol. 3, Book 31, # 154).

373

Comment: But forgetting things here, as in many other cases, is not a good thing; it is from the Satan (18:63); it cannot be from God.

3. One Hadith narrated by Ursa says that Aisha allegedly reported to her, in clarifying one Quranic verse (4: 3) that a person who is the custodian of an orphan girl, and who is attracted by her wealth and beauty, cannot marry her if he cannot give her proper dowry (*Sahih Bukhari,* Vol. 7, Book 62, # 2). Another Hadith in the same Vol. and book at # 35 disqualifies the guardian of an orphan girl to marry her if he mistreats her and does not manage her property well.

    Comment: But this negates and clouds the real and clear point made by the particular Quranic verse, which says that if one fears that he is unable to do proper justice to an orphan in regard to her wealth, he should rather marry her. And this verse should also be understood in light of the preceding verse that urges the believers to do justice to orphans and not devour their property (4:2). The two Hadith texts create an obstacle in the way of a guardian wishing to marry an orphan girl under his care, which is basically against the spirit of the Quranic message.

4. Does it help anybody to understand how divine revelation is revealed when the Hadith says that sometimes it is revealed like the ringing of a bell, or that it commences in the form of good dreams, or the angel Gabriel sometimes visited the Prophet at the cave Hira sitting on a chair between the sky and the earth (*Sahih Bukhari,* Book 1, # 2 and 3)?

The Hadith provides unsatisfactory *shan-i-nazul* (context or genesis) of revelations

A classic example of a misleading *shan-i-nazul* of a verse is as follows:

Narrated Abdullah: We used to participate in the holy wars carried on by the Prophet and we had no women (wives) with us. So we said (to the Prophet): Shall we castrate ourselves? But the Prophet forbade us to do that and thenceforth he allowed us to marry a woman (temporarily) by giving her even a garment, and then he recited: O you who believe! Do not make unlawful the good things which Allah has made lawful for you. (*Sahih Bukhari,* Vol. 6, Book 60, # 139)

As mentioned above in the context of flawed Hadith messages on marriage, the suggestion that the revelation, which is at (5:87), was occasioned to permit *muta* (temporary) marriage in the battlefield must be a figment of the imagination. The Quran does not allow temporary marriage which is prostitution pure and simple.

Look at another example of a weird *shan-i-nazul* of another verse:

Narrated Ibn Masud: A man kissed a woman and then came to Allah's Apostle and told him of that, so this divine inspiration was revealed to the Prophet 'And offer Prayers perfectly at the two ends of the day, and in some hours of the night; Verily, the good deeds remove the evil deeds (small sins) That is a reminder for the mindful.' (11.114) The man said, Is this instruction for me only?' The Prophet said, "It is for all those of my followers who encounter a similar situation." (*Sahih Bukhari,* Vol. 6, Book 60, # 209)

Divine admonition for prayer is so general and important a message for humankind that the information that the revelation about it was occasioned by a man telling the Prophet of a story of his kissing a woman reads rather silly, if not fully confusing. Such an instruction for prayer at specified timings cannot be merely for such people "who encounter a similar situation".

The *shan-i-nazul* of the revelation about *tayammum* (the wiping of hands and face with earth) in place of ablution with water is that a delay was caused in performing the regular ablution, as the stated time for prayer became due, because of an event of a loss of pieces of jewellery of one of the Prophet's wives (*Sahih Bukhari,* Vol. 7, Book 62, # 93). However, this *shan-i-nazul* is clearly unacceptable, since the Quran clearly states that the occasion for *tayammum* arises only when one is sick or on a journey, or when one cannot find water (5:6).

According to one Hadith text, fasters had sexual intercourse with their wives during Ramadan nights, which occasioned the revelation "God is aware that you were deceiving yourselves but He accepted your repentance and forgave you ..." (2: 187) (*Sahih Bukhari,* Volume 6,

Book 60, Number 35). But this is a confusing *shan-i-nazul*. The Quran's reference to believers' deceiving themselves appears more logically to have been the fact that they were observing complete abstinence during Ramadan, which was not essential.

One Hadith suggests that three revelations came to the Prophet from God allegedly because of the wishes of Umar bin al-Khattab – the revelation (2:125) about making the station of Abraham the place of worship; that about veiling of women from men; and that (66: 5) about divorcing women, and God giving better than existing wives (*Sahih Bukhari*, Vol. 1, Book 8, # 395 and 396, repeated also at *Vol. 6, Book 60, # 10- narration by Anas*). This *shan-i-nazul* does not appear to be a satisfactory one in light of the Quranic message that religious message does not go by one's wishes. The Quran says that the Prophet did not speak (any revelation) out of his own desire, and by implication, out of anybody else's desire (53:3).

Look at another Hadith giving a *shan-i-nazul*:

> Narrated Sahl bin Sad: The Verse: "And eat and drink until the white thread appears to you distinct from the black thread." was revealed, but: '... of dawn' was not revealed (along with it) so some men, when intending to fast, used to tie their legs, one with white thread and the other with black thread and would keep on eating till they could distinguish one thread from the other. Then Allah revealed' ... of dawn,' whereupon they understood what meant the night and the day. (*Sahih Bukhari*, Vol. 6, Book 60, # 38)

This Hadith sounds ridiculous since it is not conceivable that the relevant Quranic verse was revealed in the first place without the words "of dawn".

The Hadith makes bizarre predictions

Numerous texts are found in the Hadith literature (*Bukhari, Muslim*, etc.) that predict the coming of the *Dajjal* (a disbelieving misleader or a false prophet), and that of the *Mahdi* (a divinely guided person), or the coming back of Jesus, who would kill the *Dajjal*. Such texts can hardly be taken seriously in light of the Quran, where there is no such reference. In several of its texts, Bukhari makes reference to the *Dajjal* who will appear on earth in the last days before the eventual Hour (the *qiyamat*) takes place (*Sahih Bukhari*, Vol. 9, Book 88, # 237-248). He will be a one-eyed person according to some of these texts. Some Hadith texts state that some thirty *Dajjals* will appear, each of whom will falsely claim that he is a messenger of God (*Sahih Bukhari*, Vol. 9, Book 88, # 237). One of these Hadith texts is worth citing:

> Narrated Abu Sa'id: One day Allah's Apostle narrated to us a long narration about Ad-Dajjal and among the things he narrated to us, was: "Ad-Dajjal will come, and he will be forbidden to enter the mountain passes of Medina. He will encamp in one of the salt areas neighboring Medina and there will appear to him a man who will be the best or one of the best of the people. He will say 'I testify that you are Ad-Dajjal whose story Allah's Apostle has told us.' Ad-Dajjal will say (to his audience), 'Look, if I kill this man and then give him life, will you have any doubt about my claim?' They will reply, 'No,' Then Ad-Dajjal will kill that man and then will make him alive. The man will say, 'By Allah, now I recognize you more than ever!' Ad-Dajjal will then try to kill him (again) but he will not be given the power to do so." (*Sahih Bukhari*, Vol. 9, Book 88, # 246)

The Hadith says that this *Dajjal* will have power to give back life to a man whom he kills, but a question arises why this evil person should have life-giving power in the first place? Note also that from time to time, the *ulama* often declare that the *Dajjal* has come, or that this person or that person is a *Dajjal*. It is unfortunate, that they often refer to people who try to bring about some reforms in the practiced religion (which often deviates from true religion, say of the Quran) as *Dajjals*.

Along with the appearance of the *Dajjal*, the Hadith mentions other signs of the last Hour, which include disappearance of religious knowledge; an increase in earthquakes; quick passing of time; appearance of afflictions; an increase in killing; an increase in material abundance when there would remain none to accept *zakat*; the sun rising from the west; etc. Such reports are at odds with what the Prophet was commanded in the Quran to say about the Last Hour: the knowledge of it is only with God (7:187, 10:48-49; 31:34).

Disappearance of religious knowledge and prevalence of ignorance is predicted in several Hadith texts (*Sahih Bukhari*, Vol. 1, Book 3, #80, 81, 85, 98-100). One of these texts predicts that the number of men will decrease, and that of women will increase to such an extent that fifty women will be looked after by one man (*Sahih Bukhari*, Vol. 1, Book 3, # 81). Such predictions are hard to comprehend. The one that religious knowledge will disappear is counter to the spirit of the Quranic messages that say that good (religious) people prevail over the bad, and that truth will triumph over falsehood (8:7-8; 9:48; 20:68-70; 26:45-48; 21:18; and that this earth will be inherited by good people (21:105). Also, the predictions that the sun will rise from the west, and that the number of women will increase considerably disproportionately with men are scientifically unthinkable.

The Hadith predicts a future of degeneration and gloom for the Muslim *ummah*. Notice the following Hadith in particular:

> Narrated Abu Huraira: Allah's Apostle said, "There will be afflictions (in the near future) during which a sitting person will be better than a standing one, and the standing one will be better than the walking one, and the walking one will be better than the running one, and whoever will expose himself to these afflictions, they will destroy him. So whoever can find a place of protection or refuge from them, should take shelter in it" (*Sahih Bukhari,* Vol. 9, Book 88, # 202-203).

Another classic example of a Hadith text pointing to a future period of despondency is as follows:

> Narrated Abu Said Al-Khudri: Allah's Apostle said, "A time will come that the best property of a Muslim will be sheep which he will take on the top of mountains and the places of rainfall (valleys) so as to flee with his religion from afflictions" (*Sahih Bukhari,* Vol. 1, Book 2, # 18).

Similar Hadith predicting a bleak period are also in other Hadith compilations by Muslim and Tirmidhi. Some Hadith texts predict the coming of a *Mahdi* toward the Last Days, who will come as a savior of the Muslim *ummah*, and who will establish a just order. As Kassim Ahmad notes, such Hadith texts paint a pessimistic future for Muslims, which encourage them to be inactive, docile, non-partisan, and passive in

378

existing public affairs, texts that appear to have been politically motivated. Such texts are clearly against the general and political philosophy of the Quran. We do not need someone to come to save us. We can change our own lot with our own efforts, as the Quran unequivocally points out that God does not change the condition of a people unless and until they themselves change their own condition (13:11). The Quran urges us always to remain vigilant, strive in the way of God, and not remain as silent spectators. According to Ahmad, it is no surprise, why Muslims experienced degeneration and decline.[402]

Another good example of a bizarre prediction, falsely attributed to the Prophet, is as follows:

> Narrated Sahl bin Sad: The Prophet said, "Verily! 70,000 or 700,000 of my followers will enter Paradise altogether; so that the first and the last amongst them will enter at the same time, and their faces will be glittering like the bright full moon." (*Sahih Bukhari*, Vol. 4, Book 54, # 470).

The reader can very well judge whether this Hadith about the number of Muhammad's followers going to Heaven has any grain of truth in it.

The Hadith makes much ado about nothing, sends inconsistent and confusing messages, or narrates idle tales of little or no religious significance

There are numerous instances where the Hadith makes much of petty things. It speaks of what the Prophet used to do with his hands in prayer (*Sahih Bukhari*, Vol. 1, Book 12, # 702-706); whether or not one should insert water in the nose and blow it out, since Satan is supposed to reside there (*Sahih Bukhari*, Vol. 4, Book 54, # 516); whether or not one should pay any attention to the passing of wind from one's anus while praying (*Sahih Bukhari*, Vol. 1, Book 4, # 137, 139, 176); whether or not one should spit or throw nasal secretions, expectoration or sputum while praying, or if so, do on which side of the body (*Sahih Bukhari*, Vol. 1, Book 8, # 399-409); that the Prophet used to start every thing from the right (for good things) whenever it was possible in all his affairs; for example: in washing, combing, or wearing shoes. (*Sahih Bukhari*, Vol. 1, Book 8, # 418); that the things that annul prayer are a dog, a donkey, and a woman (*Sahih Bukhari*, Vol. 1, Book 9, # 493). One might wonder why a real worshiper should have to be reminded about, or should pay any close attention to, such petty things.

We have noted above several instances of either self-contradicting Hadith texts, or mutually inconsistent Hadith texts, e.g., the texts about how the number of *salat* times was reduced; about the possible date of the Night of *qadar*; about whether or not a person's current wife can seek divorce if her husband seeks to take another wife; etc. Here are more such examples.

An example of a self-contradictory Hadith is at (*Sahih Bukhari*, Vol. 1, Book 9, # 493) reportedly narrated by Aisha, which says that three things that annul prayer are a dog, a donkey and a woman. But Aisha said she used to lie between the Prophet and the *qiblah* when he prayed.

Note two mutually inconsistent Hadith texts. One is at *Sahih Bukhari*, Vol. 1, Book 3, # 100 narrated by Abdullah bin Amr bin Al' As, which says that due to the death of religiously learned men, there will remain no men with real knowledge to guide people, and hence they will go astray as they will consult wrong people without knowledge. The other is at *Sahih Bukhari*, Vol. 1, Book 3, # 71 narrated by Muawiya, which states that the Muslim nation will keep on following God's teachings, and they will not be harmed by anyone going on a different path till God's order (Day of Judgment) is established.

Hadith texts saying horses are among bad omens conflict with other Hadith texts that say there is good in the foreheads of horses till the Day of Resurrection (*Sahih Bukhari*, Vol. 4, Book 52, # 102-104).

Another Hadith narration from Abu Huraira at (*Sahih Bukhari*, Vol. 4, Book 54, # 538) states that a prostitute is forgiven by God simply because she drew out some water with her shoes, and gave it to a dog about to die of thirst. It is unthinkable that God will condone one's sins of indecency based on a little generous work for a dog. Note that this Hadith conflicts with another (at *Sahih Bukhari*, Vol. 4, Book 54, # 540), where the Prophet is reported have ordered killing of dogs.

God says that there are people who indulge in idle or funny tales to divert man's attention to more mundane things, and to make a mockery of religion (31:6). The Hadith is full of such funny tales. There are numerous such examples.

One example is a narration from Abu Huraira attributing the following saying to the Prophet:

> The main source of disbelief is in the east. Pride and arrogance are characteristics of the owners of horses and camels and those Bedouins who are busy with their camels and pay no attention to religion; while modesty and gentleness are the characteristics of the owners of sheep" (*Sahih Bukhari*, Vol. 4, Book 54, # 520).

Does this Hadith make any sense, since horses and camels are also God's gifts, and animals of utility to humankind? The Hadith diverts attention to futile things. Another good example is as follows:

> Narrated Abu Huraira: (The Prophet) Solomon son of (the Prophet) David said, "Tonight I will go round (i.e. have sexual relations with) one hundred women (my wives) every one of whom will deliver a male child who will fight in Allah's Cause." On that an Angel said to him, "Say: 'If Allah will.' "But Solomon did not say it and forgot to say it. Then he had sexual relations with them but none of them delivered any child except one who delivered a half person. The Prophet said, "If Solomon had said: 'If Allah will,' Allah would have fulfilled his (above) desire and that saying would have made him more hopeful." (*Sahih Bukhari*, Vol. 7, Book 62, # 169)

It is inconceivable that the Prophet Muhammad could speak of the Prophet Solomon in such a ludicrous and degrading manner. One does not need to invent a crazy story to explain the purpose of saying "If Allah will". Note also that this Hadith is vulgar, casting aspersion on the character of a greatly honored prophet. It belongs to the same genre of traditions that glorify sex, and invite Muslims' attention to worldly pleasures. More examples of idle tales are noted as follows:

1. Narrated 'Ata: We presented ourselves along with Ibn 'Abbas at the funeral procession of Maimuna at a place called Sarif. Ibn 'Abbas said, "This is the wife of the Prophet so when you lift her bier, do not jerk it or shake it much, but walk smoothly because the Prophet had nine wives and he used to observe the night turns with eight of

381

them, and for one of them there was no night turn." (*Sahih Bukhari*, Vol. 7, Book 62, # 5)

Comment: What is the message here for believers? Isn't it both an idle tale and one that stains the noble character of the Prophet with an oblique reference to the glorification of sex?

2. Narrated 'Aisha: I said, "O Allah's Apostle! Suppose you landed in a valley where there is a tree of which something has been eaten and then you found trees of which nothing has been eaten, of which tree would you let your camel graze?" He said, "(I will let my camel graze) of the one of which nothing has been eaten before." (The sub-narrator added: 'Aisha meant that Allah's Apostle had not married a virgin besides herself.) (*Sahih Bukhari*, Vol. 7, Book 62, # 14)

Comment: Can a sensible believer ever believe that the Prophet's wife would engage in such idle talk?

3. Narrated Sahl bin Sa'd: A man said, "O Allah's Apostle! If a man finds another man with his wife, (committing adultery) should the husband kill him?" Later on I saw them (the man and his wife) doing *lian* [giving an oath] in the mosque. (*Sahih Bukhari*, Vol. 1, Book 8, # 415).

Comment: What religious guidance does this Hadith give us?

4. Narrated Jabir bin 'Abdullah: Allah's Apostle said, "When any one of you is away from his house for a long time, he should not return to his family at night." (*Sahih Bukhari*, Vol. 7, Book 62, # 171, also repeated at # 170)

Comment: What kind of a message is this? Does it give any good guidance?

5. Narrated Sad bin Abi Waqqas: Allah's Apostle forbade 'Uthman bin Maz'un to abstain from marrying (and other pleasures) and if he had allowed him, we would have gotten ourselves castrated. (*Sahih Bukhari*, Vol. 7, Book 62, # 11; also repeated at # 12)

382

Comment: Can the Prophet give such advice? Another idle tale!

6. Narrated 'Aisha: Abu Bakr admonished me and poked me with his hands in the flank, and nothing stopped me from moving at that time except the position of Allah's Apostle whose head was on my thigh. (*Sahih Bukhari,* Vol. 7, Book 62, # 177)

Comment: What sensible message does it convey?

7. Narrated Ibn Umar: During the lifetime of the Prophet we used to avoid chatting leisurely and freely with our wives lest some divine inspiration might be revealed concerning us. But when the Prophet died, we started chatting leisurely and freely (with them) (*Sahih Bukhari,* Vol. 7, Book 62, # 115).

Comment: What religious message does it convey? An idle tale no doubt!

8. One Hadith narrated by Aisha says that the Prophet reportedly disliked garments with marks; such garments divert one's attention from prayer (*Sahih Bukhari,* Vol. 1, Book 8, # 369, a similar Hadith repeated at # 370; Hadith at #371 speaks similarly of curtains with marks).

Comment: It speaks in a very shallow way about what *salat* or prayer really means. How can a printed cloth become a source of distraction for a real worshiper, let alone for a man of the stature of a prophet? These must be concocted Hadith (tales).

9. One Hadith narrated by Uqba bin Amir speaks of the Prophet's dislike for silk garments, and attributed to him the saying: "It is not the dress of Allah-fearing, pious people." (*Sahih Bukhari,* Vol. 1, Book 8, # 372).

Comment: This must also be a fabricated Hadith, since why should the Prophet dislike a thing which God says will be a dress of the dwellers of Heaven (76:21)?

10. One Hadith narrated by Anas mentions that he found the Prophet in the mosque along with some people, who said to him, "Did Abu Talha send you for a meal?" When Anas replied in the affirmative, the Prophet said to his

companions, "Get up." They set out and Anas was ahead of them. (*Sahih Bukhari,* Vol. 1, Book 8, # 414).

Comment: Does this Hadith convey any religious message?

11. According to a Hadith narrated by Abu Huraira, one night a big demon from the Jinn came to the Prophet, and wanted to interrupt his prayers, but the Prophet overpowered him (*Sahih Bukhari,* Vol. 1, Book 8, # 450m).

Comment: But this Hadith story negates – is entirely opposed to – the very message of the Quran that a group of Jinn came to him, and listened to him carefully, and accepted the religion of the Quran (46:29-32; 72:1-19).

12. Narrated 'Aisha: Sada bint Zam'a gave up her turn to me ('Aisha), and so the Prophet used to give me ('Aisha) both my day and the day of Sad (*Sahih Bukhari,* Vol. 7, Book 62, # 139).

Comment: A typical idle tale of no religious significance.

13. A very good example of a very long idle tale (translated text of 43 standard lines) of eleven women telling about their husbands can be seen at a Hadith allegedly reported by Aisha at (*Sahih Bukhari,* Vol. 7, Book 62, # 117). The Hadith says that Aisha was to the Prophet like the eleventh lady was to one Abu Zar who gave her many ornaments, and pleased her fully, and who brought her from a poor family to a wealthy one, etc. Note also, the Hadith says, that Abu Zar was also a character who "married another woman after seeing her with two sons like two leopards playing with her two breasts", after divorcing the eleventh lady.

Comment: Here Abu Zar is not after all a good character. How could the Prophet liken him to Abu Zar and Aisha to the eleventh lady? Also, Aisha did not come from a poor family; she was a daughter of Abu Bakr who was a very wealthy person. The comparison is misleading, and gives a very wrong impression about the Prophet. The reader should wonder what significance this Hadith has for a Muslim. And also, one should try if one can remember this long Hadith *ad verbatim* after hearing it from another. Note that Bukhari claims that his team of Hadith transmitters remembered this whole Hadith from generation to generation without any mistake. A feat indeed! A classic example of a long idle tale!

Conclusion

Examples of Hadith texts that are absurd, weird, or suspect could be multiplied. Thus, what Muslims know as the Hadith, coming as it did more than two centuries after the Prophet's death, cannot legitimately claim to be genuine Prophetic discourse. This author has considered texts mostly from Bukhari, which is generally held to be the most authentic. If one can find serious problems with texts in *Bukhari*, it is more likely that problems are even more serious with the other compilations such as *Muslim, Abu Dawud, Tirmidhi*, etc. Other Hadith critics have cited other Hadith texts that they considered as inauthentic.[403] The whole Hadith is full of misleading, distorted, irresponsible and light, mutually contradictory, and confusing messages, which have given us an entirely misleading and distorted view of Islam. This literature is riddled with inconsistencies with the Quran, and with reason and observed scientific truths. The tenor of the Hadith is essentially anti-modernity and anti-progress, anti-women, anti-peace, and anti-tolerance. The roots of religious fanaticism, and religious violence, intolerance, and terrorism are to be found right in such literature. It should not, therefore, be surprising if the enemies of Islam use such Hadith texts to defame the Prophet Muhammad, and ridicule Islam, and if an inquisitive Muslim observer should label the so-called *sunnah* represented by the Hadith as a "misconceived dogma that poisoned Islam".[404] And where the Hadith provides genuine religious guidance or advice, it is either ritualistic or fragmentary in nature, which goes against the very substance or spirit of the Quran, and its universal character. The Hadith is anachronistic.

XIII. EPILOGUE: THE RISE OF RELIGIOUS FANATICISM AND THE DIRECTION FOR TRUE ISLAMIC REVIVAL

Now verily We have caused the Word to reach them, that they might take heed. – 28:51

Now hath come unto you from God Light and a Profound Book. – 5:15

Muslims once led the world in science, mathematics, literature, art, morality, and justice. What has happened to these great people, and how can they recover? – seen earlier on www.ProgressiveMuslims.Org.

Introduction

Like Bernard Lewis, author of *What Went Wrong? Western Impact and Middle Eastern Response,* Muslims should wonder what has gone wrong with them. Once the torchbearer of human progress and civilization, Muslims have reduced themselves to a global underclass. Name any area of progressive human activity; it is not difficult to pinpoint their failure or stark underperformance in that area as a community. In recent years, months, and days, Muslim "fundamentalists" or extremists excel in one thing – terrorism and violence. The recent spate of terrorist attacks, and sectarian violence and atrocities has probably no parallel in modern history. Hardly a day passes by when we do not hear of a bomb blast or some form of violence taking place in some corner of the globe – India, Pakistan, Afghanistan, Iraq, or some part of the developed world – with a toll of human life and immense human suffering. It is lamentable, but undeniable that Muslim extremists are orchestrating much of this violence. No doubt, by doing so they are tarnishing the image of Islam, and making Muslims in general despicable in the eyes of other communities.

Indeed it may not be an exaggeration to say that the biggest threat to peace and security facing the world today is not "the clash of civilizations", but the clash of ideas that has led to a rise of religious fanaticism and extremism among some people who claim to be Muslims. Civilization should not be classed into different categories such as the Western Christendom, the Muslim World, the Hindu Civilization, the Sinic Civilization, etc., as Samuel Huntington has done.[405] Civilization in proper sense of the term has essentially the same pattern with a

386

convergence of some core characteristic features. So-called Western civilization is built upon the bedrock of some core human values that are the values of religion – Islam, Christianity, Judaism or any earlier religion – values of truthfulness and honesty, fairness and justice and the rule of law, and respect for human dignity, freedom and human rights. It is a civilization where human decency and social harmony are the norms, and peaceful and prosperous living conditions prevail, and where all men and women can uninterruptedly pursue their spiritual, social, cultural, intellectual, and political and economic goals for all round human progress and development. It is precisely because of this that modern Muslim thinker Muhammad Abduh of Egypt lamented that there was Islam in the Western society though he could not find Muslims there, but he could not find Islam in his own country though there were "Muslims" there.[406] Religion in a proper sense embraces all elements of modernity that make things better, more fair and just for all people with proper checks against the bad elements. Many of such elements of modernity have been embraced by the Western civilization. Other religious groups like Muslims have lagged behind because of their obsession with wrong traditions. Once Muslims also become modernized with adoption of all the progressive ideas, the current divide between the so-called Western civilization and the Islamic civilization will wither away. Such radical features found in Western societies as promiscuity, homosexuality, co-habitation without marriage, etc., should be considered aberrations, and not integral parts of the Western civilization.

Many scholars have characterized religious extremism among some Muslims as "Islamic" fundamentalism or "Islamic" militancy, or simply, "Islamism". Though the self-proclaimed Muslims perpetrating acts of intolerance and violence and fostering a climate of militancy are giving a negative image of Islam itself, it will be wrong to equate their activities with having anything to do with Islam. As explained in this book, Islam as professed by the Holy Quran is far above their professed ideology of intolerance and violence. Hence, and since "fundamentalism" has come to be used in a derogatory way, "Islamic fundamentalism" or "Islamic militancy" or, for that matter, "Islamism" is, in a way, an inappropriate term to use, or a contradiction in terms. As Ahmad Mansour notes, "A religion should be judged by the teachings of its holy book, not by the actions and the opinions of its followers. […] If, for example, we were to judge Christianity as presented by the opinion of Christian scholars in the medieval era of Europe, or by the actions of Christian people throughout the ages, we must conclude that Christianity is a terrible religion. Yet we know that Jesus was a peace-loving person who preached peace and love."[407]

Religion has been a living, nourishing and driving force for humankind. There are many who wrongly think that religion is an obstacle to civilization. In fact, religion has been the most important contributing factor of civilization. We should distinguish between religion and those who claim to be its followers. A contemporary writer on Islam has rightly emphasized the point that one needs to differentiate between religion as such and its human understanding.[408] Religion as the Revealed Word of God has essentially always remained the same (3:19). However, human understanding, perception or interpretation of what constitutes religion has been different from person to person and even from time to time for the same person depending on the level of his understanding and knowledge. We also need to concede the fact that some versions of religion have embraced spurious ideas or elements that really do not belong to proper religion. Such factors – differences in human understanding of religion and infiltration of non-religious ideas into religion – precisely explain the existence of different religions on earth, and of different versions of the same religion originating from the same source, the same prophet. Thus while religion has been an essential instrument for spiritual and social development of man and has had a beneficial effect on human civilization at large, religion as understood and practiced has often also had a negative and deleterious effect on cultural, social, political and economic developments of particular religious groups. For example, the wrong fatalistic attitudes fostered and cultivated among Muslims, which are not part of religion but wrongly attributed to religion, are largely to blame for their lack of initiative and drive for their own development. There are also wrong notions of *jihad* (holy war) spread among extremist Muslim groups, which are leading some of them to implant bombs in cars and drive and explode them, and leading even some of them to become live exploding human bombs, for barbarously killing and injuring innocent people. And why after all should one religious or ethnic group be after the blood of another religious or ethnic group in any part of the world? Are fanaticism, bigotry and intolerance what religion teaches us?

The Rise of Muslim Fanaticism

As noted scholar of comparative religion Karen Armstrong points out, the militant form of religiosity known as "fundamentalism" is not unique to the Muslim faith. It "is a global fact and has surfaced in every major faith in response to the problems of our modernity. [... And it] exists in a symbiotic relationship with a coercive secularism."[409] "But the desperation and fear that fuel fundamentalists", she further notes, "also tend to distort the religious tradition, and accentuate its more aggressive aspects at the expense of those that teach tolerance and reconciliation."[410] As examples of the exponents of Muslim fundamentalism, Armstrong cites the names of twentieth-century Islamic writers and political activists Abul Ala Mawdudi, the founder of the Jamaat-i Islami in Pakistan, and one of his ardent followers Sayyid Qutb of Egypt, who at one time joined the Muslim Brotherhood of Egypt. Mawdudi encouraged religious fanaticism and extremism by advocating the punishment of renegades or apostates by death, and by declaring Ahmadiyas renegades from Islam, even though the Quran nowhere speaks of punishing renegades or apostates in such a manner, and even though the Quran gives man the freedom of choice in matters of religion: *"And say, `It is the truth from your Lord; then whoever will, let him believe, and whoever will, let him disbelieve (in it)"* (18:29). Mawdudi also disregarded the clear directions of the Quran for tolerance and no coercion in religion (2:256; 10:99; 109:1-6).[411] Mawdudi's writings provided the inspiration for the passage of highly problematic "blasphemy" and *"hudud"* (or rigid *shariah*) laws that have led to many human-rights violations committed against religious minorities, especially the Ahmadiyas of Pakistan, and women. In 1953, because of writing a seditious pamphlet against Ahmadiyas, which led to rioting, he was sentenced to death by the martial law authorities, who then held sway in Pakistan, but under public pressure, this sentence was first commuted to life imprisonment and then totally withdrawn. About Qutb, Armstrong notes:

> The violent secularism of al-Nasser had led Qutb to espouse a form of Islam that distorted both the message of the Quran and the Prophet's life. Qutb told Muslims to model themselves on Muhammad: to separate themselves from mainstream society (as Muhammad had made the *hijrah* from Mecca to Medina), and then engage in a violent *jihad*. But Muhammad had in fact finally achieved victory by an ingenious policy of non-violence; the Quran adamantly opposed force and coercion in religious matters; and its vision - far from preaching exclusion and separation – was tolerant and inclusive. Qutb insisted that the Quranic injunction to toleration could occur only after the

political victory of Islam and the establishment of a true Muslim state. The new intransigence sprang from the profound fear that is at the core of fundamentalist religion. [...] Every [subsequent] Sunni fundamentalist movement has been influenced by Qutb.[412]

Though Armstrong did not see the existence of "a militant, fanatic strain" of fundamentalism in Islam, and though Muslims who represent mainstream and moderate Islam are admittedly peace-loving and law-abiding, an evidently fanatic and militant version of "Islam" called Wahhabism surfaced in the Middle East during the eighteenth century, and spread throughout the world over the years. Mawdudi and Qutb basically followed and espoused this Wahhabism. This is "a radically ultraconservative and puritanical ideology", based on a strictly literal interpretation of the Quran and the Hadith, which was aggressively promoted by Muhammad ibn Abd al-Wahhab and his followers and vigorously championed by the Saudi Kingdom after it had been founded in 1932. Armstrong notes, "Because the Ottoman Sultans did not conform to his true vision of Islam, Abd al-Wahhab declared that they were apostates and worthy of death."[413] Reza Aslan notes that King Ibn Saud and Abd al-Wahhab entered into an unholy alliance. They, in addition to "destroying the tombs of the Prophet and his Companions, including those pilgrimage sites that marked the birthplace of Muhammad and his family", were guilty of killing any Muslim "who did not accept their uncompromisingly puritanical version of Islam." And Abd al-Wahhab was guilty of publicly stoning a woman to death in a village, wherefrom he was expelled by the stunned, shocked villagers. Among other things, the Wahhabis also "sacked the treasury of the Prophet's Mosque in Medina and set fire to every book they could find, save the Quran. They banned music and flowers from the sacred cities and outlawed the smoking of tobacco and the drinking of coffee. Under the penalty of death, they forced the men to grow beards and the women to be veiled and secluded [even though the veiling and secluding of women had not been the case in the Prophet's time]." The Wahhabis – the most fanatic of Sunni Muslims – were also guilty of massacring two thousand Shiite worshipers when they were celebrating Muharram in Karbala.[414] Even in modern times, the Wahhabi-inspired fundamentalists were responsible for the slaughter of tens of thousands of Algerians. In Egypt, modern Muslim thinkers have been subjected to Wahhabi-instigated and often government-supported killing, torture and harassment, including banning of their works. Recent notable examples

390

are the stabbing and maiming of Nobel Laureate Naguib Mahfouz, the assassination of human rights defender Farag Foda, the arrest and incarceration of the Ibn Khaldun Center's head Saad Eddin Ibrahim, and of many of his colleagues, and the court ruling of apostasy on the Cairo University Professor Nasr Abu Zayd which called for divorcing of his Muslim wife, a ruling that led the couple to seek exile in a foreign country.[415] Al-Azhar University Professor Dr. Ahmad Mansour and his followers who follow only the Quran and reject the traditions also became victims of harassment, persecution and tortures at the hands of the Wahhabi followers in Egypt.[416]

In the tradition of Ibn Taymiyyah[417], the Wahhabis call for rigid adherence to *shariah* as literally found in the Quran and the Hadith. But they encourage only outward piety; they discourage and suppress Muslims' inner search to know and experience God and their quest and endeavor for spiritual development and real wisdom (*marefat*). Muslim Sufis and saints have been the targets of their persecution and torture. In their zeal to enforce puritanical Islam, they have flagrantly flouted the finer and more fundamental human values enshrined in the Quran and they committed horrendous crimes against humanity. They blocked human thinking urging blind imitation of past traditions (*taqlid*), discouraged studies of science, fine arts and culture and created hurdles in the way of human progress and modernization. In his recent book, Khaled Abou El Fadl provides a detailed critique of the narrowly defined, archaic, inherently incoherent, and essentially extreme, intolerant and militant and fundamentally perverted nature of this ideology's interpretation of Islamic teachings.[418] This Wahhabi version is still followed today in Saudi Arabia and is being preached as an official version of Islam, even though the Quran does not support their archaic extreme and militant positions. Following the Wahhabi dictates, the Saudi Government enforces rigid adherence to archaic *shariah* punishments, such as the mutilation of thieves. Note also that the Quran does not support monarchical or authoritarian rule, which is a major violation of the Quranic principles by the Saudi regime. The Saudi monarchs are also guilty of having ostentatious living styles in contravention of fundamental Islamic values. Over the years, with newfound oil wealth, the Saudi government has distributed lavish funds throughout the world to build mosques and *madrasahs*, and even to finance religious teachers and preachers to preach and spread their version of Islam in all Muslim countries as well as in developed countries like the United States and Europe. Osama bin Laden's Al-

391

Qaeda group and other terrorist organizations have also benefited from the Saudi dole-outs. An enquiry instituted by the National Security Council of the United States government in late 1998 revealed that "Over the past 25 years, the desert kingdom has been the single greatest force in spreading Islamic fundamentalism, while its huge, unregulated charities funneled hundreds of millions of dollars to jihad groups and al Qaeda cells around the world."[419] The story of the Saudi patronization of fanatic Wahhabism has been forcefully brought out in a recent book by contemporary Muslim writer and journalist Stephen Suleyman Schwartz, who is currently the founder Director of a Washington-based organization, the Center for Islamic Pluralism (CIP), which was founded in 2005 to disseminate and promote the message of moderate Islam and to confront the influence of militant Islam in the United States and abroad. Schwartz argues in his book that "Wahhabism, vigorously exported with the help of Saudi oil money, is what incites Palestinian suicide bombers, Osama bin Laden, and other Islamic terrorists throughout the world."[420] A recent Newsweek article suggests that "at least 50 percent of American mosques may receive some funding from foreign governments or institutions, mostly Saudi Arabia. [...] Whatever its source, fundamentalist Islamic ideology is readily available on the Internet as well as in U.S. mosques."[421]

Thus what some historians and scholars of comparative religions have termed as contemporary Islamic revival or resurgence in the world is in large part a Wahhabi phenomenon fueled by Saudi patronization. As a result of this resurgence, as John Esposito notes, "In recent years, tensions and clashes between Muslim and non-Muslim communities have [rather] increased"; the minority religious groups such as "the Copts in Egypt, Bahai and Jews in Iran, Chinese in Malaysia, and Christians in the Sudan, Pakistan, and Nigeria" have become targets of attacks by Muslims. "The creation of more Islamically oriented societies, especially the introduction of Islamic laws, has resulted in varying degrees of tension, conflict, violence, and killing in the name of religion. [...] The Bahai of Iran and the Ahmadiya of Pakistan, on the other hand, are regarded as apostates or heretics."[422]

What has become a more ominous trend currently is that some fundamentalists among Muslims are continuing to increasingly use the aggressive techniques of Wahhabism, and are systematically conducting terrorist attacks in various countries. Abdel Rahman al-Rashed, a Saudi journalist in London, appropriately comments: "It is a certain fact that not all Muslims are terrorists, but it is equally certain, and exceptionally painful, that almost all terrorists are Muslims. [...] We cannot clear our names unless we own up to the shameful fact that terrorism has become an Islamic enterprise; an almost exclusive monopoly, implemented by Muslim men and women."[423] Amir Taheri, an Iranian-born journalist, points out that "the Muslim world today is full of bigotry, fanaticism, hypocrisy and plain ignorance – all of which create a breeding ground for criminals like bin Laden."[424] Bassam Tibi, a Syrian Professor of International Relations at the University of Göttingen, Germany forcefully argues in his book written prior to the September 11 attacks that "Islamic fundamentalism [or, Islamism in contrast to Islam] ... poses a grave challenge to world politics, security, and stability."[425] Indeed, starting with the September 11, terrorist attacks perpetrated by Muslim extremists have proliferated in recent years, months and days. Recent episodes of post-September Eleven ghastly suicide, car or other bomb attacks in Indonesia, Saudi Arabia, Turkey, Morocco, Spain, the United Kingdom, Egypt, Jordan, Iraq, India, Pakistan and Bangladesh – and more frequently in more recent time in Iraq, Afghanistan and Pakistan – highlight trends of dangers worldwide that have to be effectively confronted to strive for enduring peace in the world.[426]

Muslims still dote on their glorious past. In the peak of their civilizational role, Europe was in the Dark Ages, and dependent on Muslims for their enlightenment. What is the reason for Muslims' decay and degeneration? Today all Muslims need to dispassionately ponder what has gone wrong with them. Bernard Lewis observed, "For many centuries the world of Islam was in the forefront of human civilization and achievement. [...] In most of the arts and sciences of civilization, medieval Europe was a pupil and in a sense a dependant of the Islamic world, relying on Arabic versions even for many otherwise unknown Greek versions."[427] Then he pondered about the decline and degeneration in Muslim civilization, and legitimately asked the question: What went wrong with them? Certainly this question is more pertinent today after the September Eleven and subsequent tragic events. Observing the stark differences between the West and the Middle East in economics, politics, reforms in various fields such as education and law, and modernization, Lewis appropriately thought that the underlying reasons were not so much the differences in the visible sources of power and prosperity – military, economic and political as the "more profound, yet somehow for long overlooked [...] crucial differences in approach, in attitude, and in perception between two neighboring civilizations" with regard to topics covering women, science and music (or arts), and slavery.[428] Attitudinal differences between Muslims living in Muslim countries and non-Muslims of the West, especially after the Renaissance and the Enlightenment, make considerable difference in explaining the backwardness of Muslims. Also, as emphasized by Hassan Hanafi, an Egyptian Professor of Philosophy at Cairo University, what Muslims lack most is "thinking". Their first duty should be thinking, "Because to say "There is no God but Allah" you have to think. You have to know what that means. It's an act of consciousness. It's thinking. This is our Cartesianism. I think therefore I am."[429] The "most urgent problem facing us, the Muslims, is neither political nor economical, but a crisis of our own thinking and learning process in relation to ourselves, Islam, Muslims and humanity at large," wrote Leith Kubba, an Iraqi-born Islamist thinker. "Without an objective, relative and rational Islamic discourse, our relationship to Islam will remain as that of a sentiment to the past or a mere slogan at present but it will not become an alternative towards a better future."[430]

The Direction for True Islamic Revival

Islam's real revival is yet to take place. And this can take place only when Muslims start to seriously think about their own predicament. They need to do a lot of their own soul searching. It is as early as fourteen centuries ago that the Quran laid so much emphasis on thinking: *"Do they not then think in their own minds?* ..." (30:8) ... *"Do they not then ponder the Quran? Or is it that there are locks upon their hearts (or minds)?"* (47:24). While the vast majority of Muslims have stopped thinking, some thinking has no doubt already begun among some modern educated Muslims, despite the deplorable fact that such thinking is brutally suppressed and repressed in many Muslim countries. Richard Bullet, writing in 1994, observed, "We are currently living through one of the greatest periods of intellectual and religious creativity in Islamic – and human – history."[431] This is even truer after the September 11 events: "[...] more Muslims than ever before are reexamining their faith in light of the political, economic, and intellectual challenges of contemporary life. They are reshaping Islam for the next millennium."[432]

In recent years and contemporary times, many Muslims have been engaging in *ijtihad* (rethinking and reinterpretation) of Islam, the doors of which were closed by the tenth century. Evidently, the absence of *ijtihad* for many centuries has had a lot to do with the backwardness of

Muslims in terms of civil norms – respect for human dignity, freedom, human rights, pluralism and tolerance, and reason and justice, as well as in scientific, technological and economic developments. Muqtedar Khan, a contemporary staunch exponent of *ijtihad,* aptly notes, "If Muslims wish to unite and revive the great spirit of Islam and its civilizing ethos, then we must learn to be more tolerant and more open minded in our approach to contending arguments. Strength, legitimacy and vitality come from openness, tolerance of difference and from the willingness to create rather than to burn bridges. [...] *The present rigid and inflexible approach to Islamic legal opinions of the past must be discarded and replaced with a more open and compassionate understanding of Islam.*"[433] "The practice of hero-worship of past scholars," Muqtedar Khan further notes, "determines which interpretation is accepted. I believe that this traditionalist approach is counter-productive. It merely recycles past opinions without actually making Islam relevant to specific times and circumstances."[434] He also observes:

> The biggest disservice that Muslims do to Islam and Muhammad is their uncritical approach to Islamic sources. [...] It is time Muslims revisited their sources with a critical perspective and discarded what is false, improbable and inconsistent with the values of mercy, tolerance and justice. [...] *By adhering to irrational, anachronistic — and often meaningless — traditions, they obscure the power and beauty of Islam and deprive themselves and the rest of the world from its message.*[435]

These observations beautifully capture the gist of one of the main points this book has tried to expound: we Muslims do need to rethink and reevaluate the so-called Prophetic traditions, which are "irrational and anachronistic – and often meaningless" and misleading. However, the proponents of *ijtihad* have come only half way to discard the Hadith. They need to come the full way to embrace the idea that the so-called Hadith, which contains anti-Quran, anti-Muhammad, anti-women, anti-reason, anti-progress, anti-peace and anti-tolerance ideas, cannot be claimed as authentic prophetic discourse, and hence must be discarded as part of Islam. Contrary to the view of some scholars, *ijtihad* is not the exclusive domain of the Muslim *ulama*. They have in fact proved to be ill-equipped and incapable of doing *ijtihad*. Because of the wrong and anachronistic teachings in traditional religious schools – *madrasahs,* their knowledge, and consequently their vision, has become limited and bigoted, and their minds closed. The leadership for *ijtihad* has mostly come from Muslim intellectuals who have received modern education, and it is they who should carry forward this *ijtihad*. As a Pakistan-born professor of an American university legitimately points out, Islam's interpretation should "no longer be left to the most regressive segment[s] of Muslim society. Muslims who believe that their faith is compatible with progressive humanist ideals must express themselves – not as apologists of Islam to the West but as proponents of new possibilities for Muslims."[436]

Madrasahs, where only traditional religious instruction is imparted and no modern subjects in science and arts are taught, instead of becoming real learning centers of Islam, have rather become breeding grounds of religious fanatics. Fourteen centuries ago, the Prophet Muhammad came with the Quran to civilize and purify mankind and make them wise (62:2; 36:2). It is ironic that *madrasahs* have failed to produce wise people, and their alumni, being deprived of education and training in modern subjects, have failed to become men of any real practical utility to themselves and to their families in particular, and to humankind in general. With fanatically oriented education, it should not be surprising to see that some of these alumni would turn into extremists to embrace militant techniques.[437]

One of the most important first steps to revive and revitalize Islam would, therefore, be to thoroughly remodel these *madrasahs* on the pattern of modern schools, which should include religious education as well; but such education should be purged of the teaching of traditional material (such as the Hadith) as sacred religious sources. Also, religion should be a special subject in general education at the university level.

At the same time, a vigorous campaign for genuine reform within Islam needs to be launched and continued – the kind of campaign that one scholar has termed "the Fourth *Jihad*' " – one that requires a relentless fight against meaningless dogmas the Muslim society is possessed with.[438]

As always, the clash of ideas will always be there. In the book, I have made reference to what I interpreted as the Quranic (or, basically any religious) idea of the clash of good elements (or ideas) with bad elements (or ideas) and that the good will ultimately prevail over the bad (8:7-8; 9:48; 20:68-70; 26:45-48; 21:18).[439] Today, as Neier has put it, the real

396

clash is between fundamentalism and modernity.[440] Fundamentalism does not belong to Islam. Religion and modernity are not necessarily antithetical. Islam properly understood does embrace the elements of modernity that define the western economic system – the ideas of liberty, competition, free enterprise, integrity and business ethics, etc.

This book has tried to explain what it means to be a true and devout Muslim in light of the Quran. The light of human guidance the Quran brought fourteen centuries ago is as luminous and bright today as when it came (5:15). To learn how to become a good Muslim, one does not need another book. The Quran provides right and complete guidance (2:2; 17:9; 10:57; 16:89). For long, Muslims have neglected the Quran, and followed spurious messages from the Hadith, and misguided teachings from sectarian teachers. It is time they return to their only Holy Book – the Quran – and understand and follow its message. The return to the Quran will mark Islam's true revival.[441] None should think that reciting the verses of this Holy Book without understanding the meaning is any virtue. This is utter misguidance to keep Muslims ignorant of the true message of Islam. Both Muslims and non-Muslims should read this Holy Book to get Islam's true message, which remains as true, civilizing and relevant to our time as before. Mere observance of some rituals does not make one a good Muslim. To become a good Muslim, one needs first to be a good human being, and a thoroughly moral, and ethical person. A fifteenth century Bengali poet-priest Chandidas wrote this strikingly modern word of wisdom: Above all is Man – respect for humanity or human values; nothing is above it (*Shobar upor manush shotto; tahar upore nai*). The Quran has laid a lot of emphasis on our becoming just and kind to fellow human beings. We need to serve humanity, just as God serves humanity. Unfortunately, the human aspect of Islam has been overshadowed by spurious religious teachings, which amply explain our deplorable plight.

APPENDIX

SELECT THEMES WITH QURANIC REFERENCES

Theme   **Page**

1. Economy, the; the economic system
2. God, the conception of
3. Heaven and Hell
    The characteristics of Heaven
    The characteristics of Hell
4. Human rights and freedoms
5. *Jihad*, war and peace
6. Justice, criminal justice
7. Marriage, divorce
    Marriage
    Divorce
8. Muhammad
9. Muslims, believers
10. Orphans, the treatment of
11. Prayer (*salat, dua*)
12. Predestination (predetermination), determinism
13. Quran, the
14. Resurrection (*akhirat, qiyamat*), hereafter
15. Righteousness
    General introduction
    Getting the *iman* (mindset) right
    Getting actions right
16. Satan, the devil
17. Slaves, the status of
18. Social reforms
19. Spending in God's way (*zakat* or *zakah, sadaqa*)
20. Tolerance
21. Women, the status of

SELECT THEMES WITH QURANIC REFERENCES

Economy, the; the economic system

The basic foundation of the Quran-supported economic system is establishing justice and fairness in all dealings with others, including economic dealings, avoiding exploitation and ensuring distributive equity:

- General call for establishing justice and fairness in all dealings and for not causing any harm or injury to others, any injustice, exploitation or cheating of any kind, or any corruption in the land, 16:90; 5:8; 4:58; 2:188; 17:35; 26: 181-183, 151-152; 7:56, 74; 13:25; 47:22-23

- Sanction for individual property rights - direction for not devouring, or encroaching upon, others' property, 2:188; 17:34

- Direction for not approaching orphans' (by implication, others') property except with good intentions, 17:34

- Call for returning trusted properties in due time, 17:34; 4:6, 58; 2:283

- Call for managing the property of those weak in understanding (by implication, property mismanaged by the owners), 4:5

- Legal requirements for credit transactions – to be written down with recording of witnesses or just a pledge in hand when on a journey and writing facilities not available, 2:282-283

- Hoarding strongly condemned, 3:180

- Direction for competition in all good work, which includes economic transactions by implication, 5:48

- Private property rights are subject to the condition that everything indirectly belongs to God, and thus by implication stark economic inequalities are not justified, 22:64

- God asks us not to be oblivious of the basic needs of the orphans, the poor, the needy, and the disadvantaged (e.g., wayfarers, homeless people and people heavily laden with debt), and wants us to be good and kind also to our parents, relatives, the neighbors - whether relatives or strangers, fellow-travelers and the wayfarers, and the slaves, 4:36; 6:151; 17:23-24; 2:83, 215; 4:36; 19:14, 32; 29:8; 31:14-15; 46:15; 71:28; 93:9-10 - urgings for spending in God's way (*sadaqa* or *zakat*), i.e., for a social security and social welfare system. Also see below under "Spending in God's way"

- Interest or usury charged to people who deserve humanitarian treatment forbidden, 2:275-276, 278-280; 3:130; 30:39

- Interest or usury (charged to poor people) not to be equated with profit on trading, 2:275

- Ground for banning interest or usury – causes exploitation of the poor and disadvantaged, whereas *zakat/sadaqa* benefits them; the latter is far better in terms of virtue, 30:39

- Call for remission of usury, and for write-off of loans in deserving cases, 2:278-280

- Direction for interest-free loans (*qarz-hasana*) on humanitarian grounds to deserving people/institutions, 2:245; 57:11, 18; 64:17; 5:12; 73:20
- But not charging interest (in lieu of profit) on commercial and investment project bank loans involves injustice to the depositors of money in banks, injustice that is not warranted, 4:135; 5:2, 8; 9:24; 26:151-152, 181-183; 7:56, 74; 13:25

God, the conception of
- One, unique and unrivalled, 2:163, 255; 3:18, 79-80; 112:1-4; 16:51; 17:42; 42:11; 4:48; 6: 22-24, 100-101; 31:13; 59:22; 72:3; etc.
- He neither begets nor is begotten; has no son or daughter; has no partner, 112:3; 2:116; 3:79-80; 4:171; 5:73; 6:22-24, 100-101, 163; 19:35; 7:190-198; 9:30-31; 10:66, 68; 17:111; 72:3; etc.
- He epitomizes the perfection of all good qualities – love, truth, justice, mercy (compassion, forgiveness), seeing and hearing capabilities, knowledge, creative power, power over everything, and so on:
  - Loving, 11:90; 85:14; 2:195, 222; 3:76, 134, 146, 148; 5:13, 93; 9:4, 7; 9:108; 5:42; 49:9; 60:8; 61:4
  - Truthful, represents Truth, 4:87, 122; 18:44; 24:25; 20:114; 22:6, 62; 23:116; etc.
  - Just, source of balance and justice, 39:75; 40:20; 55:7-9
  - Beneficent, Merciful, 1:1, 3; 2:37, 54, 160, 163, 173, 182, 192, 199, 218, 226; 5:39; 9:117-118; 13:30; 59:22; etc.
  - Mercy is His rule, 6:12
  - His Mercy is for those who are righteous, 7;156
  - All-Seeing, All-Hearing, 2:137, 224, 256; 3:34; 4:58; 2:96, 110; 4:58, 134; 8:72; 17:1,18; 42:11; 59:22; etc.
  - All-Knowing, Aware, Wise, 2:32, 77, 129, 209, 220, 224, 227, 228, 234, 240, 256, 271; 3:34; 58:7; 42:12; 3:153,180; 6:103; 59:22, 24; etc.
  - Creator, Fashioner, 2:21, 29, 117; 6:73,102; 130:16; 59;24; etc.
  - Powerful, Mighty, has power over everything, 2:20; 3:26, 189; 4:149; 6:18,61; 12:39; 38;65; 18:45; 43:42; 54:42; 64:1; etc.
  - Living, Self-Subsisting, Eternal, 2:225, 255; 3:2; 20:111; etc.
  - Indestructible, Eternal, 28:88; 55:26-27
  - Sustainer, 1:2; 2:255; 6:45,164; 27:64; etc.
  - He feeds, but is not fed, 6:14
  - Omni-present, 2:115; 7:7; 57:4
  - Guide, 5:16; 16:9; 27:63; 42:13
  - Oft-returning, Forgiving, 2:37, 54, 160, 173, 182, 187, 192, 199, 218, 225-226, 235; 5:39, 71; 9:117-118; 20:122; 40:3; etc.
  - Neither slumber nor sleep overtakes Him, 2:255
  - Source of all good, 3:26

- He does not create or act irrationally or whimsically – there is no flaw in His system of creation, 67:3-4

- He is the creator of nature, and His Laws are the Laws of Nature, 77:20-23; 67:3-4; 20:50; 87:2-5; 7;54; 54:49; 15:21-23; 21:22; 27:60-61, 64; 36:33-40

- He is always right, on the straight path (sirat al mustaqim), 11:56

- Most worthy of praise and adoration by us, 1:2; 2:267; 4:131, 6:1, 45; 10:10; 11:73; 14:1,8, 39; 15:98; 16:75; 64:1; etc.

- He responds to our prayer; helps us if we seek His help; relieves our suffering; forgives our sins; and guides us to the straight path, 2:45, 107, 153, 186; 3:160; 40:60; 27:62; 11:61; 37:75; 17:25; 42:13, 26; 44; 66:8

- He forgives only those who do not persist in their sins, 3:135; 4:17-18; 9:80; 16:119; 66:8

- His mercy is only for those who believe and are righteous, 6:155; 7:156-157; 42:26; etc.

- God helps those who help themselves; He does not change the condition of a people unless they change it themselves or change their own selves, 13:11; 8:53

- He responds to the call of those who believe and are righteous, 42:26

- He guides only those who turn to Him truly repentant, and are just, righteous, 2:213; 3:135; 13:27; 25:70-71; 28:56; 42:13

- He increases in guidance those who walk aright, 19:76

- He does not guide unbelieving, unjust, wrongdoing people, 2:26, 258, 264; 3:86; 5:67, 108; 6:144; 9:19, 37, 80, 109; 12:52; 16:37, 107; 28:50; 39:3; 40:28; etc.

- He turns man whichever way he wants to go or turn, 4:115

- He could have made us all rich, guided us all aright, or made us one nation if He willed, 36:47; 6:149; 10:99; 5:48

- But He does not will like this; He does not directly determine our affairs; He has given us free will to decide between good and evil, 13:11; 18:29; 76:3

- Man has only that for which he makes effort; God does not predetermine our fate but rewards and punishes us according to our work alone, 20:15; 53:39; 2:148, 286; 28:84; 42:30; 6:132; 46:19; 17:19; 5:35

- God does not do (least) harm or injustice to men; it is men who do it to themselves, 3:117; 4:40; 7:23, 160; 10:44; 27:44; 28:16; 65:1; etc.

For more ideas on the attributes and qualities that define God, see Annex to Chapter 3.

Heaven and Hell

The characteristics of Heaven:

- A place or state of bliss and rejoicing for the dweller, 22:59; 52:17-18
- A state of no fear, no grief, 43:68; 46:13; 35:34
- A place or state of no toil, no fatigue, 35:35

401

- A place or state where the dweller is well protected from the torment of Hell-fire, 52:18, 27
- A state where the dweller gets whatever he/she wants, 25:16; 42:22
- A place or state where there is no death after first death, 37:58-60; 44:56
- A place where there is no boredom or weariness, 35:35
- An abode of peace and security, 6:127; 15:46; 89:29-30
- A garden with an abundance of fruits, 56:32
- The likes of fruit enjoyed before, i.e., in the earth, are enjoyed in Heaven, 2:25
- A place where there is no futile conversation and no lying, 78:35
- A place where there is purity and no foul play, 56:25
- A place where there is peace and salutations of peace, 19:62; 56:26
- A place where there is no feeling of rancor, but only brotherhood, 7:43; 15:47
- A place of grace and beauty, 55:70
- A place of pure companionship and love, 56:36-37
- A place where it is neither too cold nor too hot, 76:13
- A place where the dwellers pray for perfection of their light, 66:8
- A state wherefrom no one wants to go backward, 18:108
- God's righteous servants inherit and rule the world, 21:105; 24:55; 7:128-129; 10:14
- If we seek this world alone, we lose the Hereafter, 20:131; 33:28
- Those who seek the good of both worlds can expect to get both, 2:200-202
- The righteous get good in this world as well as in the Hereafter, 10:64; 16:30, 97
- We, of course, need to pay greater attention to the seeking of the Hereafter or the future, 17:18-21
- It is through our good efforts/deeds that we can transform this earth into a Garden, which the righteous inherit and live in, 39:73-74
- It is a changed earth, 14:48
- It is as wide as the heavens and the earth, 3:133
- The earth is continually purified by replacement of bad people with good ones, 10:13-14; 21:105; 47:38
- Truth will triumph, falsehood will vanish, 8:7-8; 21:18
- The party of God will be victorious, 5:56

The characteristics of Hell:
- Hell is a fire – punishment - upon hearts, 104:6-9
- A fire where the dweller neither lives nor dies, 20:74; 87:12-13
- It is fire for disbelievers/rejecters of truth/wrongdoers; 2:24; 3:131; 4:56; 6:27; 25:11; 40:71-72; etc.
- Disgrace and fear will grip them, 42:45
- It is a prison for the disbelievers, 17:8

- A state or place where the guilty will remember and realize their guilt and the truth of what God promised them, 79:34-36; 6:130; 7:44; 40:11; 69:25-29
- A state where the sufferer will regret his wrongdoing and want to ransom everything in the world in exchange for his suffering, 10:54
- The dwellers will be denied all comfort - any good food or drinks, 44:43-48; 69:36-37; 10:4; 38:57; 47:15; 56:41-44, 52-56, 92-94
- Sighing and wailing will be their lot, 11:106
- A state where asking for lightening of the suffering will not be of any avail, 35:36-37; 40:49-50; 43:75
- Frustration will be the dwellers' lot, 43:75
- The dwellers will want their end or death will knock them, but they will not die, 43:77; 14:17; 69:27
- A state or place wherefrom the dweller would want to get out, 35:37; 40:11; 42:44; 23:107
- Worldly wealth and authority or power and honor will be of no avail to the dweller of Hell, 69:28-29; 44:49; 69:28-29
- None can save, or should plead for, one who is already in Hell or destined for Hell, 39:19; 9:80, 113-114; 11:45-46
- The dwellers will abide in Hell as long as the heavens and the earth endure, or as long as God wishes, 11:107
- The ears, eyes, and skin of the sinners will bear witness against them, 41:20-23

Human rights and freedoms
- The right to life - each life is precious, 4:29-30, 92-93; 35:32; 17:31, 33; 6:151
- No human injury or torture is warranted – torture and persecution is even worse than slaughter, 2:190-193, 217
- The right to human dignity, 17:70; 4:19
- The right to freedom of religion - no compulsion in religion, 2:62, 256; 5:69; 10:99; 109:6; 50:45; 88:21-22; 11:28; 6:108; etc.
- The right to property, 2:188; 4:2, 5-6, 10, 29; 17:34; 26:183
- The right to property is subject to the considerations that everything after all belongs to God (i.e., for godly purpose or for all mankind's benefit) and that He is our sustainer and giver of livelihood, which underscores the need for caring for the poor and disadvantaged groups in society and for other God's causes, 2:57, 172, 212, 284; 3:27, 37, 109, 129; 4:126, 130-132, 170-171; 5:114; 6:12, 151; 7:160; 8:26; 9:50; 10:31, 66, 68, 93; 11:88; 14:2; 16:52, 72, 75; 17:31, 70; 20:6, 81, 132; 21:19; 22:64; 23:84-85; 24:32, 38, 64; 53:48; 93:6, 8; etc.
- All humans are equal before God; no distinction/discrimination among them is warranted except on grounds of righteousness or piety, 3:195; 4:124; 16:97; 33:35; 49:11-13; 2:197; 9:55, 69; 10:58, 88-89; 28:76-81; 30:39; 34:3-4, 37; 43:32-35; 111:2; etc.
- Safeguarding human rights and freedoms require tolerance on the part of each person or community toward every other person or community; see references under tolerance below.

403

- Safeguarding such rights and freedoms also requires establishing the rule of law and justice in society, see references above under criminal justice, and those below under jihad, war and peace.

Jihad, war and peace

- Jihad is struggle or striving for God's cause – an all–out effort with wealth and lives to make God's cause succeed, 4:95; 9:24, 41; 22:78; 29:69; 61:11
- The purpose of jihad: to establish a just, godly order, 22:41
- The ultimate purpose of jihad (striving or fighting for good) on one's part is to prepare him/her to go to Heaven, 3:142; 4:95; 9:16, 24, 86; 47:31
- Jihad is more important than blood relationship and material and business interests, 9:24
- When one can go for jihad (war) against whom, 2:190-191; 9:12-13; 22:39-40; 25:52; 60:1; 66:9
- Admonition for properly identifying the enemies - for not branding one who offers salutation of peace as an enemy without proper investigation, 4:96
- Fighting is required to end injustice, oppression and corruption on earth, 2:216-217, 251; 22:39-41
- Fighting is prescribed only against aggressing people; no aggressive fighting is permitted, 2:190
- Fighting until there is no persecution, 2:193
- Admonition for attacking the enemies in the like manner as the others attack, 2:194; 22:60
- Admonition for accepting peace when the enemies desist fighting and offer peace, 2:192-193; 4:90; 8:39, 61-62; 9:5; 49:9-10
- Admonition for ceasefire and peace when the enemies propose peace, even though they may deceive thereby, 8:61-62
- Treaties, if made with the enemy, need to be honored, 5:1; 16:91-92; 8:55-56
- Urging for honoring agreements with other communities as long as they keep up those agreements; permission for fighting on breach of an agreement by the other party, 9:7, 12-13
- How to treat the prisoners of war –set them free as an act of grace or against ransom after overcoming enemies, 47:4
- Urging for not stirring mischief in the land after it has been set aright (after order and peace has been established), 7:56, 85
- However, an agreement with a party may be broken on fears of treachery on the part of the other party, 8:58
- Urging for arbitration - its rejection by one party to be resolved by force, 49:9-10
- Encouragement for condoning and forgiving the enemies where possible and appropriate, 5:45; 7:198-199; 42:40, 43; 45:14, 73:10
- Urging for cooperative venture for godly work with others, other communities, 3:64; 4:114; 5:2
- Charity, kindness and peace among communities are God-loved virtues, 4:114

Justice, criminal justice

- General call for establishing justice and for not doing any wrong to others, 16:90; 4:58, 135; 5:8, 2; 2:188; 9:24; 26:151-152, 181-183; 7:56, 74; 13:25; 17:35; 26: 181-183, 151-152; 27:48-49; 47:22-23

- God is Just; He does no injustice to man; he does it to himself, 39:75; 2:54, 57, 231; 3:117; 7:23, 160, 177; 4:40; 27:44; 28:16; 46:19; 65:1

- God enjoins upon us justice, fairness and kindness to all involved, 16:90, 76; 5:8; 42:41-42; 2:188; 17:34; 49:9; 4,127, 135; 58; 55:9; 60:8; 65:2

- God exhorts us to uphold the cause of justice, if necessary by testifying against ourselves, parents and relatives, and not to let the hatred (or enmity or injustice) of others make us stray from justice, 4:135; 5:8

- God exhorts us to give the right measure, and not to deceive or exploit others, 26:181-183

- Deceiving others is really deceiving one's own self, 2:9; 63:1-2

- God cautions us against wrongfully craving others' property, 2:188; 17:34-35; 4:2; 26:181-183

- Punishment to be proportionate to the wrong done – life for life, the eye for the eye, the nose for the nose, the ear for the ear, the tooth for the tooth, and like retaliation for wounds, but if endured, it is better for the aggrieved, 5:45; 16:126; 42:40

- Exemplary corporal punishment for stealing, 5:38

- Exemption from such dire punishment if the thief repents and mends his or her conduct, 5:39

- Punishment for adultery – flogging where no leniency is warranted, 24:2

- But forgiveness, if the guilty repents and makes amends, 4:16

- Authority for capital punishment given to successors of the kin deliberately killed without a just cause (by implication such authority is given to the judicial system), 2:178-179; 17:33

- But alternatively, a remission in such punishment, i.e., a lighter punishment, by the aggrieved party, or by the judicial system, with proper compensation from the killer(s) according to usage, 2:178

- Provision for still lighter punishments for accidental killings, 4:92

- Exemplary harsh punishments for war crimes, 5:32-33

- Exemption from such punishments if they repent and desist from such crimes before they are caught, 5:34

- Slaves or servants or those with less intelligence or sense are to be treated generously and punished less harshly, 4:25

- Punishments of crimes to the extent they become deterrent to such further crimes – no excesses warranted in the name of religion, 4:171; 5:77

- God first sends lighter punishments; should these prove insufficient, He sends heavier punishments afterwards, 32:21

Marriage, divorce

Marriage

- Rationale for marriage – source of mutual comfort, help and progress, 30:21; 2:187; 4:19; 7:189; 9:71; 16:72; 25:54
- Husband and wife garment for each other, 2:187
- Marriage provides a means of acquiring offspring, 16:72
- Marriage strengthens human relationships through acquiring new relatives, 25:54
- Mutual love, understanding and mercy should characterize marital relationship, 30:21; 4:19
- Husband urged to live with wife with kindness, 4:29
- Husband urged to go to wife with the best of intentions doing something good beforehand, 2:223
- Family is the sound basis for procreation of children, and the bedrock of society and civilization, 16:72
- Marriage of unmarried people should in general be encouraged, 24:32
- Unmarried people urged to remain chaste until marriage, and postpone marriage until one has financial solvency, 24:33
- Forced taking of women against their will forbidden, 4:19
- May marry slave girls, if cannot afford to marry free girls, 4:25
- Slave girls should not be, for that matter none should be, forced into marriage or prostitution, 24:33
- Monasticism/celibacy is not a preferred or approved option unless observed properly only to seek God's pleasure, 57:27
- People one cannot marry, 4:22-24
- One can marry people other than those listed as not lawful, 4:22-24
- Marriage with women whom father has married (i.e., marriage of widows with their stepsons) is forbidden, 4:22
- Polygamy permitted to deal with orphaned girls ((by implication, women in distress), but if justice cannot be done to multiple wives, marrying just one is advised, 4:3, 129
- Husband and wife urged to live within the bounds of chastity, not seeking lewdness, 4:24; 5:5
- Careful selection of marriage partners is required – good believing men should marry good believing women, 5:5; 24:3, 26; 2:221
- For marriage, a good/believing slave/maid is better than a bad/unbelieving woman, 2:221
- Husband should in general be responsible for financially supporting wife, 4:34
- Husband should pay the dower, 5:5; 4:4; 19:21; 2:236-237; 33:50
- Wife can willingly waive some dowry if she chooses, 4:4, 24
- No room for homosexual or premarital and extra-marital sexual relationship, 7:80-84; 17:32; 4:15-16; 24:2-4
- No room for artificial birth control, 6:151; 2:223; 4:27

406

Divorce

- Mere uttering of the expression 'I divorce you' without intending or meaning it by heart, i.e., without sticking to it, is no action of divorce, 2:225
- The fair gradual way to divorce wives: husband to first wait four months if wishes to divorce his wife, and divorced wife to wait three (monthly) courses or if pregnant till child's birth; husband advised to take back wife if pregnant, 2:226-232
- The waiting period (iddat) for divorced wives, 2:228; 65:4
- Husband advised not to drive wife away from home during the waiting period unless she commits open indecency, 65:1
- Admonition to husband to take her wife back or part with her after the waiting period, 65:2
- Divorcing to be pronounced twice; after that husband is free to retain her or to release her, but not to retain her to her hurt, 2:229, 231
- If divorced wife voluntarily marries another person after the waiting period, she can go back to her former husband only after the second husband divorces her, 2:230
- No obstacle to be created on the way of a divorced wife going back to her husband if both want it – no room for the so-called hilla system, i.e., forcing a divorced wife to marry another person and allowing her to go back to former husband after the second husband divorces her, 2:232
- Divorcing a wife without consummating is allowed, 2:236
- Divorced wives are to be treated in a just and humane manner, 2:231; 4:19-21; 65:6; 2:233
- Feeding of the infant after divorce of the wife is urged, 2:233
- Women have rights over husbands similar to those of husbands over wives – by implication, women have rights to divorce their husbands, 2:228
- Husbands need to treat wives with dignity and honor, 4:19
- Wives need to be equally responsive and decent to their husbands, 4:34; 66:5
- Provision for arbitration of disputes between husband and wife, 4:35

Muhammad

- A man like us, who ate and went to the marketplace, 17:94-95; 18:110; 25:7; 41:6
- A man with a humble beginning - was an orphan and a needy person, and without guidance, 93:6-8
- Received shelter and became free of want, and received guidance, 93:6-8
- Received God's mercy, 9:117; 28:86; 48:2; 68:2; 93:3-8; 94:1-6; 108:1
- Not forsaken by God, nor was God displeased with him, 93:3
- His heart was broadened/opened up, and his burden lifted, 94:1-3
- Received abundance of good, 108:1
- Taught by the Lord of Mighty Power, 53:5

- Received divine revelation, 42:52-53, 3, 7; 53:1-18; 36:2-6; 69:38-48; 14:1; 3:7; 8:41; 10:2; 12:3; 13:30; 15:87; 16:44, 64, 89, 102; 25:1; 27:6; 29:47-49; 34:50; 41:6; 47:2; 57:9

- Received the Quran, 5:48; 15:87; 27:6; 28:85-86; 76:23

- Became a messenger (rasul) of God, 33:40; 34:28; 36:3; 48:28-29; 49:7; 63:1; 5:15, 19

- A messenger to all mankind, 34:28

- A warner to mankind, 5:19; 7:184, 188; 11:2; 13:7; 15:84; 17:105; 19:97; 21:45; 22:49; 25:56; 27:92; 28:46; 29:50; 32:3; 33:45; 34:28, 46; 35:23-24; 36:6; 46:9; etc.

- A bearer/bringer of good news and a warner to mankind, 2:119, 213; 5:19; 7:188; 11:2; 17:105; 18:2, 56; 19:97; 22:34, 37; 25:56; 33:45, 47; 34:28; 35:24; 36:11; 48:8; etc

- The seal/last of prophets (nabis who came with divine message up to his time), 33:40

- The news of a future messenger with name of Ahmad (praised) coming after him was foretold by Jesus, 61:6

- Foretold in the earlier divine books the Torah and the Gospel, and to earlier prophets, 7:157; 3:81

- Did not himself author the Quran, 29:48

- The Quran was divinely inspired to him, 2:97, 185; 3:7; 12:3; 14:1; 15:87; 16:44, 64, 89, 102; 25:1; 26:192-195; 27:6; 29:47-49; 42:52-53; 53:1-18; 36:2-6; 69:38-48; etc.

- Did not expect the Quran to be revealed to him, but it was God's mercy, 28:86

- Did not say anything of religion out of his own desire, 53:3

- His saying was divine revelation contained in the Quran, 69:38-48

- Himself was urged by God not to doubt the divine revelations to him, 2:147; 3:60; 10:94-95

- Urged by God not to make haste with the revelation but to follow the Quran exactly as it was revealed, and not try to explain it; the explanation was the responsibility of God Himself, 75:16-19

- Did not fabricate the divine message, 10:37-39; 52:33; 69:41-47

- Brings no new message - Nothing was said to him except what was said before to earlier prophets; his message is confirmation of all earlier divine messages, 41:43; 5:48; 10:37; 42:13; 22:78; 46:9

- Confirms earlier messengers, 37:37

- His sole duty was to deliver the Quran to mankind, 5:67, 92, 99; 13:40; etc.

- Faithfully delivered God's message - did not fabricate it, 10:15, 37-38; 18:27; 52:33; 69:40-47

- Specifically exhorted by God to judge between people by the revealed Book, and not follow the personal desires or opinions of any people, 4:105; 5:48-49; 6:114

- Specifically urged by God to advise people with the Quran alone, 6:51, 70; 7:2; 17:45-46; 27:92; 28:87; 50:45

- Followed naught save what was revealed to him, 6:50; 46:9
- God advised him and us to follow what was revealed to him, i.e., the Quran, 6:155; 45:6
- Was not mad or possessed, nor was he a poet or a soothsayer, 7:184; 21:5; 23:70; 34:46; 36:69; 37:36-37; 52:29-30; 68:2; 69:41-42; 81:22
- A man with great moral character, 68:4-6
- A religious and spiritual preacher, teacher, and guide, 62:2; 33:45-46
- Gentle-natured, not hard-hearted, 3:159
- An ideal in righteous conduct and piety, 36:3-4; 43:43; 73:20
- Did not crave, or ask for, any remuneration for his preaching and teaching, 12:104; 25:57; 34:47; 38:86; 42:23; 52:40; 68:46
- How he prayed, 26:218-219; 52:48-49; 73:2-8, 20
- His personal beliefs, 2:285; 42:15
- His spiritual accomplishments - miraj, 17:1; 53:5-18
- A social reformer who brought social egalitarianism 2:188; 17:34; 3:130; 2:278-280; 26:181-183; 90:12-18; 3:180; 2:177; 3:92; 92:17-21; 9:50
- A distinguished judge 4:65, 105; 24:51; 42:15
- A military leader and organizer 3:121-128, 153; 8:64-71; 33:16-20
- Assured of upcoming victory, 61:13; 110:1
- Came out victorious, 48:1-3, 18, 24, 27; 110:1
- Is on the right or straight path, 36:3-4; 43:43; 53:2
- Shows the right path – invites mankind to God's path/grace, 42:52-53; 12:108; 33:46; 34:46
- Always in God's sight, 52:48
- Urged not to grieve for what others did, 15:88; 16:127; 18:6; 26:3; 27:70; 31:23; 35:8; 36:76
- Assured of reward from God, 68:3; 93:4-5
- A man of exalted honor, 94:4
- A light-giving lamp for believers, 33:46
- A mercy of the universe, 9:61; 21;107; 28:46
- A man with great humanity and concern for fellow beings, 9:128; 15:88; 33:6; 3:159, 47:19
- Urged by God to bless believers, 3:159, 47:19
- Closer to believers than they are to themselves; has a greater claim on believers than they have on their own selves, 33:6
- Admonished for some lapses on his part, which he rectified, 80:1-10; 9:43; 33:37; 66:1
- An excellent example for mankind to follow, 33:21; 68:4-6
- Not responsible for what others do or what happens to others - not put in charge of them, 6:66, 107; 10:108; 17:54; 26:216; 39:41; 42:6; 88:21-22

- God and angels bless and support him; we should also bless and support him, 33:56; 48:9-10
- Assured by God of his return to his destination, 28:85
- Was exhorted not to follow those who have no knowledge, and not to follow the majority who follow nothing but conjecture and do nothing but lie, 45:18; 6:116

Muslims, believers
- Muslims are those who believe (in one God, His prophets and revelations), and are righteous, 2:112; 128, 136, 177, 277; 3:16-17, 84, 104, 110; 4:57-59, 162; 6:152-153; 9:71; 13:20-22; 14:31; 22:34, 77-78; 23:1-6, 8-9, 57-61; 10:9; 16:97, 128; 18:30, 107; 19:76, 96; 20:75-76; 21:94; 24:55-56; 25:63-74; 27:89; 28:53-55; 31:8; 33:35; 34:37; 41:8; 42:22-23, 26, 36-39; etc.
- Believers or Muslims can be by any other name – Jews, Christians, Sabians, etc., provided they believe in God, the Last Day, and are righteous, 2:62; 5:69
- Abraham was not a Jew or a Christian, but a Muslim, and this name was given by Abraham, 3:67; 22:78
- Muslims believe in God, His angels and His books and His prophets, 2:285; 4:136
- They do not associate any partner with God, 23:59; etc.
- They believe in, and recognize, divine signs or revelations, 2:4, 136; 4:162; 5:83; 8:2; 23:58; 28:53; 32:15; etc.
- They are not blind and deaf to good or divine advice, 25:73
- They keep up prayer, 2:3, 277; 6:92; 8:3; 9:71; 14:31; 23:9; 42:38; etc.
- They remember and glorify God, and fast, 9:112; 33:35, 41-42; etc.
- They spend the night prostrating and standing before God, and praying, 25:64-65
- They spend in God's way out of what they earn, 2:3, 277; 8:3; 9:71; 14:31; 23:4, 60; 28:54; 32:16; 33:35; 42:38; 57:7; etc.
- They provide shelter and help to others in need, 8:74
- When they spend, they are neither too extravagant nor too stingy, 25:67
- They are morally upright – they guard their modesty/chastity, 23:5; 33:35; 42:37
- They repel evil with what is good, 28:54
- They keep away from what is vain, 23:3; 25:72; 28:55
- They are truthful and just, speak straight to the point, and are always with the truthful, and for justice even if it goes against themselves, parents and near relatives, 2:26; 4:58, 135; 9:119; 25:72; 33:35, 70;
- They are staunch in justice, 4:58, 135
- They keep their word, 2:177; 3:17; 13:20; 16:91; 23:8; 33:23; etc.
- They restore things entrusted with them to owners, 4:58
- They are patient, and enjoin on one another truth and patience, 25:75; 33:35; 103:3
- They are humble, 11:23; 23:2; 25:63; 33:35
- They walk in the land with humility, and when the ignorant address them they say "Peace", 25:63

- They turn away from the ignorant, or from their idle talks, saying "Peace", 28:55; 43:89
- They seek permission of the Prophet (superiors) to leave when they are with him (them), 24:62
- They are grateful, 4;147; 24:62
- They keep limits – do not transgress limits of decency and decorum – and they give good news to other believers, 9:112
- They are staunch in their love for God, 2:165
- They defend themselves when they are wronged, 26:227; 42:39
- They struggle with life and wealth - do jihad - in the way of God, 2:218; 4:95; 8:74-75; 9:20, 88, 111; 49:15; 61:11; etc.
- They are urged to settle disputes among them and make peace, 49:9-10
- However, they are urged to fight one who acts wrongfully until he comes back to senses, 49:9
- They do not create mischief in the land after peace and order has been restored, 7:56
- They consult among themselves, 42:38
- They shun sins and indecencies, and forgive when angry, 42:37
- They are united at heart with one another and brothers to one another, 8:63; 49:10
- They are protectors of one another, 8:72; 9:71
- They do not disrespect one another – God advises them not to laugh at or ridicule one another, not to find fault with own people, and not to suspect and backbite others of own people, 49:11-12
- They seek comfort from their wives and children, 25:74
- They seek to be patterns or models for others, 25:74
- They enjoin good and forbid evil, 9:71, 112
- They say or advise others to do what they themselves do - God advises believers to say what they do, 61:2
- They are established as inheritors/rulers of the earth, 21:105; 24:55
- They, when established in the land, establish a godly and just (moral and ethical) order in society, 22:41; 2:177
- They are the most civilized people on the earth, 98:7
- Might and honor belongs to them, 63:8
- They are admonished to invite other communities to join cooperative moral ventures (to serve the cause of one God), 3:64

Orphans, the treatment of
- The Prophet himself was an orphan, and was especially advised not to oppress the orphan and chide the needy, 93:6-10
- Call for looking after the general welfare of orphans, 2:83, 177, 215, 220; 4:8, 36, 127; 89:17; 93:9; 107:2

411

- Mankind cautioned about their treatment with female orphans whom they do not give what is due but want to marry, and about helpless children, and they are urged to treat orphans equitably, 4:127
- Call for feeding orphans and making provisions for them from welfare funds, 90:14-15; 8:41; 59:7
- The curse of God is on those worshipers who are heedless of their worship, and treat orphans harshly, and neglect feeding the indigent, and do not encourage/urge others to feed them, 107:2-7
- Such people as mistreat orphans and do not feed the poor and encourage/urge others to feed them are really those who deny the Day of Judgment, 107:1-3
- The path of ascent is feeding orphaned relatives in times of hunger, and the needy in distress, and freeing slaves, 90:12-16
- Call for no fiddling with orphans' property, 2:220; 4:2, 6, 10, 127; 6:152; 17:34
- Admonition for not approaching the property of orphans till they attain maturity except with good intentions, 17:34
- Admonition for testing orphans for their puberty and maturity of understanding, and for returning their property to them if found attaining such maturity, and for not extravagantly and hastily consuming their property lest they should grow up, 4:6
- Admonition for restoring the property of orphans to them, and not to replace good with bad while handing over their property, and not to devour their property, 4:2
- Call for not returning the property of orphans to them if they are weak in understanding, but for managing their property properly, and if not so well-to-do, for taking some remuneration from such property for such management, 4:5-6
- Those who grab/devour orphans' property are swallowing fire, 4:10
- Call for marrying orphans if one fears cannot do justice to them in regard to their property, 4:3, 127
- Admonition for giving a portion of the inheritance of a deceased relative to poor relatives, orphans and the needy at the time of distribution of such inheritance, 4:8

Prayer (*salat, dua*)
- Prayer (salat/dua) is to be addressed only to (one) God, 13:14
- Prayer is for remembrance and glorification of God, 20:12-14; 7:205; 29:45; 13:28; 73:7-8; 76:25-26; 33:41-43; 52:48-49; 15:97-98; 7:180; 3:26-27
- We are urged to remember and glorify God earnestly, 33:41-42
- We are urged to remember God with utmost devotion, 2:200; 7:56
- We are urged to call upon God by any of His beautiful names or attributes, 7:180; 17:110
- Remembrance (dhikr) of God is the best of prayer, 29:45
- In the remembrance of God do hearts find rest and satisfaction, 13:28
- God and angels bless those who remember and glorify Him much, 33:41-43
- Prayer is for seeking divine help with perseverance, 2:45-46, 107, 153, 286; 1:5-7; 3:160; 72:22; 17:19; 3:147

- Prayer is for self-purification and spiritual development, 87:14-15; 91:9-10; 29:45; 5:35, 48; 66:8; 17:19
- Prayer is for expressing gratitude to God, 14:7; 39:7
- Prayer to be performed with humility, reverence and whole-hearted devotion, 7:29, 55-56, 205; 73:8; 2:45-46, 200; 6:162; 50:33
- God's mercy is for those who pray with due reverence and hope, 7:55-56
- The worshiper needs to be earnest and understand what he utters in prayer, 4:142-143; 4:43
- Prayer needs to be coupled with righteous and consistent deeds, 42:26; 29:45; 41:30; 5:35, 48; 107:2-7
- God's mercy is for those who do good (to others), guard against evil (are righteous), spend on the poor, and believe in God's revelations, 7:56, 156
- God's curse is on those worshipers who are heedless of their prayer, mistreat orphans and do not feed or help the poor and urge others to do so, 107:2-7
- Advice for ablution (wudu), bath or tayammum before performing prayer, 5:6; 4:43
- Advice for wearing decent dress for prayer, 7:31
- Advice for facing the direction of the Kabah at Mecca while performing prayer, 2:144
- Prayer timings – three timings: (1) morning; (2) afternoon from the decline of the sun to dark of the night, which includes dusk or early evening; and (3) some watches of the night, 11:114; 17:78; 73:1-8, 20; 20): 130; 30:17-18; 33:41-43; 52:48-49
- Forms of prayer – standing, bowing, and prostrating; remembrance of God that is the best of prayer can be done standing, sitting and reclining, 22:77; 39:9; 7:206; 96:19; 3:191; 4:103
- No particular form is sacrosanct by itself, 2:177, 225, 284, 62; 22:37, 67; 17:25
- God responds to sincere and devoted prayer, 40:60; 42:26; 2:186; 13:14; 27:62
- God wants to purify His servants and perfect His grace for them, 5:6
- God is closer to His devotee than his heart and life vein, 8:24; 50:16

Predestination (predetermination), determinism
- Predestination or fatalism is ruled out - God does not directly determine our affairs; man is given free will and power to choose between good and evil or to change his path or fate, 13:11; 18:29; 76:3; 91:7-10
- God helps those who help themselves; He does not change man's condition until he himself changes it or until he changes himself, 13:11; 8:53
- He turns man whichever way he wants to go or turn, 4:115
- God does not predetermine our fate - It is only work that determines one's fate; man gets only that which he deserves or for which he makes effort; he is rewarded or punished according to what he does, 2: 286; 20:15; 28:84; 53:31, 39; 42:30; 6:132; 46:19; 17:19; 5:35; etc.
- Reward/rank is proportionate to one's level of effort, 6:132; 46:19
- Any misfortune that people may experience is due to their own deeds, 42:30

413

- God does no injustice to man; he does it to himself, 2:54, 57, 231; 3:117; 7:23, 160, 177; 4:40; 27:44; 28:16; 46:19; 65:1
- God does not act irrationally or whimsically; there is perfect logic and rationality – no flaw - in God's creation or action, 67:3-4
- God could have made us all rich, guided us all aright, or made us one nation if He willed – that means that God does not will or determine (or predetermine) in the popular sense, 36:47; 6:149; 10:99; 5:48
- However, there are certain givens in man's life resulting from a variety of factors according to the natural laws of causation – natural, biological, hereditary, environmental or other causes, which can be called God-assigned or predetermined measure, proportion, or destiny, 25:2; 24:14; 20:129; 8:68; 3:178-179
- Part of what is given or predetermined for us is due to our own actions beforehand, 69:24, 33-37; 30:41; 3:11, 178, 182

Quran, the
- Divinely inspired, 2:97, 185; 15:87; 16:102; 20:114; 26:192-195; 29:47-49; 36:2-6; 42:52-53; 53:1-18; 69:38-48; etc.
- Revealed to Muhammad's heart through Gabriel, 2:97
- First revealed on a blessed night in the month of Ramadan, 44:3; 2:185
- Revealed in portions. 17:106
- Revealed in Arabic to enable the Arabs, the inhabitants of Mecca and adjoining areas, to grasp the Message, 42:7; 12:2; 20:113; 39:28; 41:3, 44; 43:3; 46:12
- Guidance for mankind, 2:2, 159, 185; 3:138; 10:57; 11:17; 12:111; 14:1; 16:64, 89, 102; 17:9, 105; 18:2; 27:2, 76-77; 31:3; 34:6, 28; 38:87; 41:44; 42:52-53; 45:20; 46:30; 68:52; 72:2; 81:27
- Guides to the most right or straightest path, 17:9; 6:126
- A Light for mankind, 42:52
- Guidance for Jinn, 46:29-32; 72:1-2
- A Message for the heart, 50:37
- A Universal Message for all mankind to prevail over all other religions, 9:33; 38:87; 48:28; 61:9; 68:52; 81:27-28
- True, not forged, 2:2; 11:17; 12:111; 16:102; 17:105; 32:3; 34:6; 35:31; 39:2, 41; 42:17; 46:30; 47:2-3; 51:23; 56:95; 57:16; 69:51
- No falsehood can approach it, 41:42
- Could not have been forged by any besides God, 10:37
- Pure and holy, 98:2-3
- Not the word of the Satan, 26:210-212; 81:25
- Guarded/protected by God, 15:9; 85:22
- Full of reminders/admonition, 38:1
- Straightforward, easy to understand, 44:58; 54:17, 22, 32, 40; 18:1; 19:97; 24:46; 39:28

- Makes things clear, detailed and self-explained, 6:38,114; 10:37; 12:111; 16:89; 18:1; 22:16; 24:1; 43:2; 44:2, 4; 2:242, 266; 3:103, 118; 5:75, 89; 6:46, 55, 65, 97-98, 105, 126; 7:32, 52, 174; 9:11; 10:5, 24; 13:2; 17:12; 24:61; etc.
- Requires no explanation; God explains, 75:16-19; 2:242, 266; 3:103, 118; 5:75, 89; 6:46, 55, 65, 97-98, 105, 126; 7:32, 174; 9:11; 10:5, 24; 13:2; 17:12; 24:61; etc.
- Logically coherent with no inconsistency, stress on reason and appeal with logical arguments, 4:82; 67:3-4; 2:44, 76, 286; 13:11; 17:42; 20:15; 53:39; 28:84; 42:30; 6:132; 21:21-23; 22:16; 23:91; 36:78-83; 2:170; 19:66-67; 29:12-13
- Not changed/forged, 10:15, 37-38; 18:27; 52:33; 69:40-47
- A Book of wisdom, 10:1; 17:39; 31:2; 36:2; 43:4; 62:2
- A glorious Book in a guarded tablet, 50:1; 85:21-22
- An honored Book with truth, 56:77-82; 80:11-16
- A Book of exalted power, 41:41
- An inimitable Book; a miracle by itself, 17:88; 74:35-37; 29:51; 59:21
- A bearer of good news to the believers, 27:2
- A Book of mercy and healing, 10:57; 17:82; 27:77; 28:86; 29;51; 41:44
- Full of blessing, 38:29
- Muhammad advised to preach/warn only with the Quran, 6:51, 70; 7:2; 17:45-46; 27:92; 28:87; 50:45
- When it is being read, we should listen to it with attention to receive God's mercy, 7:204; 41:26; 46:29
- It is for understanding and pondering, 2:242, 266; 3:118; 6:65, 97-98; 7:32; 9:11; 10:5, 24; 12:2; 24:61; 38:29; 43:3; 47;24; etc.
- Who cannot see, understand or accept its message, 2:6-7, 74-75; 6:111; 10:42-44, 101; 15:10-15; 17:45-46; 18:57; 26:198-201; 57:16; etc.
- Only the clean should touch it, 56:79
- No new message, confirmation of earlier messages, 41:43; 5:48; 42:13; 22:78; 3:19, 67; 5:15; 27:76; etc.
- Not to be accepted partially, 2:85; 15:91
- Forsaken/neglected by Muhammad's people, 25:30

Resurrection (*akhirat, qiyamat*), hereafter
- It is the Day of final judgment or decision, 22:17; 34:25-26; 37:21; 77:13-14; 78:17
- A Day of dispute resolution, 2:113; 3:55, 5:48; 6:164; 10:93; 16:39; 32:25; etc.
- It is a next creation or recreation, 14:19; 29:20; 35:16; 50:15
- The Day when the earth and the heavens will be transformed into something else, 14:48
- Sight/comprehension will be made keen on this Day so that everybody realizes what he/she has done and perceives the truth of what the prophets said, 79:34-35; 50:22; 7:53; 10:30; 81:1-14
- Ears, eyes and skin speak out and give testimony that Day, 41:20-22

415

- Individuals are alone that Day without relatives and friends to support them, 6:94; 19:80, 95; 80:34-37; 70:10-14
- A Day when there will be no bargains, no friendships, and no intercession except with His permission, 2:255
- False gods or unreal things are all gone that Day; only real things remain, 6;24, 94; 7;53, 139; 10:30; 11:16, 21; 16:87; 41:48
- Faces of the upright are brightened while those of the wrongdoers darkened or their eyes cast down that Day, 10:26-27; 68:43; 70:44; 75:22-24; 80:38-41; 83:24
- Doubts expressed by disbelievers, 23:82; 27:67-68

Righteousness: General Introduction
- Righteousness is the key to success/Paradise, 2:25; 3:15; 4:57, 122; 5:35, 100; 22:77; 23:1-6; 59:9; 64:16; 91:7-9; 15:45; 18:107-108; etc.
- Attainment of righteousness is the best provision one can make, 2:197
- It matters little if one belongs in name to any religion, race or color – only righteousness matters, 2:62; 5:69; 3:113-115
- We are accountable for whatever we do with our mind and body, 2:284
- Conscience or soul needs to be purified and those who do it succeed, 91:7-10
- Righteousness is not to be confused with low or ignoble human desires, 23:71; 53:3; 28:50; 13:37; 38:26; 4:105; 5:48-49
- Righteousness is not determined by what the majority think or do, nor by those who have no knowledge, 6:116, 119; 45:18
- God represents the highest unsurpassable ideal that we need to emulate - we need to take our color from God, 42:11; 2:138
- God is always right - on the right path or course (sirat al mustaqim), 11:56
- We need to try to mold ourselves on the model or pattern of God's own nature, 30:30
- Those who emulate God and reach a high stage where their sayings and actions are in line with God's Wishes and become aboveboard and unquestionable are very blessed indeed, 53:3; 18:79-82
- God recognizes and rewards even the minutest of good one does, 34:34
- Only virtuousness counts - Most honorable to God are the most righteous in conduct; He does not discriminate between male and female in rewarding for good work, 49:13; 3:195, 4:124; 16:97; 33:35
- God's visible ideal servant whom we should follow is the Prophet Muhammad, 33:21; 68:4-6
- Muhammad brought the message of the Quran and followed it – he was the living Quran, and we should heed God's and his call that we follow the Quran, 69:40-43; 62:2; 75:16-19; 4:105; 5:48-49, 67, 92, 99; 6:50, 114, 155; 13:40; 46:9; 45:6; 17:77; 53:3; 50:45; 7:3

Righteousness: Getting the *iman* (mindset) right

Getting the *iman* right requires us to have certain metaphysical beliefs: belief in God, His creatures (e.g., angels and Jinn), resurrection or afterlife, His revelations and prophets who brought them:

- We need to believe in God and His oneness or uniqueness and greatness and manifold qualities or attributes, 2:3, 62, 177, 186, 285; 3:179; 4:136; 5:69; 71:13; etc. Also see God's attributes under "God, the conception of," above
- Only the proud do not have any faith in God, 38:2; 7:11-12, 146; 23:46; 26:29-30
- Disbelief in what is real amounts to self-exultation or arrogance and defiance, 38:2
- We also need to believe in God's revelations and His Prophets who received them, His creations such as angels and Jinn, and the Last Day or the Day of Resurrection,
- 2:62, 177, 285; 3:179; 4:136; 5:69; etc.
- We need to believe in God's revelations, 2:4, 136; 4:162; 5:83; 8:2; 23:58; 28:53; 32:15; etc.
- The Prophet Muhammad was specifically urged not to have any doubt in divine revelations, 2:147; 3:60; 10:94-95
- Resurrection (qiyamat) into afterlife (akhirat) is necessary in order that God can reward those who are righteous and let those who do wrong get their proper recompense or rectification, 10:4; 34:3-6
- Resurrection is as real as the revival of dead earth after rainfall, 7:57; 22:5; 30:19, 50; 35:9; 41:39; 43:11; 50:11
- Those who doubt about resurrection in fact disbelieve in God and His powers, 13:5
- We need to believe in a rational God, which implies belief in reason – in divine or natural laws of cause and effect, and which rules out fanaticism and fatalism or the doctrine of predestination:
- God rewards or punishes us according to our work, 2: 286; 12:22; 20:15; 28:14, 84; 53:31, 39; 42:30; 6:132; 46:19; 17:19; 5:35; 6:132; 42:30; etc.
- God has given us free choice or will to choose between right and wrong, or between good and evil, 76:3; 13:11; 18:29; 91:7-10
- God does no injustice to man; he does it to himself, 2:54, 57, 231; 3:117; 7:23, 160, 177; 4:40; 27:44; 28:16; 46:19; 65:1
- We need to have an attitude of humility and modesty and shun pride and arrogance, 22:34-35; 6:42-43; 31:18-19; 7:146; 3:188; 17:37; 57:23; etc.
- Praying effectively to God is hard for one who is not sufficiently humble, 2:45-46
- Pride leads one to commit wrong deeds, which is the cause of one's downfall, 3:188; 7:146; 16:22-23; 40:56, 60; 30:41
- Pretension, hypocrisy or treachery is a most heinous act and a disease of the heart – hypocrites are at the bottom of the fire, 4:145; 47:29
- The actions of the hypocrites are rendered vain, 47:28
- God does not love the treacherous, 4:107; 22:38
- Frustration is not a helpful state of mind – God wants us not to despair of His mercy, i.e., of better days ahead, 39:53-54; 12:87
- Ease often comes after difficulty, 65:7; 94:5-6

417

- Patience, perseverance are traits of character that help peace and progress, 2:155-157; 3:146-147
- God wants us to seek His help with patience or perseverance, 2:45, 153
- God is with the patient, and loves the patient, 2:153; 3:146
- God wants us to condone wrongs done to us patiently as far as possible, 5:45; 16:126; 42:40, 43; 2:263; 3:134; 7:198-199; 45:14
- We need to get rid of greed – greed is an ignoble trait of character of those who are on the wrong path, 33:19; 68:13; 74:15
- God chides man who is intense in love of wealth, 100:6-8
- God cautions us against wrongfully craving others' property, 2:188; 17:34-35; 4:2; 26:181-183
- Being tolerant is another good virtue –all children of Adam deserve dignity, 17:70
- Discrimination by sex (or discrimination against, or intolerance to, women) is unwarranted – only virtuousness counts, 3:195, 4:124; 16:97; 33:35; 49:13
- Racial discrimination is unwarranted, 49:13
- There is no rationale for discrimination on the basis of religion in name, 2:62; 5:69
- There is no room for coercion in religion, 2:256; 10:99; 109:1-6; 50:45; 88:21-22; 11:28
- Strict cordiality in preaching is urged, 16:125; 29:46; 73:10
- We should not revile the gods of others, 6:108
- The diversity of nations implies inter-communal tolerance, 49:13; 5:48
- We are well advised to turn away from others who do not go well with us, wishing them peace (salam), 43:89; 25:63; 28:55
- Call for inviting others to do deeds of common good, 3:64
- Call for holding on to forgiveness and tolerance, for forgiveness and patience instead of revenge for wrongs done, 7:198-199; 5:45; 42:40; 16:126; 2:263; 3:134; 7:198-199; 42:43; 45:14
- Call for granting refuge or asylum to people of other communities seeking refuge, 9:6.
- Other reasons such as wealth, strength of manpower, or status or power in society are of no value to God, 9:55, 69; 10:58, 88-89; 28:76-81; 30:39; 34:37; 43:32-35; 111:2
- God forbids human rights abuses, 26:183
- God exhorts us to uphold the cause of justice, if necessary by testifying against ourselves, parents and relatives, and not to let the hatred (or enmity or injustice) of others make us stray from justice, 4:135; 5:8. For more on tolerance, see under "tolerance" below.
- We need to get rid of cowardice, undue fear, 20:68; 3:73, 175; 42:22; 5:54; 33:37; 4:77
- Doing some good deeds just to be seen by others, i.e., because of fear of men, is of no intrinsic merit, 107:4-7; 4:38, 108-109, 142; 8:47
- Hatred, malice, feeling of enmity or ill will against others is also a wrong attitude – it comes from devilish thoughts and actions, 3:91, 14, 64; 10:90-91

418

- People who nurture hatred do not deserve to be friends, 3:118
- It is people with malice who grieve at others' fortune, and rejoice at others' misfortune, 3:120
- Feelings of love and brotherhood prevail among believers, 7:43; 15:47; 59:10
- Jealousy or feeling of discomfort at others' superiority is also degrading to one's soul, 4:32
- Jealousy leads one to commit crimes, 12:8-9, 15
- Jealousy may lead to religious splits, 45:17
- God cautions against too much suspicion, 49:12
- Suspicion taking the form of slander is a grave sin, 24:23, 11-18; 104:1
- Restraining anger is part of righteousness, 3:134
- God rewards those who forgive even when they are angry, 42:36-37
- Rage or anger is removed from the hearts of believers, 9:14-15
- Feelings of love and goodwill for fellow believers/human beings are qualities that were well exemplified in the Prophet Muhammad's life, 9:128; 33:6; 3:159; 47:19
- An attitude of self-reliance or independence from others is a godly quality, 35:15; 47:38; 3:97
- God's prophets gave more to humanity than they received from them – they asked for no wages, 6:90; 10:72; 11:29, 51; 12:104; 23:72; 25:57; 26:109, 127, 145; etc.
- God wants us to follow those who do not ask for any remuneration, 36:21
- Feelings of contentment, gratitude and appreciation for any benefit received are good virtues, 31:12; 39:7; 14:7; 2:276; 22:38

Righteousness: Getting actions right
- God wants us to be truthful and honest – to never mix falsehood with truth nor conceal the truth, 2:26; 33:70; 4:135; 16:91
- God wants us to be with, or stand for, those who are truthful, 9:119
- God blesses those who make pledges of allegiance and support to people who do good, 48:10, 18
- God wants us to keep our promise, 16:91
- God's curse is on those who break their promise and do mischief in the land, 13:25
- We are urged at the same time not to make our promise a device for deceiving others, 16:94
- God's servants always keep their word, 2:177; 3:17; 13:20; 33:23
- God enjoins upon us justice, fairness and kindness to all involved, 16:90, 76; 5:8; 42:41-42; 2:188; 17:34; 49:9; 4,127, 135; 58; 55:9; 60:8; 65:2
- God exhorts us to uphold the cause of justice, if necessary by testifying against ourselves, parents and relatives, and not to let the hatred (or enmity or injustice) of others make us stray from justice, 4:135; 5:8
- We are urged to restore trusts and judge justly between people, 4:58
- We are urged not to devour others' property, and not to bribe judges to unjustly grab others' property, 2:188

419

- We are strongly cautioned against grabbing orphans' property, 4:10, 5-6; 17:34
- God exhorts us to give the right measure, and not to deceive or exploit others, 26:181-183
- Deceiving others is really deceiving one's own self, 2:9; 63:1-2
- Wrongdoing/unjustness of people is the cause of decay/destruction of nations, 17:16; 22:45
- We are admonished to be good particularly to parents, near relatives, orphans and the needy, neighbors, fellow-travelers, and the wayfarers, and slaves/captives, 4:36
- Admonition for kind treatment of parents, 4:11; 46:15; 17:23-24
- We do not know whether it is our children or our parents who are nearer to us in usefulness, 4:11
- We should not say a "Fie" to our parents nor chide them, but should speak kindly to them, 17:23
- However, parents must not be obeyed if they give wrong advice, 31:15
- There is no righteousness, piety without spending in God's way, 3:92, 134; 2:177
- Spending in Gods' way is a greatly virtuous act, 90:12-18; 2:261, 265
- Spending in God's way is for one's purification, 92:17-21
- Those who think that they do not need to spend on others thinking that if God willed He could have provided for all are in flagrant error, 36:47
- We need to spend on the poor and the needy, parents and near relatives, orphans, wayfarers, for relieving the burden of debt of heavily indebted persons, 9:60. For more on this, see under "spending in God's way" below.
- We need to be morally upright, which includes remaining chaste until marriage, and sexual restraint in married life, 24:33; 17:32; 5:5; 79:40-41; 7:28
- The Prophet Muhammad was advised not to pay any attention to that with which man enjoys worldly life, 20:131
- The Prophet was urged by God to give similar advice to his wives, 33:28
- The Prophet's wives were particularly advised to guard their modesty, and work toward purification, 33:32-34
- Both men and women need to lower their gaze and guard their modesty, 24:30-31
- Believing women need to put on proper dresses covering their private parts and bosoms, except what is apparent, and not to display their beauty in a way that may look like or sound invitation to indecency, 24:31; 33:59
- We need to avoid acts of indecency, whether open or secret, 6:120, 151
- Adultery or fornication (zina) is a great sin, and warrants stern punishment unless the committers of such a sin repent sincerely and mend their conduct, 17:32; 4:15-17; 24:2-5
- Slandering chaste women is a great sin, 4:112; 24:23; 104:1-9
- We need to live in peace, decency and harmony with others – we are urged to greet others with a salutation of "peace", or turn away from ignorant people in a decent manner, i.e., wishing them "peace", 6:54; 25:63; 28:55; 43:89
- God urges us to incline to peace if enemies incline to peace and make peace between feuding parties, 8:62-63; 49:9

420

- God allows us to fight aggression and injustices, and to fight until persecution is over, 2:190-193, 217; 9:13-14, 36; 22:39-40; 4:75, 91, 94; 8:39
- We are not entitled to initiate aggression and transgress limits, 2:190-193; 60:8; 4:171; 5:87; 7:55-56
- We are entitled to retaliate in like manner for any wrongs done to us, but we need to condone and forgive others' faults as far as possible, 3:134; 5:45; 8:38; 16:126; 42:40
- God strongly warns us against any act of wrongdoing, corruption or mischief in the land causing any injury or harm to others, 7:56, 74; 13:25; 26:151-152, 181-183; 27:48-49; 47:22-23
- God forbids us to cause unnecessary bloodshed in society, and characterizes killing of any man without any valid reason as like killing all mankind, and saving one soul as like saving all mankind, 4:29-30, 92-93; 6:151; 17:31, 33; 5:32
- Torture and persecution is even worse than slaughter, 2:190-193, 217
- We need to be good and courteous to others – be duly polite in conversation and arguments, 2:83; 16:125; 29:46; 31:19
- We need to greet or salute others, or return salutation, 4:86; 6:54; 24:27, 61; 25:63; 33:56
- We need to be duly courteous and respectful to those who are superior, 2:104; 4:46; 24:62-63; 33:56-57; 58:11; 49:1-5
- We should not ask superiors too many questions, 5:101-102
- We should obey superiors and those who command legitimate authority, 4:59
- We should not enter a house without the due permission and greeting of its inmates, 24:27-29, 61
- We should enter houses by their gates, not by their backs, 2:189
- We need to seek permission to enter rooms of couples at specified private times, 24:58-59
- We should make fun of others, 49:11
- We should not backbite one another of our own people, 49:12; 104:1
- God curses slanderers, backbiters, 104:1
- When death approaches us, we should leave a bequest or will for our surviving parents and near relatives according to reasonable usage, 2:180-183, 240; 5:106-108
- There are specified rules of distribution of inherited property after death, 4:7-13, 33, 176
- The rules of distribution of inherited property after death apply after consideration of the will and settlement of any debt lying outstanding against the deceased, 4:11
- At the time of distribution of our property, we need to make some special provision for the poor, orphans and the needy, including for poor relatives, 4:7-8
- We need to avoid intoxicants and games of chance, including sacrificing to stones and divining by arrows, 5:90-91; 2:219
- We should not go to prayer while intoxicated, 4:43
- We need to keep away from vain talks and activities, 6:68; 23:3

- Forbidden foods are only carrion (meat of naturally dead or unusually killed animals, i.e., through strangling, beating or falling from a height, or animals gored by horns or partially devoured by wild animals), pork, blood and meat of animals sacrificed to other than God, 2:172-173; 5:3; 6:3-5, 121, 145; 16:115-116; 22:30
- Pork is forbidden because of uncleanness of swine, 6:145
- We should not eat of animals on which the name of God is not mentioned, 6:121
- However, whoever is driven by necessity, for him eating the forbidden food is no sin, if he eats it not craving it and not exceeding the limit, 6:145
- For those who go on a pilgrimage to the Holy Kabah, gaming of animals is forbidden during the pilgrimage; but gaming of the sea and its food are lawful, 5:95-96
- God cautions us against forbidding food other those mentioned by Him, 5:87; 10:59; 16:116
- In the past some people unfairly prohibited some food without any divine authority, 6:119, 138-139, 143-144

Satan, the devil
- Resides in and around us; it is the wrong/evil suggestion/temptation coming from one's own mind or from the minds of others, and whispered to our hearts, 7:20; 20:120; 23:97; 57:14; 114:3-4
- Disobeys just dictates/commands (of God, conscience), 2;34; 7:16-18; 15:31; 18:50; etc.
- Misleads, deceives, 2:36; 4:119-120; 7:16-17; 15:39; 17:62-64; 20:120; 57:14; 59:16
- Makes false promises, promises nothing except deceit, 4;120; 14:22; 17:64
- Causes dissensions among men, 12:100; 17:53
- Promises poverty, enjoins doing evil, 2:268; 4:120; 20:120; etc.
- Makes evil deeds seem fair, 6:43; 8;48; 15:39; 16:63; 27:24; 29:38; 47:25
- Makes man forget things, 18:63
- An open enemy of man, 2;168, 208; 6:142; 12:5, 100; 17:53; 18:50; 20:117; 35:6; 36:60; 43:62
- Betrays/forsakes his own followers, 14:22; 17:64; 25:29; 59:16
- Can mislead only unwary and wrongdoing people, not the faithful and righteous, 15:39-40, 42; 16:99-100; 17:65; 26:221-223; etc.
- Satans are from among humans and the jinn, 6:112; 2:14; 12:5; 18:50
- Satans are friends/guardians of disbelievers, 7:27
- Satans' party are the losers, 58:19

Slaves, the status of
- The freeing of slaves or the abolition of slavery is strongly recommended, 2:177; 5:89; 24:32-33; 58:3; 90:12-13
- God designates the freeing of slaves as part and parcel of righteousness, and as an ascent to piety, 2:177; 90:12-13

- The freeing of slaves is expiation for wrongs done, 5:89; 58:3
- God encourages us to marry slave girls, 2:221; 4:25; 24:32-33
- One should consider marrying from among slave girls, should he find it difficult to marry a free woman, 4:25
- A believing slave girl or boy is better to marry than an unbelieving free girl or boy, even though the latter may be more attractive, 2:221
- Forcing maids or slave girls to prostitution is forbidden, 24:33
- Those who force slaves to prostitution seek this worldly life, 24:33
- Marrying war captives or slaves (whom one's right hand possesses) along with or as an alternative to marrying orphans is more appropriate, 4:3
- Getting male and female slaves along with other singles married is encouraged, and allowing slaves to purchase their freedom is urged, 24:32-33
- Slave girls are lawful in the same way as our cousins and other believing women, 33:50
- God asks us to marry from among orphans, not to enslave them, 4:3
- We are not entitled to take any as paramours or concubines, 4:25; 5:5

Social reforms

The Quran's social welfare reform prescriptions are aimed at ameliorating the social and economic situation of the weaker segments of society – the poor and the deprived, orphans, the homeless and wayfarers, those laden with debt, women, and slaves. See under spending in God's way, orphans, women and slaves.

Spending in God's way (*zakat* or *zakah*, *sadaqa*)

- Spending in God's way is part and parcel of righteousness and is a highly virtuous act, 2:177, 254, 261, 265; 3:134; 17:26; 24:22; 33:35; 47:38; 90:12-18; 92:17-21; 107:1-7; 57:10
- Wealth should not circulate only among the rich, but should be shared with the poor, 59:7
- The virtuous are those who give part of their wealth to the poor and the deprived, 51:19; 70:25
- No happiness without sharing one's earnings and possessions with others, 92:21
- Giving is the very worship of, and thanksgiving to, God, 76:8-9; 92:18-20; 107:1-7; 14:7; 2: 172; 3:27, 37; 6:141
- Giving is for love of God, not for any reward in return, 2:177, 3:134; 76:8-9; 92:19-21
- Charity is for one's purification; no piety without giving, 92:18; 9:103; 3:92; 107:1-7
- Spending in God's way is to be out of income and wealth, 6:141; 2:177, 254, 267; 9:41; 34:39
- Such spending (sadaqa or zakat) to go where, 2:177, 215, 273; 8:41; 9:60; 24:22; 59:9; 70:25
- We should not swear against helping near relatives and others in want, 24:22

- We need also to spend on those in need who are unable to move through the land and who do not beg importunately, 2:273
- We should be neither too stingy in spending nor too generous, 33:19; 92:8-10; 25:67
- The curse of God is on those who are too stingy in spending, 33:19; 92:8-10
- God does not love the extravagant, 7:31; 6:141; 17:26-27
- Spending, but not with a grudge, insult or injury, 2:262-264; 9:54
- God loves those who spend not only when they are in affluence or ease, but also when they are in hardship, 3:134
- Spending in secret, i.e., without undue publicity, is still more virtuous, 2:271
- Spending for God's cause – defense, economic and social development, and other social welfare, 9:41, 50; 2:273; 57:10; 24:22; 47:38; 90:12-18
- Spending in God's way (zakat or sadaqa) from both wealth and income or assets, production and earnings, 34:39; 36:47; 6:141; 8:41; 9:41; 92:17-18; 2:119, 267
- How much to spend in God's way, 2:219; 25:67; 8:1, 41; 33:19; 47:38; 92:8-10
- Beautiful lending (qarz-hasana) is also urged, 2:245; 57:11, 18; 64:17; 5:12; 73:20

Tolerance
- All men being the children of Adam deserve the same honor and dignity, 17:70
- Racial prejudice or discrimination is unwarranted; only righteousness counts, 2:62; 5:69; 3:195
- Discrimination by sex is unwarranted; only righteousness counts, 30:195; 49:13; 4:124; 16:97; 33:35
- Discrimination by religion in name is unwarranted; all religions are basically the same, 2:62; 5:69; 60:8; 2:136; 6:83-96; 3:144; 3:113-115; 4:123-124; 29:46; 5:44, 47, 68
- Discrimination by wealth, manpower and societal status or power is unwarranted, 9:55, 69; 10:58, 88-89; 28:76-81; 30:39; 34:37; 43:32-35; 111:2
- Human rights abuse is forbidden, 26:181-183
- No coercion or compulsion in religion, 2:256; 10:99; 109:1-6; 50:45; 88:21-22; 11:28, 10:41; 18:29
- Diversity in human beings – colors, tongues and races - is recognized, 49:13; 5:48; 10:99; 30:22; 11:118
- Cordiality and decency in religious preaching is urged, 16:125; 29:46; 73:10; 6:108; 28:55; 3:64; 7:198-199
- Avenging a wrong in like manner is permitted, but forgiving the offender is preferred, 5:45; 42:40; 16:126; 2:263; 3:134; 7:198-199; 42:43; 45:14
- Taking a life except for a just reason is forbidden, 5:32
- Persecution is worse than slaughter, 2:191
- Aggression, violence, terrorism, mischief-making is forbidden, 2:190; 5:2; 7:56, 74; 13:25; 26:183; 47:22-23
- While in war, establishing peace is urged when the enemy inclines to peace, 4:89-90; 8:62-63

- Goodness, equity and justice to all religious groups urged, 60:8; 4:114; 5:2, 8; 4:135
- Even enemies need to be treated with justice, 5:8, 2
- Efforts for cooperative moral ventures and peace – to help one another in goodness and piety - are urged, 5:2; 3:64; 25:63; 28:55; 43:89; 109:6

Women, the status of
- Women are on a par with men – they come from the same single nafs or cell, 4:1
- Man's mate is created from a single nafs so that they may incline to each other, 7:189
- Every being or thing is created in pairs, and man and woman are just parts of the same pair, 36:36; 51:49; 53:45
- Man and woman are one from another, 3:195; 4:25
- Women have rights over men similar to those of men over women, 2:228
- Men and women are equal before God; whoever does good, whether male or female, goes to Heaven; whoever is righteous, whether male or female, will be rewarded, 3:195; 4:32, 124; 16:97; 33:35; 40:40; 43:68-73
- The most righteous is the most honorable to God - a man is thus not necessarily superior to a woman; wife may excel husband in piety or specific qualities, 4:32; 49:13; 28:9; 66:11-12
- Love and mercy should characterize marital relationship, 30:21
- Husband and wife are each other's garment, 2:187
- Good (believing) husband and wife support each other in good work, and enjoin what is just and forbid what is evil, 9:71
- Husband and wife need to be conscious of obligations to each other and responsive to needs of each other, 2:233, 240-241; 4:19-21; 60:12
- Husbands urged to treat women with dignity and honor, and live with them in kindness, 2:231; 4:19
- Husband urged not to hate his wife, but to regard her as source of abundant good and comfort, 4:19; 25:74
- Husband urged not to cause any harm or injury to his divorced wife, 2:231
- Husband exhorted to financially support the divorced wife and their child for up to two years of nursing the baby, 2:233
- Wives have rights similar to those of husbands according to what is just, which imply wives' rights of divorce of their husbands similar to husbands' rights of divorce of their wives, 2:228
- Virtuous people wish to see their spouses and their children as source of comfort, and pray to God for such comfort, 25:74
- Virtuous men's wives need to be, and are in general, virtuous as well, 33:28-34
- Wives of virtuous people in general go to Heaven along with their husbands, 43:68-70
- Prophets' wives are like mothers to their followers, 33:6

- The Prophet urged to bid goodbye to his wives seeking worldly life in a fair manner, not to injure them in any way, 33:28
- If women fear mistreatment from their husbands, they can have a mutual agreement against such treatment, 4:128
- In case of rebellion from wife, husband advised to admonish her, leave her apart in bed, or turn away from (not beat or scourge, as traditionally interpreted) her, 4:34
- Call for arbitration or resolution by the judicial process in case of disputes between husband and wife, 4:35
- God derides those who make an unfair discrimination between males and females, 6:139
- Distinctions made between males and females in the case of inheritance from relatives and when taking them as witnesses in financial transactions, but these exceptions are explicable in terms of context and situation, 4:11-12; 2:282
- Modesty requirements enjoined by the Quran equally apply to men and women, 24:30-31
- Women admonished to wear decent and dignified dresses so as not to evoke men's invitation to indecency, 24:31; 33:32-33

REFERENCES

- Ali, S.V. Mir Ahmed, The Koran Translation: The Holy Koran Interpreted, United Muslim Foundation, Lake Mary, FL, 2005, Index, pp. 466-516.
- Haleem, Muhammad Abdel, Understanding the Qur'an: Themes and Style, I.B. Tauris & Co Ltd, London-New York, 1999, 2001.
- Khalifa, Rashad (Trans.), Quran: The Final Testament, Revised Edition, 1989, Appendices, pp. 374-486 and Index, pp. 489-535.
- Rahman, Muhammad Habibur, Koran Sutra (in Bengali - The Quranic Reference), the Bangla Academy, Dhaka, 1994.
- Rahman, Fuzlur, Major Themes of the Qur'an, Bibliotheca Islamica Inc., Minneapolis, 1980.
- Shakir, M.H. (trans.), The Qur'an, Tahrike Tarsile Qur'an, Inc., Elmhurst, New York, 12th edition, 2001, Index, pp. 425-467.

WORKS CITED

Books and Articles

Akyol, Mustafa, "Islamocapitalism: Islam and Free Market" in Edip Yuksel, et. al. (ed.), *Critical Thinkers for Islamic Reform*, Brainbow Press, United States of America, 2009.

Ahmad, Aksaruddin, *Musings of the Heart in Songs* (Bengali manuscript *Gaan-e Praaner Kotha*, undated).

--------------------------, *The Holy Quran: Bengali Translation and Word Rendering* (*Pabitra Quran: Banganubad o Shabdartha,* the first of the thirty parts of the Quran, undated).

-------------------------, *Whither are Muslims Today* (Bengali manuscript *Mussalman Aj Kon Path-e*? undated).

Ahmad, Kassim, *Hadith: A Re-Evaluation*, Translated from his original book in Malay *Hadis — Satu Penilaian Semula* by Monotheist Productions International, Tucson, Arizona, U.S.A. 1997, © Copyright Kassim Ahmad, 1996, first published in 1986. Available on the internet website www.free-minds.org.

Ahmad, Panaullah, *Creator and Creation*, Islamic Foundation, Bangladesh, 1986.

Ahmed, Akbar S., *Islam under Siege: Living Dangerously in a Post-Honor World*, Polity Press in association with Blackwell Publishing Ltd., Cambridge, UK and Malden, MA, USA, 2003.

Ahmed, Shahab, "A General Introduction (to the Hadith)", available on the website: www.iranica.com/articles/v11f4/v11f4072a.html.

Al-Shibli, *Sirat al-Numan*, Lahore, n. d. Trans. Muhammad Tayyab Bakhsh Badauni as *Method of Sifting Prophetic Tradition*, Karachi, 1966.

Anonymous author, "Hadith Authenticity: A Survey of Perspectives", website: http://www.rim.org/muslim/hadith.htm, or at http://www.rim.org/muslim/islam.htm.

Armstrong, Karen, *A History of God: The 4000-Year Quest of Judaism, Christianity and Islam*, Gramercy Books, New York, 1993.

------------------------, *Islam – A Short History*, Random House Inc., New York, Modern Library Paperback Edition, 2002, pp. 164-66.

Asad, Muhammad (trans.) *Sahih al-Bukhari: the Early Years of Islam*, Dar al-Andalus, 1981.

Aslan, Reza, *No god but God: The Origins, Evolution and Future of Islam*, Random House, New York, 2005.

Azami, M. A., *Studies in Hadith Methodology and Literature*, Islamic Book Trust, Kuala Lumpur, cited in Akbarally Meherally, undated.

Barq, Ghulam Jilani, "Hadith ke bare men mera mawqaf," Chatan, Lahore, January 9, 1956.

------------------------, *Do Islam* (Two Islams), 1950.

Bashar, M. Jamilul, *Reformation* (in Bengali: *Sangsker*), Young Muslim Society, New York, 2002.

Berk, Jan Marc, "Book Review" (Review of two books by A.L.M. Abdul Gafoor: *Interest-Free Commercial Banking*, Apptech Publications, Groningen, 1995, and Participatory Financing through Investment Banks and Commercial Banks, Apptech Publications, Groningen, 1996), *De Economist* (Quarterly Review of the Royal Netherlands Economic Association), Vol. 146, No. 1, April 1998.

Brown, Daniel W., *Rethinking Tradition in Modern Islamic Thought*, Cambridge University Press, 1996 (Paperback 1999).

Buccaille, Maurice, *The Bible, the Qur'an and Science*, Seghers Publishers, Paris, 1977. Also published as *The Bible, the Quran and Science – the Holy Scriptures Examined in the Light of Modern Knowledge, Translated from French by Alastair D. Pannell and the Author*, the American Trust Publications, 1979.

Bullet, Richard W., *Islam, the View from the Edge*, New York, Columbia University Press, 1994.

Einstein, Albert, *The Human Side: (New Glimpses from his Archives),* Selected and edited by Helen Dukas and Banesh Hoffmann, published by Princeton University Press, Princeton, New Jersey, 1979.

Esposito, John L., *Islam- The Straight Path*, New York, Oxford University Press, 1991.

--------------------, *What Everyone Needs to Know About Islam*, Oxford University Press, 2002.

--------------------, *"Ten Things Everyone Needs to Know about Islam,"* website: http://arabworld.nitle.org/texts.php?module_id=2&reading_id=62&sequence=1.

Fadl, Khaled Abou El, *And God Knows the Soldiers: The Authoritative and the Authoritarian in Islamic Discourses*, University Press of America, Inc., Lanham and Oxford, 2001.

---------------------------, *Speaking in God's Name: Islamic Law, Authority and Women*, Oneworld Publications, Oxford, 2001

---------------------------, *The Great Theft: Wrestling Islam from the Extremists*, HarperSan Francisco, A Division of Harper Collins Publishers, New York, 2005.

--------------------------- et. al, *The Place of Tolerance in Islam*, Beacon Press, Boston, 2002.

---------------------------, "The Ugly Modern and the Modern Ugly: Reclaiming the Beautiful in Islam", in Omid Safi (ed.), *Progressive Muslims: On Justice, Gender, and Pluralism*, Oneworld Publications, Oxford, 2003.

Farooq, Dr. Muhammad Umar, "Dr. Farooq's Study Resource Page" in website: http://globalwebpost.com/farooqm/study_res/islam/hadith/akramkhan_hadith.html.

Feynman, Richard P. *The Pleasure of Finding Things Out and the Meaning of It All*, Perseus Books, Massachusetts, 1998 (also paperback 1999 by Perseus Books).

Goldziher, Ignaz, *Muhammedanische Studien,*. 2 vols., Leiden, 1896. Trans. by S.M. Stern as *Muslim Studies*, 2 vols., London, 1967.

Grof, Stanislav, *Toward a New Paradigm of the Unconscious*, a video presentation in the website: http://www.thinking-allowed.com/2sgrof.html.

Guillaume, Alfred, *The Traditions of Islam*, Pakistan 1977.

Huntington, Samuel, "The Clash of Civilizations", *Foreign Affairs*, 1993, expanded into a book *The Clash of Civilizations and the Remaking of World Order*, Simon and Schuster, New York, 1996.

Iqbal, Muhammad, *The Reconstruction of Religious Thought in Islam*, edited by M. Saeed Sheikh, Adm Publishers and Distributors, Delhi, 1997; also published earlier (in 1934) by the Oxford University Press.

Jayrajpuri, Muhammad Aslam, *Ilm-i-hadith* (Knowledge of Hadith), Lahore, not dated.

Juynboll, G.H.A., *Muslim Tradition - Studies in Chronology, Provenance and Authorship of Early Hadith* (New York: Cambridge University Press, 1983.

Kazi, Mazhar U., *A Treasury of Ahadith*, Jeddah, Saudi Arabia, Abul-Qasim Publishing House, 1992.

Khalifa, Rashad, *Quran, Hadith and Islam*, reproduced in the Internet in 1982, website: www.submission.org.

Khan, Aasma, "How Muslims can Combat Terror and Violence" in Michael Wolfe & Beliefnet (ed.), *Taking Back Islam: American Muslims Reclaim Their Faith*, Rodale Inc and Beliefnet Inc, 2002, p. 51.

Khan, Ahmad, *Maqalat*, as cited in Daniel W. Brown, 1996 (paperback 1999).

Khan, Haroon A., "The Clash of Civilization[s] Thesis and Bangladesh: A Case Study", *Asian Profile*, Vol. 32, No. 2, April 2004.

Khan, M.A. Muqtedar, *American Muslims: Bridging Faith and Freedom*, Amana Publications, 2002.

Khan, M. Muhsin (trans.), *Sahih Bukhari*, available on the website: http://www.usc.edu/dept/MSA/fundamentals/hadithsunnah/bukhari/.

Khan, Sayyid Ahmad, *Tafsir al-Qur'an*, Aligarh, 1297 A.H.

Lang, Jeffrey, *Losing My Religion: A Call for Help*, Amana Publishers, Beltsville (Maryland), 2004.

Lewis, Bernard, *What Went Wrong? Western Impact and Middle Eastern Response*, Oxford University Press, New York, 2002.

MacDonald, Duncan B., *Development of Muslim Theology Jurisprudence and Constitutional Theory* (George Routledge and Sons), London, 1903.

Majid, Raja F. M., "Ghulam Jilani Barq: A Study in Muslim 'Rationalism,'" M.A. thesis, McGill University, Institute of Islamic Studies, 1962.

Malek, M.A., *A Study of the Qur'an: The Universal Guidance for Mankind*, 1997, third edition 2000, Sutton, Surrey, UK.

Manji, Irshad, , *The Trouble with Islam: A Muslim's Call for Reform in Her Faith*, St. Martin's Press, New York, 2003.

Mansour, Ahmed Subhy, "Islamic Tolerance: A Comparison between Egypt and America: Reverting Islam back to its Tolerant Roots" in the website: www.islamicpluralism.org/texts/2005t/islamictolerance.htm.

-----------------------------, "The Culture of Slaves", website: http://www.islamicpluralism.org/texts/2005t/egyptslavecult.htm#Culture_of_Slaves

-----------------------------, *Penalty of Apostasy: A Historical and Fundamental Study*, English translation by Mostafa Sabet, Original title in Arabic: *Haddur*

429

Riddah: Dirasah Usooliyya Tareekhiyya. Website: http://ahmed.g3z.com/researches/redda.htm.

Mashriqi, Inayat Allah Khan, *Tadhkira*, Amritsar, 1924.

Mauro, Paolo, "The Persistence of Corruption and Slow Economic Growth", 2002 International Monetary Fund *Staff Working Paper* (IMF WP 02/213).

Meherally, Akbarally, *Myths and Realities of Hadith* – A Critical Study, (published by Mostmerciful.com Publishers), Burnaby, BC, Canada, available in the website http://www.mostmerciful.com/hadithbook-sectionone.htm.

Melloan, George, "Making Muslims Part of the Solution", the *Wall Street Journal*, issue of March 29, 2005.

Miller, Lisa, "Islam in America: A Special Report", *Newsweek*, July 30, 2007.

Minai, Ali, "A Time for Renewal" in Michael Wolfe (ed.), *Taking Back Islam: American Muslims Reclaim Their Faith*, Rodale Inc. and Beliefnet Inc., 2002, p. 10. Reprinted from www.chowk.com.

Muir, William, *The Life of Mahomet and the History of Islam to the Era of Hegira*, 4 vols., London, 1861; repr. Osnabruck, 1988.

Murphy, Caryle, *Passion for Islam: Shaping the Modern Middle East: The Egyptian Experience*, Simon & Schuster, New York, 2002.

Musa, Aisha Y., *Hadith as Scripture: Discussions on the Authority of Prophetic Traditions in Islam*, Palgrave Macmillan, 2008.

Mustafa, Ibrahim, "Hadith and the Corruption of the Great Religion of Islam", website: http://www.submission.org/had-corruption.html.

Neier, Aryeh, "The Real Clash is Fundamentalists vs. Modernity", *International Herald Tribune*, October 10, 2001.

Palmer, Helen, *Personality Development and the Psyche*, transcript of a conversation with Dr. Jeffrey Mishlove under the auspices of the Intuition Network, A Thinking Allowed Television Underwriter. Can be seen in the website: http://www.intuition.org/txt/palmer.htm

Parwez, Ghulam Ahmed, *Muquaam-e-Hadith* (in Urdu - *The True Status of the Hadith*), 2nd edn., Karachi, 1965.

-----------------------------------, *Salim ke nam khutut*, Karachi, 1953.

Pipes, Daniel, "Identifying Moderate Muslims", *New York Sun*, November 23, 2004; website: http://www.danielpipes.org/article/2226.

------------------, "Calling Islamism the Enemy" *Weblog*, June 13, 2002, website: http://www.danielpipes.org/blog/300.

Rahim, M. Abdur, *The History of Hadith Compilation* (in Bengali), date not known.

Rahman, Fazlur, *Major Themes of the Qur'an*, Bibliotheca Islamica, Minneapolis, Chicago, 1980.

Rauf, Imam Feisal Abdul, *What's Right with Islam: A New Vision for Muslims and the West*, HarperCollins Publishers Inc., New York, 2004.

Rippin, Andrew, *Muslims: Their Religious Beliefs and Practices* vol. 1 (New York: Routledge, 1990.

Safi, Omid (ed.), *Progressive Muslims: On Justice, Gender, and Pluralism*, Oneworld Publications, Oxford, 2003.

Schacht, Joseph, *Muhammadan Jurisprudence*. Oxford University Press, Oxford, 1950.

Scriven, Michael, *Explanations of the Supernatural* (1998 Thinking Allowed Productions), discussion in the website: http://www.intuition.org/txt/scriven3.htm.

Schwartz, Stephen, *The Two Faces of Islam: Saudi Fundamentalism and its Role in Terrorism*, Knopf Publishing Group, paperback published by Anchor, 2003, cited in Website: http://www.islamicpluralism.org/books.htm.

Shaw, George Bernard, *The Genuine Islam*, Vol. 1, No. 8, 1936.

Siddiqui, Abdul Hamid (trans.), *Sahih Muslim*, available on the website: http://www.geocities.com/ahlulbayt14/sahih-mb.html.

Sidqi, Muhammad Tawfiq, "al-Islam huwa al-Qur'an wahdahu," *al-Manar* 9, 1906.

Spencer, Robert, *Islam Unveiled: Disturbing Questions about the World's Fastest-Growing Faith*, Encounter Books, San Francisco, 2002.

Sprenger, Alois, "On the Origin of Writing Down Historical Records among the Musulmans', *Journal of the Asiatic Society of Bengal 25*, 1856.

Soroush, Abdolkarim, *Reason, Freedom, and Democracy in Islam*, Oxford University Press, Oxford-New York, 2000.

Taheri, Amir, *Spirit of Allah: Khomeini and the Islamic Revolution*, Adler and Adler, 1986.

Taher, Amiri, "Islam can't Escape Blame for Sept. 11," *Wall Street Journal*, 24 October 2001.

Tibi, Bassam, *The Challenge of Fundamentalism: Political Islam and the New World Disorder*, Berkeley University Press, 1998, updated edition 2002.

Uddin, Mesbah, "Sunnah – the Misconceived Dogma that Poisoned Islam", first published in the Daily News Monitoring Service: *News From Bangladesh*, on December 12, 2004, also available on the website: www.submission.org.

United Nations (United Nations Office for the High Commissioner for Human Rights (OHCHR)), *Report of the World Conference against Racism, Racial Discrimination, Xenophobia and Related Intolerance*, held in Durban during 31 August - 8 September 2001, January 25, 2002.

------------------, (UNAIDS), *AIDS in Africa*, March 4, 2005.

von Grunebaum, G.E., *Classical Islam: A History 600-1258*, (Translation by Katherine Watson), Barnes and Noble Books, 1996, originally published in 1970 by Aldine Publishing Company.

Wadud, Amina, *Qur'an and Woman: Reading the Sacred Text from a Woman's Perspective*, Oxford University Press, New York, 1999.

Wolfe, Michael & Beliefnet (ed.), *Taking Back Islam: American Muslims Reclaim Their Faith*, Rodale Inc and Beliefnet Inc, 2002.

Yuksel, Edip, *Manifesto for Islamic Reform*, 2nd revised and enlarged edition, Brainbow Press, U.S.A., 2009.

................, *Peacemaker's Guide to War Mongers: Exposing Robert Spencer, Osama bin Laden, David Horowitz and Other Enemies of Peace*, Brainbow Press, U.S.A., 2010.

................, Layth Saleh al-Shaiban and Martha Schulte-Nafeh, *Quran: A Reformist Translation*, Brainbow Press, 2007.

Other Publications

British Prime Minister Tony Blair's talk to a Labour Party policy forum, July 16, 2005.

The Economist magazine, March 6th-12th, 2010.

Middle East Quarterly, March 2000.

President Discusses War on Terror at National Endowment for Democracy, October 6, 2005.

The Concise Columbia Encyclopedia, Columbia University Press, 1995.

The New International Pocket Quotation Dictionary of the English Language, Trident Press International, 2000.

Time magazine, December 3, 2005.

The Wall Street Journal, Online Edition, March 4, 2005.

ENDNOTES

[1] Viorst, Milton, "Puritanism and Stagnation" in Khaled Abou El Fadl (ed.), *The Place of Tolerance in Islam,* Beacon Press, Boston, 2002, pp. 27-28.

[2] This is what modern Muslim and non-Muslim scholars generally have attempted to do, as reflected in many of their works. See in particular the cover page introduction to the book Michael Wolfe and the Producers of Beliefnet (ed.), *Taking Back Islam: American Muslims Reclaim Their Faith*, Rodale Inc. and Beliefnet Inc., 2002.

[3] The abbreviation stands for "Peace be upon him", an expression of reverence and well wishing used by Muslims for the Prophet Muhammad. Muslims use this expression also in the case of other prophets.

[4] Muhammad lost his father while he was still in the mother's womb, and his mother died when he was only six years old.

[5] Ahmad, Panaullah, *Creator and Creation*, Islamic Foundation, Bangladesh, 1986, p. 29. For this Quranic idea, see (41:34).

[6] Lang, Jeffrey, *Losing My Religion: A Call for Help*, Amana Publishers, Beltsville (Maryland), 2004, p. 72.

[7] He was manager in a caravan trade operated by his wife Khadijah.

[8] Guillaume, A., *The Life of Muhammad*, trans., London, Oxford University Press,p.107, cited in John L. Esposito, *Islam- The Straight Path*, New York, Oxford University Press, 1991, p. 9.

[9] Ahmad, Kassim, *Hadith: A Re-Evaluation*, Translated from his original book in Malay *Hadis — Satu Penilaian Semula* by Monotheist Productions International, Tucson, Arizona, U.S.A. 1997, © Copyright Kassim Ahmad, 1996, first published in 1986. Available on the internet website www.free-minds.org.

[10] This was a clan of the larger Quraysh tribe.

[11] This was an invitation to him to serve as a judge to settle a bitter feud among some Medinan tribes.

[12] Esposito, John L., *What Everyone Needs to Know About Islam*, Oxford University Press, 2002, p. xiii. A summarized version is available in the internet under the title "Ten Things Everyone Needs to Know about Islam."

[13] Esposito, John L., *What Everyone Needs to Know About Islam*, Oxford University Press, 2002, p. 1.

[14] von Grunebaum, G.E., *Classical Islam: A History 600-1258*, (Translation by Katherine Watson), Barnes and Noble Books, 1996, originally published in 1970 by Aldine Publishing Company, p. 32.

[15] God often refers to Him in the plural, though He is singular. This reference is due to the fact that God acts through His very many agents – angels, human beings, Jinns, other living beings, as well as His other creations, including Nature itself.

[16] Although this male pronoun is generally used for God, it should never be understood to mean that God is male. God is neither male nor female. The conception in which we can understand God does never warrant that we should conceive Him in sex terms. For a conception of God, see Chapter 3.

[17] Lang, Jeffrey, *op. cit.*, 2004, p. 73.

[18] Lang, Jeffrey, *op. cit.*, 2004, p. 71.

[19] Lang, Jeffrey, *op. cit.*, 2004, p. 69.

[20] For a well recognized work on the signs of the Quran, see Maurice Buccaille, *op. cit*, 1977 or 1979.

[21] The term has been used by the noted Eastern Poet-Philosopher Muhammad Iqbal, who has elaborately discussed the significance of religious experience as the basis of Divine revelation and religion in his monumental work "The Reconstruction of Religious Thought in Islam", edited by M. Saeed Sheikh, Adm Publishers and Distributors, Delhi, 1997; also published earlier (in 1934) by the Oxford University Press.

[22] Iqbal, Muhammad, *op. cit.*, 1997, p. 13.

[23] This was a subject matter of Salman Rushdie's infamous book the *Satanic Verses*, a contention that was certainly malicious and misleading.

[24] For details, see Edip Yuksel, *NINETEEN: God's Signature in Nature and Scripture*, Brainbow Press, 2010, Chapter 7.

[25] Buccaille, Maurice, *The Bible, the Qur'an and Science*, Seghers Publishers, Paris, 1977. Also published as *The Bible, the Quran and Science – the Holy Scriptures Examined in the Light of Modern Knowledge, Translated from French by Alastair D. Pannell and the Author*, the American Trust Publications, 1979.

[26] For a full description of the thesis, see Edip Yuksel, *NINETEEN: God's Signature in Nature and Scripture*, Brainbow Press, 2010.

[27] An issue precisely because it is at odds with the Quranic claim that it is divinely protected from possbile corruption and change. Also, the verses in question look quite consistent with the worldview of the Quran.

[28] It seems that "Nineteen" could instead well be interpreted to denote a possible number of the stages of a human being's progress in knowledge and power, based on a similar approach to human progress made by Panaullah Ahmed in his book, *Creator and Creation*, *op. cit.*, 1986. In line with his thinking, eighteen stages can be derived as follows:

The Quran states that we are of three kinds (56:7). Following this clue we can say that existence/creation is in three kinds, and that our progress/evolution or knowledge goes through **three** stages:

- Act on another particular or other particulars;
- Act on the universal, i.e., on God Who represents the universal; and
- Allow the universal to act on the particular.

When one person works with some object or comes into contact with another person, the result is always some new experience or knowledge. This is the first stage of knowledge. The second stage is signified by the worker working selflessly or on behalf of or for the universal, i.e., acting on the universal. The third stage is when his knowledge is strengthened or fortified by gaining insight from the universal.

Another **three** stages are for application of such knowledge to others: acting on particulars, acting on the universal, and allowing the universal to act on the particulars.

These **six** stages confirm or complete one's *knowledge*.

The application of this knowledge thereafter requires another **six** stages, **twelve** in all, to get *real power*.

Power needs application, which means another **six** stages in each act. This gives creation in **eighteen** stages. Ahmad did not indicate still another stage, which would give us **nineteen** stages. But there could conceivably be one such step or stage, which would give us **nineteen** stages in all, which can enable us to decisively overcome hell fire.

[29] For more illumination on the relation between religion and science, see the relevant section in the next chapter.

[30] Esposito, John L., *Islam- The Straight Path*, New York, Oxford University Press, 1991, pp. 30-31.

[31] The expression *"nabiul ummi"* has most often been translated as "unlettered Prophet". However, the Quran itself testifies that the Prophet did learn how to read, though he could not read at first (96:1-5). "The unlettered" is not then the right word for the Prophet. "The gentile or pagan" pointing to his Arab origin thus seems an appropriate rendering of the expression *"nabiul ummi"*.

[32] von Grunebaum, G.E., *op. cit.*, 1996, p. 39.

[33] This confusion has been caused by the Hadith literature, as shown in Chapter 12.

[34] Iqbal, Muhammad, *op. cit.*, 1997, p. 134; also cited in John L. Esposito, *op. cit.*, 1991, p. 138.

[35] Esposito, John L., *op. cit.*, 1991, p. 138.

[36] These comments of Dr. Nasr Hamid Abu Zayd are cited by Caryle Murphy, *Passion for Islam: Shaping the Modern Middle East: The Egyptian Experience*, Simon & Schuster, New York, 2002, p. 190; emphasis is mine. Note that Abu Zayd's writings while he was a teacher in Arabic literature and Quranic studies in Cairo University, notably his *Concept of the [Quranic] Text* published in 1990, irked the Egyptian *ulama* (traditional learned men in Muslim religion) and drew a ruling from an Egyptian court declaring him an apostate and ordering him to divorce his Muslim wife, which forced the couple to flee the country in 1995. He was invited to teach as Visiting Professor at the University of Leiden, the Netherlands, and currently he holds the Ibn Rushd Chair of Humanism and Islam at the University for Humanistics, Utrecht, the Netherlands.

[37] Taken from the website: http://www.freerepublic.com/focus/news/792720/replies?c=2.

[38] For a good discussion of this debate, see Reza Aslan, *No god but God: The Origins, Evolution and Future of Islam*, Random House, New York, 2005, Chapter 6, pp. 140-170.

[39] Khan, Sayyid Ahmad, *Tafsir al-Qur'an*, Aligarh, 1297 A.H., I, pp. 31-34; cited in Daniel W. Brown, *Rethinking Tradition in Modern Islamic Thought*, Cambridge University Press, 1996 (Paperback 1999), p. 44.

[40] Sayyid Ahmad Khan, *Muqalat*, II, 197-258; cited in Daniel W. Brown, *ibid*, Cambridge University Press, 1996 (Paperback 1999), p. 44.

[41] Esposito, John L., *op. cit.*, 1991, p. 21.

[42] Lang, Jeffrey, *op. cit.*, 2004, p. 46.

[43] Iqbal, Muhammad, *op. cit.*, 1997, p. 1.

[44] Iqbal, Muhammad, *op. cit.*, 1997, pp. 1-2.

[45] Iqbal, Muhammad, *op. cit.*, 1997, p. 12.

[46] Iqbal, Muhammad, *op. cit.*, 1997, p. 10.

[47] Lang, Jeffrey, *op. cit.*, 2004, pp. 64-70.

[48] Ahmad, Panaullah, *op cit.*, 1986, p. 113.

[49] For more comments on this, see the section on the relation of religion to science in the next chapter.

[50] Iqbal, Muhammad, *op. cit.*, 1997, p. 16.

[51] Lang, Jeffrey, *op. cit.*, 2004, p. 137.

[52] Iqbal, Muhammad, *op, cit.*, 1934, 1997, Lecture III; also available on the web link: http://www.tolueislam.com/BazmdrIqbal/AI_Reconstruction.htm.

[53] For more on this, see Chapter 3 (The section on "Turning to God and the Conception of God"). For a fuller treatment of the subject, see the author's article "Divine Will and Human Freedom – Part 1. Divine Predestination: How Far Real?" published on OpedNews web link: http://www.opednews.com/articles/Divine-Will-and-Human-Free-by-Abdur-Rab-100102-748.html, and also on free-minds.org website link: http://www.free-minds.org/node/223. It can be read also on the Deen Research Center blog link: http://deenresearchcenter.com/Blogs/tabid/73/EntryId/93/Divine-Will-and-Human-Freedom-Part-I-Divine-Predestination-How-Far-Real.aspx.

[54] Note that this view of the Quran is that of the Rationalists, which is at odds with that of the Traditionalists. The origins of the Rationalists' argument are most clearly traceable to the Mutazilite group during the time of Shafi'i (d. 820), the founder of one of the four schools of thought in Sunni Islam. The Mutazilites were the first to oppose the Hadith theory that it was divinely inspired, as claimed by Shafi'i. The Traditionalists' position is dominated by the Asharite group who accepts the notions of predestination, and *taqlid* (blind acceptance of juridical precedent). For a good discussion of this debate, see Reza Aslan, *No god but God: The Origins, Evolution and Future of Islam*, Random House, New York, 2005, Chapter 6, pp. 140-170.

[55] Lang, Jeffrey, *op. cit.*, 2004, p. 64.

[56] Lang, Jeffrey, *op. cit.*, 2004, p. 65.

[57] Lang, Jeffrey, *op. cit.*, 2004, p. 66.

[58] For own admission in this regard of a scientist as great as Albert Einstein on the relative position of religion *vis-à-vis* science and that of prophets *vis-à-vis* scientists, see the citations from Einstein in the next chapter.

[59] For documentation of this point as well as for that of the overall distortion of the Quranic message by the Hadith, see Chapter 12.

[60] Iqbal, Muhammad, *op. cit.*, 1997, p. 7.

[61] For explanation of the plural pronoun used for God, see Endnote 15 above.

[62] Einstein, Albert, *The Human Side: (New Glimpses from his Archives)*, Selected and edited by Helen Dukas and Banesh Hoffmann, published by Princeton University Press, Princeton, New Jersey, 1979, pp. 32-33.

[63] Einstein, A., *ibid*, 1979, p. 95.

[64] Einstein, A., *ibid*, 1979, pp. 70-71. It looked rather unseemly on Einstein's part not to have mentioned the Prophet Muhammad's name along with Jesus and Moses, especially since Muhammad preached the same religion as Moses and Jesus did.

[65] For some elaboration of the rationale for such beliefs, see Chapter 7.

[66] Ahmad, Panaullah, *op. cit.*, 1986, p. 53.

[67] Ahmad, P. 1986, *op. cit.*, p. 17.

[68] These *iman* or mindset constituents are discussed in some detail in Chapter 7.

[69] For example, the Hadith encourages fatalism, which blunts individual initiative and enterprise. For details, see Chapter 12.

[70] Esposito, John L., *op. cit.*, 1991, p. 138.

[71] Feynman, Richard P. *The Pleasure of Finding Things Out and the Meaning of It All*, Perseus Books, Massachusetts, 1998 (also paperback 1999 by Perseus Books), p. 41.

[72] Feynman, Richard P., *ibid*, 1998, p. 41.

[73] Feynman, Richard P. 1998, pp. 37, 43.

[74] Einstein, A., *op. cit.*, 1979, pp. 69-70.

[75] Einstein, A., *op. cit.*, 1979, pp. 69-70.

[76] Einstein, A., *op. cit.*, 1979, p. 66.

[77] Einstein, A., *op. cit.*, 1979, p. 69.

[78] Scriven, Michael, *Explanations of the Supernatural* in the website: http://www.intuition.org/txt/scriven3.htm, an interesting television transcript of conversation between Michael Scriven and Jeffrey Mishlove on the former's *Explanations of the Supernatural* (1998 Thinking Allowed Productions).

[79] Grof, Stanislav, *Toward a New Paradigm of the Unconscious*, a video presentation in the website: http://www.thinking-allowed.com/2sgrof.html.

[80] See the subject "The Multi-Dimensional Psyche" – an interview with Stan Grof by Russell E. DiCarlo on the website: http://www.healthy.net/scr/Interview.asp?Id=290.

[81] Palmer, Helen, *Personality Development and the Psyche*, transcript of a conversation with Dr. Jeffrey Mishlove under the auspices of the Intuition Network, A Thinking Allowed Television Underwriter. Available on the website link: http://www.intuition.org/txt/palmer.htm.

[82] Feynman, Richard P., *op. cit.*, 1998, pp. 32, 43.

[83] Feynman, Richard P., *op. cit.*, 1998, p. 45-46

[84] Ahmad, Panaullah, *op. cit.*, 1986, p. 200.

[85] Ahmad, Panaullah, *op. cit.*, 1986, p. 238.

[86] Ahmad, Panaullah, *op. cit.* 1986, p. 239.

[87] Lang, Jeffrey, *op. cit.*, 2004, p. 97.

[88] Ahmad, Panaullah, *op. cit.*, 1986, p. 68.

[89] Ahmad, Panaullah, *op. cit.*, 1986, p. 97.

[90] Lang, Jeffrey, *op. cit.*, 204, pp. 112, 113 and 117.

[91] Ahmad, Panaullah, *op. cit.*, 1986, pp. 235-236.

[92] Ahmad, Panaullah, *op. cit.*, 1986, p. 107.

[93] Lang, Jeffrey, op. cit., 2004, p. 141.

[94] As noted before, such points are elaborately dealt with in Chapters 11 and 12.

[95] For a partial list of God's names and attributes, see Annex to this chapter. One thing that may be noted in this context is that Muslims seem generally to believe that God has 99 names or attributes. The partial list provided in this annex suggests that the number of God's attributes considerably exceeds 99, even if some of the attributes might be considered as overlapping with one another.

[96] This viewpoint is contested by the traditionalists. Shafii, a founder of one of the four Sunni schools of thought (*madhhabs*), contended that hadith or *sunnah* was also divinely inspired. But Shafii's point has been effectively rebutted by Ghulam Ahmad Parwez and other Hadith critics. See Daniel W. Brown, *Rethinking Tradition in Modern Islamic Thought*, Cambridge University Press, 1996. For further discussion, see Chapter 11.

[97] Note the golden calf worshipped by Moses' people in his absence.

[98] For more on this, see Chapters 7 and 8 on righteousness.

[99] Ahmad, Panullah, *op. cit.*, 1986, p. 9.

[100] Ahmad, Panaullah, *op. cit.*, 1986, p. 15.

[101] Feynman, Richard P., *op. cit.*, 1998, p. 38.

[102] Ahmad, Panaullah, *op. cit.*, 1986, p. 12.

[103] Bergson, Henri Louis, Creative Evaluation, translated by Arthur Mitchell, London , 1911, as quoted in Muhammad Iqbal, *op cit.*, 1997, pp. 37-38.

[104] Iqbal, Muhammad, *op. cit.*, 1997, p. 38.

[105] Ahmad, Panaullah,. *op. cit*, p. 223.

[106] Ahmad, Panaullah,. *op. cit*, pp. 59, 436.

[107] One meaning of *zakat* is purity or purification. In the Quran God has not advised about where and how we should pay *zakat*. On the other hand, God explicitly mentions about *sadaqa* as charity to the poor and deserving people and causes. The Quran explicitly mentions that sadaqa has been made *fard* or obligatory. And it has fully described where this sadaqa should go. For more elaboration on this, see Chapter 6.

[108] Some details of what makes righteousness are provided in Chapters 7 and 8.

[109] Soroush, Abdolkarim, *Reason, Freedom, and Democracy in Islam*, Oxford University Press, Oxford-New York, 2000, pp. 96-97.

[110] This theory is, according to our knowledge, originally attributable to a little known Eastern sage Shah Aksaruddin Ahmad, who verbally explained its broad outlines to some of his students, and some description of it was found scribbled in some of his unpublished manuscripts. Later in the work of Mr. Panaullah Ahmad (Ahmad, Panaullah, *op. cit.*, 1986, pp. 249, 370-378), who was one of Shah Aksaruddin Ahmad's students, we find some sketchy outlines of this theory.

[111] Ahmad, Panaullah, *op. cit.*, 1986, p. 249.

[112] Iqbal, Muhammad, *op. cit.*, Lecture IV: The Human Ego – His Freedom and Immortality; also available on the web link: http://www.tolueislam.com/BazmdrIqbal/AI_Reconstruction.htm.

[113] Ahmad, Panaullah, *op. cit.*, 1986, pp. vii.

[114] Ahmad, Panaullah, *op. cit.*, 1986, p. 50.

[115] Ahmad, Panaullah, *op. cit.*, 1986, p. 34.

[116] Ahmad, Panullah, *op. cit.*, 1986, p. 8.

[117] The translated text of the *tashahud* reads as follows: All the compliments, prayers and good things are due to Allah. Peace be on you, O Prophet and Allah's mercy and blessings be on you. Peace be on us and on all righteous slaves of Allah. I bear witness that no one is worthy of worship except Allah. I bear witness that Muhammad (peace be upon him) is his slave and Messenger.

[118] Note that *salat* and *dua* are virtually synonymous. *Dua* means calling upon or imploring God for help. Both signify prayer. In fact *salat* should contain *dua*, and should be consistent with *dua* all along, since that is the basic purpose of *salat* (2:153).

[119] For some elaboration of this point, the reader is referred to the section on "the Conceptions of Heaven and Hell" in Chapter 4.

[120] Note, however, that the devil can mislead only unwary and wrongdoing people (26:221-223). The devil resides in us and around us. It is the wrong suggestion coming from one's own mind, or from the minds of others, and whispered to our hearts (114:3-4).

[121] For reasons why we should follow the Quran alone to understand *salat*, and not rely on the Hadith, see also Chapters 11 and 12.

[122] For some detailed description of what constitutes righteousness, the reader is referred to Chapters 7 and 8.

[123] Ahmad, Aksaruddin, *"Musings of the Heart in Songs"* (Bengali Manuscript *Gaan-e Praaner Kotha*, undated), translation by the author.

[124] The reader is referred to Chapter 4 for some elaboration of these points.

[125] Ahmad, Panaullah, *op. cit.*, 1986, pp. 435, 439.

[126] For detailed discussion of such points, the reader can refer to Chapter 5, which is devoted to a fuller treatment of the topic of *salat*.

[127] von Grunebaum, G. E., *Classical Islam: A History 600-1258*, Aldine Publishing Company, 1970, translation by Katherine Watson, published by Barnes & Noble Books, 1996, p. 47. According to Karen Armstrong, the Prophet first enjoined two times and later three times *salat* (prayer). See her *A History of God: The 4000-Year Quest of Judaism, Christianity and Islam*, Gramercy Books, New York, 1993, pp. 142, 153.

[128] Fadl, Khaled Abou El, *The Great Theft: Wrestling Islam from the Extremists*, HarperSan Francisco, A Division of Harper Collins Publishers, New York, 2005, p. 117.

[129] Ahmad, Panaullah, 1986, *op. cit.*, p. 324.

[130] Ahmad, Panaullah, 1986, *op. cit.*, p. 9.

[131] Ahmad, Panaullah, 1986, *op. cit.*, p. 323.

[132] Note, however, that there are divisions among Muslims such as Sunnis, Shiites, etc., who pray in separate congregations; and segregation between men and women is generally maintained in mosques and other public religious gatherings.

[133] It is always preferable however, though not essential, that one's spiritual pursuit is carried forward under the guidance of an adept spiritual teacher, and monitored by him. But one should be very careful to choose a spiritual guide.

[134] Ahmad Panaullah, 1986, *op. cit.*, p. 324.

[135] For some specific examples of distortion of the *salat* conception and practice caused by the Hadith, see Chapter 12.

[136] Ahmad, Aksaruddin, *"Musings of the Heart in Songs"* (Bengali Manuscript undated), translation by the author.

[137] A little more concise version of this chapter, drawn on the relevant sections of the first edition of the book, under the title "Understanding Spending in God's Way (*Zakat* or *Sadaqa*) in the Quranic Light," was published in Edip Yuksel et. al. (ed.), *Critical Thinkers for Islamic Reform*, Brainbow Press, USA, 2009.

[138] The word *zakat* is generally understood as a kind of obligatory poor-due at a certain fixed fraction of one's wealth. The word has also another meaning – purification. In the Quran, the word *"zakat"* is found to have been used in the same verse after "spending for the poor". This suggests that the word *"zakat"* in this verse should be taken to mean purification, rather than poor-due. In that case the meaning of the later part of the verse *"akimus-salat o-atuz- zakat"* should be "establish prayer and attain purification."

[139] Current earnings make up income, and wealth is accumulated earnings and/or inherited assets.

[140] Real resources are land and other natural resources, labor, machinery and equipment, appliances, goods or merchandise, etc. The distinction between real resources and monetary resources (cash money or other monetary assets such as stocks, bonds, etc.) is often not of much substance as the either kind can be converted or exchanged into, or for, the other.

[141] Ahmad, Panaullah, 1986, *op. cit.*, pp. 61-62.

[142] I am grateful to Layth Al-Shaiban, who manages the Internet website http://free-minds.org and is also a co-author of *Quran—A Reformist Translation*, for a comment

on an earlier interpretation of mine, which has helped to rephrase the interpretation into the present one.

[143] One important case in point is the system of protection that the developed countries themselves provide to their domestic activities through government tariffs on imports from developing countries and government subsidies to their farmers for production of agricultural products, and in some cases, through subsidies on exports of certain agricultural products. According to recent World Bank estimates, such trade restrictions of both developed and developing countries hurt the poor [143] The word *zakat* is generally understood as a kind of obligatory poor-due at a certain fixed fraction of one's wealth. The word has also another meaning – purification. The use of the word *zakat* in the same verse after "spending for the poor" suggests that the word *zakat* in this verse should be taken to mean purification, rather than poor-due. In that case the meaning of the later part of the verse "*akimus-salat o-atuz- zakat*" should be like "establish prayer and attain purification".

[144] Einstein, A., *op. cit.*, 1979, pp. 70-71.

[145] Shaw, George Bernard, *The Genuine Islam*, Vol. 1, No. 8, 1936, cited in Mesbah Uddin, "Sunnah – the Misconceived Dogma that Poisoned Islam", first published in the Daily News Monitoring Service: *News From Bangladesh, on December 12, 2004*, also available on the website: submission.org.

[146] Ahmad, Panaullah, *op. cit.*, 1986, pp.199-200, 201.

[147] von Grunebaum, G.E., *Classical Islam: A History 600-1258*, Aldine Publishing Company, 1970, translation by Katherine Watson, published by Barnes and Noble Books, 1996, p. 33.

[148] Refers to the sin committed by the earliest forefathers of humankind Adam and Eve.

[149] von Grunebaum, G.E., *op. cit.*, 1996, p. 33; the article used in parentheses and the emphasis are mine.

[150] Ahmad, Panaullah, *op. cit.*, 1986, p. 219.

[151] Quoted in *The New International Pocket Quotation Dictionary of the English Language*, Trident Press International, 2000, p.119.

[152] For more on this, including a discussion on what is the real meaning of God-given *taqdir*, i.e., predestined or predetermined outcomes and meaning of true reliance on God, see Chapter 3, the section on the meaning of 'turning to God' and the conception of God.

[153] Quoted in Abd al-Ghafir al-Khatib, *Ghazali*, trans. MacCarthy, pp. 15-17, 75; also cited in Imam Feisal Abdul Rauf, *What's Right with Islam: A New Vision for Muslims and the West*, HarperCollins Publishers Inc., New York, 2004, p. 73.

[154] "A depressive disorder is an illness that involves the body, mood, and thoughts. It affects the way a person eats and sleeps, the way one feels about oneself, and the way one thinks about things. A depressive disorder is not the same as a passing blue mood. It is not a sign of personal weakness or a condition that can be willed or wished away. People with a depressive illness cannot merely "pull themselves together" and get better. Without treatment, symptoms can last for weeks, months, or years. Appropriate treatment, however, can help most people who suffer from depression. Some of the signs and symptoms of this disease are:

- Persistent sad, anxious, or "empty" mood;
- Feelings of hopelessness, pessimism;
- Feelings of guilt, worthlessness, helplessness; and

- Loss of interest or pleasure in hobbies and activities that were once enjoyed.

Depressive disorders come in different forms, just as is the case with other illnesses such as heart disease. However, within these types there are variations in the number of symptoms, their severity, and persistence.

Major depression is manifested by a combination of such symptoms that interfere with the ability to work, study, sleep, eat, and enjoy once pleasurable activities. A variety of treatments including medications and short-term psychotherapies have proven effective for depression.

A less severe type of depression, *dysthymia*, involves long-term, chronic symptoms that do not disable, but keep one from functioning well or from feeling good. Many people with dysthymia also experience major depressive episodes at some time in their lives.

Another type of depression is *bipolar disorder*, also called manic-depressive illness. Not nearly as prevalent as other forms of depressive disorders, bipolar disorder is characterized by cycling mood changes: severe highs (mania) and lows (depression). Sometimes the mood switches are dramatic and rapid, but most often they are gradual. When in the depressed cycle, an individual can have any or all of the symptoms of a depressive disorder. When in the manic cycle, the individual may be overactive, over talkative, and have a great deal of energy. Mania often affects thinking, judgment, and social behavior in ways that cause serious problems and embarrassment. For example, the individual in a manic phase may feel elated, full of grand schemes that might range from unwise business decisions to romantic sprees. Mania, left untreated, may worsen to a psychotic state." (Website: http://www.nimh.nih.gov/publicat/depression.cfm#intro)

[155] Saying of Pliny the Elder, cited in *The New International Pocket Quotation Dictionary of the English Language*, Trident Press International, 2000, p. 26.

[156] This subject has been discussed in detail in Chapter 7, and will again be touched in the next chapter.

[157] Einstein, Albert, *The Human Side*, 1979, *op. cit.*, p. 70-71.

[158] United Nations (United Nations Office for the High Commissioner for Human Rights (OHCHR)), *Report of the World Conference against Racism, Racial Discrimination, Xenophobia and Related Intolerance,* (held in Durban, during 31 August - 8 September 2001), January 25, 2002.

[159] The UN report cited in the preceding endnote.

[160] Some of the worst human tragedies and crimes against humanity of the last century include the Holocaust during the nineteen thirties and forties, the world's largest and most gruesome genocide, which involved, in addition to torture, killing of more than 6 million people, mostly Jews – extermination of some two thirds of the Jews of Europe - by the Nazis; the genocide of Armenians up to 1.5 million (estimated by historians) by Ottoman Turks around the time of World War I, an event widely viewed by scholars as the first genocide of the 20th century (but. denied by Turkey that the deaths constituted genocide, saying the toll has been inflated and those killed were victims of civil war and unrest); the Cambodian genocide of 1975-1979, in which approximately 1.7 million people lost their lives (21% of the country's population); mass killings in Bangladesh (then East Pakistan) in 1971 by the Pakistan

army; and those in East Timor in 1979-80 involving killing of over one fifth of its population; the Rwanda genocide in 1994 involving killing of nearly I million, mainly of the Tutsis by the Hutus; Hindu Muslim communal riots in undivided British India just prior to its independence and partition in 1947 involving arson, mass human slaughter and massive human displacements; and ethnic cleansing in Bosnia in the last decade of the century. As reported by the Wall Street Journal Online Edition (dated April 21, 2005), since 2003, government-backed militias have waged a campaign against rebels (Christians and non-Arab Muslims) in the Darfur region of Sudan, resulting in at least 180,000 deaths and leaving more than two million people homeless. In the course of their counter-insurgency, they have been accused of committing all manner of atrocities, including murder, rape and the destruction of villages. Despite recent peace efforts with ceasefire, atrocities against displaced persons put in camps and against aid workers are still continuing.

[161] Ahmed, Akbar S., *Islam under Siege: Living Dangerously in a Post-Honor World*, Polity Press in association with Blackwell Publishing Ltd., Cambridge, UK and Malden, MA, USA, 2003, pp. 36-37.

[162] Statement of Rev. Jesse Jackson at Durban Racism Conference on August 30, 2001, the day before the start of a U.N. conference against racism.

[163] Khan, M.A. Muqtedar, *American Muslims: Bridging Faith and Freedom*, Amana Publications, 2002, pp. 67-68.

[164] Reference may be made of the United Nations Report cited in Endnote 158, which mentions the actions that were taken before, and the follow-up actions that are being taken afterward.

[165] For an elaborate treatment of this point, see Chapter 9, section on the status of women.

[166] Khan, Aasma, "How Muslims can Combat Terror and Violence" in Michael Wolfe & Beliefnet (ed.), *Taking Back Islam: American Muslims Reclaim Their Faith*, Rodale Inc and Beliefnet Inc, 2002, p. 51.

[167] Soroush, Abdolkarim, *Reason, Freedom, and Democracy in Islam*, Oxford University Press, Oxford-New York, 2000, p. 97.

[168] Fadl, Khaled Abou El, *The Great Theft: Wrestling Islam from the Extremists*, HarperSan Francisco, A Division of Harper Collins Publishers, New York, 2005, p. 209.

[169] Esposito, John L., *What Everyone Needs to Know About Islam*, Oxford University Press, 2002, pp. 70-71. A summarized version is available in the Internet under the title "Ten Things Everyone Needs to Know about Islam." The following brief account on the record of religious intolerance of Christians provides a sharp contrast: "Many of the Nazis who slaughtered millions of civilians during World War II were Christians (in that they were of the Christian religion); many of the Crusaders who massacred unarmed Muslim men, women, and children in the name of God were devoted Christians; the Spanish inquisitors who tortured and murdered non-Christians were committed Christians; the white soldiers who brought about the genocide of native American peoples in North and South America – often accompanied by missionaries – were Christians; and so were the armies of Charlemagn who eagerly slaughtered tens of thousands of pagan Anglo Saxons." (Jeffrey Lang, *op, cit*, 2004, p. 302, Footnote 206.

[170] Where, as Esposito rightly notes, the blame for such clashes cannot always be pinned down or put on Muslims. See Esposito in the previous endnote.

[171] Esposito, John L., *Islam – The Straight Path*, Oxford University oppress, 1992, p. 192, the expression in parentheses is mine. He writes: "In recent years, tensions and

clashes between Muslim and non-Muslim communities have increased: the Copts in Egypt, Bahai and Jews in Iran, Chinese in Malaysia, and Christians in the Sudan, Pakistan, and Nigeria. The creation of more Islamically oriented societies, especially the introduction of Islamic laws, has resulted in varying degrees of tension, conflict, violence, and killing in the name of religion. For militant Muslims, Christian minorities are often seen as those who cooperated with colonial powers, benefited from their protection, and were the fruit of Christian missions. The Bahai of Iran and the Ahmadiya of Pakistan, on the other hand, are regarded as apostates or heretics who rejected and broke away from Islam." *Ibid*, p. 192.

[172] This led the couple to seek exile in the Netherlands.

[173] See Mansour, Ahmed Subhy, "Islamic Tolerance: A Comparison between Egypt and America: Reverting Islam back to its Tolerant Roots" in the website: www.islamicpluralism.org/texts/2005t/islamictolerance.htm. Because of his views, Mansour, a Professor in Al-Azhar University, was removed from the University, harassed with imprisonment, and threatened with life, which led him to seek exile into the United States. Mansour's extended family members and his fellow Quranists were also subjected to harassment, persecution and torture.

[174] Khan, M.A. Muqtedar, 2002, *op. cit.*, p. 38. For more illumination on the backlash against Muslims, see Akbar S. Ahmed, *op. cit.*, 2003, pp. 39-41.

[175] Taken from American writer George Melloan, "Making Muslims Part of the Solution", the *Wall Street Journal*, issue of March 29, 2005.

[176] See the latest July 30, 2007 Newsweek article "Islam in America: A Special Report" by Lisa Miller.

[177] Only a handful of people were executed due to breach of law. A few rich men were persuaded to make a contribution to compensate the poorer followers who were deprived of the booty. See G.E. von Grunebaum 1970, *op. cit.*, p. 44.

[178] Incidents of such sectarian strife, violence and killing have been recurrent notably in Pakistan, and more recently and markedly in Iraq.

[179] Fadl, Khaled Abou El et. al, *The Place of Tolerance in Islam*, Beacon Press, Boston, 2002, pp. 21-22.

[180] Yuksel, Edip, *Peacemaker's Guide to Warmongers: Exposing Robert Spencer, Osama bin Laden, David Horowitz, Mullah Omar, Bill Warner, Ali Sina and Other Enemies of Peace*, Brainbow Press, USA, 2010, p.41.

[181] Armstrong, Karen, *A History of God*, Gramercy Books, New York, 1993, pp. 155-156.

[182] One hadith text refers to a killing of a sleeping man in his house by a group of Muslims sent by the Prophet (*Sahih Bukhari*, Vol. 4, Book 52, # 264, 265), and another text encourages Muslims to kill youths with foolish thoughts and ideas (*Sahih Bukhari*, Vol. 6, Book 61, # 577; repeated at Vol. 9, Book 84, # 64). The Hadith also prescribes that apostates should be punished with killing. There are also texts that are clearly anti-Semitic. All these hadith texts are contradictory to what the Quran states. For citation of the relevant hadith texts, see Chapter 12.

[183] Cited in *The New International Pocket Quotation Dictionary of the English Language*, Trident Press International, 2000, p.70.

[184] William Shakespeare, *Julius Caesar* (II, ii, 32-37). Also cited in *The New International Pocket Quotation Dictionary of the English Language*, Trident Press International, 2000, p. 70.

[185] Taken from *The New International Pocket Quotation Dictionary of the English Language*, Trident Press International, 2000, p. 121.

[186] Taken from *The New International Pocket Quotation Dictionary of the English Language*, Trident Press International, 2000, p.122.

[187] See Ahmed Subhy Mansour, "The Culture of Slaves", website: http://www.islamicpluralism.org/texts/2005t/egyptslavecult.htm#Culture_of_Slaves.

[188] A saying of Mahatma Gandhi, cited in *The New International Pocket Quotation Dictionary of the English Language*, Trident Press International, 2000, p. 19.

[189] A generally applied but partial measure of corruption is given by the misuse of public power for private gain in forms such as bribing of public officials, kickbacks in public procurement, or embezzlement. Since 1995, an international organization the Transparency International has been producing annual corruption scores (called CPI – Corruption Perceptions Index) for many countries of the world, starting with as many as 97 countries in 1995 and covering 133 countries in 2003. Such scores suggest that the most corrupt countries in the world are those located in Asia and Africa.

Also note that a recent 2002 International Monetary Fund Staff Working Paper (IMF WP 02/213) titled "The Persistence of Corruption and Slow Economic Growth" authored by Paolo Mauro) examined the questions why the economic costs of corruption are high with substantial adverse effects on economic growth, and why many countries appear to be stuck in a vicious circle of widespread corruption and low economic growth, often accompanied by ever-changing governments through revolutions and coups. A possible explanation explored in the paper is that when corruption is widespread, individuals do not have incentives to fight it even if everybody would be better off without it.

[190] For some discussion of the possible implications of the Quranic message for the economic system, see Chapter 10.

[191] For more material on this topic, see Chapter 6 on spending in God's Way and Chapter 10 on the implications of the Quranic message for the economic system.

[192] For more on this, see Chapters 3 and 9.

[193] Putting on a dress in a decent or dignified way should not be interpreted as wearing a headdress or headscarf and a "*burqa*" or veil all over the body, even covering one's face. The Qur'an clearly states that such dresses can leave such parts of the body uncovered as are normally apparent such as head, face, hands and feet. It specifically mentions the private parts and bosoms for covering by the dress. It does not mention head, face, hands and feet.

[194] HIV stands for Human Immuno-deficiency Virus.

[195] AIDS stands for Acquired Immune Deficiency Syndrome.

[196] A recently published United Nations report "*AIDS in Africa*" released on March 4, 2005 says that more than 25 million Africans have already been infected with HIV, the virus that causes AIDS. The agency UNAIDS estimates that more than 80 million Africans may die from AIDS by 2025 and infections could soar to 90 million -- or more than 10% of the continent's population -- if more isn't done soon to fight the disease. The disease is having a devastating effect on the continent. The UNAIDS reports that life expectancy in nine countries has dropped to below 40 years because of the disease. There are 11 million orphans, while 6,500 people are dying each day. In 2004 3.1 million people were newly infected. (The *Wall Street Journal*, Online Edition, March 4, 2005) WHO and UN reported more recently (in November 2005) that an estimated 40 million people worldwide are HIV-positive, including a record 1 million in the United States. In New York City, doctors were alarmed to discover a particularly powerful strain of HIV in a sexually active gay man. Resistant to all but

one of the classes of anti-AIDS drugs, that fast-working virus appears to lead to a full-blown AIDS in a matter of months. (*Time* magazine, December 3, 2005)

[197] The statements attributed to the Prophet Jesus are that "You have heard that it was said, 'An eye for an eye and a tooth for a tooth.' But I say to you: Do not resist an evil-doer. But if anyone strikes you on the right cheek, turn the other also." (*Matthew* 5:1-2, 38-39).

[198] For more on this, see the section on tolerance in the preceding chapter.

[199] For some description of these rules regarding the shares that should go to females *vis-à-vis* males, see Chapter 9.

[200] The Qur'an mentions that certain foods were forbidden especially for the Jews because of their rebellion. These were animals which had undivided hoofs and fat of cattle and sheep except some specified fat (6:146).

[201] Yuksel, Edip, Layth Saleh al-Shaiban and Martha Schulte-Nafeh, *Quran: A Reformist Translation*, Brainbow Press, 2007.

[202] Iqbal, Muhammad, *op, cit.*, 1997 (Oxford University Press, 1934), pp. 136-137. Also cited in Daniel W. Brown, *Rethinking Tradition in Modern Islamic Thought*, Cambridge University Press, 1996 (Paperback 1999), p. 25.

[203] Fadl, Khaled Abou El, *op. cit.*, 2005, p. 131.

[204] According to distinguished contemporary scholar Khaled Abou El Fadl, the current practice of Islamic or *shariah* law suffers from the deficiencies of both "a lack of competency [on the part of those who apply it] in the usage of legal objectives and methodologies [of *shariah*]" and the non-development of such objectives and methodologies "to meet contemporary advances in epistemology, hermeneutics, or social theory. In the contemporary age, Muslims end up with a rather ironic and painfully nonsensical paradigm." Cf., Khaled Abou El Fadl, *op. cit.*, 2001, p. 111.

[205] Esposito, John L., *op. cit.*, 2002, p. 149.

[206] Ahmad, P. *op. cit.*, p. 246.

[207] Ahmad, Aksaruddin, *"The Musings of the Heart in Songs"* (Bengali manuscript *Gaan-e Praan-er Kotha* undated), translation by the author.

[208] Some countries such as the Netherlands, Belgium, Norway, Sweden, South Africa and, since just recently, Spain and Canada officially recognize same-sex (gay or lesbian) couples (the Netherlands since 2001, Belgium since 2003 and Spain and Canada since July 2005). In the United States, same-sex marriages are not recognized federally, but several states (New Hampshire, Iowa, Massachusetts, Vermont, and Connecticut) have recently legalized such marriages.

[209] "Gendercide" and other articles, The Economist, March 6th-12th, 2010 issue, pp. 13, 77-80 and 104-105. The seriousness of the gender imbalance in China is illustrated by a statistic: there are almost as many unmarried young men in China as the total number of (both married and unmarried) young men in the United states – ibid, p. 13.

[210] Lewis, Bernard, *What Went Wrong? Western Impact and Middle Eastern Response*, Oxford University Press, New York, 2002, p. 71.

[211] It is unfortunate that the Hadith literature gives such a horrible impression about the Prophet.

[212] Two noted examples in the exception category are wives of Noah and Lut (7:83; 66:10).

[213] As reported in Amir Taheri, *Spirit of Allah: Khomeini and the Islamic Revolution*, Adler and Adler, 1986, p.51; cited in Spencer, Robert, *Islam Unveiled: Disturbing Questions about the World's Fastest-Growing Faith*, Encounter Books, San Francisco, 2002. p. 87.

214 In recent years, notable reforms have been carried out in the Muslim marriage and divorce laws in a number of countries such as limitation of polygamy rights, expansion of rights for women seeking divorce, including the right to financial compensation, expansion of rights for women to participate in contracting their marriage and to stipulate conditions favorable to them in the marriage contract, the requirement that the husband provide housing for his divorced wife and children as long as the wife holds custody over the children, raising of the minimum age for marriage for both spouses, prohibition of child marriage, and expansion of the rights of women to have custody over their older children. Cf., John L. Esposito, *op. cit.*, 2002, p. 93.

215 Armstrong, Karen, *op. cit.* 1993, pp. 157-158.

216 Esposito, John L., *op. cit.*, 2002, pp. 90-91.

217 Fadl, Khaled Abou El, *op. cit.*, 2005, p. 268.

218 For some illumination on this point, see Irshad Manji, *The Trouble with Islam: A Muslim's Call for Reform in Her Faith*, St. Martin's Press, New York, 2003, pp. 160-167.

219 Wadud, Amina, *Qur'an and Woman: Reading the Sacred Text from a Woman's Perspective*, Oxford University Press, New York, 1999, p. 76.

220 Aslan, Reza, 2005, *op. cit.*, pp. 69-70.

221 Yuksel, Edip, Layth Saleh al-Shaiban and Martha Schulte-Nafeh, *op. cit.*, 2007, p. 93, verse 4:34.

222 Lang, Jeffrey, *op. cit.*, 2004, p. 430.

223 It is also extended to other than humans (2:116; 30:27).

224 Wadud, Amina, *op. cit.*, 1999, p. 74.

225 Wadud, Amina, *op. cit.*, 1999, pp. 69-74.

226 Wadud, Amina, *op. cit.*, 1999, pp.95-99.

227 Fadl, Khaled Abou El, *op. cit.*, 2005, pp. 263-264.

228 Esposito, John L., *op. cit.*, 2002, p. 92.

229 Lewis, Bernard, 2002, *op. cit.*, p. 71.

230 Esposito, John L., *op. cit.*, 1991, p. 144.

231 Aslan, Reza, 2005, *op. cit.*, pp. 73-74.

232 Aslan, Reza, 2005, *op. cit.*, p. 74.

233 Esposito, John L., *op. cit.*, 2002, pp. 93-94.

234 Esposito, John L., *op. cit.*, 2002, pp. 96.

235 Esposito, John L., *op. cit.*, 2002, p. 95.

236 Aslan, Reza, 2005, *op. cit.*, p. 69.

237 Fadl, Khaled Abou El, "The Ugly Modern and the Modern Ugly: Reclaiming the Beautiful in Islam", in Omid Safi (ed.), *Progressive Muslims: On Justice, Gender, and Pluralism*, Oneworld Publications, Oxford, 2003, p.44. For a systematic analysis of the deprecating treatment of women, see Khaled Abou El Fadl, *Speaking in God's Name: Islamic Law, Authority and Women*, Oneworld Publications, Oxford, 2001, pp. 170-249.

238 Lewis, Bernard, *op. cit.*, 2002, p. 73.

239 Lewis, Bernard, *ibid.*, 2002, pp. 64-75.

240 Esposito, John L., *op. cit.*, 2002, p. 148.

241 *Source*: The Concise Columbia Encyclopedia, 1995 by Columbia University Press from MS Bookshelf, as cited and compiled by Eddie Becker in the Internet.

242 Lewis, Bernard, 2002, *op. cit.*, p. 69.

243 Manji, Irshad, *op. cit.*, 2003, p. 37.

[244] For some illumination on this point, see Endnote 189 above.

[245] This is an economic argument. It states that tinkering with taxes and subsidies that may affect production itself or prices (of goods, services or factors of production) would distort the appropriate allocation and efficiency of productive resources, resulting in less than optimal production and growth in the economy. Hence public assistance programs should be devised in such a way that they do not distort production and prices in the economy.

[246] The neo-classical position that market-clearing activities under laissez faire leads to an optimal solution is valid only when the given distribution of income and wealth in society can be considered as sacrosanct or optimal. If, however, the given wealth and income distribution is considered to be highly or significantly inequitable, there should be a prior redistribution of such wealth and income. For example, there are countries, where the existing distribution of land resources is highly unequal, which requires redistribution in favor of the landless. This is dictated also by good economics from the point of view of maximizing or optimizing production in the economy.

[247] Akyol, Mustafa, "Islamocapitalism: Islam and Free Market" in Edip Yuksel, et. al. (ed.), *Critical Thinkers for Islamic Reform*, Brainbow Press, United States of America, 2009.

[248] For some discussion of this point, see Chapter 6.

[249] Rauf, Imam Feisal Abdul, *What is Right with Islam: A New Vision for Muslims and the West*, HarperCollins Publishers, Inc., New York, 2004, pp. 3-4.

[250] Akyol, Mustafa, *op. cit.*, 2009.

[251] This happens as follows: As long as an individual's marginal time preference (i.e., time preference at the margin of his spending, i.e., time preference when he spends his last dollar) is larger than the current interest rate, he will continue to spend on his current consumption until his marginal time preference (which falls with higher and higher spending) becomes equal to the interest rate. He cannot increase his marginal spending on current consumption beyond this point, since in that case interest cost of present consumption would be larger than his time preference. Thus interest plays the essential role of an allocative device between consumption and saving of individuals.

[252] A higher rate of growth in the economy, which is associated with higher profits or returns on invested capital, thus gives rise to a higher real rate of interest.

[253] Capital can be used in alternative ways. One will invest in ways where the return on capital is the highest to the point where the return at the margin, i.e., return on the last dollar invested becomes equal to the existing interest rate. The interest rate thus plays both as a rationing device, i.e., it helps ration the uses of the capital to the amount of the existing available capital and it also allocates capital resources between different uses so that the possible maximum profit potential can be realized, and possible misuses avoided.

[254] See Berk, Jan Marc, "Book Review" (Review of two books by A.L.M. Abdul Gafoor: *Interest-Free Commercial Banking*, Apptech Publications, Groningen, 1995, and Participatory Financing through Investment Banks and Commercial Banks, Apptech Publications, Groningen, 1996), *De Economist* (Quarterly Review of the Royal Netherlands Economic Association), Vol. 146, No. 1, April 1998.

[255] Berk, Jan Marc, *ibid*, 1998.

[256] *hadith* – sing. (pl. *ahadith*), lit., a report, account or statement. In generally used Islamic law and discourse, it refers to traditions attributed to the Prophet Muhammad.

447

[257] *sunnah* – lit., the way, course or conduct of life. In general Muslim belief, it refers to the way of Prophet Muhammad.

[258] Other alleged sources of Islam are the *qiyas* and the *ijma*. *Qiyas* refers to comparative or analogical deduction in a particular case derived from the analogy of similar cases. Qiyas is used to provide parallels between similar situations or principles when no clear text is found in the Quran or Sunnah. Ijma, regarded as the fourth source of law, originated from Muhammad's reported saying, "My community will never agree on an error." This came to mean that a consensus among religious scholars could determine permissibility of an action. The Fiqh literature is an anthology of Islamic law or jurisprudence derived from the Hadith sources. The reader should note that this author does not believe that Islam should be understood by any other book except the Quran, which only brought Islam and perfected Islam (5:3).

[259] This is what modern Muslim and non-Muslim scholars generally have attempted to do, as reflected in many of their works. See in particular the cover page introduction to the book Michael Wolfe and the Producers of Beliefnet (ed.), *Taking Back Islam: American Muslims Reclaim Their Faith*, Rodale Inc. and Beliefnet Inc., 2002.

[260] Ahmad, Panaullah, *op. cit.*, 1986, p. 295.

[261] Some might still contend, the Hadith contains good words as well. Well, that is no good or sufficient defense for the Hadith thesis, for such good words are either submerged in, or overshadowed by, a sea of misleading or worthless texts. One is more likely to be overwhelmed by the worthless texts than the really worthwhile ones, which one can find much more easily in the Quran.

[262] Brown, Daniel W., *Rethinking Tradition in Modern Islamic Thought*, Cambridge University Press, 1996 (Paperback 1999), pp. 15-16.

[263] Brown, Daniel W., *ibid*, 1996 (Paperback 1999), p. 15.

[264] Azami, M. A., *Studies in Hadith Methodology and Literature*, Islamic Book Trust, Kuala Lumpur, p. 92, quoted in Akbarally Meherally, *Myths and Realities of Hadith – A Critical Study*, (published by Mostmerciful.com Publishers), Burnaby, BC, Canada, p. 6, available in the website http://www.mostmerciful.com/hadithbook-sectionone.htm.

[265] Azami, M. A., *Studies in Hadith Methodology and Literature*, Islamic Book Trust, Kuala Lumpur, p. 92, quoted in Akbarally Meherally, *Myths and Realities of Hadith – A Critical Study*, (published by Mostmerciful.com Publishers), Burnaby, BC, Canada, p. 6, available in the website http://www.mostmerciful.com/hadithbook-sectionone.htm.

[266] Esposito, John L., *Islam – The Straight Path*, Oxford University Press, 1991, p. 134.

[267] Cited in Daniel W. Brown, *op. cit.*, 1996 (paperback 1999), p. 88; the emphasis is mine.

[268] Khan, Ahmad, *Maqalat*, I, pp.27-28; cited in Brown, Daniel W., *op. cit.*, 1996 (paperback 1999), p. 97; the emphasis is mine.

[269] Ahmad, Kassim, *Hadith: A Re-Evaluation*, Translated from his original book in Malay *Hadis — Satu Penilaian Semula* by Monotheist Productions International, Tucson, Arizona, U.S.A. 1997, © Copyright Kassim Ahmad, 1996, first published in 1986. Available on the website: free-minds.org. Information about Abu Rayya is also mentioned in Shahab Ahmed, "A General Introduction" to the Hadith, available on the website: www.iranica.com/articles/v11f4/v11f4072a.html..

[270] Sidqi, Muhammad Tawfiq, "al-Islam huwa al-Qur'an wahdahu," *al-Manar* 9 (1906), p. 515; cited in Brown, Daniel, 1996, *op. cit.*, pp. 88-89.

[271] Brown, Daniel, 1996, *op. cit.*, pp. 47, 40-41.

[272] Sidqi, Muhammad Tawfiq, "al-Islam huwa al-Qur'an wahdahu," al-Manar, 9, 1906, p. 515. Also see Ghulam Ahmed Parwez, Maqam-i-hadith, 2nd edn., Karachi, 1965, p. 350. Cited in Brown, Daniel, 1996, *op. cit.*, p. 54.

[273] Brown, Daniel, 1996, *op. cit.*, p. 89.

[274] Brown, Daniel, 1996, *op. cit.*, p. 38.

[275] Brown, Daniel, 1996, *op. cit.*, pp. 38-39.

[276] He was the founder of a Bengali Daily *"The Azad"* and writer of a biography of Prophet Muhammad *"Mustafa Charit"* in Bengali.

[277] Cited in Farooq, Dr. Muhammad Omar, "Dr. Farooq's Study Resource Page" in website: http://globalwebpost.com/farooqm/study_res/islam/hadith/akramkhan_hadith.html.

[278] Cited in M. Jamilul Bashar's book in Bengali "Sangsker" (Reformation), published by Young Muslim Society, New York, 2002, p. 49.

[279] He wrote many books in Urdu covering the Quranic teachings. He is also author of "Islam – A Challenge to Religion" in English. His position on the Hadith is detailed in his Urdu work "Muquuam-e-Hadith" (The True Status of the Hadith). His English book and English translations of other books in Urdu are available in the website www.tolueislam.com/Parwez/mh/mh_01.htm.

[280] Rippin, Andrew, *Muslims: Their Religious Beliefs and Practices* vol. 1 (New York: Routledge, 1990), p. 74; cited in *Hadith Authenticity: A Survey of Perspectives* (by anonymous author), at website: http://www.rim.org/muslim/hadith.htm, or at http://www.rim.org/muslim/islam.htm.

[281] Parwez, Ghulam Ahmed, *Salim ke nam khutut*, Karachi, 1953, Vol. 1, p. 43; cited in Brown, Daniel, 1996, *op. cit.*, p. 54.

[282] Rippin, Andrew, *op. cit.*, p. 74; Andrew Rippin, *Muslims: Their Religious Beliefs and Practices* vol. 1 (New York: Routledge, 1990), 78; cited in *Hadith Authenticity: A Survey of Perspectives* (by anonymous author), at website: http://www.rim.org/muslim/hadith.htm, or at http://www.rim.org/muslim/islam.htm.

[283] Parwez was an admirer of, and took inspiration from, the great Muslim thinker and philosopher Muhammad Iqbal. At his request, he published and founded in 1938 the *Tolu-i- Islam* in Urdu, a monthly magazine.

[284] Author of *Do Islam* (Two Islams), 1950 and other works.

[285] Barq, Ghulam Jilani, "Hadith ke bare men mera mawqaf," Chatan, Lahore, January 9, 1956; cited by Majid, Raja F. M., "Ghulam Jilani Barq: A Study in Muslim 'Rationalism,'" M.A. thesis, McGill University, Institute of Islamic Studies, 1962, p. 80; cited in Daniel W. Brown, *op. cit.*, 1996 (Paperback 1999), p. 128.

[286] The book he published contesting the Hadith is titled *"Quran, Hadith and Islam"*, which was reproduced in the Internet in 1982. He has a good and easy to understand English translation of the Quran. His works are available in the website under www.submission.org, or under *"The Computer Speaks: God's Message to the World, Quran, Hadith and Islam."*

[287] In addition, I found the "index" provided at the end of his translation as the most detailed and useful for Quranic reference purposes.

[288] See his *Quran, Hadith and Islam, op. cit.*, 1982.

[289] The books in Bengali he was trying to write are titled (1) *Pabitra Quran: Banganubad o Shabdartha (The Holy Quran: Bengali Translation and Word Rendering)*, its first part of the thirty parts was completed and printed), (2) *Mussalman Aj Kon Path-e?* (*Whither are Muslims Today?*, and (3) *Gaan-e Praaner Kotha (The Musings of the Heart in Songs)*".

[290] It was rather unusual but encouraging seeing that the Bangladesh Islamic Foundation, which is found generally to represent the traditional view, published his book *Creator and Creation* in 1986.

[291] Ahmad, Panaullah, *op. cit.*, 1986, pp. 138-140, 295, 328-330, 347-348; emphasis is mine.

[292] His book is titled: *Hadith: A Re-Evaluation*, Translated from his original book in Malay *Hadis — Satu Penilaian Semula* by Monotheist Productions International, Tucson, Arizona, U.S.A. 1997, © Copyright Kassim Ahmad, 1996, first published in 1986. Available on the internet website www.free-minds.org.

[293] Rippin, Andrew, *Muslims: Their Religious Beliefs and Practices* vol. 1 (New York: Routledge, 1990), 78; cited in *Hadith Authenticity: A Survey of Perspectives* (by anonymous author), at website: http://www.rim.org/muslim/hadith.htm, or at http://www.rim.org/muslim/islam.htm.

[294] Cited in Rippin, *ibid*, pp. 78-79; emphasis is mine.

[295] Ahmad, Kassim, *op. cit*, 1997.

[296] His book in Bengali is titled '*Sanskar*' (*Reformation*) published by the Young Muslim Society, New York, 2002. The inspiration for his book came from his father who was a very devoted disciple of Shah Aksaruddin Ahmad.

[297] Author of *A Study of the Qur'an: The Universal Guidance for Mankind*, 1997, third edition 2000, Sutton, Surrey, UK, with a chapter on "The Implications of Hadith for Islam" available in the website http://www.members.aol.com/MAmalek2/.

[298] Author of "Hadith and the Corruption of the Great Religion of Islam", website: http://www.submission.org/had-corruption.html.

[299] Author of an article "Sunnah – the Misconceived Dogma that Poisoned Islam", first published in the Daily News Monitoring Service: *News From Bangladesh, on December 12, 2004*, also available on the website: submission.org.

[300] Lang, Jeffrey, *op. cit.*, 2004, p. 475.

[301] The first edition of this book (published by iUniverse) has been, and this edition also is, aimed at making some contribution to this ongoing movement.

[302] For some description and evaluation of their contribution to Islamic reforms, see John L. Esposito, *Islam – The Straight Path*, Oxford University Press, 1991, pp. 126-147..

[303] The door of ijtihad was closed by the *ulama* by the tenth century, to which earlier scholars of Islam who took exception are Ibn Taymiyya (d. 1328) and al-Suyuti (d. 1505). Cf., Esposito, John L., *ibid*, 1991, p. 84.

[304] Esposito, John L., *ibid*, 1991, p. 138.

[305] Esposito, John L., *ibid*, 1991, pp. 81-82.

[306] Author of *The Life of Mahomet and the History of Islam to the Era of Hegira*, 4 vols., London, 1861; repr. Osnabruck, 1988. First serialized in Calcutta *Review* 19, (January- June 1853): 1-8. Also cited in Daniel Brown, 1996, *op. cit.*

[307] Sprenger, Alois, "On the Origin of Writing Down Historical Records among the Musulmans', *Journal of the Asiatic Society of Bengal 25*.(1856), 303-329, 375-381; Cited in Daniel Brown, 1996, *op. cit.*

[308] Author of *Muhammedanische Studien,*. 2 vols., Leiden, 1896. Trans. by S.M. Stern as *Muslim Studies*, 2 vols., London, 1967. Also cited in Daniel Brown, 1996, *op. cit.*

[309] Author of *Muhammadan Jurisprudence*. Oxford University Press, Oxford, 1950, especially pages 138-76; cited in John Esposito, *Islam – The Straight Path*, *op. cit.*

[310] Author of *Muslim Tradition - Studies in Chronology, Provenance and Authorship of Early Hadith* (New York: Cambridge University Press, 1983. Also cited in Daniel Brown, 1996, *op. cit.*

450

[311] Brown, Daniel, 1996, *op. cit.*, p. 21.

[312] Muir, William, *The Life of Mahomet and the History of Islam to the Era of Hegira*, 4 vols., London, 1861; repr. Osnabruck, 1988, I, xxvii; cited in Daniel Brown, 1996, *op. cit.*, p. 35.

[313] Brown, Daniel, 1996, *op. cit.*, p. 35.

[314] Ahmed, Shahab, "A General Introduction" to the Hadith, available in the website http://www.iranica.com/articles/v11f4/v11f4072a.html.

[315] Cited by Reza Aslan, *No god but God: The Origins, Evolution, and the Future of Islam*, Random House, New York, 2005, p. 68.

[316] Esposito, John L. 1991, *op. cit.*, p. 82.

[317] Juynboll, G.H.A, *Muslim Tradition - Studies in Chronology, Provenance and Authorship of Early Hadith*, 1983, p. 71. Also cited in *Hadith Authenticity: A Survey of Perspectives* (by anonymous author), at website: http://www.rim.org/muslim/hadith.htm, or at http://www.rim.org/muslim/islam.htm.

[318] Juynboll, *ibid*, 1983, pp. 15-17, 45, 52-55, 60, 70, 89; cited in Lang, Jeffrey, *op. cit*, 2004, pp.226-228.

[319] Buccaille, Maurice, *The Bible, the Quran and Science – the Holy Scriptures Examined in the Light of Modern Knowledge*, Translated from French by Alastair D. Pannell and the Author, the American Trust Publications, 1979.

[320] Buccaille, Maurice, *ibid*, pp. 2 and 5. Also cited in Ahmad, Kassim, *op. cit.*, p. 88.

[321] Cited in *Hadith Authenticity: A Survey of Perspectives* (by anonymous author), at website: http://www.rim.org/muslim/hadith.htm, or at http://www.rim.org/muslim/islam.htm.

[322] Esposito, John, L., *Islam - The Straight Path* (Toronto: Oxford University Press), 1991, p. 81, also cited in Also cited in *Hadith Authenticity: A Survey of Perspectives* (by anonymous author), at website: http://www.rim.org/muslim/hadith.htm, or at http://www.rim.org/muslim/islam.htm.

[323] Khan, M. A. Muqtedar, *American Muslims: Bridging Faith and Freedom*, Amana Publishers, 2002, p. 86.

[324] Fadl, Khaled Abou El, *op. cit.*, 2001, p. 111.

[325] See Chapters 2-7 for a discussion of such a path in light of the Quran.

[326] Ahmad, Kassim, *op. cit.*, 1997.

[327] Ahmad, Kassim, *op. cit.*, 1997.

[328] Brown, Daniel W., *op. cit.*, 1996 (paperback 1999), pp. 54-55.

[329] Mashriqi, Inayat Allah Khan, *Tadhkira*, Amritsar, 1924, p. 91; quoted in Majid, "Ghulam Jilani Barq," p.3; cited in Daniel Brown, *op. cit.*, 1996 (Paperback 1999), p. 45.

[330] See Khalifa, Rashad, *op. cit*, 1982, and Kassim Ahmad, *op. cit.*, 1996.

[331] Ahmad, Kassim, *op. cit.*, 1997.

[332] Kazi, Mazhar U., *A Treasury of Ahadith*, Jeddah, Saudi Arabia, (Abul-Qasim Publishing House), 1992.

[333] Note, however, that characteristically of many Hadith narrations, which in isolation or in relation to other Hadith narrations may look inconsistent or confusing, this full Hadith is also confusing. While the first part speaks of the prohibition of the Prophet on Hadith writing and his call for its erasure, the second part denies this in the same breath by stating that narration from the Prophet was all right so long as it was not false.

[334] Reported in Akbarally Meherally, *Myths and Realities of Hadith – A Critical Study*, available on the web site www.mostmerciful.com/hadithbook.

[335] Guillaume, Alfred, *The Traditions of Islam*, Pakistan 1977, p. 15; cited in "Hadith as a Source of Historical Information", website: borishennig.de.

[336] Rahim, M. Abdur, *The History of Hadith Compilation* (in Bengali), p. 290, quoted by Jamilul Bashar, *op. cit.*, pp. 11.

[337] Jayrajpuri, Muhammad Aslam, Ilm-i-hadith, Lahore, n. d., p. 2; cited in Brown, Daniel W., 1996 (paperback 1999), *op. cit.*, p. 86.

[338] Source: same as in the previous footnote, p.12.

[339] Brown, Daniel W., 1996 (paperback 1999), *op. cit.*, p. 96.

[340] Ahmad, Kassim, *op. cit.*, 1997.

[341] Iqbal, A. M., *The Reconstruction of Religious Thought in Islam*, First Indian Edition 1997, p. 137.

[342] Al-Shibli, *Sirat al-Numan*, Lahore, n. d. Trans. Muhammad Tayyab Bakhsh Badauni as *Method of Sifting Prophetic Tradition*, Karachi, 1966. p. 179; cited in Daniel W. Brown, 1996 (Paperback 1999), *op. cit.*. p. 114.

[343] Early books of Hadith writing are the *Muwatta* of Malik ibn Anas who died in 179 A.H. that related to legal matters, and the *Musnad* of Ahmad ibn Hanbal, who died in 241 A.H.

[344] MacDonald, Duncan B., *Development of Muslim Theology Jurisprudence and Constitutional Theory* (George Routledge and Sons), London, 1903, p. 76.

[345] MacDonald, Duncan B., 1903, *ibid*, pp. 76-77, emphasis mine.

[346] Brown, Daniel W., 1996 (paperback 1999), *op. cit.*, p. 96.

[347] Jayrajpuri, *Ilm-i-hadith*, p. 16, cited in Brown, Daniel W., 1996 (paperback 1999), *op. cit.*, p. 96.

[348] First Muslim ruling dynasty after the *Khulafai Rashidun*; it ruled during 41 A.H./661 C.E.-132 A.H./750 C.E.

[349] The second ruling dynasty of the Muslim empire after the Umayyads, who ruled during 132 A.H./750 C.E.-923 A.H./1517 C.E.

[350] Brown, Daniel W., 1996 (paperback 1999), *op. cit.*, p. 96.

[351] MacDonald, Duncan B., 1903, *ibid*, p. 81.

[352] Ahmad, Kassim, 1996, *op. cit.*, 1997.

[353] Juynboll, *op. cit.*, p. 145, cited in reference at Footnote 10.

[354] Brown, Daniel W., 1996 (paperback 1999), *op. cit.*, p. 86; citing an example of mutual vilification among the Prophet's Companions cited by Mawdudi, taking from Ibn Abd al-Barr, *Jami*.

[355] Brown, Daniel W., 1996 (paperback 1999), *op. cit.*, p. 86.

[356] Brown, Daniel W., 1996 (paperback 1999), *op. cit.*, p. 86.

[357] Mustafa, Ibrahim, *Hadith and the Corruption of the Great Religion of Islam*, undated, *op. cit*, pp. 9-10.

[358] Ibn Sa'd, *Tabaqat*, II, ii, p. 135; cited in Azami, *Studies in Early Hadith Literature*, Beirut, 1968; repr. Indianapolis, 1978, p. 285; cited in Brown, Daniel W., 1996 (paperback 1999), *op. cit.*, p. 92.

[359] MacDonald, Duncan B., 1903, *op. cit.*, pp. 77-78; the expression in brackets is mine.

[360] Malik b. Anas (716-794 A.D.) is recognized as the founder of one of the four juristic divisions of Sunni Muslims. He was a major collector of hadith.

[361] Goldziher, Ignaz, *op. cit.*, p. 45; cited in Also cited in *Hadith Authenticity: A Survey of Perspectives* (by anonymous author), at website: http://www.rim.org/muslim/hadith.htm, or at http://www.rim.org/muslim/islam.htm.

[362] Lang, Jeffrey, *op. cit*, 2004, pp. 251-252.

452

[363] Asad, Muhammad (trans.) *Sahih al-Bukhari: the Early Years of Islam*, Dar al-Andalus (1981), pp. 47-48; cited in Jeffrey Lang, *op. cit*, 2004, pp. 251-252.

[364] Lang, Jeffrey, *op. cit*, 2004, p. 253.

[365] Lang, Jeffrey, *op. cit*, 2004, p. 255.

[366] Lang, Jeffrey, *op. cit*, 2004, p. 263.

[367] Aslan, Reza, 2005, *op. cit.*, p. 68.

[368] Aslan, Reza 2005, *ibid*, p. 68.

[369] Brown, Daniel W., 1996 (paperback 1999), *op. cit.*, p. 95.

[370] Cited in *Hadith Authenticity: A Survey of Perspectives* (by anonymous author), at website: http://www.rim.org/muslim/hadith.htm, or at http://www.rim.org/muslim/islam.htm, p. 9; the expression in parentheses is mine.

[371] Jayrajpuri, *Ilm-i-hadith*, pp. 22-23; cited in Brown, Daniel W., 1996 (paperback 1999), *op. cit.*, p. 98.

[372] Lang, Jeffrey, *op. cit.*, 2004, pp. 214-215.

[373] Jayrajpuri, *ibid*, p. 26; cited in Brown, Daniel W., 1996 (paperback 1999), *op. cit.*, p. 98.

[374] Juynboll, *op. cit.*, 1983, pp. 179-180; cited in Lang, Jeffrey, *op. cit*, 2004, p. 218.

[375] Lang, Jeffrey, *op. cit*, 2004, p. 218.

[376] Lang, Jeffrey, *op. cit*, 2004, p. 222.

[377] Lang, Jeffrey, *op. cit*, 2004, p. 215.

[378] Lang, Jeffrey, *op. cit*, 2004, p. 246. To be fair to the author, note that though he displays a critical outlook to the Hadith, he is not totally disposed toward dismissing all hadith as unacceptable. He accepts those "authenticated legal traditions that do not seem to conflict with the Qur'an." He also thinks "it necessary to take into consideration the historical contexts of the Prophet's acts. [He thinks] it important to derive general ethical and spiritual lessons from them, rather than attempt to replicate the cultural and historical specifics they describe or to mimic tangential aspects of the Prophet's example." And he admits that his position on the Hadith is an evolving one. (Lang, Jeffrey, *ibid*, p. 265) He is "more wary of non-legal traditions ... [and] especially cautious with regard to the theological traditions" (The same reference, p. 267). These points are also repeated on pages 270-271 of the same reference.

[379] Cited in *Hadith Authenticity: A Survey of Perspectives* (by anonymous author), at website: http://www.rim.org/muslim/hadith.htm, or at http://www.rim.org/muslim/islam.htm, pp. 3-4.

[380] Ahmad, Kassim, *op. cit.*, 1997.

[381] Ahmad, Kassim, *op. cit.*, 1997.

[382] Ahmad, Kassim, *op. cit.*, 1997.

[383] Fadl, Khaled Abou El, And *God Knows the Soldiers: The Authoritative and the Authoritarian in Islamic Discourses*, University Press of America, Inc., Lanham and Oxford, 2001, pp. 70-71. For an academic exploration of "the earliest extant discussions on the authority of the Hadith in Islam," and for a comparison of such discussions with contemporary debates, see Aisha Y. Musa, *Hadith as Scripture: Discussions on the Authority of Prophetic Traditions in Islam*, Palgrave Macmillan, 2008.

[384] *"taqdir"* or fate is derived from the term *"qadar"*.

[385] This is not to deny, however, as argued before that there are things that may be already decided beforehand because of our own earlier work, or because of the work of our parents and forefathers (hereditary factors) or because of other predetermining external factors. Such predetermined lot is so to say God-given. But to say in a

blanket way that everything is decided beforehand by God amounts to misconceiving Him as to how He acts. For a fuller discussion of why the idea of predestination is wrong, and what is the real meaning of *"taqdir"* or given lot, see Chapters 1 and 3.

[386] See the last chapter.

[387] Available on the website:
http://www.usc.edu/dept/MSA/fundamentals/hadithsunnah/bukhari/

[388] Yuksel, Edip, et. al., *op. cit.*, 2007, p. 447.

[389] As pointed out in Chapter 8, the Quran, of course, provides for harsh or exemplary punishments, but such punishments are offered as alternative options to deal with exceptional situations such as war times when the culprits are fighting against the Muslims and causing mischief in the land with might and resources (5:33). The Qur'an also encourages forgiveness as far as possible (3:134, 159; 5:45; 16:126; 42:40).

[390] Lang, Jeffrey, *op. cit.*, 2004, p. 255.

[391] For some details on this, the reader is referred to Chapter 5.

[392] The translated text of the *tashahud* taken from the Hadith reads as follows: All the compliments, prayers and good things are due to Allah. Peace be on you, O Prophet and Allah's mercy and blessings be on you. Peace be on us and on all righteous slaves of Allah. I bear witness that no one is worthy of worship except Allah. I bear witness that Muhammad (peace be upon him) is his slave and Messenger. (*Sahih Bukhari*, Vol. 1, Book 12, # 794; repeated in # 797).

[393] Term used by Reza Aslan, *op. cit.*, 2005, p. 71.

[394] Two noted examples in the exception category are wives of Noah and Lut (7:83; 66:10). An example of the opposite exception is the wife of Pharaoh, who was a pious lady (28:9; 66:11).

[395] Aslan, Reza, 2005, *op. cit.*, p. 69.

[396] Fadl, Khaled Abou El, *op. cit*, 2001, pp. 62-82.

[397] Fadl, Khaled Abou El, *op. cit*, 2001, pp. 72-76.

[398] For some elaboration of this point, the reader is referred to Chapter 9.

[399] For some elaboration on this concept of a deterrent punishment, which may vary depending on the circumstances, see Chapter 8.

[400] For some examples of Hadith-influenced harsh punishments being enforced by *shariah* law followed in several Muslim countries, see Chapter 8.

[401] Ahmad, Panaullah, 1986, *op. cit.*, p. 329.

[402] Ahmad, Kassim, 1997, *op. cit.*, pp. 49-52.

[403] For a good collection of absurd, weird Hadith ideas and those of Muslim sectarian clerics, see Edip Yuksel, *Manifesto for Islamic Reform*, Brainbow Press; 2nd revised & enlarged edition, 2009; an earlier version is at Appendix 5 of their *Quran: A Reformist Translation, op. cit.*, 2007.

[404] Mesbah Uddin, "Sunnah – the Misconceived Dogma that Poisoned Islam", first published in the Daily News Monitoring Service: *News From Bangladesh, on December 12, 2004*, also available on the website: submission.org.

[405] See Huntington, Samuel, "The Clash of Civilizations", *Foreign Affairs*, 1993, expanded into a book *The Clash of Civilizations and the Remaking of World Order*, Simon and Schuster, New York, 1996. Huntington's central thesis is that "post-Cold War conflict would occur most frequently and violently along cultural (often civilizational, e.g., Western, Islamic, Sinic, Hindu, etc.) instead of ideological lines, as under the Cold War". Cf., *Wikipedia*, website:
http://en.wikipedia.org/wiki/Samuel_P._Huntington.

[406] Cited by Karen Armstrong in a Foreword she wrote for Imam Feisal Abdul Rauf, *What is Right with Islam: A New Vision for Muslims and the West*, HarperCollins Publishers, Inc., New York, 2004.

[407] Mansour, Ahmad Subhy, *Penalty of Apostasy: A Historical and Fundamental Study*, English translation by Mostafa Sabet, Original title in Arabic: *Haddur Riddah: Dirasah Usooliyya Tareekhiyya*. About the actions of medieval Christian priests and of other Christians throughout other ages, Mansour notes, "the atrocities committed by the Christian Priesthood in the medieval ages are unparalleled in the history of religion." and other atrocious crimes against humanity committed by Christians throughout other ages – using killing machines and weapons of mass destruction, colonization of underdeveloped countries, waging of two world wars, the killing of Jews (the Holocaust), committing inhuman crimes against indigenous people in the Americas and Australia, mass raids for enslavement of African people, mistreatment of black African-Americans, etc., and concludes "but no sensible person would condemn Christianity due to the actions of its followers. Why then condemn Islam due to the actions of its followers?" Websites: http://ahmed.g3z.com/researches/redda.htm, or, http://www.islamicpluralism.org/texts/2005t/apostasy.htm#It%20is%20not%20permissible%20for%20a%20Muslim%20to%20call%20another.

[408] Expression by Nasr Hamid Abu Zayd, an exiled Egyptian Professor teaching at the University of Leiden, the Netherlands, cited by Caryle Murphy, *Passion for Islam: Shaping the Modern Middle East: the Egyptian Experience*, Simon and Schuster Inc., New York, 2002, p. 190.

[409] See Armstrong, Karen, *Islam – A Short History*, Random House Inc., New York, Modern Library Paperback Edition, 2002, pp. 164-66.

[410] Armstrong, Karen, *ibid*, 2002, p. 167.

[411] For a detailed and comprehensive coverage of why it is wrong to kill or mistreat those who are called apostates in light of what the Quran directs us and in light of what the Prophet actually did, see Ahmad Subhy Mansour, *Penalty of Apostasy: A Historical and Fundamental Study, op. cit.*

[412] Armstrong, Karen, *ibid*, 2002, pp. 169-170.

[413] Armstrong, Karen, *ibid*, 2002, p. 135.

[414] Aslan, Reza, *op. cit.*, 2005, pp. 243-244.

[415] This led the couple to seek exile in the Netherlands.

[416] See Mansour, Ahmed Subhy, "Islamic Tolerance: A Comparison between Egypt and America: Reverting Islam back to its Tolerant Roots" in website: www.islamicpluralism.org/texts/2005t/islamictolerance.htm. Because of his views, Mansour, a Professor in Al-Azhar University, was removed from the University, harassed with imprisonment, and threatened with life, which led him to seek exile into the United States. Mansour's extended family members and his fellow Quranists were also subjected to harassment, persecution and torture.

[417] A late thirteenth-early fourteenth century Muslim preacher who declared the Mongols who converted to Islam as infidels and apostates, and who attacked as inauthentic such Islamic developments as Shiism, Sufism and Falsafah. Cf., Armstrong, Karen, *op. cit.*, 2002, p. 104.

[418] See his book, *The Great Theft: Wresting Islam from the Extremists*, *op, cit.*, 2005, especially Chapters 3 and 4, pp. 45-110. For a succinct critical review of Wahhabism, see Khaled Abou El Fadl (ed.), *The Place of Tolerance in Islam*, Beacon Press, Boston, 2002, the first article by Abou El Fadl, especially the sections on Wahhabism

and Modern Islam, and The Theology of Intolerance. Also another presentation on the same topic is available in his article "The Ugly Modern and the Modern Ugly: Reclaiming the Beautiful in Islam", in Omid Safi (ed.), *Progressive Muslims: On Justice, Gender and Pluralism*, Oneworld, Oxford, 2003, especially the section on Wahhabis, Salafis and Salafabis.

[419] "The Saudi Connection: How billions in oil money spawned a global terror network", US News and World Report in *USNews.com* dated December 15, 2003, Report by David Kaplan, website:
http://www.usnews.com/usnews/news/articles/031215/15terror.htm.

[420] Schwartz, Stephen, *The Two Faces of Islam: Saudi Fundamentalism and its Role in Terrorism*, Knopf Publishing Group, paperback published by Anchor, 2003, cited in Website: http://www.islamicpluralism.org/books.htm.

[421] See article by Lisa Miller, "Islam in America: A Special Report", *Newsweek*, July 30, 2007.

[422] Esposito, John L., *Islam- The Straight Path*, New York, Oxford University Press, 1991, p. 192.

[423] Cited in Daniel Pipes, "Identifying Moderate Muslims", *New York Sun*, November 23, 2004. See his Website: http://www.danielpipes.org/article/2226.

[424] Taher, Amiri, "Islam can't Escape Blame for Sept. 11," Wall Street Journal, 24 October 2001; cited in Robert Spencer, *Islam Unveiled: Disturbing Questions about the World's Fastest-Growing Faith*, Encounter Books, San Francisco, 2002., p. 37.

[425] Tibi, Bassam, *The Challenge of Fundamentalism: Political Islam and the New World Disorder*, Berkeley University Press, 1998 (updated edition 2002), p. xxv. Also cited in a review by Daniel Pipes in *Middle East Quarterly*, March 2000. Website: http://www.danielpipes.org/article/826. Also see his article "Identifying Moderate Muslims", *New York Sun*, November 23, 2004, Website: http://www.danielpipes.org/article/2226.

[426] Fortunately, there is now a growing awareness and realization among also statesmen that the real threat is ideological – an ideology taught in *madrasahs* and espoused by extremist groups like the al-Qaeda, which does not belong to the true face of Islam. The present US President Barack Obama, in a major speech at Cairo University in June last year designed to reframe relations, called for a "new beginning between the United States and Muslims" and for confronting together violent extremism across the globe. He emphasized the point that there is no enmity between America and the Muslim world and, quoting from the Quran, recognized that Islam is not a religion of violence. Though his tone sounds markedly friendlier to Muslims and the Muslim world than that of the previous administration, he basically supports his predecessor George W. Bush's position that the murderous ideology of the Islamic radicals is a great challenge of our time. The former British Prime Minister Tony Blair appropriately commented, "What we are confronting here is an evil ideology. It is not a clash of civilisations; all civilised people, Muslim or other, feel revulsion at it. But it is a global struggle and it is a battle of ideas, hearts and minds, both within Islam and outside it. ... This is a religious ideology, a strain within the world-wide religion of Islam, as far removed from its essential decency and truth as Protestant gunmen who kill Catholics or vice versa, are from Christianity. ... Its roots are not superficial but deep, in the madrassahs of Pakistan, in the extreme forms of Wahabi doctrine in Saudi Arabia, in the former training camps of Al Qaeda in Afghanistan; in the cauldron of Chechnya; in parts of the politics of most countries of the Middle East and many in Asia; in the extremist minority that now in every European city preach

hatred of the West and our way of life. ... It cannot be beaten except by confronting it, symptoms and causes, head-on. Without compromise and without delusion." (Taken from talk to a Labour Party policy forum, July 16, 2005). Other statesmen and diplomats of various countries have also articulated similar views. See Daniel Pipes, "Calling Islamism the Enemy", *Weblog*, June 13, 2002, Website: http://www.danielpipes.org/blog/300.

[427] Lewis, Bernard, *What Went Wrong? Western Impact and Middle Eastern Response*, Oxford university Press, 2002, pp. 3 and 7.

[428] Lewis, Bernard, *ibid*, 2002, pp. 46-53, 64-69.

[429] Cited in Caryle Murphy, Passion *for Islam: Shaping the Modern Middle East: the Egyptian Experience*, Simon and Schuster Inc., New York, 2002, pp. 189-190.

[430] Murphy, Caryle, *Passion for Islam: Shaping Modern Middle East – the Egyptian Experience*, New York, Simon and Schuster, 2002, p. 192.

[431] Bullet, Richard W., *Islam, the View from the Edge*, New York, Columbia University Press, 1994, p. 207. Cited in Note 3 of Chapter 11 in Caryle Murphy, *Passion for Islam: Shaping Modern Middle East – the Egyptian Experience*, New York, Simon and Schuster, 2002, p. 316.

[432] Murphy, Caryle, *op. cit.*, 2002, p. 191.

[433] Khan, M. A. Muqtedar, *American Muslims: Bridging Faith and Freedom*, Amana Publications, 2002, p. 86. Emphasis is mine.

[434] Khan, M. A. Muqtedar, his website: www.ijtihad.org. Also cited in Caryle Murphy, *op. cit.*, 2002, p. 316.

[435] Taken from some of Muqtedar Khan's articles on his website: www.ijtihad.org. Emphasis is mine.

[436] Minai, Ali, "A Time for Renewal" in Michael Wolfe (ed.), *Taking Back Islam: American Muslims Reclaim Their Faith*, Rodale Inc. and Beliefnet Inc., 2002, p. 10. Reprinted from www.chowk.com.

[437] A recent (2007) glaring example is the Red Mosque and *madrasah* complex in Islamabad, which housed dozens of well-armed Muslim militants led by a hard-line Muslim cleric who sought to impose a Taliban-style Islamic rule in Pakistan. The Pakistan government army's eight-day siege of, and final assault on, this complex left more than 100 dead.

[438] Voss, Richard S., "The Fourth Jihad" in Edip Yuksel et. al. (ed.), *Critical Thinkers for Islamic Reform*, Brainbow Press, USA, 2009.

[439] For some elaboration of this point, see Chapter 4 under the section "the Conceptions of Heaven and Hell".

[440] Neier, Aryeh, "The Real Clash is Fundamentalists vs. Modernity", *International Herald Tribune*, October 10, 2001. Cited in Khan, Haroon A., "The Clash of Civilization[s] Thesis and Bangladesh: A Case Study", *Asian Profile*, Vol. 32, No. 2, April 2004.

[441] For a brief recount of fundamental reasons why Muslims and non-Muslims should understand Islam through the lens of the Quran alone, see my article on one of the following web links:

http://www.opednews.com/articles/Fifteen-Great-Reasons-We-S-by-Abdur-Rab-081202-982.html

http://islamicreform.org/index.php?option=com_content&view=article&id=80:fifteen-great-reasons-we-should-embrace-and-follow-the-quran-only-islam-by-abdur-rab&catid=34:edip-yuksel&Itemid=64.